RACE, CLASS, GENDER: BONDS AND BARRIERS

Edited by
Jesse Vorst et al.

Revised Edition

Socialist Studies / Etudes Socialistes

5

EDITORIAL COLLECTIVE:
Tania Das Gupta
Cy Gonick
Ronnie Leah
Alan Lennon
Alicja Muszynski
Roxana Ng
Ed Silva
Mercedes Steedman
Si Transken
Jesse Vorst
Derek Wilkinson

MANAGING EDITOR:
Jesse Vorst

PRODUCTION:
Jesse Vorst
Lisa Allbutt
Kathleen McCallum

TRANSLATIONS:
Alice Vorst
Hubert Balcaen
Enid Marantz

Spelling, syntax and punctuation in this volume follow, in most cases, *Gage Canadian Dictionary* (Gage Educational Publishing Company Toronto 1983) and *The Canadian Style: A Guide to Writing and Editing* (Dundurn Press Limited in co-operation with the Department of the Secretary of State; Toronto 1985). Word processing was done on the University of Manitoba mainframe computer (Amdahl 5870).

Published by *Garamond Press*, 403-77 Mowat, Toronto ON M6K 3E3, Canada, in co-operation with *The Society for Socialist Studies / Société d'études socialistes* 471 University College, University of Manitoba, Winnipeg MB R3T 2M8, Canada. Phone: 204-474-9119. Fax: 204-261-0021

Cover design: Ron Rosin Production Graphics. Printed in Canada.
The publisher acknowledges the financial assistance received in aid of this volume from the Social Sciences and Humanities Research Council of Canada.

Canadian Cataloguing in Publication Data

Main entry under title:
Race, class, gender
    (socialist studies series ; 5)
    Co-published by the Society for Socialist Studies
    Includes summaries in English and French.
    Includes bibliographical references.
    ISBN 0-920059-92-9

1. Canada -- Social conditions. 2. Racism -- Canada. 3. Canada -- Race Relations. 4. Social classes -- Canada. 5. Sexism -- Canada. I. Vorst, Jesse. II. Society for Socialist Studies.

Editorial Statement

Jesse Vorst

Progressive activists and academics join forces in the fifth volume (revised edition) of *Socialist Studies/Etudes Socialistes: A Canadian Annual*. They discuss how race, class and gender combine in the oppression of millions of people, at home and abroad.

The *Society for Socialist Studies / Société d'études socialistes* is happy to contribute in this way to the identification, analysis and eradication of dividing barriers, and their replacement with strong, uniting bonds.

As Managing Editor of this series I am indebted to the authors of the eleven articles and to my colleagues on the Editorial Collective for their collaboration and cooperation toward this *Annual*. It has been a great privilege working with them over the past few years. The need for a second edition testifies to the value of their contributions.

For their diligence and wise advice, a well deserved thank-you goes to my production assistant Lisa Allbutt (who did the word processing and assisted with the editing) and to Diane Cox of the University of Manitoba Computer Centre.

The Collective does not pretend having said the final word on the issue of bonds and barriers of race, class and gender. We hope that this volume makes a valuable contribution to the debate. For reactions to the views and arguments presented in this *Annual* and for further discussion, you are invited to submit articles and follow the debate in the pages of the *Socialist Studies Bulletin*.

The *Annual* and the quarterly *Bulletin* are the official publications of the *Society for Socialist Studies / Société d'études socialistes*, an organization affiliated with the Learned Societies of Canada. Founded in 1967 as a committee, the Society now has over 400 members across the country and abroad, drawn from universities, unions and other centres of progressive thinking. The Society is non-partisan, and its activities range from local seminars to the four-day national conferences in the context of the Learned Societies held every spring at a Canadian university.

The Society acknowledges support from the Social Sciences and Humanities Research Council of Canada for this publication (Program of Aid to Learned Journals) and for conference travel and administration (Program of Aid and Attendance Grants to Scholarly Associations).

We also thank Garamond Press for their assistance in co-publishing and distributing this volume.

Of the other issues of the *Annual*, tables of contents may be found at the end of this volume.

All correspondence about the Society and its activities (including membership and publications) may be sent to:

Society for Socialist Studies / Société d'études socialistes
471 University College, University of Manitoba
Winnipeg MB R3T 2M8, CANADA

Contents

1. Introduction and Overview

Tania Das Gupta*

Choosing the Theme

The theme for this issue of *Socialist Studies* emerged from a series of events during the 1988 Learned Societies Conference at the University of Windsor.

Black and native speakers on a panel entitled "Capitalism/Patriarchy/Socialism: Theoretical Contradictions in Understanding Change" focussed on racism within the women's movement, particularly among academic feminists. The main contention at this session, organized by the Society for Socialist Studies, was that the institutionalization of feminist studies in various universities had generated a host of white, middle class women pretending to speak for *all* women, regardless of race and class backgrounds.

The ensuing discussion was very heated. Some of the white women in the audience disputed the charge and directed their criticism at the male panelists (Métis and black African). Partly at issue was whether men of colour could criticize the white women's movement without being accused of sexism. At the end of the session, there was much unresolved disagreement and anger on both sides.

Further impetus came from a workshop of "Feminism, Critical Theory and the Canadian Legal System", organized by the University of Windsor's Faculty of Law. Intense debate developed on the existence of racism within the universities, particularly the law faculties. Again, the inspiration for these debates was brought about by black and native women and men.

Participants felt that they had to guard against the institutionalization of the women's movement and its concomitant adoption of ruling class discourse. It was further stressed that the women's movement cannot and must not be appropriated and diluted by a small segment of privileged white women claiming to speak for *all* women.

Following these sessions, a number of people involved in the discussions explored the possibility of orienting the forthcoming *Annual* of *Socialist Studies* on feminism and racism. It was hoped that this would provide an opportunity to transcend the barriers of race, class and gender, and to generate dialogue.

All papers presented in sessions of the Society for Socialist Studies, focussing on at least two of the three areas of race, class and gender, were considered for inclusion in the *Annual*: some of these appear in this volume. In addition, a further call for papers was placed in the quarterly *Socialist Studies Bulletin*, and invitations were sent to a number of writers, theorists and activists in the field, particularly women of colour. The CRIAW (Canadian Research Institute for the Advancement of Women) conference on "Women and Development", held in Québec City in November 1988, provided the occasion for further contributions to this volume. Presenters addressed the impact of development on native women and on women in the Third World, and challenged the dominant themes and assumptions made by leading North American and European feminists. Altogether, a large number of articles were submitted and considered for publication.

The Editorial Committee

While outreach was continuing for the submission of articles, the editorial committee was being formed. Some of the original participants from the Learneds stayed on. Others joined in enthusiastically. Efforts were made to establish an editorial collective with proper non-elitist representation and avoid the formation of a white academic women's collective. As a result, a couple of women of colour (including myself) came into the process.

Despite great efforts to increase the participation of black, native and other women of colour, the overall rate of success was disappointing. This is indicative of the marginalization of these women in academia -- as well as their exhaustion due to community involvement, particularly their work to overcome the barriers faced by themselves and their respective constituencies. As a result, they must carefully choose the projects in which they will become involved. In this sense, a publication aimed at a predominantly academic audience might not appear to have a high priority. And invitations to join this type of editorial collective may understandably be greeted with cynicism, as legitimizing the work of academics and publishers who have decided to embrace an issue that is currently in vogue.

For whatever reason, while the impetus for this *Annual* came from women and men of colour (some of whose articles appear in this volume) and from some progressive white women and men, the composition of the editorial committee remained problematic. This is not just a commentary on the Society for Socialist Studies, but includes academic publications and institutions in general. Systemic barriers too complex to discuss here have the net result of excluding black and native women, as well as other women of colour. While individuals may be committed to the elimination of racism and sexism, established practices and structures make the task extremely difficult. It is this very dynamic that keeps the numbers of academics of colour so low in Canadian universities.

As far as possible, the editorial members endeavoured to work as a collective. Through the miracle of technology, editorial members from across the country were able to participate in a conference call to decide on criteria for the inclusion of articles, the theme areas for this issue, editing of individual papers, and so on. All materials having been circulated in advance, the group carefully reviewed each article, evaluating its positive and negative aspects and finally deciding collectively on its inclusion, exclusion or further consideration.

It was felt that in order for articles to be included, they would have to relate closely to the theme: race, class and gender. It was also decided that a consideration of at least two of these aspects was essential, with "race" being one of these. The rationale was that an anti-racist perspective to feminist and Marxist analyses and practice was the key contribution of this issue. Women of colour and black women speaking in their own voices about their own experiences were to be given high priority.

This volume of *Socialist Studies* was visualized as not just another issue of an academic journal but also as a reader for university courses in feminist, labour, socialist or anti-racism programs. It was therefore important for it to have an integrity and coherence of its own. Articles were thus grouped under three major sub-themes: (a) theoretical and methodological considerations; (b) historical development of sexism, racism and class exploitation; and (c) contemporary realities and struggles. Under (a) we have included Ng, Thornhill, Kline and Muszynski; under (b) Bourgeault, St-Onge and Calliste seemed most appropriate; Leah, Poelzer and Kopinak fall under (c).

Following the selection process each author (with the exception of Esmeralda Thornhill whose 1985 paper would be printed *verbatim*) had the opportunity of revising the original text, each working with one or two members of the editorial collective. Final versions were then submitted for final editing by the managing editor of the *Annual.*

Overview of the Articles

It is important for readers of the articles contained in this volume to understand the political context in which debates around race, class and gender are taking place today.

Women of colour have stressed that their experiences cannot be neatly fragmented by gender, race and class. These variables mediate one another, and thus take on different forms at different times. Failure to acknowledge this is itself an indication of racism, sexism and class oppression.

Roxana Ng criticizes academics who demand that the categories of gender and race be separated in order to achieve so-called "definitional clarity". She demonstrates that race, class and gender relations are made even more complex because they are further mediated and organized by the state. She rejects traditional static and ahistorical definitions of gender, ethnicity and race, arguing that they arise from the domination and subordination of the means of production over time.

Ng develops her argument by means of an examination of a concrete historical example. After they had settled in Canada, the domestic work of immigrant women was transformed. Previously, their labour had been defined in relation to subsistence activities. In Canada, it was transformed and organized by industry, mechanization and the husband's waged work. The state played a role in that it organized gender and ethnic group formation through its colonization, immigration and other "nation-building" practices.

Notions of motherhood and Christian morality based on the western European model became the cornerstones upon which the very idea of nation was constructed by the various agents of the state. Ng provides further examples of the way in which the Canadian state organized various groups, citing the experiences of native peoples and of Acadians in the Atlantic region. Racism and sexism operate through the conscious and unconscious practices that serve to include or exclude people on the basis of their gender and/or race. The resulting racism and sexism is not simply attitudinal or structural, but systemic.

Esmeralda Thornhill writes of the brutal experience of slavery and its effects on black women. Black women were forced through historical circumstances to adopt non-traditional roles. "Black women first had to be nullified as Women", often with the complicity of white women, through such barbarous acts as beatings, floggings and various forms of sexual exploitation. In response to these experiences, black women had to "toughen up fast" and had to "assume a masculine role" in order to survive. In turn, white racists redefined this reality to negatively stereotype black women as being aggressive, Amazonian and, alternatively, either asexual or "sexually loose".

Thornhill demonstrates the existence of systemic racism in the women's movement. She notes, for example, that many books on women make no reference to racial identity. Many Canadian Women's Studies courses have no perspective from or of black women. Thornhill asserts (as do Ng and Kline) that, from this vantage point, the category "woman" does not include the experiences of black women, nor is racism considered to be a feminist issue. She urges the adoption of true "sisterhood" by acknowledging and confronting the differences, as well as the similarities, among women. The notion of race, on which slavery and imperialism were built, must be acknowledged. The experiences of black women cannot be marginalized but must be incorporated within feminist discourse.

Thornhill concludes her article with a historical tribute to black women activists. She confirms the politicization of black women in response to their oppression. Racist ideology perpetuates an opposite image: the stereotype of the immigrant woman or the woman of colour as "passive" and "over-dominated". Women of colour are reclaiming their history of struggle, as several of the authors in this volume demonstrate.

Marlee Kline provides a critique of mainstream white feminists like Nancy Harstock and Nancy Chodorow, particularly their notions of "a women's standpoint" and of "common oppression" on the basis of gender. Kline argues that contemporary feminists do not consider differences among women based on other variables, such as race, class and sexual orientation. By thus denying the "multiplicity of women's experience", they marginalize and exclude women more powerless than themselves.

It is their white privileged status that causes contemporary feminists to obscure the differences and inequalities among women. Being generally highly educated and enjoying the privileges attendant to their class and race, they are not aware of race and class oppression. Thus, when they refer to *women*, they actually refer to *white women*. This is an example of racism "entrenched in our ways of thinking".

Kline further argues that white privileged women have shaped the contemporary feminist movement in their own class and race interests. To fight against inequalities stemming from race and class would require that they transfer their own power to women less privileged than themselves. The denial of these inequalities prevents solidarity among all women. To illustrate her point, Kline quotes Bell Hooks who shows that, since black women occupy the bottom rung of the social ladder and have experienced racism, sexism and class oppression, their consciousness is more wholistic and oppositional. That is, black women have developed a consciousness that allows them to build solidarity amongst themselves and to struggle against extreme poverty and despair.

That gender, race and class react upon and shape each other is a point made by both Kline and Ng. It is developed in a somewhat different fashion in the article by Alicja Muszynski who focusses on the concept of patriarchy as it developed in Western civilization. She argues that patriarchy formed the basis for class relations in Western European societies, and was also implicated in a later historical period in race relations. Like Kline and Ng, Muszynski stresses the importance of consciousness, in this case, as the development in individuals of "bifurcated ways of seeing the world" (to adopt a phrase developed by Dorothy Smith). That is, individuals come to see social relations as oppositional, in terms of male/female, white/black, bourgeois/proletariat, and so on.

Drawing on the work of Hannah Arendt, Muszynski argues that central to this dichotomized way of seeing the world is the establishment of the public/private dichotomy which is so fundamental to patriarchal relations. Men, separated from nature, created a "second nature": the public realm of politics. Only those who were "free from necessity" could participate in this realm. They excluded women and slaves. The "state" emerged at the same time to enforce this order -- which included the private realm of the household to which women and slaves were confined.

Like all women, women of colour experience gender oppression. Within the family they are subordinated to their male relatives. And they carry a double day of work as wage labourers and in their reproductive labour. However, it is important to recognize the different forms and degrees of this oppression for women of colour in contrast to white women: the historical impact of slavery (noted by Thornhill), the imposition of bachelor societies among early Asian immigrants (Muszynski notes how Chinese male domestics in British Columbia were referred to as a "feminine race"), and the forced transformation and appropriation of native labour for the fur trade (as developed by Bourgeault in his discussion of Chipewyan women used as work horses by European traders) -- all of these historical events prevented the existence of "the family" as we know it. Gender relations within family households were distorted and produced different notions of masculinity and femininity. These various notions were further reinterpreted within racist ideologies, leading to negative stereotyping of various peoples.

Ron Bourgeault studies the manner in which the state organizes race and gender relations to help capital accumulation. Specifically, he looks at how the labour power of Indian women and men was exploited to develop mercantile capitalism through the establishment of the fur trade in North America, in order to secure capital accumulation in Great Britain. The fur trade could not be pursued without a suitable and sufficient pool of labour. But before Indian labour could be exploited, the indigenous cultural, social and political organizations had to be transformed and appropriated. This was accomplished by means of the subjugation of Indian women. In the process, a relatively egalitarian kinship system was transformed and incorporated within unequal capitalist relations.

Bourgeault reveals the slow and insidious process by means of which "treaties" were used to create a male comprador class within the Dene-Chipewyan people. He presents a fascinating study of the means by which women's sexuality and their position within communal societies became tools for colonial domination. All relationships were transformed: those between Indian men and women, those among Indian women, and those between the Indian peoples and the Europeans. This transformation resulted in the creation of the "Half-breed". Racist ideology was employed to establish clear demarcations between European wage labourers and Indian fur producers, between white and Indian women, and between Europeans and the mixed blood or Métis.

Nicole St-Onge picks up the theme of the creation of race in terms of class distinctions in her study of a settlement of Métis in the Manitoba Interlake. With the encroachment of capitalist relations in the region, class and racial structures developed jointly. It was the "mixed blood" children of European or Canadian male workers and local women, those who had not been absorbed into the "Indian class", who filled the need for a wage labour pool. These children were considered to be neither Indian nor English, but were defined as the "Métis" or Half-breed.

Among the Métis, a privileged class of traders and farmers emerged. St-Onge describes the process by which these people were "whitened" by local missionaries who saw them as genetically predisposed to success. The surplus population, poverty-stricken hunters and fishers, survived precariously and were labelled "Métis" and stereotyped as being irresponsible, lazy and indolent. In this way a racist ideology was used to explain and legitimize class inequalities arising from international capitalist relations.

Women of colour have historically been assigned the hardest work at the most insecure conditions and lowest pay. One of the occupations traditionally assigned to immigrant women and women of colour is that of domestic work. In line with Ng's argument, Agnes Calliste demonstrates how the Canadian state enacted various immigration policies to actively organize this pool of labour. In particular, Calliste examines the Caribbean Domestic Scheme adopted between 1955 and 1966 by the Canadian state.

The Canadian government was blatantly racist in denying entry to black Caribbeans before 1955, while admitting whites from the same area. It was also clearly sexist, developing cultural stereotypes of black women as "promiscuous", further justifying their exclusion because they were all portrayed as being "single parents". Cultural stereotypes were reinforced by orders-in-council that legally barred Caribbean women from entering Canada. Calliste further demonstrates how legal barriers were eradicated when the Canadian state saw the possibility that Caribbean women could fill the need for domestic labour. It collaborated with the Caribbean state to maintain trade and investment ties while developing the Domestic Scheme of limited immigration.

Calliste presents details about the life and work experiences of domestic workers, describing conditions of work, social life, relationships with black Caribbeans of other classes, and community involvement. The mediation of gender by race and class is evident in domestic work. The predominant pattern is that of white women hiring and/or supervising women of colour. These domestics work in the houses of upper-class whites, mothering white children in addition to cooking and cleaning.

In the context of contemporary struggles, Ronnie Leah addresses the theme of resistance by women of colour by examining the public world of paid work, through a case study of trade union organization in Ontario. She begins by noting how women of colour have been ghettoized into occupations that are dead-end, low-paid and insecure. Leah criticizes the labour and women's movements for treating issues around racism in a marginal fashion, and contrasts this with the community and labour struggles of immigrant women and women of colour. She presents a case study of a particular union local in metro Toronto that fought and won an important campaign against racism and sexism.

The organizing efforts by women of colour have, in the last two decades, focussed on the special needs of immigrant women -- forming networks, self-help groups, settlement services, ESL classes and so on. They drew attention to the fact that vital services were denied to them by dominant institutions and that women's organizations (and the Canadian state) were not responding to these needs, even though immigration policies have changed and larger numbers of people are now entering Canada from Third World countries. Black and native Canadian women showed their new immigrant sisters the long history of oppression and struggle against racism and sexism. Canadian citizenship and possession of language skills have not ended systemic and chronic discrimination for these women.

Leah argues that their experiences in community organizing have politicized women of colour. Further politicization has followed in response to international events and the racist nature of native politics in Canada. In turn, community pressure has been exerted on the women's movement, on organized labour and on government -- forcing all three to deal with racism and sexism. However, government response must be carefully monitored, given the history of state co-optation of popular movements.

Leah outlines the criticisms made by women of colour of the labour and women's movements. While these movements have often upheld an anti-racist policy, they have contradicted their policy by not implementing it at the grass-roots or within their own organizational structures. Workers of colour have been forced to organize independently to address their specific concerns, such as in the formation of the Ontario Coalition of Black Trade Unionists (OCBTU).

CUPE Local 79 did take up the challenge, linking struggles against the triple oppression of race, gender and class. A key element that led to success was the Local's ability to mobilize both the communities of colour and its own membership, black and white.

Irene Poelzer examines the experiences of Métis women in northern Saskatchewan. Analagous to the historical analysis by St-Onge and Bourgeault, she demonstrates how poverty is as much a fact for Métis women today as it was in the past.

Even though the structures have changed, systemic barriers are still in place, preventing Métis women from obtaining permanent and well-paid jobs. Multinationals operating in the region hire men from outside the region for the best jobs. Métis women are confined to gender-specific work, most of it in the service sector and generally very badly paid.

But their paid work means that they have little or no time for their children, especially in the absence of male help. This adds stress to their double day of work, and forces them to transform their roles as mothers, wives and housekeepers. Commodities and services introduced externally by the capitalist economy, in the form of television sets and programmes, cars and laundromats, further force them to reorganize their lives. As a result, the monetary economy becomes ever more important, and living expenses increase dramatically.

The monetary economy also serves to reorganize recreational activities, and thus, community relations. Métis women find themselves doing volunteer work, which is unpaid labour that further ties them into a capitalist economy. For example, their children are now involved in costly recreational sports like hockey which drains women's financial resources and their time. Simultaneously, relations that were part of the traditional community become transformed and commodified.

It is hard for Métis women to resist capitalist domination because of their dependence on the state during times of unemployment. Capitalism reduces a population to destitution and poverty; the state placates discontent and potential resistance by doling out transfer payments. Unlike a significant portion of the white female working class, Métis women often do not have a wage earning male partner, thus rendering them even more dependent on welfare and, thus, on the state. The bureaucratic rules and regulations attached to welfare payments also serve to institutionalize sexism.

The public/private split that is theoretically discussed in Muszynski's work is illustrated in Poelzer's article. Although Métis women are drawn into the wage economy, they continue to perform and assume responsibility for tasks attached to the household, the private realm. However, when these same tasks are performed in the public economy, they are valued not according to their value in the public domain but according to the socially defined worth of the people hired to perform them. In this way the labour of Métis women is devalued, and racist and sexist ideology is used to justify paying them very low wages. The state plays an active role here in defining, mediating and maintaining the public/private dichotomy. Poelzer illustrates, through the lives of Métis women, the close connection between the private and the public worlds.

The interplay of gender, race and class, and the fight against these oppressive forces is a global concern. While we engage in our own battles on Canadian soil, we have also become aware of the machinations of international capital and its subordination of labour, wherever possible. This exploitation is at its extreme in Third World countries, particularly in its exploitation of female and child labour. Kathryn Kopinak looks at factory or *maquiladora* workers in Juarez, Mexico, where Canadian, American, European and Japanese manufacturers have established plants in the textile, garment and electronic industries in order to take advantage of cheap labour.

Kopinak points out how Canadians often identify the women workers of *maquiladoras* as "backward" and "raw", compared to the "more advanced" workers at home. The racist, sexist and imperialist implications of such value-laden terms are clear to Canadian women of colour, who have had some of the same adjectives applied to them. She demonstrates the falsity of such negative stereotypes in her description of how Mexican women workers organized a women's centre and, subsequently, a series of cooperatives under their own leadership. Mexican women had to resist not only super-exploitative working conditions but also the power of the Mexican state. The women's centre (COMO) evolved from a philanthropic organization to one that served to raise consciousness -- before it was co-opted by the state. Kopinak also presents a fascinating discussion of the influence of liberation theology and the Catholic charismatic renewal movement in empowering women to assume leadership in religious as well as in political work.

Conclusion

The articles contained in this *Annual* treat a broad range of issues emanating from the concepts of race, class and gender. Critiques of the dominant discourse, theoretical perspectives, historical realities as well as contemporary politics are covered. Nevertheless, there are obvious gaps; for example, native women's politics and historical writings by and about Asian immigrant women are not treated. The task of filling these gaps lies, in particular, with the women of these communities.

We hope that readers will find this *Annual* useful in enhancing their analysis and understanding of race, class and gender, and of the intertwining of these variables in the daily lived experiences of black women, of Indian and Métis women, and of other women of colour. Such understanding will bring men and women of all races together to develop an open and honest dialogue, strengthening the development of an anti-racist and working-class feminist movement in Canada.

*Department of Sociology, Atkinson College, York University, 4700 Keele Street, North York ON, M3J 2R7.

2. Sexism, Racism, and Canadian Nationalism

Roxana Ng

My Starting Point

My concern about the dynamic of sexism and racism, and of the interrelation of gender, race/ethnicity and class arose out of my experience as a "visible minority" immigrant woman and a member of the intelligensia living in a white dominated Canada. Working politically in the immigrant community, I and other women of colour frequently feel that our status as women does not have weight equal to our status as members of minority groups. Our interests and experiences are subsumed under the interests of immigrant men, especially those of "community leaders". This situation is analogous to the classic position of the Left: women's issues are secondary to the class struggle. Women are often told that their interests can be taken up only after the revolution.

Working in the women's movement, on the other hand, women of colour also feel silenced from time to time. Our unique experiences as women of colour are frequently overlooked in discussions about women's oppression. At best, we are tokenized; at worst, we are told that our concerns, seen to be less advanced, have to do with a patriarchy characteristic of our indigenous cultures [1]. There is something missing in the women's movement which gives us an increasing sense of discomfort as we continue to participate in struggles in which only a part of our experiences as women of colour is or can be taken up.

Analytically, in standard social science debates (which filters to the Left and to the women's movement through people's multiple roles and locations in society), there is a tendency to treat gender, race and class as different analytic categories designating different domains of social life. While I continue to experience gender and race oppression as a totality, when I participate in academic and intellectual work I have to make a theoretial and analytical separation of my experience and translate it into variables of "sex", "ethnicity" and "class" in order for my work to be acceptable and understandable to my colleagues. It is not uncommon, when I present papers in conferences, to receive comments about the lack of definitional clarity in my use of concepts of gender, race/ethnicity and class. I am asked to spell out clearly which category is more important in determining the position of, for example, immigrant women.

It is out of these experiences and concerns that I began, over ten years ago, to search for a way of thinking about the interrelation of categories of gender, race/ethnicity and class, which would account for the lived experiences of people of colour; a way of understanding their experiences which does not fragment them into separate and at times opposing domains of social life.

Furthermore, as I continue to teach and do research in ethnic and women's studies, and especially since my two-year sojourn in New Brunswick, it became clear to me that we cannot understand gender and ethnic relations in Canada without attending to how these relations have been mediated by the Canadian state historically, and continues to be organized by state processes. (Let me remind the reader that Nova Scotia and New Brunswick are the oldest provinces in the colony of Canada, settled and dominated not only by Irish and Scottish immigrants but also by Loyalists.) Thus I would argue that it is not enough for feminist and ethnic historians to rewrite women's history and ethnic history. In order to understand how Canada came to be a nation with its present configuration, we have to rewrite the history of Canada.

This paper does not address problems of racism and sexism in the Left and of racism in the feminist movement directly. It is a methodological paper which calls for a different conceptualization of gender, race/ethnicity and class by grounding these relations in the development of the Canadian social formation. In so doing I challenge current theorizations of ethnicity and class, and show the interlocking relations of gender, race and class by means of historical examples. I make use of a method of work informed by Marx's analysis of capitalism in the nineteenth century [2] and feminist interpretations of Marx's method [3]. This method insists on locating the knower in a particular subject position in relation to her inquiry, and on situating contemporary realities in the historical development of nation states in a definite mode of production. It treats historical and contemporary moments and events, not as separate fields or areas of study, but as constiuents of a society with its own internal logic and dynamic.

In developing the present analysis I asked myself: How do I account for the silencing I and other women experience in our diverse and different social locations? How do I have to understand history in order to understand my experience as a totality lodged in a particular social formation? I don't claim to put forward a complete or definitive theory or argument. This paper is an attempt to develop a method of thinking which illuminates sexual and racial oppression from the standpoint of women of colour -- standpoint in this context referring to the the relationship between the knower's experience and the social organization generating her experience. It is also an attempt to develop a praxis for eradicating sexism and racism, not merely in structures and institutions, but more fundamentally in our unconscious thoughts and action.

Before proceeding I want to make a couple of qualifications. First, I am using the concepts "ethnicity" and "race" interchangeably throughout this paper. Although I am aware of the technical differences between the two concepts, I want to draw attention here to their socially, ideologically and politically constructed character. For instance, while the difference between people of Irish and Scottish descent in New Brunswick is seen as sub-cultural differences today, at one time they treated each other as people belonging to different races with distinct and distinguishable characteristics. Certainly, the Acadians were, and to an extent still are, treated as people from an inferior race, distinguishable from the Anglo-Saxons and the Celts by social and physical differences.

Today, the term "ethnic groups" is used primarily to refer to immigrants from non-British and non-French backgrounds, especially those from third world countries. In the past, immigrants were referred to as "Europeans", "Orientals", "Negros", etc., signifying their different racial origins. In this connection, we should remember that the change of studies in race relations to "ethnic relations" in the late 1960s and early 1970s was a political move on the part of the state to diffuse rising racial tensions among different groups in the US, notably between black and white Americans. This terminology was adopted in Canada to diffuse the antagonistic relations between Québec and English Canada, and between the Native people, other minority groups and the Canadian state. The reverse movement toward policy development in race relations in Ontario since the mid-1980s, as opposed to multiculturalism, signals the increasing militancy and political clout of minority groups in the changing political economy of that province [4]. Thus, it is important to bear in mind that definitions and meanings of ethnicity and race are social constructions that shift constantly, reflecting the changing dynamics of gender, race/ethnic and class relations over time.

Second, I am using the term "the Canadian state" as a short-hand for the multiplicity of institutions and departments which administer and coordinate the activities of ruling. It therefore includes the formal government apparatuses and the various policies and programs which come under their jurisdiction, and the functions performed therein. More importantly, I wish to advance the notion of the state as the central constituent in the developing relations of capitalism in Canada (MacIntosh 1978). This set of relations didn't appear overnight. As Corrigan correctly points out, it was constructed through time, by complicated and extensive struggles of people grouped together by their differing relationships to the emerging dominant mode of production (Corrigan 1980:xxii). Indeed, as we shall see, the history of ethnic and gender relations *is* the history of Canadian state formation.

Ethnicity, Class and Gender -- Standard Conceptual Problems

In his book *Ethnic Canada* Driedger distinguishes three views of the interrelationship of class and ethnicity. The first view states that ethnicity is a by-product of the class structure and reducible to class. The second view holds that ethnicity may or may not be reducible to class, but it certainly is a drawback to social mobility. The third view, held by Driedger himself, suggests that ethnicity and class are separate phenomena and should be examined separately (Driedger 1987:6). Certainly, ethnicity and class are observable features of social life. Both have an objective reality outside of people's subjectivity. While orthodox Marxists contend that ethnicity is a product of the class structure (Cox 1948), Depres maintains that ethnicity and class are different bases of sociality, although at times they overlap (Depres 1975).

I suggest that the difficulties encountered by these theorists in understanding the interrelationship between ethnicity and class has to do with the fact that they treat these phenomena as analytic categories whose relationship to each other can be established only abstractly, through the construction of clever analytic schema developed to discover correlations between variables. In this kind of approach, ethnicity and class are conceptualized as variables which have no actual relationship to one another in the everyday world. The indicators for "ethnicity" as an analytical category are descent, common religion, and a shared feeling of belonging to the same group. This list can be expanded and changed depending on the group the researcher is investigating; the criteria used do not change the procedures and conceptual schema adopted. Class, on the other hand, is an economic category which has to do with occupations, level of education, income, etc. Class is relevant to researchers of ethnic groups only if they wish to study the economic participation and social status of the groups. The question then becomes: how do particular groups rank in terms of this socio-economic classification (class) [5]?

Standard approaches to ethnicity, then, treat "the ethnic phenomenon" (VanderBerghe 1981) as a separate ontological and epistemological domain, much like the way scholars of Orientalism treat the study of the Orient according to Edward Said (Said 1979:2). What is considered as the ethnic phenomenon is severed from the relations which give rise to it. Its ontological domain is one whose relevance resides in race, kinship and -- following from these two major attributes -- a sense of belonging and a shared identity. Seen in this light, ethnicity can be considered apart from and as unrelated to the political and economic processes of any particular society; it is detached completely from the context within which the phenomenon arises. Similarly, the phenomenon of class, for these researchers, arises in terms of a person's relative position in a stratified society. Since class and ethnicity are seen to be different variables designating different social phenomena, their relationship has to be derived by examining their correlation (or the lack thereof) in a conceptual schema devised by the researcher. Their interconnection in the shaping of social life is left unexaminable.

Gender usually falls outside the realm of analytical relevance for ethnic theorists. Implicitly, like other areas of sociology, women's experiences are subsumed under those of men. More often, the significance of gender (read woman) is overlooked or is treated as a separate field of investigation. Thus, we find women being included in the study of the family or the domestic labour debate, for example, but political economy remains completely sex blind [6]. While efforts by feminists to incorporate women into the study of ethnicity and class are increasing, these efforts are only at a preliminary stage. Frequently, the similarities between racism and sexism are compared [7], and parallels between the experience of women and the experience of ethnic minorities are drawn (Juteau-Lee and Roberts 1981:1-23). Recently, feminists such as Roberts and Juteau Lee have attempted to conceptualize the relationship between gender, ethnicity/race, and class by suggesting that they are three different systems of domination which overlap (Juteau-Lee and Roberts 1981:1-23). Their inclusion of gender in ethnic studies is a major breakthrough, but the question of the *precise* relationship between these three systems of domination remains to be conceptualized and investigated.

Gender, Race/Ethnicity and Class as Relations

This paper calls for a different conceptualization of ethnicity/race, gender, and class: they must be treated as *social* relations which have to do with how people relate to each other through productive and reproductive activities. This conception is consistent with Marx's and Engels' treatment of class (Marx and Engels 1967, 1970), which refers to people's relations to the means of production, rather than as an economic category. As Braverman eloquently explains, class -- properly understood -- never precisely designates a group of people; rather, it is the expression of a process which results in the transformation of sectors of society (Braverman 1974:24). When we speak of class, then, we are referring to a process which indicates how people construct and alter their relation to the productive/reproductive forces of society, using whatever means they have at their disposal.

Reviewing the historical development of Canadian society, we find that family and kinship, perceived or real, are means people deploy to exert their domination or overcome their subordination. The deployment of kin ties and common descent is what theorists have identified as the salient features of ethnic groups. However, as Weber has pointed out, descent itself is not a sufficient condition for the formation of ethnic groups. He correctly observes:

> it is primarily the political community, no matter how artifically organized, that inspired the belief in common ethnicity. This belief tends to persist even after the disintegration of the political community, unless drastic differences in the custom, physical type, or above all, language exist among its members (Weber 1922:389).

In terms of gender relations, women's work within and outside the family is taken for granted. It is deemed not worthy of consideration in ethnic studies.

Weber's contribution lies in his identification of political and ideological factors in the formation of ethnic groups. In particular, he draws attention to the importance of colonization and emigration as an important basis for group formation. In this sense, his conception of ethnicity coincides nicely with Marx's conception of class: they both see these two phenomena as arising out of the struggles for domination and control, notably in colonization as capitalism emerged as the dominant mode of production in the western world.

Similarly, gender relations are crucial and fundamental to the division of labour in a given society -- any society. In most societies, gender is the basic way of organizing productive and reproductive activities. But gender relations are not the same in all societies. Furthermore, like ethnic and class relations, they change over time in response to changing social, political and economic relations. My investigation of immigrant women's domestic work, for example, reveals the transformation of their domestic labour after immigration to Canada. Whereas in a less industrialized setting women's work is organized organically in relation to farming and other subsistence activities, in Canada it is organized industrially by the husband's waged work outside the home, school schedules, the degree of mechanization of the household (e.g., the use of vacuum cleaner and other appliances), public transportation systems, distances to shopping facilities, and so on. The change in women's domestic labour in turn creates new areas of contestation and conflict between immigrant women and their husbands; as well, it upsets the previous balance of power among all family members (Ng and Ramirez 1981). Smith observes:

> In pre-capitalist societies, gender is basic to the "economic" division of labour and how labour resources are controlled. In other than capitalist forms, we take for granted that gender relations are included. In peasant societies for example, the full cycle of production and subsistence is

organized by the household and family and presupposes gender relations. Indeed, we must look to capitalism as a mode of production to find how the notion of the separation of gender relations from economic relations could arise. It is only in capitalism that we find an economic process constituted independently from the daily and generational production of the lives of particular individuals and *in which therefore we can think economy apart from gender* (Smith 1985a, emphasis in original).

Thus, gender as well as ethnicity and race are relations integral to the organization of productive activities. The theoretical and analytical separation of gender from the economy (productive relations) is itself the product of capitalist development, which creates a progressive separation between civil society, politics and the economy in the first place, and renders relations of gender, race and ethnicity more abstract and invisible to productive processes in the second place [8].

When we treat class, ethnicity and gender as relations arising out of the processes of domination and struggles over the means of production and reproduction over time, a very different picture of their interrelationship emerges. We find that we don't have to develop a set of criteria -- be they "economic" or pertaining to descent -- for defining gender, ethnicity and class. We see that they are relations which have crystallized over time as Canada developed from a colony of England and France to a nation built on male supremacy. Indeed, we can trace ethnic group formation and gender relations in terms of the development of capitalism in Canada, firstly through its history of colonization, and subsequently through immigration policies which changed over time in response to the demands of nation-building. People were recruited firstly from Ireland, then the Ukraine and Scandinavia to lay an agrarian base for England and Canada; they were imported from China through an indentured labour system to build the railways for Canada's westward expansion; more recently people from southern Europe were recruited to fill gaps in the construction industry. In the overall framework of immigration, men and women were/are treated differentially. For example, Chinese men were not allowed to bring their wives and families to Canada so they could not propagate and spread the "yellow menace" (Chan 1983). Even today, men and women enter Canada under different terms and conditions. The majority of third world women enter the country either as domestic workers on temporary work permits or as "family class" immigrants whose livelihood is dependent on the head of the household or on the sponsor (Estable 1986; Djao and Ng 1987:141-158).

Indeed, the emergence of the Native people as a group, not to mention the Métis sub-group, is the result of the colonization process which destroyed, re-organized, fragmented and homogenized the myriad tribal groups across the continent. Until very recently, the differential and unequal status of Indian women was set down by law -- in the *Indian Act* (Jamieson 1978). Ethnicity and gender *are* the essential constituents in the formation of the Canadian class structure.

The treatment of gender and ethnicity as relations constituted through people's activities helps us to observe the differential work carried out by men and women in nation building. Barbara Roberts divides the work of national building during the period between 1880 and 1920 into two aspects. The first aspect had to do with developing the infra-structure of the economy: the building of a nation-wide transportation system, the development of a manufacturing base and a commodity market, and so forth. The development of this aspect of the economy was the domain of men. The second aspect had to do with the building of the human nation: the development of a population base in Canada. Women reformers (whom Roberts calls upper class "ladies") were the active organizers of this aspect of nation building. To ensure the white character and guarantee Christian morality of the nation, upper class women from Britain worked relentlessly to organize the immigration of working-class girls from that country to serve in the new world as domestics and wives (Roberts 1990; Lay 1980:19-42). These "ladies" thus established the first immigration societies in the major cities of Canada, attending to the plight of immigrants.

Similarly, Kari Dehli's research on school reforms in Toronto at the turn of the century shows how middle class mothers of (mainly) British background worked to enforce a particular version of motherhood on working class immigrant women. In the 1920s Toronto experienced a serious depression. Many working class immigrant women were forced to engage in waged work outside the home. Alarmed by the declining state of the family (many working class children attended school hungry and poorly dressed), middle class women worked hard to propagate and enforce "proper" mothering practices in working class families. It was in this period that the notion of "proper motherhood" gained prominence in the organization of family life through the school system [9].

These examples point to the class-based work done by men and women to preserve Canada as a white nation and to enforce a particular ideology to guarantee white supremacy.

But as ruling class men consolidated their power in the state apparatus, they also began to take over and incorporate women's work into the state. Roberts found that, by 1920, control over immigration and the settlement of immigrants had shifted from the hands of the ladies to the hands of state officials. As state power was consolidated, women's work was relegated more and more to the domestic sphere (Roberts 1990; Smith 1985b:156-198). Similarly, community work has been incorporated into the local state -- in boards of education. The central role played by middle class women in school reform was supplanted by the rise and development of an increasingly elaborate bureaucracy within different levels of the state. Interestingly, it is also as the state consolidated its power that sexuality became legislated by law. During this time, homosexuality became a crime, and sexual intercourse was legitimized within legal marital relationship only (Kinsmen 1987).

I am not arguing that gender and ethnicity are reducible to class. I maintain that the examination of gender, ethnicity and class must be situated in the relations of a specific social formation, which have to do with struggles, by groups of people, over control of the means of production and reproduction over time. An examination of the history of Canada indicates that class cannot be understood without reference to ethnic and gender relations; similarly, gender and ethnicity cannot be understood without reference to class relations.

On the basis of the foregoing one can see why I maintained, at the beginning of this paper, that gender, ethnic and class relations are inextribly linked to the formation of the Canadian state, if we see the state as the culmination and crystallization of struggles over the dominant -- in the case of Canada: capitalist -- mode of production. The history of the Native people, from the fur trade period to their entrapment in reserves, is the most blatant example. (The expulsion of the Acadians -- a primarily agrarian group with a subsistence economy -- by the British colonizers, including the Loyalists, from the richer arable lands of the Atlantic region offers another historical testimony of consolidation of power and control by the Anglo-Saxons and the Scots.) The struggles of groups of Irish, Scottish and English descent in the Maritimes is yet another example (Acheson 1985).

Although we don't have an encompassing picture of the detailed interplay of gender, ethnicity, class, and Canadian state formation -- because few systematic studies making use of the above conceptualization have been carried out -- we can begin to see the centrality of gender, ethnicity and class in the formation of the Canadian state by reviewing selected historical studies. Armstrong's research on the Family Compact during the 18th and 19th centuries, for example, begins to pinpoint the genesis of the Ontario Establishment. He describes ways in which groups from Scottish and English origins consolidated their power through acquisition of land and wealth, marriage, and connections in the officialdom in Britain, which eventually culminated in the formation of the Canadian elite. He ends his investigation by suggesting that, once in power, the elite tended to "de-ethnicize" themselves (Armstrong 1987:290).

The process that Armstrong describes becomes, in the 20th century, what Porter has called "the vertical mosaic" (Porter 1967). Although Porter's empirical study of the interrelationship between ethnicity and class is essentially correct, his positivism has prevented him from coming to grips with the *actual* connection between ethnicity, class and the state. While he correctly points out that the upward mobility of certain groups tends to be curtailed by their ethnicity, he does not perceive ethnic relations as part of the organization of productive relations in Canada, nor does he see the state as the culmination of the struggles between the various groups over time. The framework proposed here, on the other hand, explains the emergence of what some researchers have called "ethnic nationalism" (Richmond 1983; Nagel 1987), being played out in the present historical conjuncture when capital is undergoing global restructuring.

In sum, I have presented some historical sketches of gender, race/ethnicity and class dynamics as relations which underpin the development of Canada as a nation-state. It is important to note that these historical events are not presented as instances to support a particular theoretical proposition. Rather, I made use of a way of understanding the world which does not splinter the different historical events and moments into compartmentalized fields or areas of study [10]. In the latter approach, what upper class women did would be seen as "women's history", which has little to do with the organization of the labour market, and as the continuance of Anglo supremacy in nation building, which would be treated as "imperial history". The framework I put forward enables us to put together a picture of the formation of Canada as a nation-state with strong racist and sexist assumptions and policies -- out of the seemingly separate pieces of history which are in fact pieces of the same jigsaw. It is thus that we come to see racism and sexism as the very foundation of Canadian nationhood.

Political Implications

On the basis of the above discussion I want to explore how we may work to eradicate sexism and racism from our praxis as feminists, as intellectuals, and as people of colour.

The first thing that needs to be said is that gender, race/ethnicity, and class are not fixed entities. They are socially constructed in and through productive and reproductive relations in which we all participate. Thus, what constitutes sexism, racism, as well as class oppression, changes over time as productive relations change. While racism today is seen in discriminatory practices directed mainly at coloured people (the Blacks, South

Asians, Native people, for example), skin colour and overt physical differences were not always the criteria for determining racial differences. Historically, the Acadians were treated, by the Scots and the Irish, as people from a different race, and were discriminated and suppressed accordingly. Their experience of racial oppression is no less valid than that encountered by the Native people and today's ethnic and racial minorities. Within each racial and ethnic group, men and women, and people from different classes are subject to differential treatments. For example, while virtually no Chinese labourer or his family was allowed to enter Canada at the turn of the century through the imposition of the head tax, Chinese merchants and their families were permitted to immigrate during this period (Chan 1983).

Thus, it seems to me that it is not our project to determine whether gender, race/ethnicity, class or the economic system is the primary source of our oppression. The task is for us to discover how sexism and other forms of gender oppression (e.g., compulsory heterosexuality [11]), racism, and class oppression are constituted in different historical conjunctures so that the dominant groups maintain their hegemony over the means of production and reproduction. Meanwhile, it is important to see that the state in modern society is a central site of the struggles among different groups. Recognizing the way in which the state divides us at each historical moment would enable us to better decide how alliances could be forged across groups of people to struggle against racial, sexual and class oppression.

Secondly, from the above analysis, it becomes clear that racism and sexism are not merely attitudes held by some members of society. I am beginning to think that they are not even just structural -- in the sense that they are institutionalized in the judicial system, the educational system, the workplace, etc. -- which of course they are. More fundamentally, they are systemic: they have crystallized over time in the ways we think and act regardless of our own gender, race and class position. Indeed, sexist, racist and class assumptions are embodied in the way we "normally" conduct ourselves and our business in everyday life [12].

Thus, we cannot simply point our finger at, for example, the media or the school, and accuse them of gender and racial discrimination. While we begin from a recognition of the fundamental inequality between women and men, and between people from different racial and ethnic groups, at the everyday level we have to recognize that we are part of these institutions. We must pay attention to the manner in which our own practices create, sustain and reinforce racism, sexism and class oppression. These practices include the mundane and unconscious ways in what and to whom we give credence, the space we take up in conversations with the result of silencing others, and the space we don't take up because we have learned to be submissive. We need to re-examine our history, as well as our own beliefs and actions, on a continuous basis, so that we become able to better understand and confront ways in which we oppress others and participate in our own oppression. While this in itself will not liberate us completely from our own sexist, racist and class biases, it is a first step in working toward alternate forms of alliances and practices which will ultimately help us transform the society of which we are a part.

Endnotes

*Department of Sociology in Education, Ontario Institute for Studies in Education, 252 Bloor Street West, Toronto, ON, M5S 1V6. This paper is based on a lecture entitled, "Conceptual difficulties of the interrelation of gender, race/ethnicity, and class - a discussion" given in a course on Critical Philosophy of Science, University at Bergen, Bergen, Norway, May 24-27, 1988. I wish to thank the organizers of the course, Anka Broch-Due and Ann Nielson, for inviting me to be part of the course, and the participants for their feedback and support. I also want to thank members of the editorial board of this Annual, especially Ronnie Leah and Derek Wilkinson, for suggestions toward improving an earlier draft of this paper.

1. See, for example, the charge of racism by Native and Black women of Toronto's International Women's Day Committee (IWDC) in 1986, and the subsequent debates in socialist feminist publications such as *Cayenne* in 1986 and 1987.

2. See Karl Marx 1954 and 1967:475-495. For a critique of contemporary Marxists and a concise discussion of Marx's method, see Derek Sayer 1979.

3. Sandra Harding has called this "the standpoint approach" in her book *The Science Question in Feminism* 1986. The major proponents of this approach, according to Harding, are Nancy Hartsock and Dorothy Smith. See Nancy C.M. Hartsock 1983, and Dorothy E. Smith 1987. While both Hartsock and Smith insist on the primacy of women's standpoint in social analysis, their theories differ in important ways. The way I make use of their work is to begin from the experiences of women of colour and to situate their experiences in the social organization of Canadian society. I make no claim to follow their theories exegetically. See Roxana Ng 1982:111-118.

4. See various Ontario Ministry of Education documents released since the mideighties. A pivotal document is "The Development of a Policy on Race and Ethnocultural Equity", Report of the Provincial Advisory Committee on Race Relations, September 1987.

5. See, for example, Peter C. Pineo 1977:147-157; Peter C. Pineo and John Porter 1985.

6. For a critique, see Dorothy E. Smith 1987.

7. See Roxana Ng 1984, Endnotes 1 and 3 for a discussion on the exclusion of gender from ethnic studies.

8. See the works of Dorothy E. Smith, cited in this paper; lectures given by David Mole in the Dept. of Sociology, Ontario Institute for Studies in Education, 1979-80; and Derek Sayer 1979.

9. See Kari Dehli 1990; and Anna Davin 1978:9-65, for discussion on a similar phenomenon in Britain.

10. For a critique of sociology, see Dorothy E. Smith 1974:7-13; for a critique of political economy, see Dorothy E. Smith 1987.

11. This term is used by Adrienne Rich to describe the institution of heterosexuality which discourages and stifles intimate relationships among women. See Adrienne Rich 1983:139-168.

12. In examining racism embodied in feminist praxis, Himani Bannerji calls this form of racism "common sense racism". See Himani Bannerji 1987:10-12.

BIBLIOGRAPHY

Acheson, T.W. 1985. *Saint John: The Making of a Colonial Urban Community*. Toronto: University of Toronto Press.

Armstrong, Frederick H. 1987. "Ethnicity and the Formation of the Ontario Establishment". In *Ethnic Canada. Identities and Inequalities*. Leo Driedger, ed. Toronto: Copp Clark Pittman.

Bannerji, Himani. 1987. "Introducing Racism: Notes Towards an Anti-Racist Feminism", *Resources for Feminist Research* 16:1, pp. 10-12.

Braverman, Harry. 1974. *Labor and Monopoly Capital. The Degradation of Work in the Twentieth Century*. New York and London: Monthly Review Press.

Chan, Anthony B. 1983. *The Gold Mountain. The Chinese in the New World*. Vancouver: New Star Books.

Corrigan, Philip, ed. 1980. *Capitalism, State Formation and Marxist Theory*. London: Quarter Books.

Cox, Oliver C. 1948. *Caste, Class and Race: A Study in Social Dynamics*. Garden City, N.Y.: Doubleday.

Davin, Anna. 1978. "Imperialism and Motherhood", *History Workshop* 5, pp. 9-65.

Dehli, Kari. 1990. "Women in the Community: Reform of Schooling and Motherhood in Toronto", pp. 47-64. In *Community Organization and the Canadian State*. Roxana Ng, Gillian Walker and Jacob Muller, eds. Toronto: Garamond Press.

Depres, Leo, ed. 1975. *Ethnicity and Resource Competition*. The Hague: Mouton.

Djao, Angela W. and Roxana Ng. 1987. "Structured Isolation: Immigrant Women in Saskatchewan". In *Women: Isolation and Bonding. The Ecology of Gender*, pp. 141-158. Kathleen Storrie, ed. Toronto: Methuen.

Driedger, Leo, ed. 1987. *Ethnic Canada. Identities and Inequalities.* Toronto: Copp Clark Pittman.

Estable, Alma. 1986. "Immigrant Women in Canada, Current Issues". A Background Paper prepared for the Canadian Advisory Council on the Status of Women. March.

Harding, Sandra. 1986. *The Science Question in Feminism.* Ithaca: Cornell University Press.

Hartsock, Nancy C.M. 1985. *Money, Sex and Power. Toward a Feminist Historical Materialism.* Boston: Northeastern University Press.

Jamieson, Kathleen. 1981. *Indian Women and the Law in Canada: Citizens Minus.* Ottawa: Advisory Council on the Status of Women and Indian Rights for Indian Women, April 1978.

Juteau-Lee, Danielle and Barbara Roberts. "Ethnicity and Femininity: (d')après nos experiences", *Canadian Ethnic Studies* 13:1, pp. 1-23.

Kinsmen, Gary. 1987. *The Regulation of Desire. Sexuality in Canada.* Montreal: Black Rose Books.

Lay, Jackie. 1980. "To Columbia on the Tynemouth: The Emigration of Single Women and Girls in 1862". In *In Her Own Right: Selected Essays on Women's History in B.C.*, pp. 19-42. Barbara Latham and Cathy Kess, eds. Victoria: Camosum College.

Marx, Karl. 1954. *Capital.* Vol. 1. Moscow: Progress Publishers.

Marx, Karl. 1967. "The Metaphysics of Political Economy: The Method". In *Writings of the Young Marx on Philosophy and Society*, pp. 475-495. Lloyd Easton and Kurt Guddat, eds. New York: Anchor Books.

Marx, Karl and F. Engels. 1967. *The Communist Manifesto.* Translated by Samuel Moore. Penguin Books.

Marx, Karl and F. Engels. 1970. *The German Ideology.* New York: International Publishers.

McIntosh, Mary. 1978. "The state and the oppression of women". In *Feminism and Materialism. Women and Modes of Production*, pp. 254-289. Annette Kuhn and AnnMarie Wolpe, eds. London: Routledge and Kegan Paul.

Nagel, Joan. 1987. "The Ethnic Revolution: Emergence of Ethnic Nationalism". In *Ethnic Canada. Identities and Inequalities.* Leo Driedger, ed. Toronto: Copp Clark Pittman.

Ng, Roxana. 1982. "Immigrant Housewives in Canada: A Methodological Note", *Atlantis* 8:1, pp. 111-118.

Ng, Roxana. 1984. "Sex, Ethnicity or Class: Some Methodological Consideration", *Studies in Sexual Politics* 1.

Ng, Roxana and Judith Ramirez. 1981. *Immigrant Housewives in Canada.* Toronto: Immigrant Women's Centre.

Ontario. Ministry of Education. 1987. "The Development of a Policy on Race and Ethnocultural Equity". Report of the Provincial Advisory Committee on Race Relations. September.

Pineo, Peter C. 1977. "The Social Standing of Ethnic and Racial Groupings", *Canadian Review of Sociology and Anthropology* 12:2, pp. 147-157.

Pineo, Peter C. and John Porter. 1985. "Ethnic Origin and Occupational Attainment". In *Ascription and Achievement: Studies in Mobility and Status Attainment in Canada*. M. Boyd, J. Goyder, F.E. Jones, P.C. Pineo and J. Porter, eds. Ottawa: Carleton University Press,.

Porter, John. 1965. *The Vertical Mosaic*. Toronto: University of Toronto Press.

Rich, Adrienne. 1983. "Compulsory Heterosexuality and Lesbian Existence". In *The Signs Reader -- Women, Gender and Scholarship*, pp. 139-168. Elizabeth Abel and Emily K. Abel, eds. Chicago: University of Chicago Press.

Richmond, Anthony. 1983. "Ethnic Nationalism and Postindustrialism". In *Two Nations, Many Cultures. Ethnic Groups in Canada*. Second Edition. Jean Leonard Elliot, ed. Scarborough: Prentice-Hall Canada.

Roberts, Barbara. 1990. "Ladies, Women and the State: Managing Female Immigration, 1880-1920", pp. 108-130. In *Community Organization and the Canadian State*. Roxana Ng, Gillian Walker and Jacob Muller, eds. Toronto: Garamond Press.

Said, Edward. 1979. *Orientalism*. New York: Vintage Books.

Sayer, Derek. 1979. *Marx's Method. Ideology, Science and Critique in 'Capital'*. Sussex: The Harvester Press.

Smith, Dorothy E. 1987a. *The Everyday World as Problematic. A Feminist Sociology*. Toronto: University of Toronto Press.

Smith, Dorothy E. 1987b. "Feminist Reflections on Political Economy". Paper presented at the annual meeting of Political Science and Political Economy, Learned Societies Meetings, Hamilton, June.

Smith, Dorothy E. 1985a. "Women, Class and Family". In *Women, Class, Family and the State*. Varda Burstyn and Dorothy E. Smith. Toronto: Garamond Press.

Smith, Dorothy E. 1985b. "Women's Equality and the Family". In *Inequality: Essays on the Political Eonomy of Social Welfare*, pp. 156-198. Allan Moscovitch and Glenn Drover, eds. Toronto: University of Toronto Press.

Smith, Dorothy E. 1974. "Women's Perspective as a Radical Critique of Sociology", *Sociological Inquiry* 44:1, pp. 7-13.

VanderBerghe, Pierre L. 1981. *The Ethnic Phenomenon*. New York: Elsevier.

Weber, Max. 1978. *Economy and Society*. New York: Bedminister.

3. Focus on Black Women!

Esmeralda Thornhill*

We women share a common concern, a common commitment, and a common goal (Thornhill 1985). Yet when we think of *Women*, what images and role models immediately come to mind? Let us contemplate the present portrait of Women. Let us run our eyes over the collage of the female experience. We must quickly conclude that Black Women are *not* in the picture. We Black Women either have been left out, or, where there is a hint of presence, we remain an undeveloped negative, unacknowledged as a negative -- but a negative which is being passed off in its distorted state as a truthful and fully developed picture.

We Black Women have shared a very unique experience which can be most instructive in better understanding the oppression of women. Firmly believing that all of us must band on the basis of a shared understanding of Women's varied collective and individual plight (Hooks 1981:151, 10-12, 121-122), I invite you to come with me on a short visual journey as I aim the spotlight at the obfuscated image of Black Women, buried under the cobwebs of oblivion, indifference, and racism. Throw open your perception field and allow your mind's eye to rove with me, like the lens of a camera, panning the backdrop of our human story, zooming in here and there on Black Women, so that our experiences may bring added dimension, colour, and richness to the present incomplete picture of Woman.

The quest for the illusory true image of Black Woman of necessity is a journey of discovery and rediscovery, but more importantly, it is a journey of *personal introspection*. To salvage from history the true picture of Black Women, we must first confront and dispel the distortions, stereotypes, and groundless myths that pervade and obscure the images of Black Women.

Getting the Proper Perspective

As Women, we live in a sexist world order. However, we Black Women and other Women of Colour in addition live in a racist world order which so far has denied us entry into the mainstream of the Women's Movement (*Visible Minority Women* 1983:61).

> [T]here is an on-going "dialogue" of frustration employed
> by White [Women] and Black [Women] towards each oth-

er. Whites want to know why Blacks always bring up the
racial issue and refuse to see "people as people" -- and
Blacks want to know why Whites are so resistant to facing
the reality of being "colour conscious products" of a racist
society (Cheek 1977:24).

The racism underlying this dialogue of frustration so clouds the lens of our
mind's eye and so blurs our vision, that before we can begin our viewing,
we must first address the issue of racism.

This Western hemisphere was colonized on a racially imperialistic base
and not on a sexually imperialistic base. Racism took precedence over sexual alliances in the White world's interaction with both Native Nations and
African Canadians, just as racism overshadowed any bonding on the basis
of sex between Black Women and White Women. While one can arguably
maintain that sexual imperialism is more endemic to all societies than
racial imperialism, yet when it comes to this Western hemisphere, North
American society is one in which racial imperialism supercedes sexual
imperialism (Hooks 1981:122).

The force that allows White feminist authors, for example, to make no
reference to racial identity in their books about Women that are in actuali-
ty about White Women, is the same force that would compel any author
writing exclusively about Black Women to refer explicitly to their identity.
That force is racism. For, in racially imperialistic societies such as ours, it is
the dominant group that automatically reserves for itself the luxury of dis-
missing racial identity. It is the dominant group that has the power to make
it seem that their own experience is wholly representative (Hooks
1981:138).

For all these reasons, *Woman* has become synonymous with White
Women, whereas Women of Colour, such as myself, are seen as *Others*, as
nonpersons, as dehumanized beings -- or sometimes not seen at all. There
persists a dogged unwillingness to acknowledge and distinuish between varying degrees of discrimination, despite the self-evident reality that *not all
women are equally oppressed* (Hooks 1981:145).

Let us start by screening the present vision of Women. This vision is
clearly colour-blind, short-sighted, and tunnel-visioned (Thornhill 1985).
We Black Women, it would appear, have no role in the finalized script of
Canadian Women's Studies. We have no speaking parts. Despite our
unique experience of Triple Oppression -- on the counts of race, sex, and
class -- and despite our special survival skills, which are indispensable cornerstones to the evolving documentary of female experience, the Women's
Movement has failed to generate any in-depth analysis of the Black female

experience (Hooks 1981:11). The silhouettes of Black Women are footnoted in books, dismissed in marginal asides, and relegated to obscure corners -- the hesitant hint of a presence hovering on the periphery of the total picture of Sisterhood.

In addition, patronizing (or rather, "matronizing") attitudes towards Black Women, as well as the language and concepts that White feminists use, effectively exclude us. A case in point: When White feminists draw analogies between *Women* and *Blacks*, the message that we Black Women receive loudly and clearly is: "We do not acknowledge *your* presence as women in this society!" Would it not make good ideological sense for White feminists to zoom in on the Black female experience when drawing such an analogy?

Certain assumptions take neither Black Women nor our issues into consideration. Consequently, there is a belief and a presumption that Women's issues need not address racism. White women insist that sex and race are two separate issues (Hooks 1981:12-13). And yet, in the words of Black feminist writer Bell Hooks: "At the moment of my birth, two factors determined my destiny, my having been born Black, and my having been born female" (Hooks 1981:10-12, 121-122). Clearly, race and sex are two immutable facets of human identity and the struggles to end them are naturally entwined.

Yet, let us look at the prevailing picture of Woman!

It is a picture -- currently being marketed, a number one box office attraction for government, groups, and individuals -- of women being treated as a single oppressed group for purposes of such correctives as Affirmative Action programs. This further perpetuates the presumption that the social status of *all* women in Canada is the same.

This presumption is wrong.

It is a picture of endless argument and debate as to whether racism is even a feminist issue.

Such a point is moot.

It is a picture of Women's Studies programs being established with all-White faculty teaching literature almost exclusively by White Women, about White Women, and frequently from racist perspectives.

Such a program is biased and discriminatory.

It is a picture of White Women doing research and writing books that purport to be about the experience of Women, when in fact they concentrate solely on experiences of White Women.

Such a one-track agenda is dangerous.

It is a picture of White Women being given grant money to do research on Black Women when Black Women do not receive and have never received funds to research either White Women's history or our own history.

Such a practice constitutes a double standard.

It is a picture of articulate discourse on the historical aspects of psychological, physical, and sexual oppression and aggression against women -- a discourse that nimbly sidesteps, ignores, minimizes, and excludes any analysis (scholarly or otherwise) of systematic, legalized, and institutionalized oppression and aggression against Black Women.

Such a discourse falsifies the facts.

Importance of Black Woman's Experience

We Black Women have a great many cultural, historical, and experiential differences that need to be recognized, acknowledged, shared, and accorded their rightful place (Thornhill 1985:6). By way of illustration: We Black Women have a long history of "nontraditional" roles forced upon us primarily because of racism: breadwinner, sole provider, *poto mitan* of the family, surrogate mother to many young offspring (Rodgers-Rose 1980:296). Pioneers in many ways, long have we been in the forefront of struggle, trailblazing and pathfinding. As affirms Black political writer Manning Marable, "Black Women have carried the greatest battle for democracy in North America" (Marable 1983:74). Our special coping and surviving skills in the face of Triple Oppression set us apart from White Women. With the unique experience of being caught in the interstices between race and sex comes also a unique vulnerability (Ellis 1981:30-45).

As Women in struggle, we cannot limit ourselves to merely selectively borrowing certain pages from the Black Struggle, adverting conveniently to certain examples and principles expressed by the Black experience. Before doing that, we must first train our camera on Black Women. Our feminist lens must be readjusted so that the blurred negative of Black Women is brought into the total picture of Women. Our strengths, stamina for survival, self-respect, courage, conviction, and independence must be properly recognized. And we Black Women must be allowed to *take and wield* OUR share of "appraisal power" in helping to define, within a Canadian context, the emerging picture of Woman.

Meaning of SISTERHOOD

We North American Women have undergone years of racist and sexist socialization that has brought us to trust blindly our knowledge of the facts and interpretations that go to make up history. We accept unquestioningly its impact and effect on present reality. De facto Sisterhood today reflects inevitably the same hierarchical patterns of race and sex relationship (Hooks 1981:121). Despite the lip-service and rhetoric of feminism, we Black Women perceive as highly dubious the quality of today's Sisterhood as professed by certain White feminists. We are not automatically thrilled when we hear White Women express a desire for Sisterhood or merely voice a desire to have Black Women join their White Women's groups. White Women perceive themselves as acting in a generous, open, nonracist manner and become shocked when we Black Women respond to such magnanimous but empty overtures with anger or outrage.

We Black Women expect OUR White Sisters' commitment to Sisterhood to go beyond hollow lip service. All women are oppressed. Yes. *But not all women are equally oppressed!* Varying degrees of oppression have to be distinguished because the oppressed could in turn become the oppressor by using their class, race, education, privilege, and political options in such a way that they effectively oppress others (Nicola-McLaughlin 1984).

I maintain that real Sisterhoood should mean a willingness, a political and personal will -- collectively and individually -- to assume responsiblity for the elimination of racism. This willingness need not be engendered by feelings of guilt, moral responsiblity, or rage. It might be. But it need not be. For it can spring from a heartfelt desire for Sisterhood and the personal and intellectual realization that racism among women undermines and weakens our collective power. It can spring from our knowledge that racism is an obstacle that divides us and that women -- all women -- are accountable for the racism that divides us (Hooks 1981:159).

This true Sisterhood begins with the revelation, acknowledgement, and confrontation of the myths, stereotypes, and false assumptions that cloud the real image and deny the existence of Black Women. This true Sisterhood means that we have to be supportive of justice for all Women, which in turn means opposing injustice against Women of Colour (*Visible Minority Women* 1983:23). This true Sisterhood means that we must contribute to the building of a New World Order that eliminates the international underclass status of Women of African descent. This true Sisterhood means that we must stop playing ostrich and start acknowledging the shared commonness of our human experience, our common oppression as females, *and* our common differences (Hooks 1981:157).

Discovery and Rediscovery

Now, having prepared and established the necessary "mindset" and framework for the emerging picture of Black Women, let us embark on our journey of discovery and rediscovery of the Black Woman. Let us readjust and refocus the lens of our mind's eye, as, with brief glimpses into the past, we strive to reclaim from the ruins the priceless and unique image of Black Women and to restore to it its inherent and splendid lustre. We must understand our past in order to comprehend our present and better face our future. But where we Black People are concerned, "History has many cunning passages, contrived corridors and issues, deceives with whispering ambitions, guides us by vanities" [1]. Therefore, come with me on a short flashback. Throw wide open your perception field. Let your eyes, like the lens of a camera, pan the vast tableau of history.

Ancient Africa!   Black female heads of state, warriors, tacticians and militarists.   Queen Hatshepsut, who ruled Egypt for twenty-one years; Queen Nzingha, great Angolan head of state who ruled in 1583 and was the symbol of early Mbundu resistance to the Portuguese.   Queen Yaa-Asantewa, inspiring force behind the Ashante people (Wilson 1980:310; Joseph and Lewis 1981:87-89).

Ancient America!   The early presence of Black Africans (Van Sertima 1976) in this hemisphere ... long before Columbus touched these shores by mistake is eloquently and irrefutably attested by numerous archaeological finds: the multiple massive Negroid stone heads in the Olmec heartland of Central America; pottery and sculptures bearing facial scarification unearthed from Pre-Christian and Pre-Columbian Mexico; Peruvian techniques of mummification and trepannation, identical to those of Africa; particular weaving techniques and design found only in the Motherland.

The Middle Passage!   Come venture with me aboard the slave ship *Pongas* where 250 Black Women, many of them pregnant, are squeezed into a lightless compartment 16' x 18' for the duration of voyage from Africa to America (Hooks 1981:18-19). Unknown are the numbers of our foremothers who died during childbirth or the number of stillborn children. Countless are the numbers whose bodies succumbed to the ravages of disease and malnutrition, broke under physical torture (rape, beatings, brandings), sought release in a suicidal jump overboard.... Traumatic experiences such as these were the initial stages of indoctrination necessary to transform human beings into slaves. The slave ship experience had a tremendous psychological impact on the psyches of both Black Women and Black Men. Psychological warfare and terrorization were -- *and still are* -- used in an effort to "break in" Black Women and Men.

The Americans and Slavery! Let us zoom in for a close-up because much of what we Black Women are and appear to be was conditioned and shaped by this "peculiar institution" known as slavery. Truly the first "bionic" women were our slave foremothers -- super-exploited workers as labourers in the field, as workers in the domestic household, as large scale breeders, as objects of White male sexual assault, and as the ever-handy victim of physical and psychological abuse by both White Men and White Women.

Priceless Black female slave narratives graphically recount first hand how Black Women suffered and incontrovertibly show us how Black Womanhood has been devalued and the Black Woman devalorized through slavery. We Black female slaves, unprotected by law, public opinion, or family, were singularly easy targets for the antiwoman sexual politics of the colonial, patriarchal, and racist Americas -- North, Central, and South. In order for us to function as slaves, we Black Women first had to be nullified as Women. As White North American men idealized White Womanhood, they correlatively assaulted and brutalized Black Women. Beaten as harshly as male slaves, Black Women, like Montréal's Marie-Joseph-Angélique, were often stripped naked, tied to a stake, and whipped with a hard saw or club -- not to mention being put naked "on the block" to be impersonally peered at, pawed over, poked at in public before being sold off to the highest bidder. These sadistic floggings and exposures of naked Black Women frequently took place while more privileged White Women looked on.

And so, to survive, our slave mothers were forced to assume a masculine role, somewhat like a surrogate man. They had to toughen up fast. We Black Women have not had the opportunity to indulge in the parasitic dependence upon the male that is expected of females in a patriarchal society. We have been always obliged to struggle for individual independence. Whether under slavery or under the Canadian government's Domestic Scheme of the 1950's, we Black Women have been forced to raise White families at the same time that we had to find time to care for and nurture our own extended families -- thus becoming mother, sister, aunt, each one responsible for the other.

Getting the True Picture

Because of widespread and distorted assumptions, White people too often cannot see us as we are but become all too eager to impose upon us an identity based on any number of negative stereotypes. All of these myths and stereotypes are rooted in racism and sexism: the superstrong Amazon woman enduring hardships, the likes of which no "lady" could endure; the tough, domineering, aggressive matriarch; the asexual, slow, cow-like mammy; the evil, treacherous, nagging shrew; the passive submissive slave girl; the sexually loose, immoral and earthy sexual savage ... and the list runs on and on. These false and obsolete stereotypes so obfuscate the picture of Black Woman that we risk missing the very essence, the real emerging image of strength, courage, conviction, awesome fighting spirit, and stamina of Black Women. Down through the centuries, the silenced screams of resistance of our foremothers, our grandmothers, our mothers, and indeed our own voices of protest today, have never ceased.

From African rulers to the revolting slave Marie-Joseph-Angélique [2], to bold Harriet Tubman [3], to articulate Sojourner Truth [4], our foremothers have survived, our families have survived, and our collectivity has survived. We need to readjust our lens and rethink our vocabulary. Confusing words make for confusing thoughts. We have to stop confusing *assertive* with *aggressive*; *matrifocal* with *matriarchal*; *masculinized* with *emasculating*; *passive resistance* with *submissiveness*; *self-respect* with *arrogance*.

We Black Women are proud. We Black Women have reason to be proud. We Black Women are the proud daughters of Black Women who have endured *and are still enduring* over three hundred years of mistreatment. From the youngest girl-child to the most senior Community Elder, we Black Women are politicized. Oppression is a thorough teacher. To know oppression is to become politicized. We are very much aware of the varying ways in which we are still oppressed, as well as of the new insidious forms of oppression.

Woman up until today in Canada, for all intents and purposes, has been synonymous with *White Woman*. If we consider ourselves to be truly Sisters in Struggle, we must come together in harmony after once having understood and eliminated the obstacles that divide us.

You, White Sisters, who already share a certain amount of power and are finding yourselves with increasing frequency in positions of relative influence, must struggle to avoid becoming a new oppressor emerging from the ranks of the oppressed.

Future feminist discourse must take into account the silenced screams of Black Women. Feminist discourse on such issues as sexual harassment or aggression must be back-tracked, re-played, and re-edited in order to take fully into account the systematic and legalized physical and sexual aggression experienced by Black Women. Corrective measures targeting Women, such as Affirmative Action programs, must have their parameters expanded to include policies that accommodate Women who have been disadvantaged by race-sex. The rich and insightful experiences of Black Women must *not* be tacked on as window-dressing, dismissed in parentheses, or hidden in footnotes. Norms of Womanhood must be extended and widened to embrace images with which Women of Colour such as myself can identify positively. And above all, valid and more visible partnerships must be struck to ensure that Black Women exercise our fair share of "appraisal power".

As Women we share a common concern, a common commitment, and a common goal. In the words of Rosemary Brown, the first Black Woman to be elected to a Canadian legislature,

Until all of us have made it, none of us has made it!

Endnotes

*Commission des droits de la personne du Québec, 360 rue Saint-Jacques, Montréal, QB, H2Y 1P5. Reprinted with permission from *Canadian Journal of Women and the Law* 1(1985), pp. 153-162. (Women and Equality Issue).

1. T. S. Elliot, "Gerontion", *The Wasteland and Other Poems* (New York: Harcourt, Brace, Jovanovich, 1979), p. 20. Quoted in Marable, *How Capitalism Underdeveloped Black America*, pp. 231-232.

2. Marie-Joseph-Angélique: Black Woman and slave who, in 1734, on learning that she would be sold the next day, set fire to her mistress' house and took flight. She was captured and executed.

3. Harriet Tubman: Most famous "conductor" of the Underground Railroad, she returned nineteen times to the slave holding South to lead out to freedom in the North and Canada over three hundred slaves, without ever losing a single "passenger".

4. Sojourner Truth: Black Women and slave, the outstanding orator of Black liberation during the nineteenth century; pioneering abolitionst and feminist.

BIBLIOGRAPHY

These materials will give a basic background in the history of North American Black Women.

Allen, Lillian. 1982. *Rhythm and Hard Times*. Toronto: Is Five Press.

Bearden, Jim and Linda Jean Butler. 1977. *Shadd: The Life and Times of Mary Shadd Cary*. Toronto: NC Press Ltd.

Bennett, Lerone Jr. 1966. *Before the Mayflower: A History of the Negro in America, 1619-1964*. Baltimore: Penguin Books.

"Black Women Novelists: New Generation Raises Provocative Issues", 1984 *Ebony* 40 (November), pp. 59-60ff.

Braithwaite, Bella. 1975. *The Black Woman*. Toronto: no publisher.

Campbell, Maria. 1973. *Half-Breed*. Halifax: Goodread Biographies.

Cheek, Donald. 1977. *Assertive Black ... Puzzled White: A Black Perspective on Assertive Behavior*. San Luis Obispo, California: Impact Publishers, Inc.

Clairmont, Donald H. and Dennis William Magill. 1974. *Africville: The Life and Death of Canadian Black Community*. Toronto: McClelland and Stewart.

Davis, Angela Yvonne. 1981. *Women, Race and Class*. New York: Random House.

Davis, Angela Yvonne. 1974. *Autobiography*. New York: Random House.

Davis, Angela Yvonne. 1971. *If They Came in the Morning: Voices of Resistance*. New York: Signet Books.

Dixon, Bob. 1978. *Catching Them Young: Sex, Race and Class in Children's Fiction*. New York: Pluto Press Ltd.

Duckmaster, Henrietta. 1969. *Let My People Go! The Story of the Underground Railroad and the Growth of the Abolition Movement*. Boston: Beacon Press.

Ellis, Judy Trent. 1981. "Sexual Harassment and Race: A Legal Analysis of Discrimination", *Journal of Legislation* 8 (Winter), pp. 30-45.

"Focus on Visible Minority Women". 1984 (special issue). *Currents: Readings in Race Relations*, 1, p. 4.

Fumas, J.C. 1956. *Goodbye to Uncle Tom: An Analysis of the Myths Pertaining to the American Negro From Their Origins to the Misconceptions of Today*. Toronto: George J. McLeod Ltd..

Genovese, Eugene. 1972. *Roll, Jordan, Roll: The World The Slaves Made*. New York: Pantheon Books.

Hooks, Bell. 1981. *Ain't I A Woman? Black Women and Feminism*. Boston: South End Press.

"How to Handle a Racist: Experts Give Their Advice". 1984. *Ebony* 40 (November), pp. 51-52 ff.

Hughes, Langston. 1973. *Good Morning Revolution: Uncollected Writings of Social Protest*. Edited by Faith Berry. Westport, Conn: Lawrence Hill and Co.

Hull, Gloria, Patricia Bell Scott, and Barbara Smith. 1982. *All the Women are White, All the Blacks are Men, But Some of Us are Brave: Black Women's Studies*. Old Westbury, N.Y.: Feminist Press.

Jordan, Winthrop. D. 1971. *White Over Black: American Attitudes Toward the Negro. 1550-1812*. Baltimore: Penguin Books Inc.

Joseph, Gloria I. and Jill Lewis. 1981. *Common Differences: Conflicts in Black and White Feminist Perspectives*. New York: Anchor Press, Doubleday.

Kogawa, Joy. 1984. *Obasan*. Markham, Ontario: Penguin Books.

Kouka-Ganga, Jane. 1982. "A Different Approach is Necessary When Researching Controversial Issues About Women in the Third World". Paper delivered to the First International Conference on Research and Teaching Related to Women. Montréal, Institut Simone de Beauvoir. Concordia University.

Mannix, Daniel P. and Malcolm Cowley. 1978. *Black Cargoes: A History of the Atlantic Slave Trade, 1518-1865*. New York: Penguin Books.

Marable, Manning. 1983. *How Capitalism Underdeveloped Black America*. Boston, South End Press.

Nicola-McLaughlin, Andrée. 1984. "Can the Oppressed be the Oppressor? Meeting the Challenge of a New Reality". Paper Delivered at the International Conference of African Women. Conference on Racism and Power, Washington, D.C., January.

Naylor, Gloria. 1983. *Women of Brewster Place: A Novel in Seven Stories*. New York: Penguin Books.

Obbo, Christine. 1980. *African Women: Their Struggle for Economic Independence*. London: Zed Press.

Rodgers-Rose, La Frances. 1980. *The Black Woman*. Beverly Hills: Sage Publications.

Schwartz, Barry N. and Robert Disch. 1975. *White Racism: Its History, Pathology and Practice*. New York: Dell Publishing Co.

Stampp, Kenneth M. 1956. *The Peculiar Institution: Slavery in the Anti-Bellum South*. New York: Vintage Books.

Staples, Robert. 1984. "The Mother-Son Relationship". *Ebony* 39 (October), pp. 74-78.

The   Visible Minority Women. 1983. Toronto Human Rights Commission Race Relations Division. Proceedings of the Conference on Racism, Sexism and Work, September 30 to October 2, 1983.

Thornhill, Esmeralda. 1985. "Black Women's Studies in Teaching Related to Women: Help or Hindrance to the Universal Sisterhood?" In *Black Women, Double Dilemma*. Montréal: Québec Human Rights Commission. Education Department.

UNESCO. 1983. *Second Medium Term Plan 1984-1989*. Paris: UNESCO.

Van   Sertima, Ivan. 1976. *They Came Before Columbus*. New York: Random House.

Watkins, Mel and Jay David. 1970. *To be a Black Woman: Portraits in Fact and Fiction*. New York: William Morrow and Company Inc.

Wilkinson, Doris Y. 1975. *Black Male/White Female: Perspectives on Interracial Marriage and Courtship*. Cambridge, Massachusetts: Schenkman Publishing Company.

Wilson, Geraldine L. 1980. "The Self-Group Actualization of Black Women". In *The Black Woman*, Rogers-Rose ed. Beverly Hills: Sage Publications.

Wilson, Harriet E. 1983. *Our Nig: Sketches from the Life of a Free Black*. New York: Vintage Books.

Wilson, William J. 1976. *Power, Racism and Privilege: Race Relations in Theoretical and Socio-historical Perspectives*. New York: Macmillan Publishing Co., The Free Press.

"Women of Colour". 1983 (special issue). *Fireweed: A Feminist Quarterly* 16 (Spring).

4. Women's Oppression and Racism: Critique of the "Feminist Standpoint"

Marlee Kline*

> Our vision of women working together is not the vision of reducing us to our similarities but to addressing our contradictions, respecting our political positions and coming to a politics which is mindful of those things...
> -- Black Women's Collective of Toronto [1]

I.

My purpose in this paper is to examine some of the ways that white middle-class privilege finds expression in contemporary feminist thought. In particular, I will discuss the assumption that there is "a women's standpoint", grounded in some sort of common experience of oppression of women, from which it is possible to generate a feminist theory of social relations. I want to demonstrate how this assumption serves to focus attention on the concerns and priorities of white middle-class women, and obscure the forms of oppression experienced by women of colour [2]. I will discuss my concerns in the context of the work of Nancy Hartsock (1983a), a major proponent of the idea of a feminist standpoint [3]. Hartsock argues that the different life activities and material experiences of women and men generate different world views, with a women's standpoint providing a broader, deeper and less distorted understanding of the reality of social relations than that of men. Moreover, Hartsock understands the women's standpoint as a source for developing a liberatory vision of social relations. I will argue that the "women's standpoint", as an approach to feminist theorizing, is not sufficiently attentive to the complexity of women's experience [4]. It suggests that there is an essential or universal experience of being a woman and thereby obscures differences that exist between women. To this extent, there is a risk that the "women's standpoint" will function to generalize falsely the particular experiences and perspectives of those who use it in their analyses.

I hope to build upon the important insights of Hartsock by complicating her analysis of a feminist standpoint in much the same way that she has complicated the Marxist conception of a proletarian standpoint. I will argue that, by insisting on the existence of a feminist standpoint arising from women's universal experience of oppression caused by the sexual division of labour, Hartsock opens herself to the same charge of false generalization that she has raised against Marx from the perspective of gender. A feminist standpoint, when viewed from perspectives attentive to considerations of race, class, ethnicity, religion, sexual identity, physical ability, etc., appears limited and essentialist in the same way the proletariat perspective appears limited from a perspective attentive to considerations of gender. Because of space constraints, I will discuss and illustrate my points in reference to the complications that inevitably arise when issues concerning race and racism are considered in the analysis of the feminist standpoint. It should be understood, however, that a similar critique could be based upon the consideration of concerns of class oppression, heterosexism and other forms of oppression. By relying on the insights of feminist women of colour into the complex interconnections between race, class and gender, I hope to show that the assumption of a feminist standpoint, grounded in the common experience of women of the sexual division of labour, is an insufficient basis for feminist theorizing and, ultimately, an impediment to women's solidarity [5].

My discussion will begin with a description of Hartsock's notion of a feminist standpoint, and of certain assumptions that underlie her theorizing. Next I will consider how the incorporation of racial differences among women into Hartsock's theory challenges these assumptions. This will demonstrate the serious problems one imposes on feminist theorizing when the complexity of women's experience is oversimplified through reliance on universalized, ahistorical and essentialist conceptions of women's reality. I then focus on the white privileged status of most contemporary feminist theorists and consider some of the reasons why this has led to a tendency to emphasize the commonalities among women rather than our[6] differences. I will conclude by urging those engaged in feminist theorizing and practice to confront, rather than fear or ignore, the complexity of women's experience of oppression and the consequent differences in women's priorities and concerns, and thus maintain a historically-based and contextual approach to analyzing, strategizing and actively working for women's liberation.

II.

In *Money, Sex and Power* [7], Nancy Hartsock begins the project of constructing a feminist standpoint on which to ground a specifically feminist historical materialism. Her goal is to develop a deeper understanding of the social relations of power and domination (Hartsock 1983a:151-152), particularly with respect to the question of how relations of domination along gender lines are constructed and maintained (Hartsock 1983a:2). She adopts Marxist analysis as a methodological source while not accepting it as "an adequate theorization of domination" (Hartsock 1983a:139). Marxist analysis, in her view, is both gender-blind and gender-biased; it has, therefore, serious limitations in its capacity to account for relations of domination (other than those of "class") [8]. It provides, however, the important insight that a person's understanding of the relations of domination and oppression is deeply shaped by his/her material reality. In constructing her feminist theory of power, Hartsock relies on Marx's emphasis on the need to expose the material epistemological level at which a theory of power is based (Hartsock 1983a:139). She then expands and modifies Marx's analysis in order to understand the gender as well as class dimensions of relations of domination (Hartsock 1983a:151). Hartsock shows how feminists can use Marx's emphasis on the vantage point of the oppressed. By relying on this method feminists would understand how women's material experience as structured by the sexual division of labour lays the foundation for a feminist standpoint from which the institutional bases and ideologies of sexist oppression can be seen as partial and perverse representations of human relations.

A standpoint, according to Hartsock, as opposed to a "world view" or a "perspective", structures epistemology in a particular way [9]. It is based on the notion that differences in material experience construct knowledge and understanding of social relations in complex and often contradictory ways (Hartsock 1983a:118). The result is that "there are some perspectives on society from which, however well intentioned one may be, the real relations of humans with each other and with the natural world are not visible" (Hartsock 1983a:118). Thus, not all forms of life activity can form the basis of a standpoint. Ideas generated by the dominant group, on the one hand, will give a distorted account of reality, an account only of the surface of appearances [10]. The concept of a standpoint, on the other hand, posits a series of levels of reality "in which the deeper level or essence both includes and explains the 'surface' or appearance and indicates the logic by means of which the appearance inverts and distorts the deeper reality" (Hartsock 1983a:118). A standpoint, therefore, provides a vantage point that should be privileged. It is a deeper epistemological level, from which one can see beneath the dominant ideology and reveal the perverseness and inhumanity of human relations. The concept captures why -- despite the partial nature and perversity of a ruling group's interpretations of reality -- those constructions can still "be *made real* because of the power of the ruling groups to define the terms of the community as a whole" (Hartsock 1983a:132). Because oppressed groups suffer directly from the system that abuses them, however, their experience motivates them to discover how distorted accepted interpretations of reality are and to develop new and less distorted ways of understanding the world (Jaggar 1983:371). A standpoint also provides an ontological base from which to move beyond those relations in more liberatory directions by offering the possibilities inherent in its own material experiential base for generalization to the rest of society (Hartsock 1983a:226, 231).

In building her argument for a feminist standpoint, Hartsock begins with Marx's conception of the proletariat "but enriches this notion immeasurably by her proper insistence that the proletariat is not an abstract group but a *gendered* reality" (O'Brien 1984:9-10). Hartsock considers women to suffer a special form of exploitation and oppression in contemporary society. This distinctive social position provides women with a unique epistemological standpoint. Hartsock sees the feminist standpoint as emerging from the contradiction between the differing structures of men's and women's life activity in Western cultures. The material conditions of women that generate a feminist standpoint begin, for Hartsock, with the institutionalized sexual division of labour that defines women as responsible for both housework (including child-rearing) and wage work. It is this multiple experience and activity of women, rather than the merely "doubled" [11] experience of Marx's (male) proletariat, that constitutes the "real material ground of human existence" (Hartsock 1983a:10). Women's lives provide a deeper, broader, more wholistic and, therefore, more adequate epistemological base for understanding the power relations of domination and oppression.

Hartsock also considers the feminist standpoint to provide an ontological base for moving beyond an understanding of oppressive social relations towards a more liberatory vision. She relies on Nancy Chodorow's work to examine the differences in men's and women's experience of self, resulting from the sexual division of labour in childrearing. This differential life activity is seen to give rise to the "abstract masculinity" of men and the feminist standpoint of women (Hartsock 1983a:240). It is abstract masculinity that has structured the hierarchical and dualistic institutions which have generated the oppressive and destructive social relations characterizing Western societies (pp. 240-242). In contrast, women's material experience -- particularly the directly sensuous nature of much of women's work, their activity of "transforming both physical objects and human beings" (p. 242), their experience of carrying a fetus as part and yet not part of themselves -- is thought to generate a construction of self that leads in an opposite direction: "toward opposition to dualism of any sort, valuation of concrete, everyday life; a sense of a variety of connectednesses and continuities both with other persons and with the natural world" (p. 242). Thus, women are thought to have a "relationally defined existence" (p. 242), to "experience others and themselves along a continuum..." (p. 242). Thinking of the world and human nature in terms of dichotomies is foreign to the world view emerging from the experience of women (p. 242). Thus, Hartsock believes that women's experience carries greater liberatory potential than that of the (male) proletariat:

> Generalizing the human possiblities present in the life activity of women to the social system as a whole would raise, for the first time in human history, the possibility of a fully human community, a community structured by a variety of connections rather than separation and opposition (p. 247).

To emphasize the positive aspects of women's experience and activity and the liberatory possibilities which flow therefrom (in contrast with the negative experiences generated by sexist oppression), Hartsock uses the term "feminist" as opposed to "women's" standpoint (p. 232).

Hartsock concludes that women's life activity forms the basis of a specifically feminist materialism, "a materialism that can provide a point from which to both critique and work against phallocratic ideology and institutions" (p. 232). However, the vision available to women "must be struggled for ... and represents an achievement that requires both science to see beneath the surface of the social relations in which all are forced to participate and the education that can only grow from struggle to change those relations" (p. 232). The ability to go beneath the surface of appearances to reveal the real social relations thus requires both theoretical and political activity [12].

III.

Hartsock bases her concept of a feminist standpoint on the existence of a material experience that women have in common and thereby claims a certain universal validity for the feminist standpoint. She explicitly acknowledges that her "effort to uncover a feminist standpoint *assumes that there are some things common to all women's lives* in Western class societies" (p. 234, emphasis added). Even when faced with marked differences in women's contribution to subsistence along the lines of race and class (such as the greater amount of paid domestic labour of women of colour that replicates the domestic work also undertaken in their own households) Hartsock still focuses on highlighting the experiences she believes all women share (p. 236). She locates the alleged common experience ahistorically in women's life activity as structured by the sexual division of labour that marks "every society" (pp. 232-233) [13]. The feminist standpoint is based, Hartsock insists, on the consequences of this sexual division of labour for epistemology and ontology (p. 232). She not only advocates the generalization of women's experiences of oppression as the "ground for critique" (p. 232), but submits further that "the potentiality made available by the activity of women" (p. 247) should be generalized to the rest of society in order to develop the theory and practice that will transform the presently oppressive nature of human relations. The important task for feminist theorists is the process of "revaluing the female experience" by "searching for the common threads that connect the diverse experiences of women, and searching for the structural determinants of these experiences" (p. 246). The universal nature of the Hartsock's conception of the feminist standpoint is evident in her repeated references to feminist standpoint in the singular: "*a* standpoint" (pp. 152, 226ff.), "*a* feminist standpoint" (pp. 152, 226, 231, 232ff.), "*the* feminist standpoint" (pp. 233, 240ff., emphasis added).

Implicit in Hartsock's treatment of women's experience as common rather than differentiated and in her related understanding of the feminist standpoint as being universal, is the assumption that one can examine and theorize about gender separately from race and class. As pointed out above, throughout her argument in support of a feminist standpoint Hartsock insists on dealing only with experiences that women share in common because of their gender. She recognizes there are "important differences among women" but insists on "lay[ing] them] aside" (p. 233). While acknowledging "that domination occurs along lines of race and sex, or that race and sex affect class domination" Hartsock emphasizes that her "particular concern" is with "how relations of domination along *gender* lines are constructed and maintained" (p. 1, emphasis added). She is not unaware of the danger involved in ignoring differences among women, "the danger of making invisible the experience of lesbians or women of colour" (p. 234), and she admits some "reluctance" to risk such danger. In the end, however, Hartsock limits her pursuits to the search for the "central commonalities across race and class boundaries" (p. 233).

Hartsock's unwillingness to incorporate race, class and other differences among women into her analysis of a feminist standpoint seems to follow from her belief that gender oppression underlies oppression based on race and class. She acknowledges the suggestion in her argument that gender oppression provides the foundation for other forms of oppression (p. 259). In her conclusion, she goes further, proposing that continued development of her analysis will eventually enable Marx's famous statement to be amended to read: "Though class society appears to be the source, the cause of the oppression of women, it is rather its consequence" (p. 262). Thus, Hartsock appears to believe that development of her feminist historical materialism would not only adopt Marx's method but also incorporate much of Marx's analysis of class domination (p. 259). In other words, she understands the feminist standpoint to be wholistic: it allows for the recognition of economic bases of power, as well as the gendered forms of power relationships. Hartsock thus finds it unimportant, and perhaps unnecessary, to discuss class differences among women, and does not consider the possible implications this power relationship would hold for the epistemological and ontological components of her theory [14].

Hartsock's reasons for focussing on gender oppression independent of race oppression are related to those concerning her treatment of class issues, but somewhat different. She finds support (for not incorporating race into her historical materialism of gender) in Marx's similar strategy when analyzing capitalism. The deletion of such important factors as imperialism and gendered power relationships did not affect Marx' two most fundamental theories, those of surplus value and alienation. On the same basis, she considers it unnecessary to deal with issues of race in her development of a theory concerning "the extraction and appropriation of women's activity and women themselves" (p. 233). Hartsock seems to believe, therefore, that the incorporation of racial differences into her analysis would not affect her general theoretical premises and conclusions.

IV.

> Much feminist theory emerges from privileged women who live at the center, whose perspectives on reality rarely include knowledge and awareness of the lives of women and men who live in the margin. As a consequence, feminist theory lacks wholeness, lacks the broad analysis that could encompass a variety of human experiences. Although feminist theorists are aware of the need to develop ideas and analysis that encompass a larger number of experiences, that serve to unify rather than to polarize, such theory is complex and slow in formation.
>
> -- Bell Hooks (1984:x)

By applying Marxian concepts to the material experience of women, Hartsock has provided us with a perceptive and insightful way to theorize about the perspectives of women on social reality. To the extent that she attempts to disregard the complexity of women's experience, however, her analysis is limited. In particular, Hartsock is too quick to dismiss race and racism as factors in her analysis. She appears to assume that the recognition and incorporation of racial differences among women and the attendant power relationships would have no impact on the assumptions that constitute the theoretical core of her argument. I want to problematize this assumption by complicating Hartsock's analysis of the division between men's activity and women's activity, through a consideration of the division between the life experiences of women of colour and the life experiences of white women. My purpose here is to demonstrate that differences in women's experiences of oppression must be considered in feminist theorizing, and that serious consideration of issues concerning race and racism changes the nature of the assumptions that can be made about, and the conclusions that can be drawn from, a feminist standpoint.

Hartsock's assumption that one can consider and theorize about experiences based on gender separately from those related to race or class, creates problems when the particular oppression of women of colour is acknowledged and considered. Descriptions and analyses by black women, First Nations women, Asian women, South Asian women, and other women of colour clearly demonstrate that these women cannot overlook or dismiss the complexity of interaction between racism, sexism and class oppression in their lives [15]. Women of colour tend to experience various forms of oppression simultaneously [16]. As a result, they find it difficult, if not impossible, to separate experiences they attribute to their gender from those ascribed to their race, class or other differentiating characteristics. In the words of Patricia Monture:

> Whenever something like this happens in discussion of race and gender, I cannot separate them. I do not know, when something like this happens to me, when it is happening to me because I am an Indian, or when it is happening to me because I am an Indian woman (Monture 1986:167).

Other feminist women of colour emphasize a similar understanding of the simultaneity of experience of different forms of oppression in their writing [17].

While Hartsock acknowledges the potential for differences between the experiences of white women and women of colour, she fails to seriously incorporate into her theorizing these discrepancies and their implications. She leads us to believe instead that women's experiences of sexist oppression can be considered independently from their experiences of racism and class oppression. The difficulty here is that race, class and gender are not independent variables that can be tacked onto each other or separated at will: they are "concrete social relations, [that] ... are enmeshed in each other and the particular intersections involved produce specific effects" (Anthias and Yuval-Davis 1983:63). The assumption of common oppression, relied upon by Hartsock to ground her theoretical analysis, can be contrasted to the the approach taken by women of colour who recognize from the outset that they "can point to no single source for [their] oppression" (Carby 1982:213). The observations of Audre Lorde in this regard are particularly helpful:

> The oppression of women knows no ethnic nor racial boundaries, true, but that does not mean it is identical within those differences (Lorde 1984:70).

> Some problems we share as women, some we do not. You fear your children will grow up to join the patriarchy and testify against you, we fear our children will be dragged from a car and shot down in the street, and you will turn your backs upon the reasons they are dying (Lorde 1984:119).

When feminist theorists ignore the different experiences of sexist oppression of white women and women of colour, relying instead on a notion of common oppression of women, we obscure and deny the particular reality of the experience of women of colour (Spelman 1982:43). Bell Hooks thus regards "[t]he idea of 'common oppression' ... [as expressed by bourgeois white women as] a false and corrupt platform disguising and mystifying the true nature of women's varied and complex social reality" (Hooks 1984:44).

An important consequence of Hartsock's approach is that the role of white women in the process of subordinating and exploiting other women (and men) is repressed. Although she refers at one point to differences between white women and women of colour [18], her commitment to determining a universal basis for women's oppression prevents her from realizing and incorporating into her analysis the complicity of white women in the oppression of women of colour. Anthias and Yuval-Davis, for example, point out that dominant white women are quite involved in the exploitation of other women's reproductive labour (Anthias and Yuval-Davis 1983:71). Recognition of such complicity complicates Hartsock's view of the liberatory possibilities inherent in the particular life experience of women. Hartsock assumes that women in general have a relationally defined existence and a sense of others and themselves along a continuum. When white women's complicity in the oppression of women of colour is incorporated into the analysis, however, we recognize that relations among women are hierarchical: in a white dominated social order, white women enjoy positions of privilege as part of the dominant culture, and women of colour exist in positions of subordination because of their race. In Hartsock's assessment of the importance of one's material experience to the depth of one's understanding of reality, dominant white women must have a distorted understanding of reality because of their interest in concealing their position of domination over others. One would expect, for example, that the suffering of those subordinate to dominant white women would be ignored or, at least, de-emphasized. Such a distorted perception of reality would necessarily limit the liberatory potential of white privileged women's actual existence and conception of self. If their experience were fully generalized to the rest of society, it would merely replicate present structures of racist oppression, rather than provide a means by which to move beyond the present state of oppressive human relations.

Hartsock does not avoid this complication by grounding her notion of a feminist standpoint at what she terms the epistemological level defined by reproduction (Hartsock 1983a:9). The concept of "reproduction" appears, at first, to tie the feminist standpoint to a specifically gendered experience [19]. Hartsock even tries to connect the potential for developing new ways of understanding human differences to the epistemological level of reproduction:

> The capacity for a variety of relations with others that
> grows from the experience of being mothered by a woman
> may help feminists to develop new understandings of both
> the differences and similarities among us, and new ways of
> working with those differences (Hartsock 1983a:258-259).

Whatever one calls the material level at which the liberatory potential of
women's experience is supposed to emerge, however, the consequences of
acknowledging white women's participation in oppression do not change;
whether white women's conception of self is considered to emerge from
our experience of pregnancy and child-rearing (Hartsock 1983a:243), or
our having been mothered by a woman, or from some other developmental
experience, the fact remains that we participate in the oppression of others,
with consequent distortions of our interpretation of the reality of social
relations, and limitations in our potential to imagine less oppressive ways
of understanding the world [20].

Hartsock's notion that a liberatory standpoint comes out of an experience of oppression means that those women most victimized by sexist
oppression should be the ones to ground a liberatory standpoint. According to Bell Hooks and Sandra Harding, it is the lived experience of black
women that must carry the liberatory potential on which Hartsock bases
her conception of the feminist standpoint (Harding 1986:191; Hooks
1984:ix, 14). Hooks argues that, because black women are positioned at the
very bottom of the social ladder, it is they who bear the brunt of racist,
sexist and classist oppression, it is they who "are allowed no institutionalized 'other' that [they] can exploit or oppress" (Hooks 1984:14). Black
women's understanding of reality, as a result, should be recognized as
much deeper, less distorted and more wholistic that that of privileged white
women.

> ... Living as we did -- on the edge -- we developed a par-
> ticular way of seeing reality. We looked both from the
> outside in and from the inside out. We focused our atten-
> tion on the centre as well as on the margin. We under-
> stood both. This mode of seeing reminded us of the exis-
> tence of a whole universe, a main body made up of both
> margin and center. Our survival depended on an ongoing
> public awareness of the separation between margin and
> center and an ongoing private acknowledgment that we
> were a necessary, vital part of that whole.

> This sense of wholeness, impressed upon our consciousness
> by the structure of our daily lives, provided us an opposi-
> tional world view -- a mode of seeing unknown to most of

our oppressors, that sustained us, aided us in our struggle
to transcend poverty and despair, strengthened our sense of
self and our solidarity (Hooks 1984:ix).

The internal logic of the feminist standpoint as articulated by Hartsock
would appear to demand that the lived experiences of black women be considered to provide the *best* vantage point from which "to criticize the dominant racist, classist, sexist hegemony as well as envision and create a count-
er-hegemony" [21]. Even on its own terms, then, Hartsock's theory of a
feminist standpoint is not taken far enough.

These complications illustrate the difficulties inherent in Hartsock's
attempt to find a universal basis for a feminist standpoint. Because women
are divided by race, class, ethnicity, religion, sexual identity and other differences, there can be no consensus among women as to how things are
(Grimshaw 1986:95) or should be. There is, therefore, no unitary category
of "woman" to whose experience Hartsock can appeal, but only particular
women and groups of *women* (Anthias and Yuval-Davis 1983:71; Grimshaw
1986:96); not simply one female reality but multiple female realities
(Grimshaw 1986:96); not one female standpoint but multiple female standpoints. Neither in her use of the term "feminist" (rather than the more
general term "women") nor in her reliance on women's reproductive activity, can Hartsock avoid the complications following from her assumption of
a universally based standpoint, once the complexity of women's experience
is recognized. Indeed, Hartsock's theory is vulnerable to the same critique
she developed of Marx's proletariat standpoint. She considered Marx's
analysis to be gender-blind and gender-biased and, therefore, seriously limited in its capacity to provide an adequate understanding of domination and
oppression. Similarly, Hartsock's analysis is racially-blind and, hence,
racially-biased; it subsequently fails to provide an adequate understanding
of domination and oppression. Whereas Hartsock insists that reality is
"three-tiered" (Hartsock 1983a:10), as opposed to Marx's "bi-leveled"
(Hartsock 1983a:9) reality, the above analysis suggests that reality is multi-
tiered, and the layers themselves are complexly interwoven. Not only must
one consider the proletariat as a gendered reality but one should also view
gender as a racially-divided reality [22]. Race is class-divided; class is divided along lines of sexual identity; sexual identity along lines of race; etc.
Oppression is multi-layered, and attempts to find a universalized standpoint of the oppressed will sacrifice insight for the sake of simplicity.
Instead, each element "exists in the context of the others and [thus] any
concrete analysis has to take this into account" (Anthias and Yuval-Davis
1983:65).

It is true that Hartsock does not claim her theory of a feminist standpoint to be in any sense complete. Rather, she considers her theory to be
"only *one part of a collective effort* to construct an account of women's

oppression from the ground up..." (Hartsock 1983a:151, emphasis added). She also refers to her focus on the sexual division of labour as the point at which "one *could begin, though not complete*" the construction of a feminist standpoint on which to base a specifically feminist historical materialism (Hartsock 1983a:231). Both of these statements contemplate the need for further development of this approach, and possibly leave her theory open to the incorporation of differences in the material experience of women of colour and others into her analysis [23]. In her concluding chapter, Hartsock insists that "much remains to be done" (Hartsock 1983a:254) in feminist theorizing, and refers specifically to the effort being made by contemporary feminists to "understand and remake difference" as potentially providing resources to contribute to the development of a more adequate and liberatory feminist understanding of power (Hartsock 1983a:258). In this reference to difference she does not mean "the mere tolerance of difference" but "the creative function of difference in our lives ... [the] fund of necessary polarities between which our creativity can spark like a dialectic" [24]. At first glance this appears to be a recognition of the necessity to incorporate the differences among women into a theory of power and feminist historical materialism. This reference to "difference", however, focuses only on the importance of the creative function of difference. At no place in her argument does Hartsock seriously acknowledge and consider the oppressive meaning and results which difference (and in particular racial difference) engenders in North-American society and the implications that this source of oppression carries for her conclusions with respect to a feminist standpoint. Hartsock herself states that a more adequate and liberatory theory of power "must ... no[t] ignore systematic domination to stress only energy and community" (Hartsock 1983a:255). And yet this is what she appears to do in her discussion of difference. Again, she does not deal with the institutionalized domination of women (and men) of colour by white women (and men), stressing instead a simplistic understanding of unity among women and the potential for positive uses of power [25]. Indeed, as noted earlier, Hartsock appears to believe that sexism is prior to and responsible for class oppression and racism, implying that the latter would be eliminated with the elimination of the former.

None of this is to suggest that the idea of common oppression is not a helpful concept for feminists. Some distinction must be made in regard of the question as to who uses the notion of "common oppression" and for what purposes. It is clear that "what unifies women and justifies us in talking about the oppression of women is the overwhelming worldwide historical evidence of the subordination of women to men" (Spelman 1982:58). We must be careful, however, not to claim generality for any particular statements we make about the oppression of women. Whenever we assert that all women are oppressed, we should explain such subordination in terms of the many varieties of oppression that different groups of women endure (Spelman 1982:58). Failure to do so can lead to further tyranny in the form of silencing and marginalization. My concern is that the concept of "common oppression" on the basis of gender can, when over-generalized, itself be a source of oppression. When those with the social power to define the criteria of relevance in feminism -- for the most part white middle-class women -- rely on the notion of common oppression as a basis for determining common interests and concerns on the part of all women, there is a danger that the different experiences, concerns and interests of exploited women (who do not have power to make themselves heard) will be marginalized, excluded, and ignored [26]. I believe the notion of common oppression has to some extent been used in this way by contemporary feminist theorists.

It is possible that, upon listening to accounts of the oppression of a particular group of women, others may recognize and acknowledge aspects of commonality between that account and their own experiences. We must be careful, however, to distinguish between a situation in which we recognize commonality in the experiences of oppression, and the case of our mere belief in the commonality of oppression -- only because we refuse to acknowledge important differences. The danger in relying on a notion of common oppression comes when we simply assume as a theoretical starting point that the pain and oppression of others is the same as our own.

V.

Hartsock is not unique among contemporary feminist theorists in her failure to consider seriously the possible effects of race and racism in her account of gender oppression [27]. This tendency in feminist theory is, I believe, partly a consequence of the particular material circumstances in which much of contemporary feminist theory has been produced. Most dominant contemporary feminist theorists are women cushioned by high education, material privilege and the benefits of white domination. However disadvantaged we may feel as women, we experience great privilege in terms of race and class (Ramazanoglu 1986:86). We are "unusual" in the extent to which we can exercise choice in our own lives, in the lack of contradiction we personally experience (Ramazanoglu 1986:86). White feminist theorists, as a result, have tended to "underrat[e] ... the complexity of the contradictions in which most women are embroiled."[28]. As Bell Hooks points out, it is certainly easier for "women who do not experience race or class oppression to focus exclusively on gender" (Hooks 1984:14). Perhaps because racism and classism do not negatively factor in our own lives, as white privileged women we have little to make us aware of our own race and class. As Marilyn Frye has observed, white people tend not to think of themselves "as *white*" (Frye 1983:117) but only as people. In racist societies such as ours, though, it is only the dominant group that can reserve for itself this luxury of ignoring racial identity [29]. The result is that white people tend to treat our particular experiences as universal [30]. This may play out in contemporary feminist thought through, among other things, the assertion that women share a common experience of oppression, which effectively "whitewashes" [31] the differences that exist among women.

Some critics have understood the tendency among white feminist theorists to overlook the implications of the particular experiences of women of colour as a manifestation of ethnocentricism (see Barrett and McIntosh 1985:23-46). The problems resulting from ignoring or submerging the different experiences of oppression of women of colour are, however, not merely the result of ethnocentricism. They are, rather, a reflection of the structures of racism in Western society, from which white feminists, with our assertions of the common bonds between women, have not been able to escape. As Caroline Ramazanoglu points out:

> It seems to me that black women are not accusing white feminists so much of ethnocentricism, which could perhaps be corrected by extending the field of vision, but of a crushing, institutionalized racism which is so totally and deeply entrenched in our ways of thinking and being that we cannot see clearly how we help to justify and perpetuate it (Ramazanoglu 1986:84).

Although recent white feminist writing does not explicitly advance positions of white domination, much of it reflects and thus helps to reinforce the racism that characterizes our society. In this paper I have concentrated on one particular approach to feminist theorizing -- namely, the emphasis on a feminist standpoint -- which omits focus on the ways racism structures the experience of all women. Other tendencies in feminist theory are similarly problematic and, together, have contributed to the creation of feminist theory and practice that often disregards racism as an important and relevant concern of feminists [32].

In trying to understand the emphasis placed by Hartsock and others on common oppression, it is important to understand that we (white privileged women) have had the power to inject our ideas into academic and political discourse and construct feminist theory largely as a consequence of our race in a social order which "unfairly distribute[s] ... benefits and burdens to whites and blacks" (Spelman 1982:41, quoted in Hooks 1984:53). It may be that white privileged feminists deny differences among women, focusing instead on a source of common oppression, in order to justify, whether consciously or unconsciously, our own power to direct feminist theory and decide political priorities in our particular interests [33]. Emphasis on the commonalities of women's experience not only obscures the particular experiences of women subject to racist and class oppression, but, by way of corollary, also reinforces the invisibility of the racial and class privilege of white middle-class women [34]. It is precisely because the theoretical structures of this form of feminist inquiry have not emphasized the identities and experiences of particular groups of women, that white privileged women have been able to claim identification with all discrimination against women and the authority to speak for all women. This submerges the structures of racism that divide women, and serves to further legitimize the priorizing of white women's concerns and interests in feminist theory and practice [35].

VI.

The complexity of women's experience means most fundamentally that women's interests and priorities are cut across by race and class, ethnicity, sexual identity, and so on (Ramazanoglu 1986:85). Rather than pretending unity, we must recognize and confront the barriers that racism, heterosexism and class oppression construct for feminist solidarity, and struggle to overcome the divisions that exist amongst women. The building of a truly representative women's movement requires that there no longer be hegemonic control by a dominant group of women over feminist discourse and strategy (Hooks 1984:162). If women subject to race, class and other barriers are to trust the feminist movement to deal with their particular concerns with respect to ending sexist oppression, then they must be involved in the development of practical strategy and the theory to inform such strategy (Hooks 1984:160-161). Acknowledgement of the complexity of women's experience (and the differences in interest that follow) means that we as white feminists cannot merely invite women of colour to join already established agendas [36]. Rather, we must relinquish the power to define what feminism means [37].

This will involve, among other things, abandoning the notion of a universal feminist standpoint or universal feminist epistemology [38]. We can no longer speak of gender relations as though they can be separated from race and class relations, nor continue to focus on women's alleged common experiences, common interests and common enemies, nor assume the feasibility of a universal and all-encompassing feminist theory. The various facets of social relations cannot be abstractly dissociated from one another, nor can the importance of one social division be abstractly prioritized over that of another. On the contrary, we must consider the ways that structures of racism, sexism, heterosexism and class oppression and their ideological formations are historically implicated within a particular context [39]. In doing so we will confront, rather than fear or ignore, the complexity of women's experience of oppression and the consequent differences in women's priorities and concerns, and will thus maintain a historically-based and contextual approach to analyzing, strategizing and actively working for women's liberation.

Endnotes

*Faculty of Law, University of British Columbia, 1822 East Mall, Vancouver, B.C., V6T 1Y1. I would like to thank the following people for their helpful comments on an earlier draft of this paper: Joel Bakan, Jenny Abell, Brenda Cossman, Judy Fudge, Shelley Gavigan, Hans Mohr, Patricia Monture, Mary Jane Mossman, Mary O'Brien, Andrew Petter, Toni Pickard, Jackie Sealy, Farida Shaikh, Toni Williams, the "M O'B Alumni" group, and the Editorial Collective of this *Annual*, especially Roxana Ng.

1. Statement by the Black Women's Collective of Toronto, as published in their newspaper, *Our Lives* 1:1(1986), and distributed just prior to International Women's Day, March 8, 1986; excerpts are printed in *Cayenne* 2:2/3(1986), pp. 25-43, (p. 25).

2. In this paper I use the phrase "women of colour" whenever I want to refer to the unity of non-white women as a political phenomenon against the oppression of white supremacy and racism, recognizing at the same time that the particular experiences of non-white women are far from monolithic but reflect a "diversity of origin and variation in geographical, historical and cultural reference points": Amina Mama 1984:25. I am aware of the concern expressed by some women that the terms "women of colour" and "non-white" are themselves problematic since the former assumes that white is not a colour and both establish white as the norm against which other skin colours are distinguished. In this paper, however, I have chosen to use the term "women of colour" because that is the term of identity chosen by many women of colour both in Canada and in the United States. See, e.g., Esmeralda Thornhill 1985 (reprinted in this volume) and Bell Hooks 1984. In addition, I use the term "black" to refer to women of African descent, "South Asian" to refer to women of Indian, Pakistani, and Bangladeshian descent, "Asian" to refer to women of Chinese, Japanese, Korean, and Southeast Asian descent, and "First Nations" to refer to women who are descendants of the peoples indigenous to the land we now call Canada, the United States, and Mexico. I used the same terminology in a recent paper: Kline 1989:115-150.

3. There are other contemporary feminist theorists who also develop the notion of a feminist or women's standpoint. See Dorothy E. Smith 1979; Mary O'Brien 1981; Hilary Rose 1983; Jane Flax 1983. For a general discussion of the emergence of standpoint epistomologies in the writing of feminist theorists see Sandra Harding 1986:136-62.

4. My reliance on the concept of "experience" is not itself unproblematic. For an interesting and insightful discussion of issues raised by the concept of experience in feminist analysis, see Michèle Barrett's consideration of "difference as experiential diversity" (1987:30-33), discussing the privileging of experience in certain feminist work with its attendant emphasis on identity construction and pluralism and the confidence in "empirical method and ontological reality" which this tendency presupposes, and contrasting this approach to the relationship between theories of ideology and experience.

5. As I noted in a recent article which also critiqued white feminist scholarship from a perspective attentive to considerations of race and racism: "I approach this project with some hesitation, arising from the fact that I am a white woman. Would consideration of white feminist ... theory not best move from women of colour themselves? And why is a white woman again being given public space to address issues concerning race and racism?": Kline 1989:118 (footnotes omitted). The way I attempted to resolve this dilemma in that article is also relevant to this discussion. I recognize that:

... I am only able to undertake this project because women of colour have, for many years, developed critiques of mainstream feminist scholarship. My critique, then, is an attempt to apply ... many of their insights concerning the limits of feminist theory and practice in [another] context[ ]... I believe it is important that white women take responsibility to identify our racism and help to eliminate it, rather than leaving all of the work to women of colour. In fact, this has been the prescription of many of the critiques by women of colour. It is necessary that we apply the critiques developed by women of colour in the specific fields in which we work, both to our own work and to the works on which we rely. I am not, therefore, attempting to speak for women of colour. Rather my intention in this analysis is to move from an examination of my own experience of white supremacy (pp. 119-20, footnotes omitted).

And to clarify further:

By "my own experience of white supremacy" I mean that, as a white woman, I tend to take for granted the benefits I derive from the simple fact that I am white as well as the assumptions and beliefs underlying this position of privilege... To move from my own experience of white supremacy ... means that I will focus on identifying aspects of contemporary white feminist legal scholarship which overlook the impact of racism on women of colour but seem to have gone previously unnoticed by myself and other white feminists (p. 120 fn 16).

6. I take a similar approach here as in a recent article:

The following discussion is largely directed toward white women from a white woman. The references to "we", "us", and "our" include all of us who are white middle-class women. I use these terms both to situate myself in white middle-class scholarship and to recognize the need for white feminists to take responsibility for the elimination of racism... I do not, however, to mean this discussion to be exclusively among white women. Rather, I hope this article will be one part of a continuing dialogue among all women (Kline 1989:116 fn 5).

7. See also Nancy C.M. Hartsock 1983b.

8. Hartsock (1983a) summarizes her critique of Marx in this way: "By ignoring the genderedness of power relations he presents an incomplete account of relations of domination and of the possibilities for a more humane community" (pp. 5-6).

9. Hartsock appears to equate the terms "perspective" and "world-view" in her analysis. For her these terms represent the general category, of which a standpoint is a particular subset. Every perspective (or world-view), in other words, will not satisfy the requirements for a standpoint. Colin Sumner defines a "world-view" as:

a total way of looking at the world. It is a "model" or "paradigm" which produces "interpretations". It is an overall philosophy which structures and ranks all other mental forms in an individual's head... It is clearly implicit in the notion of a world-view that human subjects carry a total vision to all their practices which assimilates every new impression into its grand pattern (Colin Sumner 1979:88).

In Sumner's view, the concept of "world-view" is a highly undifferentiated concept which, in Marxist theory, is superceded by a number of concepts and premises including those of ideology, ideological formation, spontaneous consciousness, philosophical consciousness and the connections between ideology and practical social relations. A much more complicated understanding of Hartsock's concepts of a standpoint, world view, and perspective, then, might be developed through a consideration of the concept of "ideology"; see, e.g., Centre for Contemporary Cultural Studies 1977; Stuart Hall et al. 1978; Michele Barrett 1980; Alan Hunt 1985:11-37; Shelley A. M. Gavigan 1988.

10. Hartsock 1983a:9; also see Alison Jaggar 1983:370-71:

> Because the ruling class has an interest in concealing the way in which it dominates and exploits the rest of the population, the interpretation of reality that it presents will be distorted in characteristic ways. In particular, the suffering of subordinate classes will be ignored, redescribed as enjoyment or justified as freely chosen, deserved or inevitable. Because their class position insulates them from the suffering of the oppressed, many members of the ruling class are likely to be convinced by their own ideology... They experience the current organization of society as basically satisfactory and so they accept the interpretation of reality that justifies that system of organization.

11. Hartsock 1983a:123. "This doubled experience [of the worker], the doubled experience of being both a commodity and an active human subject, form the basis for the recognition of double level of determination."

12. Hartsock 1983a:261. As Sandra Harding notes, engaging a feminist standpoint is not merely an intellectual action, but involves a political commitment to understanding the world from the perspective of the lives on which the standpoint is based (1986:149).

13. Hartsock explicitly recognizes that her description of the sexual division of labour is a "schematic and simplified" one, yet persists in relying upon it "in order to explore the epistemology contained in the institutionalized sexual division of labour" (p. 232).

14. There is, however, some ambiguity in Hartsock's treatment of class issues. On the one hand, Hartsock insists she is incorporating Marx's analysis of class domination into her own analysis. This view is implicitly accepted by Mary O'Brien when she considers Hartsock as having accepted Marx's analysis of the privileged vantage point of the proletariat, and yet has gone deeper to acknowledge the proletariat as "not an abstract group but a gendered reality". On this basis one might consider Hartsock to have sufficiently acknowledged and incorporated into her theorizing the class differences among women. On the other hand, Hartsock's assumption that gender oppression underlies oppression based on class clearly works to diminish the importance to her analysis of class differences among women.

15. See, e.g., Barbara Smith 1984:81. "[A]s Third World feminists we know that sexual oppression cuts across all racial, class, and nationality lines, at the same time we understand how race, class, ethnicity, culture and the political system under which one lives determine the specific content of that oppression."

16. I have considered the simultaneity of the experiences of oppression of women of colour elsewhere as well and the following discussion is based in part on my earlier analysis; see Kline 1989:121-23.

17. See, e.g., Hazel V. Carby 1982:213: "[B]lack women are subject to the simultaneous oppression of patriarchy, class, and 'race'...". The Combahee River Collective (1982:13): "We also often find it difficult to separate race from class from sex oppression because in our lives they are most often experienced simultaneously. We know there is such a thing as racial-sexual oppression which is neither solely racial nor solely sexual e.g. the history of rape of black women by white men as a weapon of political repression." Hamida Kazi (1986:88): "It is being a woman and simultaneously black that gives an added dimension to black women's oppression. In every black woman's life there are innumerable occasions when she is not only sexually but also racially discriminated against." Sue Lees (1986:94): "In particular situations it is often very difficult to weigh the importance of different systems of stratification. Is a black woman, for example, denied a job on the basis of class, race or sex?"

18. Hartsock's reference to the differences in power between white women and women of colour comes at a point when she is considering the understanding of the notion of power by the contemporary feminist movement. In her view, the contemporary feminist movement has accepted that the exercise of power is the exercise of domination. In contrast, power might be understood in its creative function, as energy and ability. According to Hartsock, "the feminist acceptance of the phallocratic understanding of power [as domination] functioned as a justification for a series of separatist strategies." Splitting into separate groups for blacks, whites, lesbians, working-class women, etc. "meant that no woman had to work with others who might be in a position -- whether through class, race, or heterosexual privilege -- to exercise power over her." Hartsock's tone in discussing this issue is almost apologetic, not (it seems) because she acknowledges that even feminists were dominating one another on the basis of race, etc., but because she finds their understanding of power misguided. Apparently, she is so concerned with advancing her new understanding of power that she completely misses the importance of this fact for her analysis (1983a:2, 13 fn 4).

19. Hartsock attempts to support and reinforce her treatment of gender issues as independent of concerns of race by relying on Nancy Chodorow's work on human development: Nancy Chodorow 1978; Hartsock 1983a:237-239. Elizabeth Spelman, however, has demonstrated that Chodorow's work itself suffers from an inadequate consideration of the interconnections between race, class and gender oppression: Elizabeth V. Spelman 1988:80-113. Most importantly, Chodorow narrowly defines the social context within which mothering takes place as limited to the mother's experiences of gender oppression. As Spelman argues, however, a mother's mothering is also informed by her relation to people of other classes and races, as well as her experiences of living in a society in which there are race and class hierarchies. By ignoring these other elements, Chodorow is able to portray gender identity as distinctive and unrelated to class or race identity. The difficulty, however, is that her conclusion of the distinctiveness of gender identity is assumed at the point she defines "social context", and it is unclear on what basis she can support the narrowness of her definition of social context. In view of this, Hartsock's reliance on Chodorow only compounds the problem.

20. Hartsock's use of the term "feminist" as opposed to women's standpoint, to emphasize the positive experiences and nature of women as opposed to the negative experiences resulting from sexist oppression, does not avoid this conclusion.

21. Hooks 1984:15. It appears that Hartsock was inhibited from arriving at this conclusion by her commitment to the universalization of women's experience and a feminist politics of unity on the basis of common oppression.

22. The category of "women" is also divided by class, sexual identity, handicapping condition, and other differences.

23. These reservations, however, do not avoid the fact that Hartsock specifically dismissed the relevance of race and racism to her assumptions about the grounding of a feminist standpoint.

24. Hartsock 1983a:258, quoting Audre Lorde 1981:99. ("Advocating the mere tolerance of difference between women is ... a total denial of the creative function of difference in our lives. For difference must be not merely tolerated, but seen as a fund of necessary polarities between which our creativity can speak like a dialectic. Only then does the necessity for interdependency become unthreatening.")

25. At the end of her argument, Hartsock does acknowledge for the first time the importance of developing a feminist historical materialism that could "provide the terrain on which both the commonalities of women's situations and differences of race, class and sexuality could be understood." (Hartsock 1983a:254-255). This recognition, however, does not change the fact that differences among women are not incorporated into the feminist historical materialist theory that Hartsock develops. I have demonstrated that development in this direction will necessarily involve an acknowledgement of racial differences among women and incorporation into the notion of a feminist historical materialism the multiplicity of feminist standpoints this recognition necessarily entails.

26. Audre Lorde, for example, has observed that "As white women ignore their built-in privilege of whiteness and define woman in terms of their own experience alone, then women of colour become 'other', the outsider whose experience and tradition is too 'alien' to comprehend." 1984:117.

27. See, for example, the following critiques of the work of white feminist theorists other than Hartsock: Carby 1982; Hooks 1984; Anthias and Yuval-Davis 1983; Kline 1989.

28. Ramazanoglu 1986. It may also be that we are alarmed by what is entailed by recognizing seriously the complexity of women's experiences. As Martha Minow has observed: "[F]ull acknowledgment of all people's differences threatens to overwhelm us" (1987:64).

29. Thornhill 1985:155. In contrast, the identy of those who are subject to racism will not be so easily forgotten or overlooked.

30. Frye 1983:117. Adrienne Rich calls this phenomenon "white solopsism": "to think, imagine, and speak as if whiteness described the world", "Disloyal to Civilization: Feminism, Racism, Gynephobia": Adrienne Rich 1979:299, as quoted in Spelman 1982:36.

31. "[T]he definition of 'whitewash' -- a concealing or glossing over of flaws -- does not imply improving or correcting an object or situation but the covering of reality with a cheap, inferior disguise (whiteness).": Ran Hall 1982:40, as quoted in Frye 1983:115. But, of course, the important point is that white women have the power in our society to ignore the experience of others when deeming our own perspectives as reality.

32. The lack of concern with issues of race and racism in feminist theory and practice is demonstrated by, e.g., Hooks 1984:51; Thornhill 1985:155; Spelman 1982; Kline 1989; LaChapelle 1982:261-2; Ng 1982:249-56; Stasiulis 1987:7; Bannerji 1987:11.

33. Hooks 1984:6 ("[F]eminist emphasis on 'common oppression' in the United States was less a strategy for politicization than an appropriation by conservative and liberal women of a radical political vocabulary that masked the extent to which they shaped the movement so that it addressed and promoted their class interests."); Spelman 1988:112 ("It is because white middle-class women have something at stake in not having their racial and class identity made and kept visible that we must question accepted feminist positions on gender identity [which reinforce the invisibility of race and class identity].").

34. Spelman 1988:112 ("...[H]owever logically, methodologically, and politically sound such [emphasis on women's commonality] seems, it obscures the ways in which race and class identity may be intertwined with gender identity. Moreover, since in a racist and classist society the racial and class identity of those who are subject to racism and classism are not obscured, all it can really mask is the racial and class identity of white middle-class women.")

35. As Himani Bannerji poignantly states: "[T]o speak in the name of all confers a legitimacy without which such a stand of authority could not have been constructed.": Bannerji 1987. See also Kline 1989:143.

36. Hooks 1984:53 ("Many white women have said to me, 'we wanted black women and other non-white women to join the movement', totally unaware of their perception that they somehow 'own' the movement, that they are the 'hosts' inviting us as 'guests'.")

37. The process involved in relinquishing such power is a often difficult one. Two recent situations in Toronto illustrate the conflict and resistance often felt by white feminists when women of colour attempt to exercise control over strategy formation in feminist organizations previously controlled by white women. The first example concerns the coalition of activist women that organized International Women's Day 1986 around the theme "Women Say No to Racism from Toronto to South Africa". The organizing that led up to this event generated charges of racism by women of colour against their white co-organizers, and resulted in a great amount of tension, conflict and hostility. For a good description of the events as they developed, as captured in excerpts from the various documents and articles generated by the organizational steps, see: "Racism and International Women's Day in Toronto" 1986:25.

The second example involves the Toronto Women's Press. Here conflict initially arose when two women of colour joined different sections of the Press. One woman, Larissa Cairncross, joined the fiction group but had very little impact on the directions of the group because she was regarded, not as a representative of black women, but as only one individual out of ten, and a minority voice at that. "The one black person or woman of Colour is reduced to a minority voice and in the collective process that means one vote ... one voice. It is quite difficult for one voice to speak out as loudly as it should ... there is an undermining of self-confidence and you are constantly on the other side of the discussion facing nine or ten people who have an opposing point of view. It is always a minority situation... I would like to see real involvement not just a token presence." For a more indepth description of the particular problems that arose under these circumstances see the interview with both Larissa Cairncross and Nila Gupta by Ayanna Black 1987:30-1.

More recently, a controversy developed at the Women's Press over the definition of racism, when three stories originally selected for a fiction anthology were subsequently rejected due to their allegedly racist overtones. This decision sharply divided the members of the collective into a majority group that supported the rejection of the problematic stories and a dissenting minority which held to a narrower definition of racism. In addition to overruling the minority by deciding not to print the three problematic stories, the majority fired a member of the minority who had been working full-time for several years, and took over the press. See *Globe and Mail*, Aug. 9, 1988, p. C5, col. 1. The minority group has since started a new feminist publishing house: "Second Story Press", *Broadside*, vol. 10, no. 3, p. 4, col. 3 (Dec. 1988 - Jan. 1989)(Letter to the Editor). These two examples also appear in a previous article of mine to illustrate a similar point: Kline 1989:147 fn 131.

38. As Nancy Fraser and Linda Nicolson argue: "since women's oppression is not homogeneous in content, and since it is not determined by one root, underlying cause, there [can be] no 'feminist method', no 'feminist epistemology'" (1988, as quoted in Minow 1987:63-4).

39. As Lees argues, we will not "get very far looking at race, class and sex as categories and trying to see what the relationship between them 'should be' from a theoretical standpoint. Rather, we should try and see that the relationship between them is a question of historical experience and struggle through which these identities take on a real historical existence" (1986:96).

BIBLIOGRAPHY

Anthias. Floya, and Nira Yuval-Davis. 1983. "Contextualizing feminism -- gender, ethnic and class divisions", *Feminist Review* 15, pp. 62-75.

Bannerji, Himani. 1987. "Introducing Racism: Notes Towards an Anti-Racist Feminism", *Resources for Feminist Research* 16:1, pp. 10-12.

Barrett, Michèle. 1980. *Women's Oppression Today: Problems in Marxist Feminist Analysis*. London: Verso.

Barrett, Michèle. 1987. "The Concept of 'Difference'", *Feminist Review* 26, pp. 29-41.

Barrett, Michèle, and Mary McIntosh. 1985. "Ethnocentricism and Socialist-Feminist Theory", *Feminist Review* 20, pp. 23-46. Black, Ayanna. 1987. "Working With Collectives: An Interview with Larissa Cairncross and Nila Gupta from Toronto's Women's Press", *Tiger Lily* 1:3, pp. 29-32.

Bulkin. Elly, Minnie Bruce Pratt and Barbara Smith. 1984. *Yours in Struggle: Three Perspectives on Anti-Semitism and Racism*. Brooklyn: Long Haul.

Carby, Hazel V. 1982. "White women listen! Black feminism and the boundaries of sisterhood". In *The Empire Strikes Back*, pp. 213-35. Centre for Contemporary Studies. London: Hutchinson.

Centre for Contemporary Cultural Studies. 1977. *On Ideology*. London: Hutchinson.

The Combahee River Collective. 1982. "A Black Feminist Statement". In *All the Women Are White, All the Blacks Are Men, But Some of Us Are Brave*, pp. 13-22. Gloria T. Hull, Patricia Bell Scott, and Barbara Smith, eds. New York: The Feminist Press.

Chodorow, Nancy. 1978. *The Reproduction of Mothering: Psychoanalysis and the Sociology of Gender*. Berkeley: University of California Press.

Flax, Jane. 1983. "Political Philosophy and the Patriarchal Unconscious: A Psychoanalytic Perspective on Epistemology and Metaphysics". In *Discovering Reality: Feminist Perspectives on Epistomology, Metaphysics, Methodology and Philosophy of Science*, pp. 245-81, Sandra Harding and Merrill B. Hintikka, eds. Dordrecht, Holland: D. Reidel.

Fraser, Nancy, and Linda Nicholson. 1988. "Social Criticism Without Philosophy: An Encounter between Feminism and Postmodernism", *Communication* 10, pp. 345-366.

Frye, Marilyn. 1983. *The Politics of Reality: Essays in Feminist Theory*. New York: The Crossing Press.

Gavigan, Shelley A.M. 1988. "Law, Gender and Ideology". In *Legal Theory Meets Legal Practice*, pp. 283-297. Anne F. Bayefsky, ed. Edmonton: Academic Printing and Publishing.

Grimshaw, Jean. 1986. *Philosophy and Feminist Thinking*. Minneapolis: University of Minnesota Press.

Hall, Ran. 1982. "dear martha", *Common Lives Lesbian Lives: A Lesbian Quarterly* 6 (Winter), p. 40.

Hall, Stuart, Chas Critcher, Tony Jeffereson, John Clarke, and Brian Roberts. 1978. *Policing the Crisis: Mugging, the State, and Law and Order*. London: MacMillan Press.

Harding, Sandra. 1986. *The Science Question in Feminism*. Ithaca: Cornell University Press.

Hartsock, Nancy C.M. 1983a. *Money, Sex and Power: Toward a Feminist Historical Materialism*. Boston: Northeastern University Press.

Hartsock, Nancy C.M. 1983b. "The Feminist Standpoint: Developing the Ground for a Specifically Feminist Historical Materialism". In *Discovering Reality: Feminist Perspectives on Epistomology, Metaphysics, Methodology and Philosophy of Science*, pp. 283-310. Sandra Harding and Merrill B. Hintikka, eds. Dordrecht, Holland: D. Reidel.

Hooks, Bell. 1984. *Feminist Theory: from margin to center*. Boston: South End.

Hooks, Bell. 1981. *Ain't I A Woman: black women and feminism*. Boston: South End.

Hull, Gloria T., Patricia Bell Scott and Barbara Smith. 1982. *All the Women Are White, All the Blacks Are Men, But Some of Us Are Brave*. New York: The Feminist Press.

Hunt, Alan. 1985. "The Ideology of Law: Advances and Problems in Recent Applications of the Concept of Ideology to the Analysis of Law", *Law and Society Review* 19, pp. 11-37.

Jaggar, Alison. 1983. *Feminist Politics and Human Nature*. Totowa, N.J.: Rowman and Allanfeld.

Kazi, Hamida. 1986. "The Beginning of a Debate Long Due: Some Observations on 'Ethnocentricism and Socialist Feminist Theory'", *Feminist Review* 22 (Spring), pp. 87-91.

Kline, Marlee. 1989. "Race, Racism and Feminist Legal Theory", *Harvard Women's Law Journal* 12, pp. 115-50.

LaChapelle, Caroline. 1982. "Beyond Barriers: Native women and the Women's Movement". In *Still Ain't Satisfied*. M. Fitzgerald, C. Guberman and M. Wolfe, eds. Toronto: Women's Press.

Lees, Sue. 1986. "Sex, Race and Culture: Feminism and the Limits of Cultural Pluralism", *Feminist Review* 22 (Spring), pp. 92-102.

Lorde, Audre. 1984. *Sister Outsider*. Trumansburg: The Crossing Press.

Lorde, Audre. 1981. "The Master's Tools Will Never Dismantle the Master's House". In *This Bridge Called My Back*, Cherrie Moraga and Gloria Anzaldua, eds. Watertown, Mass.: Persephone Press.

Mackinnon, Catherine. 1987. *Feminism Unmodified: Discourses on Life and Law*. Cambridge, Mass.: Harvard University Press.

Mackinnon, Catherine. 1983. "Feminism, Marxism, Method, and the State: Towards a Feminist Jurisprudence", *Signs: Journal of Women in Culture and Society* 8, pp. 635-658.

Mackinnon, Catherine. 1982. "Feminism, Marxism, Method, and the State: An Agenda for Theory", *Signs: Journal of Women in Culture and Society* 7, pp. 515-44.

Mama, Amina. 1987. "Black women, the Economic Crisis and the British State", *Feminist Review* 17, pp. 21-35.

Minow, Martha. 1987. "The Supreme Court: 1986 Term -- Foreword: Justice Engendered", *Harvard Law Review* 101, pp. 10-95.

Minh-ha, Trinh T. 1987. "Difference: 'A Special Third World Women Issue'", *Feminist Review* 25, pp. 5-22.

Monture, Patricia. 1986. "Ka-Nin-Geh-Heh-Gah-E-Sa-Nonh-Yah-Gah", *Canadian Journal of Women and the Law* 2:1, pp. 159-71.

Ng, Winnie. 1982. "Immigrant Women: The Silent Partners of the Women's Movement". In *Still Ain't Satisfied*, pp. 249-56. M. Fitzgerald, C. Guberman and M. Wolfe, eds. Toronto: Women's Press.

O'Brien, Mary. 1981. *The Politics of Reproduction*. London: Routledge and Kegan Paul.

O'Brien, Mary. 1984. "Between Critique and Community", *The Women's Review of Books* 7:1, pp. 9-10 (review of Nancy Hartsock, *Money, Sex and Power: Toward a Feminist Historical Materialism*).

"Racism and International Women's Day in Toronto: Cayenne Takes Up the Debate". 1986. *Cayenne* 2:2/3, pp. 25-43.

Ramazanoglu, Caroline. 1986. "Ethnocentricism and Socialist-Feminist Theory: a Response to Barrett and McIntosh", *Feminist Review* 22 (Spring), pp. 83-86.

Rich, Adrienne. 1979. *On Lies, Secrets and Silence: Selected Prose 1966-78*. New York: W.W. Norton.

Rose, Hilary. 1983. "Hand, Brain and Heart: A Feminist Epistemology for the Natural Sciences", *Signs: Journal of Women in Culture and Society* 9, pp. 73-90.

Smith, Barbara. 1984. "Between a Rock and a Hard Place: Relationships Between Black and Jewish Women". In *Yours in Struggle: Three Perspectives on Anti-Semitism and Racism*, pp. 67-87. Elly Bulkin, Minnie Bruce Pratt, and Barbara Smith, eds. Brooklyn: Long Haul.

Smith, Barbara. 1982. "Toward a Black Feminist Criticism". In *All the Women Are White, All the Blacks Are Men, But Some of Us Are Brave*, pp.157-175. Gloria T. Hull, Patricia Bell Scott, and Barbara Smith, eds. New York: The Feminist Press.

Smith, Dorothy E. 1979. "A Sociology for Women". In *The Prism of Sex: Essays in the Sociology of Knowledge*, pp.135-187. Julia A. Sherman and Evelyn Torton Beck, eds. Madison: University of Wisconsin Press.

Spelman, Elizabeth V. 1988. *Inessential Woman: Problems of Exclusion in Feminist Thought*. Boston: Beacon Press.

Spelman, Elizabeth V. 1982. "Theories of Race and Gender: The Erasure of Black Women", *Quest: A Feminist Quarterly* 5:4, pp. 36-62.

Stasiulis, Daiva K. 1987. "Rainbow Feminism: Perspectives on Minority Women in Canada", *Resources for Feminist Research* 16, pp. 5-9.

Sumner, Colin. 1979. *Reading Ideologies: An Investigation into the Marxist Theory of Ideology and Law*. London: Academic Press.

Thornhill, Esmeralda. 1985. "Focus on Black Women!", *Canadian Journal of Women and the Law* 1, pp. 153-162. (Women and Equality Issue). Reprinted in this volume.

5.   What Is Patriarchy?

Alicja Muszynski*

Introduction

One of the most difficult problems in critical feminist theory today is conceptualizing the interconnections of race, class and gender. Feminist research has shown the actual interplay of the three in women's lives [1]. Much more difficult is the task of theoretically thinking about race, class and gender in a way that does not subsume one or two within the third: such that race and gender, for example, are explained solely through class relations. It is imperative that all three concepts stand alone. It is equally imperative, however, that we recognize their interdependence. For example, we cannot understand sexism within an advanced capitalist nation-state like Canada without taking into account the dynamics of class relations and of racism. That is, we need to make creative use of material dialectics without giving primacy to class.

Most Marxists, and many feminists who adopt the traditional Marxian paradigm, reject the idea that patriarchy can be useful in understanding women's oppression *within* the capitalist mode of production [2]. I propose to treat patriarchy with the following precautions.

First, historical specificity is crucial. Since the capitalist mode of production first emerged in western Europe, and since it is the Canadian context that informs the current discussion, I will discuss patriarchy only as it emerged and developed within what is known as Western civilization. Patriarchy has a number of different variants in, for example, China and India. Each historical form requires its own analysis.

Second, the feminist movement acquired momentum in the 1960s, marked by diversity in the decades that followed. A number of different strands have emerged, along with many disagreements on the theoretical, political and practical levels. For example, radical feminist accounts feature patriarchy as the cause of woman's oppression, while socialist feminists have concentrated on class analysis. I draw on the more recent radical feminist work, like that of Gerda Lerner (1986), that treats patriarchy as a historical phenomenon. Earlier feminist work that treats patriarchy as transhistorical and universal is omitted from this discussion [3].

Third, a note of caution is needed. Giving attention to the concept of patriarchy as it relates gender to class and race analyses does not mean that an argument is being made for its primacy. What I wish to argue is that patriarchy, as it emerged within Western civilization, underlay class relations in Western European societies. Its most important effect was the incorporation into the consciousness of people of what Dorothy Smith has called bifurcated ways of seeing the world [4]. Class relations thus came to be embedded within patriarchal relations, although class relations pertinent to any particular mode of production affected and altered patriarchal relations while being shaped, at least partially, by the latter.

Finally, I assume that race is also socially constructed, and embedded in both patriarchal and class relations. Like patriarchy and class, it has a unique historical development, stemming from the mercantilist expansion that prefigured the emergence of the capitalist mode of production in western Europe. Colonialism and imperialism led to a redefinition of patriarchal consciousness to include race as an exclusionary category. Simultaneously, nascent capitalist class relations introduced the commodification of human beings as slaves. A connection was made between the institution of slavery and a pseudo-scientific hierarchical ranking of racial groups to justify white enslavement of certain races.

> Racism, particularly in the context of black-white relationships, is often portrayed as universal and natural, not just by white supremacists, but also by some scholars. Yet that is not true ... Racism constitutes an elaborate and systematic ideology; it acts as a conceptual tool to rationalize the division of the world's population into the privileged and the deprived. It is inherently a political phenomenon. Racism in this sense is a relatively recent thing. It did not exist ... in ancient Greece and Rome. Most specialists agree that it emerged with the advent of the colonization of the Third World by European nations, and thus coincided too with the development of capitalism (Barrett 1987:5-6).

Following from this definition, then, race must be understood in its historical manifestation within the capitalist moments connected with colonization and imperialism. It stands apart from class relations, while at the same time becoming embedded within them, particularly in the transition from slave labour to wage labour; that is, from the commodification of human beings to the commodification of their labour power [5].

At the same time, the bifurcated consciousness that can split the world into white/black is patriarchal in origin. Bifurcations arise along class lines (e.g., proletariat/bourgeoisie) and along racial lines (for example, white/Indian). The dichotomy male/female is also redefined and filtered through class exploitation and racism. Working class women, for instance, constitute a labour force that is paid wages below those received by men. However, black working class women face different job opportunities, in worse conditions and at even lower wages, than white working class women [6].

Class relations are intertwined with those that emerge from patriarchy and racism. Class struggle is thus fought on a multitude of different fronts, not all of which relate directly to class consciousness as elaborated by traditional Marxists [7]. Thus, to assume that all working class struggles can be understood solely through class analysis is already to exclude from discussion other forms of oppression.

One of the ways we can study the connections between patriarchal forms of oppression and class exploitation is through a re-examination of labour. Hannah Arendt's critique of Marx's use of the concept of labour is useful in indicating the need to situate labour within *both* a class analysis *and* as already defined by patriarchal oppression.

The Importance of Labour in the Work of Marx and Arendt

In his later work on the political economy of the capitalist mode of production, Marx's starting point is the seemingly simple proposition that humans beings must labour in order to survive. And because labour entails group cooperation, it underlies all human relations, whether cooperative or exploitive.

Class relations, then, are rooted in the primacy of the human need to labour and the corresponding relations that develop around the survival needs of the species, including the conceptualization of what those needs are and how they can be satisfied. Classes emerge when one group forces another to labour in order to satisfy the subsistence needs of both groups.

In *The Human Condition* (1958) Arendt challenges Marx's proposition. Specifically, she argues that Marx treated the primacy of the need to labour in a transhistorical and universal fashion: while the need to labour is basic to human survival, the way in which people (men) come to define themselves *may* deny labouring activity as defining human (and, in particular, political) relations. She credits Marx with pinpointing the driving force of a capitalist economy, which (she agrees) is based on extracting surplus from labour and turning it into profit. In the process, social and political relations become subsumed within economic class exploitation. But Arendt argues that this phenomenon, including the priority given to economic relations as the basis upon which all human relations are patterned, is historically unique.

For example, she contrasts Marx's concept of history as a process with the classical Greek definition of history as "remembrance". She focusses particularly on the meaning of history in the Athenian polis, and in the distinction that was made there between man and nature. Men created history to reflect a world that they made themselves in opposition to the world forced upon them by nature, i.e., by their animal need to survive. The needs imposed upon men by their mortality made them prisoners of nature's cycles. Men broke the cycle by erecting a space, the polis or public realm, in which single great acts were to be remembered. All that related to the natural cycles and rhythms attached to the needs of the body was to be banished from the public realm. Arendt uses the term necessity to cover these needs, and she sees labour as part of necessity:

> In the beginning of Western history the distinction between the mortality of men and the immortality of nature, between man-made things and things which come into being by themselves, was the tacit assumption of historiography. All things that owe their existence to men, such as works, deeds, and words, are perishable, infected, as it were, by the mortality of their authors. However, if mortals succeeded in endowing their works, deeds, and words with some permanence and in arresting their perishability, then these things would, to a degree at least enter and be at home in the world of everlastingness, and the mortals themselves would find their place in the cosmos, where everything is immortal except men (Arendt 1987a:43).

Arendt thus argues that the Greek notion of politics (the creation of the polis, of the public realm) was marked precisely by the rejection of labour as defining *human* endeavour. According to Arendt, labouring is an activity that ties humans to the cycles of nature and renders them animal-like. The utility of Arendt's definition of labour (as filtered through the Athenian exclusion of labouring activity as defining the political realm of man) is to indicate that at the roots of Western civilization (represented in Greek philosophy and political theory) there was a concept of labour that served to exclude those who were seen as tied to it from political participation in the world of "man". Western civilization marked the emergence of a distinctly human activity: politics defined as a distinct series of acts unique to the polis. Speech and reason, as opposed to necessity, were to form the basis for collective action in the public realm.

Arendt acknowledges the fact that the creation of the polis was based on the enslavement of those excluded from membership. In order to participate as free and equal beings, citizens had to have their needs satisfied elsewhere, and by others. She notes: "The *polis* was distinguished from the household in that it knew only 'equals', whereas the household was the center of the strictest inequality" (Arendt 1958:32).

Thus the polis was marked by boundaries between itself and the private realm of the household, where the needs of the citizen were satisfied by forcing others to labour for him.   The relationship between these two spheres was "that the mastering of the necessities of life in the household was the condition for freedom of the *polis*" (Arendt 1958:30-31). Arendt further notes that Greek philosophers viewed the violence that characterized the relations within the private realm of the household as both necessary and positive [8].

> What all Greek philosophers, no matter how opposed to *polis* life, took for granted is that freedom is exclusively located in the political realm, that necessity is primarily a prepolitical phenomenon characteristic of the private household organization, and that force and violence are justified in this sphere because they are the only means to master necessity -- for instance, by ruling over slaves -- and to become free. Because all human beings are subject to necessity, they are entitled to violence towards others; violence is the prepolitical act of liberating oneself from the necessity of life for the freedom of world (Arendt 1958:31).

Thus Arendt argues that the emergence of polis life was in opposition to all that tied humanity to nature.   But modern life has witnessed a complete reversal.   Necessity has intruded into the public realm, and now defines it.   Reason is now used to satisfy the needs of the body and has been employed to harness nature to these needs.   And because the needs of the body are cyclical, process becomes valued as an end in itself and becomes part of all human endeavour.   For example, the capitalist is never satisfied with accumulated profit but seeks to keep expanding it.   The aim of all politicians is to get re-elected, not to become known for a single great achievement.

Arendt views this development as a negative one to the extent that politcal theorists have not rethought the meaning of this redefined public/ private dichotomy.   To her, the invasion of economic self-interest in the world of politics has had enormous consequences in terms of the growing "irrationality" of the public realm [9].   However, my own interest in her discussion has little to do with whether or not "labouring activity" should be part of the public realm.   Counterposed to Marx's discussion, Arendt's re-evaluation of modern politics shows that the definition of public and private is itself subject to change.   While the reality of what comprises the public realm has changed significantly, there has been a certain blind spot in our theoretical thinking that has overlooked the dynamic components of how public and private mutually define each other -- *both* in terms of economic relations *and* in the ways in which these economic relations are interpreted politically and ideologically. Thus, while economic relations were transformed in the capitalist mode of production, entailing corresponding changes in the political structure, the thinking about the public/ private dichotomy continued to reflect more ancient patriarchal relations. These have, in turn, continued to affect and transform, in their own way, material reality. Thus, labour as a concept has come to have both a private and a public character.

The cyclical pattern so unique to the capitalist economy now dominates *all* human endeavour, including politics. Process is seen as a universal force when, for Arendt at least, it used to characterize only nature's cycles and, as such, was banned from the way in which men thought themselves to be human and different from other animals. For Arendt, man has not only fallen prey to his animal needs but has come to define his humanity through them. What I wish to add to Arendt's discussion is the necessity of recognizing the devalued aspect of labour which continues *despite* its partially public component as wage labour. In particular, labouring as necessity and, therefore, as non-human activity continues to be attached to the work of women whether in the private realm of the household or in the public realm of salaried employment.

O'Brien's Critique of Arendt and of Marx

As O'Brien makes clear in *The Politics of Reproduction* (1983), both Marx's analysis and Arendt's critique of it ignore the unique place of woman, whether in the Athenian polis or in the capitalist economy [10]. While O'Brien finds much that is useful in Marx's work, she is quick to dismiss Arendt as a "female male-supremacist ... who perceives childbirth as animal" (O'Brien 1983:3). What O'Brien finds particularly abhorrent in Arendt's analysis is her evaluation of polis life as a positive event and her lament for its passage.

I agree with O'Brien that Arendt is too readily dismissive of the inequalities which she sees as necessary aspects of polis life and of citizenship, justifying the use of violence and force against those who are imprisoned in the private realm. However, I think that O'Brien rejects Arendt's analysis too quickly and too thoroughly. For there is much that feminists can learn from Arendt's work. In particular, without acknowledging that she is doing so, Arendt in fact connects the idea of what Western civilization is in political and philosophic thought with an explanation of the simultaneous emergence of patriarchy.

While Marx defines class exploitation in terms of the appropriation of labour, Arendt connects labour to necessity. The dawn of Western civilization, at least as represented in classical Athens, was marked by the freeing of those men who created the polis (in recognizing one another as citizens) from the need to labour. But this was not so much an economic relation as it was a political event. What the citizen could claim as part of his right to participate in polis life was ownership of those who belonged in his household: slaves, wives and children. What we see here, although Arendt does not name it as such, is the establishment of patriarchy, the private realm of the household controlled by the head who is simultaneously father-husband *and* citizen.

In order to free himself from necessity, man defines woman as other. He has reason while she is bound by her body to reproduce his heirs and to labour for him in the realm of necessity. While O'Brien seizes this point, I think she fails to see its full significance. She asks rather why men need to claim women's bodies in order to be able to name their own biological male heirs. Her answer is tied to her argument that men and women have a different reproductive consciousness:

> Male reproductive consciousness is a consciousness of discontinuity. Underlying the doctrine that man makes history is the undiscussed reality of why he must. The alienation of his seed separates him from natural genetic continuity, which he therefore knows only as idea. To give this idea substance, man needs praxis, a way of unifying what he knows as real with an actual worldly reality. Men must therefore make, and have made, artificial modes of continuity (O'Brien 1983:53).

O'Brien goes further to argue that Marx's analysis of capitalism shows how men reproduce artificially, through the mechanisms of capital accumulation, to compensate for their lack of connection to the human species. In the process, men have appropriated women and the products of their labour: their children.

While O'Brien makes some brilliant insights, in the end she is left with the argument that the consciousness of men and women is different because their role in biological reproduction is oppositional. This conclusion informs much of radical feminist analysis. Unfortunately, it makes reconciliation between men and women an impossibility.

O'Brien remains caught in an analysis of cyclical process, using Marxian analysis to show the transition from dependence on the natural cycles of a woman's body (which allow the propagation of the human species) to dependence on the economic cycles of capitalism, which allow the propagation of profit while threatening to destroy the human species.

What Arendt argues, and which provides us with an escape from reasoning that sometimes becomes circular, is that the creation of the polis, and thus of the entire political and philosophic superstructure related to ideology, denied cyclical time. This important insight can, I think, be used to develop and push forward feminist analysis [11]. For what happened here -- at what has been celebrated as the dawn of Western civilization -- was an event of massive importance for the *processes* that were to mark social, cultural, political and economic change in the following centuries; that is, the transformation of consciousness itself.

The establishment of the polis, of the public realm (including the emergence of the state), required the corresponding establishment of the private realm. What was established here was not process but dichotomy. And fundamental to that dichotomy was the one between man and woman. As Simone de Beauvoir notes in *The Second Sex*: "He is the Subject, he is the Absolute -- she is the Other" (de Beauvoir 1970:xvi). Man has reason. Woman has nature. Process is linked to nature, to necessity, to woman. Man thus frees himself from natural process by establishing the category of woman as Other.

The only men who could participate in polis life were those who had been freed from necessity and could thus qualify for citizenship.   But because men can never be entirely free from necessity, since their life is given them by nature, they assign others to necessity, appropriating their labour and freeing themselves from the need to labour in nature.   Women, in their ability to give birth, remind men of their origins *in* nature, and of their mortality. Men thus separate themselves from women and nature, while appropriating for themselves the products of women's labour, including their children (O'Brien 1983:56).

Women are thus tied -- by the political, legal, philosophic and religious systems erected by men -- to first nature, while second nature becomes this man-made realm of idea-systems, with its corresponding spheres of action, divorced from acting in the world (that is: in nature) and divorced from process. It is important to note here that not all men can enter this realm of second nature. Only the citizen is so privileged. And since it is primarily heroic acts of war that are celebrated in the public sphere and enter history, those captured in warfare are not only denied citizenship but are enslaved. Embedded in these idea-systems is, in addition to the irreconcilability of the man/woman dichotomy, the possibility of race hatred (which flourishes later under colonial domination).

Arendt defines freedom as *freedom from*, in particular freedom from necessity. Man must liberate himself from his own nature in order to be free. O'Brien shows that this idea underlines not only the thought of Arendt but the entire history of political theory. Political theorists root the essence of the human condition, its ontology, in this historic event. Dallmayr also develops this point:

> Together with Arendt, Heidegger presents human existence as governed by neither external constraints nor individual (or collective) whims or impulses; overarching the antimony of fatalism and subjective designs, freedom is found to mark man's "essence" -- which consists in care for, or attentiveness to, "Being." Likewise, power in Heidegger's thought does not primarily signify strategic manipulation or coercion; nor is it a proprietary adjunct of human will. As presented in his works, power signifies first of all an ontological potency or "empowerment," that is, a condition of possibility of human and public life -- a view which does not rule out, but rather supports, the "agonal" operation of power in concrete political settings (Dallmayr 1984:102).

For Arendt, then, history is manmade in the sense that man inserts himself into nature and into time. Man cuts into the cyclical pattern of natural events with his own man-made words and deeds: polis life. This is Arendt's definition of the public realm and of politics.

Connecting Class Exploitation with Patriarchal Oppression

We can glean from the preceding analysis that a particular form of consciousness has come to organize our perception of ourselves, our relations with one another, our place in the world and in nature. That is, our understanding of what constitutes reality (the very ways in which we think) is organized dichotomously, in either/or terms (e.g.. male/female, man/nature, public/private [12]. And, in turn, our consciousness cuts across class relations, shaping our idea of what labour is and who performs it. The category of woman is created and made equivalent to necessity, thus redefining labour according to male/female. Labouring in necessity is woman's nature and woman's work. As such, it has no value because it is not considered to be a human activity. Further, both woman and her labour are defined in biological terms. Simone de Beauvoir (1970:1) captures this idea very well when she writes: "The term 'female' is derogatory not because it emphasizes woman's animality, but because it imprisons her in her sex." Woman has no history, however defined. Woman's labour is natural, endless, and mindless, without even the means/end instrumentality introduced by the modern idea of history.

But as feminist historians, both socialist and radical, are finding out in their research exploring the origins of Western patriarchy, history (redefined once more as the documentation of those revolutionary moments which have tranformed human societies and human relationships) becomes at this point extremely important [13]. For example, Coontz and Henderson argue that the connection between woman and necessity must be documented (Coontz and Henderson 1986:110). They develop the connection through an examination of how a division of labour by sex developed. Saliou examines dichotomous relations between men and women as they developed beyond the period of time represented by classical Greece, for example, in traditional European agriculture (Saliou 1986:184). Lerner carefully searches ancient legal codes and various extant pieces of documentary and archealogical evidence to show women's struggle against this move by men who were redefining power in new terms and disqualifying women (Lerner 1986:4). She argues that this move, which encompassed centuries of struggle, required the revolutionary overthrow of woman and was marked by the emergence of history as a record written by and for man.

Thus, what we see as the birth of Western civilization is actually the triumph of patriarchy. Arendt's formulation of the ancient concept of history can be seen as the act of remembering that which celebrates the feats of men (in, for example, warfare) and by excluding the history of women, children, slaves (that is, all non-citizens), declaring them as not worth remembering. Banned from history, women were condemned to repeat their struggles against patriarchal oppression as if each new struggle was the first [14].

The various contributors to *Women's Work, Men's Property* (Coontz and Henderson 1986) also point to the connection between the subjugation of women and emerging class relations that subordinated and redefined kin relations. There is considerable evidence that in the centuries (perhaps millenia) preceding the emergence of patriarchy, the mode(s) of production were based on kin ties, and that women as well as men held important positions. Labouring, even if divided between men and women, was a shared activity. While men and women may have performed different types of work, these authors and others argue, there is nothing natural about sexual or gendered division of labour [15].

For example, Leibowitz provides persuasive evidence to suggest that in early hominid societies there was no basis for a sexual division of labour. Life spans were extremely short, with few individuals living to full adulthood. Thus, it is very likely that children took care of the subsistence needs of the group, freeing nursing mothers to look after the youngest and most vulnerable members of the group. She concludes that productive activity was characterized by sharing and notes:

> Short life spans, a relatively late age of sexual maturation, and rates of population growth which suggest that fertility levels were low combine to indicate that early hominid populations were composed primarily of young, non-dimorphic members. Species survival could not, then, have hinged on the subsistence activities of the few adults in the group, but must have depended on the development of cooperative production by all and for all (Leibowitz 1986:55).

Leibowitz concludes that divisions of labour based on physiological characteristics like age or sex are not inherent to the human species but are rather created by humans as they develop new methods of production. For example, she argues that the invention of fire and cooking must have had a profound impact for the organization of labouring activity and of human relationships [16].

Combining these various strands of thought and research, then, what can be said is that, previous to the establishment of patriarchy, labouring was an activity shared by men and women, although it took different forms. The establishment of patriarchy was accompanied by the simultaneous establishment of the state (part of the public realm) to ensure the forcible subjugation of women as well as dominated classes.

> As part of this institutionalization of civil power at the expense of aristocratic kin groups, there grew up a new emphasis on the conjugal bond and the civil legitimacy of marriage. Where marriage once united corporate kin groups, it now broke them up, as husband and wife were urged -- and often legally obliged -- to identify with each other rather than with their kin. The state wished to deal with separate households, which it could control more easily than extended kin corporations. Thus ancient states regularly restricted inheritance rights of distant kin and attempted to deal directly with individual household heads in matters of taxation, labour mobilization, military service, politics, and law (Coontz and Henderson 1986:150-151).

Classes were also emerging from the dissolution of kin-based communal groupings. But those who created the ancient structures of the state apparatus appear to have been dealing directly with the heads of households. The latter had a stake in the evolving system of class exploitation because their own status as head of household was legally based and destroyed the older kin ties. That is, while the citizen-head could command the labour in his own household, he in turn was subject to exploitation since not all citizens ruled as equals in the polis. This may have represented a perversion of the initial vision of the Athenian polis, but it came to reflect reality in Western Europe.

The subjugation of women by means of confining them to the private realm of household was accompanied by establishing and devaluing the category of woman as tied to nature, to necessity and to labour. But men also continued to labour, and the development of class relations laid the conditions for the appropriation of the surplus of men's labour. However, men's labour was not defined as such. We can return once more to Arendt's work for insight.

Arendt uses in *The Human Condition* the term *vita activa* to designate three fundamental human activities. We have already briefly examined two of these: action (which she connects to politics) and labour. What we haven't examined is an activity that she situates in terms of importance midway between the two: work. By work she essentially means craftsmanship. Work differs from labour because it is an activity that breaks into nature's cycle and creates manmade objects that endure beyond their immediate use. The activity associated with work is not as important as political action because it is still part of the world; men (she uses the term *homo faber*) must use nature to fashion these artifacts.

Returning to the assignment of woman to labouring in necessity, we can interpret Arendt's concept of work as man's separation of his activity in nature from that of woman. What men do is work. What women do is labour. Actual historical research shows us just how relative these two concepts can be. But the important point is that whatever woman does that is seen as somehow naturally part of her being a woman is valued as worthless by men, including the artifacts she produces through her skills.

It is important to keep in mind that what I am discussing here are the differences between *perceptions* of men's and women's work/labour. The reality shows that women can and have engaged in almost all spheres of work activity undertaken by men (especially in times of war when there is a shortage of men to do skilled craft work). And when social, cultural, political and/or economic transformations take place, women rally to the changed reality and demand a place of equality in the new order. As Marilyn French documents, though, in Western countries patriarchal attitudes have always been reasserted to assign women to a lesser position than that occupied by men (French 1985). The justification for declaring women to be inferior to men has often been based on the perception that the work assigned to women requires little skill or knowledge, *despite* the material reality.

If we jump several centuries to the Industrial Revolution, we see that it was the products of woman's work that were transformed, for example, in the textile mills of Lancashire. And it was the commodification of the use values previously performed in the household that gave impetus to capitalism, because a huge market of consumers was created with the dispossession of people from control over their means of subsistence. What previously had no value because it was woman's work was now taken into the factory and acquired both exchange and surplus value, as Marx documented so well. But capitalism did not annihilate or even transform bifurcated consciousness. Rather, it fed off it, incorporating it into waged labour and using it to divide the working class against itself. Indeed, Arendt credits the beginnings of the Industrial Revolution to *homo faber*. The technology that gave rise to mechanization is credited to the skilled craftsmanship of men [17].

Let us return to bifurcated consciousness. O'Brien argues that men and women have different consciousness based on their different relationship to biological reproduction. She argues that Marx omitted from his analysis of labour women's labour in bringing forth and nursing children. Smith conceptualizes it in a different manner when she uses Hegel's parable of the master-servant relation and applies it to women. That is, those who labour develop a different consciousness from those who, in ruling, appropriate the labour of others:

> There are parallels then between the claims Marx makes
> for a knowledge based in the class whose labor produces
> the conditions of existence, indeed the existence, of a ruling
> class, and the claims that can be made for a knowledge of
> society from the standpoint of women (Smith 1987:79).

Smith's argument allows us to dissociate bifurcated consciousness from biological imperatives. While women's reproductive functions contribute to the formation of their consciousness, the way in which women cooperate with one another around the birthing process is social and cultural. To see this in a dichotomous way is to adopt and reproduce patriarchal ways of seeing reality. What O'Brien demonstrates so well is the gulf that exists currently in Western societies between men and women -- a sexism based on the non-valuation of the labour of women. This is not to argue that women do not develop a consciousness that is specific to their situation; quite the opposite. But I am arguing that woman's consciousness is not rooted in her biology, but rather in her conditions of oppression and in her struggles against it.

The Private and the Public

With capitalism, economic activity entered into and transformed the public realm. And women entered the labour force as wage workers. However, throughout its history, capitalism has maintained patriarchal relations, transforming them to reflect the new class realities. Thus, the work women do in the paid labour force -- while acquiring value because it produces exchange and surplus value -- is devalued in relation to the work men do. Jobs get typed as women's work, with lower pay scales which employers justify on the basis that there are no or few skills involved. These are jobs associated with the labour of women in the household; for example, feeding others as waitresses, serving men as secretaries, nursing, teaching very young children, etc. When men do similar work, the job classifications change (women nurse, men doctor). Their work is craft work and requires skill. When women do it, it is seen to be mindless and thus effortless because it is tied to their "natural" abilities as women.

This kind of valuation, which serves to differentiate working class jobs according to gender typing, is rooted in patriarchal relations. Marx himself was generally blind to this because he examined the capitalist mode of production as an abstract system, looking at the laws of the economy. The relations we have been examining here in that sense have nothing to do with class relations in the abstract. But the reality since ancient times has been that class and patriarchal relations have always been intertwined.

The ideas examined here may also throw a bit of light on another dichotomization that has plagued feminist analysis: the public/private split. Marxist feminists have been hard pressed to reconcile women's unpaid labour in the home with capitalist relations of production where labour acquires exchange value and can be used to realize surplus value. The domestic labour debate reflects this conundrum [18].

What I am suggesting is that we must begin to treat the public and private realms in the same way that many socialist and radical feminists are now treating patriarchy: as historically variable. Once again, Arendt's analysis is useful here because she compares the establishment of the Athenian polis with the nature of the private and the public in modern society. While the latter had roots in the former, the public sphere was completely transformed when advanced industrialization incorporated economic activity as a fundamental aspect of public life. Arendt views this development as the destruction of the public realm. Critical theorists in the Frankfurt School have also paid attention to the impact of the commodification of all human relations on private life.

These studies illustrate the *connection* between the private and public spheres, their mutual interdependence and interplay, and, in modern life, the fluidity between their boundaries. Much of what was once defined as private has become part of public life, with serious consequences for the household and the type of lives people now live. What is significant, however, is that the notion remains intact that there is still a boundary line between private and public.

For example, one of the most significant aspects of neoconservative ideology today is its glorification of "the family". As the number of nuclear family households decreases, conservatives blame the ills of society (largely the result of their own policies) on the decline of the traditional family unit of stay-at-home mother, wage-earning father and their biological offspring who live in their own separate household. The continuous re-election of conservative governments in England, the United States and Canada testifies at least in part to the power of this ideology [19]. Patriarchy remains a powerful element in the way in which Western consciousness is organized.

We are now in a position to be able to answer the question: What is patriarchy? Patriarchy is a form of consciousness that defines material reality through dichotomizing people, their relations to nature and to each other. Patriarchy shapes and transmits the idea-systems and the culture that underlies the capitalist mode of production. It also shapes the idea of labour: what it entails, the relations to which it gives rise, and the division of labour (who does what). Labour has had a long historical development, not only in the relations arising from material production but also in the very consciousness that in turn organizes that production (as well as being organized by it). Its material manifestations in capitalism are rooted in patriarchal relations of domination. The specific class relations that emerge with capitalism are economic relations of exploitation built upon relations of oppression related to both patriarchal forms of domination and previous relations of class exploitation.

Connecting Racism to Patriarchal Oppression and Class Exploitation

Having connected patriarchal oppression with class exploitation allows us to examine racism as a further development of the inequalities connected with the emergence of the capitalist mode of production. Again, the concept of labour throws some light as to how these connections have been made and how they shape one another.

The racism so characteristic of capitalist societies is unique. That is to say, other modes of production subjugate peoples identified as alien, often through the institution of slavery. But slaves are captives taken in warfare.

Mercantilist expansion took this pre-existing institution and commodified it. It was not war that was being glorified, with captives giving testimony to the prowess of the victors; rather, the capture of slaves became an end in itself because there was an unfulfilled demand for labour in nascent capitalist economies in other parts of the globe [20].

While the function of slaves (the commodification of slavery) can be situated within the relations of class exploitation that marked the capitalist mode of production, the fact that a whole race of people (black Africans) was so enslaved and kept separate from other races requires further explanation. Patriarchal consciousness helped organize, rationalize and justify racial categorization, and was itself transformed in the process. The same mentality that created woman as Other could be further pushed to create racial dichotomization. It was not that certain blacks were forced into slavery on the American cotton plantations. All blacks were slaves because they were not suited for the activities pursued by their white masters. It is amazing how the same pseudo-scientific theories used to justify the inferiority of women to men are used to justify the inferiority of non-white races to whites: brain size, intelligence, emotionality, irrationality, etc. In fact, there is historical evidence to show that the category of woman was applied to non-white peoples, as well as to slaves.

For example, Chevillard and Leconte demonstrate "that the role and place of women is in every respect fundamental in the historical process leading to the appearance of slavery" (Chevillard and Leconte 1986:156). In ancient times, and in lineage societies, most slaves were in fact women since men captured in warfare were generally killed, considered to be too dangerous to be kept alive. The authors note that when a man is enslaved in lineage societies, his status becomes problematic. In these particular societies, the status of women has already been degraded (although patriarchal relations have not yet been fully developed). The solution adopted, then, is to have the male captive take on female status:

> To resolve this contradiction, the male captive will, except
> in particular circumstances, acquire female status: he will
> not be entitled to a wife, will not have progeny, and in
> practice, will be required to perform "women's work". If
> he is given a wife after some time, he will then lose his
> captive status. (Chevillard and Leconte 1986:157).

While lineage societies are not patriarchal, those societies in which women as a group have been subordinated can provide us with clues as to how patriarchy becomes established. The important point in terms of Chevillard and Leconte's analysis is the connection between the individual and the group. Where an entire group has been subordinated -- as is here the case with women -- individuals, whether male or female, can be assigned to the group to which they do not belong biologically. Here male slaves take on female status while in captivity. Individual women can escape their subordinated position and, in a sense, become men; for example, some European monarchs were women when there was no male descendent and where royal blood lines had to be preserved at all costs. Individuals can escape the fate of the category to which they have been assigned precisely because that category exists in the first place.

When patriarchal oppression is filtered through class relations we see the complexity of the position of women in the upper classes. Clearly, these women are far more privileged than women and men of the lower classes. And women in class societies have owned and/or controlled the labour of others in their own households. But these women do not constitute a separate class, even though they are subordinated to the men who hold power in their society and to whom they are married. Nor do they belong to the subordinated classes. Here is one instance where patriarchal and class relations together produce a complicated situation, but one which serves to further divide rather than to unite people, even of the same class.

And race further complicates and divides people. Within capitalism, racial categorization leads to the perception that peoples of different nations are irreconcilably different. When Europeans colonized the world they reproduced the dichotomy between men and women and applied it to conquered peoples -- who were then judged to be inferior, not as individuals, but as a society. And they sometimes equated non-white races with the category of woman. An example from my own research illustrates this point and shows how patriarchal consciousness has been applied in the creation of industrial labour forces.

When the province of British Columbia was established in 1871, an imbalance existed in the gender composition of the population. Apart from aboriginal peoples, very few women lived in the province. In an industrializing economy certain jobs had to be filled. These had been typed as "women's work" in western Europe, but there were not enough women to fill them. Chinese men were employed -- for example as domestics, in the salmon canneries, and in laundries. But in the Royal Commissions of 1885 and 1902, provincial politicians and employers referred to them as a "feminine race". Rather than acknowledging that these Chinese were men, those with political and economic power conflated the race with the gender of women [21].

These Chinese male labourers came to the Pacific Northwest from China and maintained ties with their kin and with their society. Their passage money was often paid by benevolent societies to whom they became endebted. Chinese merchants also came to control large amounts of capital. As Ward makes clear in his work *White Canada Forever*, the European population living in British Columbia was determined that power, whether political or economic, would reside with whites. This led to a set of exclusionary acts to deny Chinese immigrants access to entry into Canada. But by that time there were enough women to fill the new job classifications created through the continuous mechanization of canning lines.

Thus, in the end, Chinese men were still perceived to be a greater threat to the new industrial order being established in British Columbia than were women. Throughout the history of the B.C. fisheries, Indian women have been employed in large numbers in the salmon canneries. But they have been paid wages inferior to those of Chinese labourers, to Indian men, and to white women [22]. However, wages were not determined according to racial or gender identity. Rather, employers created new job classifications and then used gender and racial criteria to fill them. These jobs came to be seen as work that could only be done by the group hired. For example, the machine that was invented and which displaced Chinese butchers from the industry was called the "Iron Chink". The creation of jobs and employment of labour in this industry, then, was marked by the interplay of race, class and gender.

Conclusion

From the foregoing discussion, the following can be concluded about the concepts of gender, class and race. First, class as treated by Marx and those Marxians who study it as a complex set of relationships (rather than simply as a category that can be measured empirically) is the notion with which I have worked here. Fundamental to it is the primacy of the human need to labour and the relations that develop around the survival needs of the species, including the conceptualization of those needs.

But labour does not tell us everything about the human condition. And while labour is a central component within the capitalist mode of production, it was not always acknowledged as defining what was considered to be human (as opposed to animal) activity. As Arendt and others have argued, for much of Western history labour was devalued, as were those who were made to labour for others -- rather than for themselves. I have argued that the concept of patriarchy becomes important to understand how this historical event came into being.

The emergence of race categorization -- with the commodification of human beings as slaves and with the European conquest of peoples around the world -- has introduced yet another set of relations which simultaneously stem from class exploitation and patriarchal oppression while reacting to and reshaping the latter. Our theoretical conceptualization of what this all means in terms of the potential liberation of all humans must take account of this complexity, rather than simplify matters in the interest of pursuing one or another set of prescribed orthodoxies.

Endnotes

*Sociology, University of Waterloo, Waterloo ON, N2L 3G1. This article has taken shape around my efforts to come to terms with Marx's labour theory of value and its historical application to the labour requirements of the British Columbia fishing industry, especially the need for cheap wage labour in the shore plants. I thank my colleague Phillip Hansen for introducing me to the work of Hannah Arendt, although he may not agree with my interpretations of Arendt's work. I would also like to thank Roberta Hamilton and Cy Gonick for their helpful suggestions on how to strengthen the ideas contained in earlier drafts of this paper. Finally, I am grateful to my former students who have taken an interest in this topic and engaged in challenging discussions of the readings in this area. In particular, I thank Susan Lyons and Ron Bourgeault who broadened my understanding of this complex issue.

1. There is a growing literature that attests to the reality of gender, race and class as both separate yet interconnected, including several articles in this volume. My own research for my doctoral dissertation also made this clear to me.

2. For a summary of the history of how the concept of patriarchy was introduced into Marxist analysis see R.A. Sydie 1987:115-120. However, the analysis I develop in this paper differs considerably from Sydie's discussion of patriarchy.

3. There are a number of socialist feminist critiques of patriarchy. One of the most influential arguments is that of Barrett 1985. Unfortunately, while she provides an insightful summary of the radical feminist literature on the subject, she dismisses the concept because of its treatment by *some* radical feminists as a universal and transhistorical concept. Specifically, these feminists argue that male domination is itself "natural". Gayle Rubin (1975) also dismisses the term patriarchy and substitutes what she calls the "sex/gender system".

4. For an interesting treatment of bifurcated consciousness, see the collection of essays by Dorothy Smith 1987.

5. There is an important interconnection between racism and the creation of cheap wage labour. This is treated in my doctoral dissertation as well as by Bolaria and Li 1985.

6. See the articles by Roxana Ng and Agnes Calliste in this volume.

7. Part of the inspiration for this volume grew from the accusation by Indian, Métis and black women (and men) that feminism is becoming academicized in Canada and appropriated by white middle-class academics. This charge was made at a number of sessions of the 1988 Learned Societies Conference at the University of Windsor. It engendered much heated and emotional discussion and the conclusion that the feminist movement is not necessarily racist, although current developments may institutionalize it and make it so. The argument developed here is that there is also a danger in the thinking which becomes accepted as "feminist", resulting in theoretical closure and compartmentalization.

8. From Arendt's discussion, it is difficult to situate her own position on these questions. For an interesting discussion of the possible racism and sexism in Arendt's work, see Dossa 1989. He compares Arendt's views on European imperialism in Africa to her treatment of the mass killings of Jews in the Holocaust. He asks (p. 34): "In what way could one approach, wonders Arendt, strange and alien people who seemed to have the most tenuous claim to humanity?" He notes further: "What becomes strikingly apparent in the Holocaust is the murder of eminently 'civilized' victims by equally 'civilized' killers." Dossa (p. 68) also appears to accuse Arendt of being anti-feminist: "She does not think it was an accidental feature of ancient Greek life that 'women and slaves' were seen as belonging in the 'same category'... Implicit in her theory is the claim that most women are naturally unable to transcend their laborious and routine condition."

9. For a fuller discussion, see Arendt 1987b. However, Arendt does acknowledge the continued existence of "purely political action" in, for example, the Free Speech movement and the Anti-war movement that occurred in the 1960s on American university campuses, as well as the civil rights movement of the previous decade. Arendt 1958:202-203.

10. My use of the term "man" is deliberate. I do not use it to refer to humanity but to the equation of human with man and the resulting exclusion of women, as well as of children, slaves and, in modern times, of non-white races.

11. This is also the reason for my calling this paper "What Is Patriarchy?" I do not hope to give a definitive treatment of this phenomenon. Rather, I try to suggest that "what" questions rather than "how" questions (which are connected to process) might inform our understanding of patriarchy. Arendt (1987a:57) notes that "modern science was born when attention shifted from the search after the 'what' to the investigation of 'how'." I am suggesting that our understanding of patriarchy might advance by drawing on those periods in history that concentrated on the "what" aspects of human existence.

12. There is an enormous literature on consciousness, much of it drawing on the work of Freud. It is beyond the scope of this paper to examine that literature, but my own understanding has been informed by the work of Mitchell (1975), Chodorow (1979), Rubin (1975), Smith (1987), Fox (1988), Mills (1987), Althusser (1971) and Barrett (1985), amongst others. Particularly relevant in this context is the work of ethnomethodologists and their concept of the "natural attitude", as developed by Garfinkel (1967) and Kessler and McKenna (1985).

13. See Lerner's critique of history as "man made" and her alternative vision of history making (1986:4).

14. Because women have been excluded from male stream thought and from history has not meant that women have not developed other forms of remembering and of passing on their past to future generations. For example, Keith Fulton draws

on the theory of the muted group to discuss how groups excluded from power develop their own meaning systems. She calls this "making sense" from "non sense" (lecture given at the University of Regina on Feb. 22, 1989). And, in another context, the African sociologist Niangoran Bouah talks about the language and history conveyed by the drum in African society. He has developed a special sub-discipline within sociology which he calls "drummology" to recreate the "civilization" of African peoples in written records, a civilization preserved and passed down through the tam-tams (lecture given at Laval University on Sept. 13, 1988).

15. Feminist criticism of Engels' *The Origin of the Family, Private Property and the State* (1981) has been directed, at least partially, around his own acceptance of sexual dichotomies. While he recognized the "world historic defeat of the female sex", he attributed it to the evolving relations of private property and the need of the bourgeois male to pass on his wealth to his biological male heirs. He did not question why men had this need to transfer property rights in this manner.

16. The authors of the articles edited by Reiter (1975) also examine the origins of the sexual division of labour.

17. For a fuller discussion of the role of *homo faber* in the Industrial Revolution, see Arendt 1987a:59. See Arendt 1958 for a more extensive discussion of the meaning of work and her contrast of it to both labour and action.

18. There has been much discussion of the domestic labour debate and the issue of whether or not there is a domestic mode of production. Summaries of the various viewpoints can be found in Paul Smith 1980, Pat Armstrong and Hugh Armstrong 1983, and Eli Zaretsky 1976. In pointing to the problem of dualism in much of the literature, Eisenstein herself gets caught in a tautological trap, for example, when she notes: "Capitalism uses patriarchy and patriarchy is defined by the needs of capital" (1979:28). Finally, for a summary of the debate within Canadian feminist circles, including the piece by the Armstrongs and their response to Patricia Connelly's critique of their argument, see Hamilton and Barrett 1986.

19. For a discussion of the eclipsing of the nuclear family household, see Margrit Eichler 1983. In the Foreword to the fourth printing of *Women's Oppression Today*, Barrett discusses the powerful force of Thatcher's ideology on the British working class.

20. For an interesting treatment of the historic transformation of slavery under mercantilism see Chapter 7 of Eric Wolf 1982.

21. This material is developed more fully in Chapter Five of my doctoral dissertation of 1986.

22. A fuller discussion of the employment of aboriginal women in the salmon canneries of British Columbia is contained in Muszynski 1988.

BIBLIOGRAPHY

Althusser, Louis. 1971. "Ideology and Ideological State Apparatuses (Notes towards an Investigation)". In *Lenin and Philosophy and Other Essays*, pp. 123-173. Translated by Ben Brewster. London: New Left Books.

Arendt, Hannah. 1987a. "The Concept of History". In *Between Past and Future: Eight Exercises in Political Thought*, pp. 41-90. London: Penguin Books.

Arendt, Hannah. 1987b. "Truth and Politics". In *Between Past and Future: Eight Exercises in Political Thought*, pp. 227-264. London: Penguin Books.

Arendt, Hannah. 1972. *Crises of the Republic*. San Diego: Harcourt Brace Jovanovich.

Arendt, Hannah. 1958. *The Human Condition*. Chicago: The University of Chicago Press.

Armstrong, Pat and Hugh Armstrong. 1983. "Beyond Sexless Class and Classless Sex: Towards Feminist Marxism", *Studies in Political Economy* 10 (Winter), pp. 7-43.

Barrett, Michèle. 1985. *Women's Oppression Today: Problems in Marxist Feminist Analysis*. London: Verso.

Barrett, Stanley R. 1987. *Is God a Racist? The Right Wing in Canada*. Toronto: University of Toronto Press.

de Beauvoir, Simone. 1970. *The Second Sex*. Toronto: Bantam Books.

Bolaria, B. Singh and Peter S. Li. 1985. *Racial Oppression in Canada*. Toronto: Garamond Press.

Chevillard, Nicole and Sebastien Leconte. 1986. "The Dawn of Lineage Societies: The Origin of Women's Oppression". In *Women's Work, Men's Property: The Origins of Gender and Class*, pp. 76-107. Stephanie Coontz and Peta Henderson, eds. London: Verso.

Chodorow, Nancy. 1979. *The Reproduction of Mothering: Psychoanalysis and the Sociology of Gender*. Berkeley: University of California Press.

Coontz, Stephanie and Peta Henderson, eds. 1986. *Women's Work, Men's Property: The Origins of Gender and Class*. London: Verso.

Dallmayr, Fred R. 1984. *Polis and Praxis: Exercises in Contemporary Political Theory*. Cambridge: The MIT Press.

Dossa, Shiraz. 1989. *The Public Realm and the Public Self: The Political Theory of Hannah Arendt*. Waterloo: Wilfred Laurier University Press.

Eichler, Margrit. 1983. *Families in Canada Today: Recent Changes and Their Policy Implications*. Toronto: Gage.

Eisenstein, Zillah R., ed. 1979. *Capitalist Patriarchy and the Case for Socialist Feminism*. New York: Monthly Review Press.

Engels, Frederick. 1981. *The Origin of the Family, Private Property and the State*. Edited with an introduction by Eleanor Burke Leacock. New York: International Publishers.

Fox, Bonnie. 1988. "Conceptualizing 'patriarchy'", *The Canadian Review of Sociology and Anthropology* 25:2 (May), pp. 163-182.

French, Marilyn. 1985. *Beyond Power: On Women, Men, and Morals*. New York: Summit Books.

Garfinkel, Harold. 1967. *Studies in Ethnomethodology*. New Jersey: Prentice-Hall, Inc.

Hamilton, Roberta and Michèle Barrett, eds. 1986. *The Politics of Diversity: Feminism, Marxism and Nationalism*. London: Verso.

Kessler, Suzanne J. and Wendy McKenna. 1985. *Gender: An Ethnomethodological Approach*. Chicago: University of Chicago Press.

Kuhn, Annette and AnnMarie Wolpe. 1980. *Feminism and Materialism: Women and Modes of Production*. London: Routledge and Kegan Paul.

Leibowitz, Lila, 1986. "In the Beginning...: The Origins of the Sexual Division of Labour and the Development of the First Human Societies". In *Women's Work, Men's Property: The Origins of Gender and Class*, pp. 43-75. Stephanie Coontz and Peta Henderson, eds. London: Verso.

Lerner, Gerda. 1986. *The Creation of Patriarchy*. New York: Oxford University Press.

Marx, Karl. 1967. *Capital, Vol 1: A Critical Analysis of Capitalist Production*. New York: International Publishers.

Mills, Patricia Jagentowicz. 1987. *Woman, Nature, and Psyche*. New Haven: Yale University Press.

Mitchell, Juliet. 1975. *Psychoanalysis and Feminism Freud, Reich, Laing and Women*. New York: Vintage Books.

Muszynski, Alicja. 1988. "Race and gender: structural determinants in the formation of British Columbia's salmon cannery labour force". In *Class, Gender and Region: Essays in Canadian Historical Sociology*, pp. 103-120. Gregory S. Kealey, ed. Canadian Journal of Sociology.

Muszynski, Alicja. 1986. "The Creation and Organisation of Cheap Wage Labour in the British Columbia Fishing Industry". Unpublished doctoral dissertation. Vancouver: University of British Columbia.

O'Brien, Mary. 1983. *The Politics of Reproduction*. Boston: Routledge and Kegan Paul.

Reiter, Rayna R., ed. 1975. *Toward an Anthropology of Women*. New York: Monthly Review Press.

Rubin, Gayle. 1975. "The Traffic in Women: Notes on the 'Political Economy' of Sex". In *Toward an Anthropology of Women*, pp. 157-210. Rayna R. Reiter, ed. New York: Monthly Review Press.

Saliou, Monique. 1986. "The Processes of Women's Subordination in Primitive and Archaic Greece". In *Women's Work, Men's Property: The Origins of Gender and Class*, pp. 169-206. Stephanie Coontz and Peta Henderson, eds. London: Verso.

Smith, Dorothy. 1987. *The Everyday World as Problematic: A Feminist Sociology*. Toronto: University of Toronto Press.

Smith, Paul. 1980. "Domestic labour and Marx's theory of value". In *Feminism and Materialism: Women and Modes of Production*. Annette Kuhn and AnnMarie Wolpe, eds. London: Routledge and Kegan Paul.

Sydie, R. A. 1987. *Natural Women, Cultured Men: A Feminist Perspective on Sociological Theory*. Toronto: Methuen Press.

Ward, W. Peter. 1978. *White Canada Forever: Popular Attitudes and Public Policy Toward Orientals in British Columbia*. Montréal: McGill-Queen's University Press.

Wolf, Eric R. 1982. *Europe and the People Without History*. Berkeley: University of California Press.

Zaretsky, Eli. 1976. *Capitalism, the Family, and Personal Life*. New York: Harper and Row Publishers.

6. Race, Class and Gender: Colonial Domination of Indian Women

Ron Bourgeault*

Introduction

The subjugation and oppression of Indian and Métis (Aboriginal) women in Canada has been a lengthy and complex process intricately involved with the development of capitalism. It has been a process which has involved the destruction of pre-capitalist Indian societies and modes of production, the development of class and race divisions, and the fashioning of an elaborate state system of segregation which has manifested these divisions. The origin of modern subordination of Aboriginal women to men (European and Indian) is not to be found in the original pre-capitalist Indian societies. Rather, Aboriginal women's subordination is rooted in early French and English colonial praxis and inextricably bound with class and race divisions of capitalist development.

This paper investigates the impact of early British colonial praxis in the sub-arctic fur trade on the subjugation of Indian and Métis women to capital, and on their subordination to men, with the creation of commodity production of fur. In the seventeenth and eighteenth centuries the Indian communal societies of the sub-arctic were radically altered to accommodate the commodity production of fur. Capitalistic relations of production were imposed on the communal societies slowly destroying in the process the egalitarian relations between Indian women and men and creating in their place divisions of class, race and gender, which had not previously existed [1].

The imposition of peripheral capitalist relations of production in the early nineteenth century, together with the continued breakdown of the collective family, had the effect of increasing the dependence of Indian women on men and in particular European men [2]. The initial development of capitalistic divisions of class, race and gender established in the previous century were further intensified with the ensuing intermarriage of European men and Indian women.

Class, Race and Gender

In Western feminism [3] there is an assumption that the global oppression of women is due to the universality of male domination within the family. It is argued that male domination has existed in all societies and at all times as a separate system of hierarchy subject to its own set of social laws (Caulfield 1981). This assumption has varied theoretical expressions, from the dichotomization of women and men based on either culture/natural divisions or biological differences with respect to reproduction, to either a male dominated sex/gender or patriarchical systems as the motive force of history (Rosaldo and Lamphere 1974; Rubin 1975; Hartmann 1976). In either case, women's oppression is seen as universal, a result of male domination which is separated from class, race (national) and other forms of oppression [4].

Much of western feminism's analysis is theorized from the rise of capitalism in Europe and North America (Eurocentric) and then projected globally as a condition for all societies (Bandarage 1984:507). In many investigations of gender relations in pre-capitalist social formations the role of women and hierarchical structures in advanced capitalist societies are projected onto these formations (Leacock 1978:247; Caulfield 1977:67-68). Power and hierarchy are made to appear as applicable to all stages of human society, assuming the evolutionary continuum to be linear rather than dialectical. Any qualitative distinction between pre-capitalist and capitalist society is lost. This results in assumptions based on a distorted and ahistorical analysis devoid of any ethnohistorical evidence (Leacock 1978:254; Sacks 1979).

Some feminist anthropologists (Marxist) are advancing a more accurate historical materialist interpretation of women's status in pre-capitalist societies [5]. According to their investigations, women in pre-capitalist societies had more relative autonomy, and a commonality in status, than they have under the influence of capitalism (Reiter 1975). These analysts also recognize that gender relations must be analyzed as part of a total system and not in terms of the structure and function of roles and relationships separate from political and economic influences (Leacock 1978:254). On this latter point, capitalism is seen as a social and economic system distinct from previous systems. The development of capitalism in western society and its expansion has altered innumerable pre-capitalist societies. As a result, the social, political, and economic relationships between women and men within these varied societies have been changed to a form required by western capitalism (Etienne and Leacock 1980).

Feminist anthropologists have also clarified the distinction between relations of domination and relations of exploitation as they apply to pre-capitalist societies. In communal formations this distinction is often not made. Men are presumed to have extracted the surplus labour and products of women throughout the ages. In many respects the belief in universal patriarchy and other sex/gender systems is based on this mistake.

In pre-capitalist communal societies relations of domination are interrelated with relations of cooperation (Siskind 1978). The kinship system and the ideology of kinship guarantees the collective appropriation of surplus labour and its products. Relations between women and men -- what they produce and how it is distributed -- are mutual and reciprocal, based upon the common ownership of the means of production (Leacock 1978). Relations of domination exist between the sexes, around certain tasks, but domination is contained within the collective appropriation of labour and produce [6].

In pre-capitalist class (tributary) societies, the domination of women assumes a permanent status -- but one which varies according to material circumstances in the development of the social formation. It is important to look at the transition to class society and how relations of domination (kinship system) interact with nascent relations of exploitation. Eventually, the latter gain precedence over the former, leading to their demise, and a new ideology of domination is imposed (Samin 1980:39, 42).

Patriarchy is not a historically universal system of gender relations common to all societies. It is, instead, a form of male domination specific to particular pre-capitalist patriarchal societies. The modern universalization of male domination stems from the spread of capitalism as a world system. Patriarchy's pre-capitalist Judeo-Christian form was transformed and dialectically reproduced as a form of male domination within expanding European capitalism. Sexism emerged in turn as the ideological expression of male dominated gender relations, propounded by the Christian church and state, as they were integrated with the social and economic interests of the rising capitalist class [7]. As the capitalist mode of production became predominant in the world system, the exploitation of labour-power assumed a value form. Pre-capitalist domestic relations and organization of the family were transformed (proletarianization of labour and nuclearization of family) and incorporated into the capitalist system. The subordination of women enabled capital to lower the value of labour-power; men dominate women, but they both are exploited (Samin 1980:39-41). Racism can be directly linked to the mercantilist period of European capitalist development. Unlike gender oppression, which is rooted in pre-capitalist societies and the transition to early class formations, race oppression is closely linked to the rise of capitalist relations of exploitation. Race oppression has its roots in the mercantile phase of capitalism when many pre-capitalst societies peripheral to Europe were conquered and their populations indentured or enslaved. Racism, then, has its historical roots in Europe's imperialistic expansion (Cox 1959:484).

Although closely linked to capitalist exploitation, the origins of racism are not to be found on the economic level of capitalist relations. Also, racism does not originate solely from conflicts because of ethnocentrism and social intolerance even when they come from colonial capitalist expansion (Cox 1959:478-9). Racism is an ideology and as such it operates at the level of the extra-economic. As is the case with sexism, the origins of racism are to be found within Christianity as a religious and nationalist ideology which became tightly meshed with the social and economic interests of rising capitalism (Cox 1964:53).

In many peripheral areas European capitalist expansion did not entirely destroy the pre-capitalist relations of production but, in fact, reproduced them in distorted form (Meillassoux 1972; Bradby 1975; Rey 1982). With communal societies in which relations of exploitation did not exist, it is important to analyse how the kinship system interacted with externally imposed relations of exploitation. The imposition of foreign relations of exploitation for capital accumulation resulted in a colonial relationship between peripheral peoples and the dominant society. European capitalist expansion, in addition to establishing class relations of exploitation as part of their colonial policy, also imposed divisions of race and gender resulting in specific forms of oppression which were and are interrelated.

To exploit labour power in the colonial areas, capitalism had to conquer pre-capitalist societies. In the course of conquest and subjugation, women were seen as maintainers and reproducers of "savage nature", a role which had to be destroyed (Leacock 1981:43-62; Mies 1986:69). The changes that occurred both to the society and to the relations between the sexes were determined by the nature of the colonialism. In turn, these changes were determined by the political and economic motives of the colonizer and the nature of the indigenous society itself (Etienne and Leacock 1980:17). Compared to women in the colonizing countries, women in the colonial areas were subjected to different sets of values and relations of exploitation, mostly in support roles to men. Generally, with the establishment of colonial relations upon the peripheral societies, the European colonizers addressed their demands and productive relations to men thereby contributing to the development of male domination. Where male domination already existed, these relations were further exacerbated and transformed (Etienne and Leacock 1980:19).

The transformations that took place with colonial capitalism were not without the participation of women. Some women benefitted from the complex relationships that developed around domination, sexual inequalities, and the creation of classes in the colonial situation. Some women gained advantage over other women (and over some men) and became members of the resident colonial elite (Etienne and Leacock 1980:20).

Indian Women and Hunting-Gathering Society

The hunting-gathering societies of the sub-arctic can, for all intents and purposes, be assumed to have been egalitarian and bilateral-bilocal (Driver 1969:266; Leacock 1981:63-81, 133, 236). Within the broad transitional period of communal formations, hunting-gathering societies had a low level of developed productive forces, incapable of producing a large surplus. Socially, they consisted of small gatherings of families grouped together in bands possessing egalitarian relations of production (Leacock 1974:220-2; Leacock 1981:67, 137-8). Relations between the sexes were economically and socially both mutual and reciprocal.

As part of the communal mode of production, the basic unit of production in the hunting-gathering societies was the migratory band governed by the kinship system (Leacock 1954:7). The kinship system defined the egalitarian social relations of production, access to resources and tools, and the collective appropriation of surplus production for its use-value (Siskind 1978:861). The Indian hunting-gathering societies were organized around the internal production and distribution of goods and services. Although an extensive pattern of trade between the groups existed, there was no specialized production of goods on the basis of exchange-value. Any production along these lines would have required and resulted in a change in the social organization of the group (Amin 1976:14). In these societies relations of production, the band, and the kinship system were not static relations, but were in fact a dynamic state of relationships subject to change (Siskind 1978:865).

The status of Indian women was rooted in the social-economic structure of these hunting-gathering societies. Indian women were autonomous to the extent that they had control and authority over their socially necessary labour in the production, distribution and consumption of the necessities of life required for the reproduction of the society. Women's authority, as it was for men, existed on the basis of group consensus and was limited to their socially necessary production. Authority as a whole was restricted by virtue of the fact there was no relationship of power by individuals or collection of individuals, either women or men, that held precedence, whether temporarily or permanently, over the kinship system and relations of cooperation (Leacock 1978:247, 249-253; Siskind 1978:863).

The sexual division of labour for Indian women was not totally restrictive. Many tasks in which men engaged, such as hunting, were also undertaken by women. Conversely, men also took part in some tasks usually performed by women, for example domestic work (Leacock 1978:249, 251; Siskind 1978:865). Indian women were not restricted to the private household work of the nuclear family, with men involved in the public work of the society. In hunting-gathering societies all individuals depended upon the collective family (the band). It was through the communal family that the production of economic surplus and biological reproduction for use-value was undertaken. What appears to be women's work within the household was in fact labour for the whole society (Leacock 1975:33; Caulfield 1981:205, 211). Any differences therefore, between women and men, are qualitative and not quantitative.

As with bilateral-bilocal societies generally, marriage was mainly band exogamy, with domestic residence taken in the household where the labour of either spouse was most needed (Leacock 1981:63-7). Marriages were formed primarily out of economic convenience and were for the most part monogamous. Polygamy existed when there was a shortage of one sex. Divorce was attainable through mutual consent, which meant that monogamous marriages were loose. Pre- and extra-marital sex was not uncommon and was concomitant with egalitarian relations and autonomy (Leacock 1975:31; Leacock 1981:123).

From Egalitarian Relations to Relations of Exploitation: the First Transformation, 1670-1760

When the fur trade was established along the shores of Hudson's Bay during the seventeenth century, two incompatible systems of political, economic, and social organization were brought together: European nascent capitalism (mercantilism) and Indian communalism. European intentions were to accumulate capital through the production and circulation of commodities on a world scale. In the area of the Hudson's Bay the commodity sought was fur. A source of labour to produce that commodity was needed.

The only available local source of labour, the Indian, was not at that time prepared to become party to that production process. Since an alternate source of labour could not be introduced in the area, the European was obliged to transform the Indian population into the desired form of labour that would produce the required commodities.

> To tap the fur resources of America, the merchants from across the seas could not sweep aside the Indians with the sword and loot secret places of the continent. Indians were necessary to the fur trade, and their skill had to be utilized (Mackay 1949:219).

British mercantilism was imposed upon Indian communalism, resulting in the domination and reorganization of the latter.

If the European wanted the commodity production and exchange of fur to occur, then the predominance of kinship systems (relations of cooperation) in the Indian societies had to end. There had to be a systematic and continued domination of capital over these societies such that the appropriation of surplus-labour and its products was no longer entirely communal, but would be directed towards the merchant capitalists. Relations of exploitation had to take precedence over relations of cooperation. The creation of trade or exchange relations by themselves were not enough. Indians would continue to trade only at their convenience for goods that they found to have use-value. In addition, to allow for the increased production of surplus fur the forces of production had to be increased.

Since the kinship system was dominant in the organization of labour and distribution of the economic surplus, the merchant capitalists had at first to use the kinship system, which included relations of authority through women and men, in order to gain control of the labour-power of the Indian. Later, as production and exchange of fur were developed, relations of authority were reinforced through Indian men.

The social and economic transformation took place over an extended period. This did not mean that pre-capitalist relations of production were destroyed completely. To the contrary, pre-capitalist relations of production were reproduced in distorted form under capital, thereby giving the appearance that communal (traditional) society continued unabated. In fact, much of communal society, such as natural subsistence, was reproduced which became a facilitating mechanism by which Indian labour was exploited.

In the 1670s, the British established trade initiatives on the west coast of Hudson's Bay and the southern portion of James Bay. The Cree, Ojibway and Montagnais were, by that time, already in varying degrees under the influence of French mercantilism. The French had initiated individual trading through the introduction of the rifle and other commodity goods as means of production and subsistence, which was leading to the breakdown of the communal band as the basic unit of production. Individual trading meant that fur became private property and was no longer communal property (Bailey 1969:88). Christianity was also introduced with the intention of breaking down ideological collectivism (kinship; Tyrell 1931:119, 125-6).

On their arrival in Hudson's Bay, the British set about developing trade relations with the Cree and Ojibways, bringing them under their influence. English rifles and other goods were traded to displace French trade goods in order to gain control over the Cree and Ojibways' means of production (Rich 1942:254-5). The British also introduced, through male authority in the public sphere, "treaties" in the 1680s as a binding trade agreement to the various bands [8].

The merchant bourgeoisie in London gave continued instructions to the resident officers to further the development of political relationships of trade through male leaders, and to reinforce these relationships with economic rewards [9]. Leading males were eventually established in authority positions as an extension of the mercantile trade, thereby undermining traditional relationships of accountability [10].

The following account of the British development of trade relationships with the Dene-Chipewyan people illustrates this process. It also provides the clearest concise evidence of the influence of Indian women in their society, and of their use by the Europeans for the purpose of penetrating and creating commodity production in Indian pre-capitalist society.

In 1714 the Hudson's Bay Company was contemplating expanding trade to the Northwest among the Chipewyan people. That year the officer in charge of York Fort obtained a Chipewyan woman, whom he called the "Slave woman", from the Crees around York Fort. The strategy of the officer was to keep the Slave woman with him on a personal basis and use her to develop a trade relationship with her people. The Slave woman was kept at the fort for one year so that she might learn the system of commodity exchange and the value of British goods and private property. She was then sent into the interior to recruit Chipewyan people to come to York Factory and commence trade. On her return she brought with her 400 of her nation, including 160 men.

Indeed, the influence of the Slave woman in her society was so great that she was able to train her people in the selection and preparation of valuable furs for trade [11]. The following observation by the Chief Officer at York Factory illustrates this point.

> [S]he has told all her country men what ever traded for
> and directed them how to stretch and clean all there skins
> and furs, etc. The time of year to kill them in telling them
> to kill no summer skins but Moose skins ... she kept all
> the Indians in awe ... she scolded at some and pushing of
> others that all stood in fear and forced them to y'r peace ...
> now she is here she doth awe her country men they dare
> hardly speak to her [12].

The officer then disclosed what was to be his overall intention and strategy. If there was to be any accumulation of wealth, then the Indian had to be dominated, and relations of exploitation created where before they did not exist. As the officer stated,

> I have now had some more discourse with those Northern
> Indian strangers and begin to think the charge as I have
> been at to bring this Place to pass is the best lay'd out of
> any as ever was in the [N.W.] for I find all things agree by
> these Indians ... there is abundance of Indians in those
> parts as never has traded either trade or commerce with
> any people ... but these Poor people have none but are
> forced to live by their bows and arrows and they cannot
> live a great many together, because they have nothing to
> subsist on but what they hunt ... but if please God when I
> have settled a trade amongst them and can bring what I am
> working upon to pass I will stop the trade with those Indi-
> ans for a year or two and let them make ? on them and
> drive the Dogg's to the Devill... [13].

The women and men were instructed in what furs were of value, the desired quality, and the time of year they were to be trapped. The men in particular were instructed in the use of the rifle, beginning the process of developing the forces of production and the displacement of their tradition- al tools of work [14]. The introduction of new tools of work, together with the displacement of some food and clothing production, meant that the exchange of these goods replaced their equivalent production for use-value [15]. These European commodity goods no longer simply held use-value for the Indian. To obtain them required that they accept exchange value. Indian labour gradually began to produce the commodity fur, which itself took on a value of exchange in order to trade for the required goods need- ed to live. The introduction of new tools of work through exchange meant that the Indians came to own their means of production. However, they could not determine their use, since control was vested with the merchant capitalists and their local agents [16].

The influence of the Slave woman extended to political affairs. She was instrumental in negotiating a peace between the Northern (Dene-Chi- pewyan) and Southern (Cree) Indians. This conflict was originally started by the British when they armed the Cree and pitted them against inland Indians to gain access to fur bearing grounds. The British later desired peace in order to draw both nations into the trade. The Slave woman was not only able to bring this peace about, but she also kept it intact. A par- ticular situation arose which the Slave woman sensed would be detrimental to this peace and, of course, to the impending trade with the British. She used her authority to immediately rectify the situation, as the Chief Officer further reported:

> I cannot omit taking Notice of one Passage today one of
> the Northern Indians meddling with one of those Indian's

> Wifes, the Slave Woman when hearing of it took such diss-
> gust at it and immediately she took up a stick and beat the
> man well, she made him roar out and told him that was not
> a way to keep peace and asked him if he had a mind to
> break out wars again [17].

So committed was the Slave woman to the development and expansion of the trade into the Interior, that she vowed not to rest until the whole of the Dene people had been engaged in the trade. She considered this task to be so important that she resolved not to return to her husband because he might impede her activities. So well did she understand the importance of using "agents" in the development of the trade, that she requested that her brother be made a trade captain to assist her in her endeavours.

In February 1717 the Slave woman died. In his remorse at her loss, the Chief Officer lauded her contribution to the development of the trade as "being chief promoter and acter in it which has caus'd respect to her and carry'd allso a Great sway among the Indians" [18]. He was also fearful for its continuation with her departure.

The officer recollected how he utilized the Slave woman in his strategy to develop the trade. The purpose of his strategy was the domination and destruction of Indian communal society, together with the domination of Indian women and the destruction of their role in that society. His procedure was to confine the Slave woman to the fort for a period of two years, where she was made to accept private property and the role of capital by European men. The following recollection illustrates the strategy of domination.

> As I have been writing about the Slave Woman (Deceas'd)
> it will not be amiss to mention one thing. Last June She
> gave away a little kettle as I had given for to carry with her
> when she went back into her country again. I ask'd her
> about it she said she had not gave it away. I sent to the
> Indian as had it and fetched it away and show'd it her. She
> told me was a lyer for he had stole it for she did not give it
> him and said that her Indians should kill men when I come
> to Churchill River and did rise in such a passion as I never
> did see the like before and I cuff'd her Ears for her but the
> next morning she came and cry'd to me and said she was a
> fool and made and told me that I was a father to them all
> and that she and all her Indians would love me and I
> should never come to any harm. She had been very good
> ever since in giving me any information and always speak-
> ing in our praise to these Indians and her own. Wee buried
> her ab't 4 a clock... [19].

The relationship between the Slave woman and the Chief Officer was political. It became a strategic practice for the leading officers of the Hudson's Bay Company to acquire Indian women as a means of developing trade relationships, as well as gaining access to the kinship system. In the words of one officer of the company -- reflecting the early period of the eighteenth century -- to the extent that they were "a great help in engaging them [Indians] to trade", these alliances with Indian women resulted in "a firm friendship" [20].

From the foregoing it appears that women were being exchanged as sexual commodities. In terms of European men this was undoubtedly the case. In the case of Indian men this was initially not applicable. Exchanges of men and young boys also took place, as symbols of peace and friendship. The exchange of women for the purposes of extending relations of cooperation around trade is quite different from their exchange on the basis of their being a sexual commodity. Besides, it was unlikely that the exchange could take place without the permission of the woman (Leacock 1981:24, 215-7). The following illustrates the importance of particular Indian women to the continuation of trade. The woman in this situation was "of ye blood Royal", that is, an important person in her own right or perhaps a relative of a leading hunter. In the past she had lived with and had a child by the previous Chief Officer of the fort:

> Ausiskashagan came in here hawling his sick wife on a Sledge, relieved them with provisions ... she having been brought up at Albany and used to these comforts, as being of ye blood Royal and has a child by Mr. Adams, is very industrious in catching Martins, I having had above two hundred from her husband already and must use them with tenderness on acc't of ye comp'ys interest [21].

The exploitation of Indian women as sexual commodities went beyond the political strategy of developing trade relationships. During this first period of the trade, clandestine relationships were not uncommon around the fur trade posts throughout the Bayside. One should bear in mind, however, that these types of relationships between Indian women and European men reflected the relationship that existed between Indian and European society as a whole. Sexual relationships preceding the creation of relations of domination and commodity production represent one thing. After domination and subjugation has taken place it represents something else. In the former case, there appears to be certain formalities that had to be followed between the two societies. Unsanctioned relationships, in which it was obvious that the Europeans were taking advantage, were met with reprisals, sometimes death, from the Indians [22].

As the society was transformed through a policy of domination, Indian women became sexual commodities to be purchased through the exchange of European goods, particularly alcohol, for their services [23]. For the Indian woman the choice to engage in these relationships was, in part, still a reflection of her autonomy arising from her society; in other respects, though, it was also the result of material dependence on the European. The following statement by a servant made to the 1749 inquiry into the Hudson's Bay Company reveals the changes that occurred. Asked whether European clandestine relationships with Indian women were detrimental to the trade, the servant responded: "the Indians were a sensible People, and agree their women should be made use of" (Great Britain 1749:219). The very fact that these relationships occurred around the exchange of goods initiated by the European represented prostitution. But it was created through the colonial imposition of relations of domination and exploitation. By the 1760s, sexual exploitation had become so prevalent around the Bayside that a recently arrived officer reported in his journal at York Factory in 1762: "the worst Brothel House in London is not so common a [stew] as the men's House in this Factory was before I put a stop to it" [24].

It was the policy of the Hudson's Bay Company in its first century not to allow European women into Rupert's Land, nor to allow mixed family formations to take place around the fur trade posts. Such formations were seen to create a population whose labour was not needed and who would therefore become a burden upon the trade. The relationships between Indian women and European servants, albeit exploitative given the colonial relations that predominated, were for the most part clandestine. Any offspring from these relationships were for all intents and purposes raised as Indians, comprising in part the homeguard Indians [25].

Exploitation of Indian women by the officer class was more disguised. It took the form of a class privilege with Indian women becoming concubines, although in some instances these relationships were originally formed to maintain trade relations. In other instances they were based solely on offering material benefits to the women in return for their companionship. These relationships, particularly when women became dependent on men, laid the bases for differences of privilege among Indian women. In terms of communal society, such relations probably became expressions of status, but eventually it was to become an expression of class as Indian labour was formallly subordinated to capital. In the absence of European women, many leading officers kept a "bedfellow" with them at all times (Graham 1969:248).

Although a few of the children born of these circumstances may have been smuggled to Britain, many other were abandoned by their officer fathers. Some officers supported their children to a certain extent but many offspring were left anonymous and destitute [26].

Since Indian women were the producers of the means of production used by men to hunt, the kinship system guaranteed their appropriation of economic surplus produced by men (Siskind 1978). The introduction of new tools as means of production gave the merchant traders the leverage they needed to control the labour power of the Indians. The introduction of these new tools, displacing the old, fractured the reciprocal relationship between Indian women and men and marked the beginning of dichotomizing the public/private spheres within Indian society. Also, the introduction of domestic goods through men in trade, displacing their equivalent production by women, had the effect of imposing male power over the domestic sphere. It also meant that women's labour in the domestic sphere could be freed and directed toward the preparation of fur for trade. Nonetheless, once economic dependence and extra-economic domination were in effect, the reproduction of domestic and public tools of work remained under the authority of the merchant capitalist. It must be clearly understood that the kinship system still continued; it was decomposing, though. The dichotomization between public and private spheres was a process that developed over time but which began from the imposition of commodity production and relations of exploitation.

With the decomposition of communal relations, continued emphasis on men as the primary agents in exchange relations elevated their social role. The creation of status along with the creation of class, through the process of exploitation, imposed hierarchical structures upon Indian society that had never existed. By using Indian men in the manner described, these hierarchical structures also came to include sexual stratification. Egalitarian relationships dissolved as men came to interfere with and then to pre-empt women's control over the conditions of their work and the distribution of their produce.

At the base of commodity production and exploitation was the value of labour power and exchange [27]. Once there was a consistency of production, the "wage" in the form of the value of goods traded was less than the value of commodities produced. Any continued subsistence was intended to make Indian labour responsible for its own social and physical reproduction, keeping the value of Indian labour power at its lowest common denominator: that of natural subsistence [28].

The specialized production and exchange of fur as a commodity also drew the Indian into the realm of the international division of labour. The imposition of relations of exploitation, and decomposition of Indian society, resulted in a new social formation (fur trade society) in which there was a fundamental social division of labour between the Indian as a primary producer and the European as a wage labourer. This division was determined by how they were subordinated to and exploited by capital, and reinforced at the economic level by the value of their labour power. Any change in production relations, such as allowing Indians access to wage labour jobs around the posts, were forbidden, since such change would contribute to the breakdown of the division of labour and remove Indians from the primary production of fur.

The economic basis of the social division of labour was reinforced on the ideological level through the use of Christianity. The obvious social differences between the Indian and British, as between pre-capitalist and capitalist forms of labour, were defined as differences between civilized and uncivilized. In the late 1680s the London merchants instruct their resident officers:

> Wee do strictly enjoyn you to have publish prayers and readings of the Scriptures ... that wee who profess to be Christians may not appear more barbarous than the poor heathens themselves who have not been instructed in the knowledge of the true God [29].

The reproduction of the social division of labour between Indians as primary producers and British as wage workers became over time a segregated division of labour. Racist ideology developed and served as an explanation. Social relations between Indian women and men and British were seen by the merchant bourgeoisie as outside the "Lawes of God or man" [30], and therefore justified enforcing a system of social segregation.

In this new relationship men were entrusted with the primary means of production as hunters and trappers. As they began to engage in commodity production of fur and food provisions, arrangements were made for the care of dependent women and children. In return for their maintenance women were cajoled into contributing their labour to the upkeep of the post, making it clear that they were no longer entirely contributing to the collective Indian society. For both women and men, surplus labour and surplus production (whether commodity production or food provision) were appropriated by the posts, thereby destroying communal appropriation and dependence. Subsistence relations continued but were incorporated within these new relations of dependency. Within ten years (1724) the Chipewyans were drawn into fur production and the officer at Fort Prince of Wales embarked on a policy of displacing the collective family.

> The Indian which come in here ye 22nd of last month went away with his wife in order to look for some deer, he leaving children by reason they would be a hindrance if he had

> taken them with him he having been employ'd all this fall
> a making things necessary for our Men which lay abroad
> this winter. So I think to entertain him he having a small
> family for to hunt for us this winter also to knitt snow
> shoes and making Indian shoes and other things is wanting
> for.   Ye men in ye winter time and itt being usuall to
> entertain an Indian for ye some purpose [31].

Indian women performed many tasks, for example, making clothing and other forms of subsistence provisioning [32]. What is important in this respect is that these tasks contributed to the accumulation of a surplus, particularly of provisions, in the posts that otherwise would have continued to be produced in the communal society. The post in turn dispensed the surplus food back in times of grave hardship to meet the basic subsistence needs of the labour force [33].

As the hunting-gathering societies were transformed through a formal policy of domination, the role and status of Indian women were also transformed. Indian women were subordinated first to the interests of European men, and then exploited in the interests of capital. In the new social formation which was created, the acts of sexual exploitation of Indian women were little more than violence, an expression of the superiority of the European over the Indian arising from the economic conquest and exploitation.

The Beginning of Peripheral Capitalism:
Class, Sex and Race, 1760-1800

During the latter part of the eighteenth century mercantilism further expanded into the interior of the continent with the Hudson's Bay Company and North West Company competing with the other. The new relations of production were entrenched around the 'Bayside' and within the 'untouched' inland societies, drawing into commodity production more Indian labour in the interior. In the case of Indian women it meant the increased exploitation of their labour and their sexuality.

Before mercantilism (particularly the Hudson's Bay Company) expanded into the interior, different Indian groups had been established as middlemen trading with inland Indians and bringing the furs to the coast. To the south were the Crees (Swampy) and to the north the Chipewyan [34]. This middleman status considerably altered the social structure. Particularly affected were relations between Indian men and women.   For example, Chipewyan men around Fort Prince of Wales were first established in the commodity production of fur and were then transformed and used as the main carriers of commodity goods between the interior and the coast (Rich 1960:47). Among the Chipewyan, "trade gangs" were involved in commodity exchange between the interior (including their own people) and the coast. One such "gang" was led by a Chipewyan by the name of Matonabee [35]. Matonabee was the leader of Samuel Hearne's excursion into the interior.

On these northern inland excursions (Hearne travelled to the Copper-mine River and the Arctic) Chipewyan women were brought along as support workers or as the acquired "wives" of Europeans. In its inland expansion, merchant's capital incorporated the sexual division of labour in communal society into its system of exploitation. Indian women's labour power, as was the case with Chipewyan women, was exploited by merchant capital along the lines of their "traditional" activity. The skills and value of Indian women's labour became inexpensive *and* invaluable. Indian women served as guides, translators, provisioners, paddlers and porters. Indeed, as Hearne describes in his journal on the eve of his departure in 1770 from Fort Prince of Wales:

> ...when all the men are heavy laden, they can neither hunt nor travel to any considerable distance; and in case they meet with success in hunting, who is to carry the produce of their labour? Women ... were made for labour; one of them can carry, or haul, as much as two men can do. They also pitch our tents, make and mend our clothing, keep us warm at night; and, in fact, there is no such thing as travel-ling any considerable distance, or for any length of time, in this country, withouth their assistance. Women ... though they do everything, are maintained at a trifling expense; for as they always stand cook, the very licking of their fingers in scarce times, is sufficient for their subsistence... (Hearne 1958:35).

The particular positions of Chipewyan men as middlemen, especially with the emergence of the "trading gangs", altered production relationships within the sexual division of labour. The original role of Indian women and their labour in communal society was redefined. Chipewyan women now became the property of particular men in the transport of commodity goods, usually in the capacity of a wife. These men (trade leaders and leading hunters) took it upon themselves to accumulate women as "tradi-tional" wives to assist them in the transport of *their* goods. (Hearne 1958:80). These men came also to see the value that numerous wives could have in their accumulation of economic surplus.

To the British traders at the time the plurality of wives and ownership of women appeared as a polygamous practice of the communal society. On

the contrary, these relationships were an expression of the material altera-
tion of the pre-capitalist kinship system arising from commodity production. The sexual division of labour and social relations of production in
communal society were being transformed and incorporated into the capitalistic relations of production taking form with the expansion of merchants' capital. Hearne describes the value of women to the mercantile
trade, and a leading trade captain acquiring another wife through trade
purchase:

> From these Indians Matonabee purchased another wife; so
> that he had now no less than seven, most of whom would
> for size have made good grenadiers ... in a country like this
> where a partner in excessive hard labour is the chief
> motive for the union, and the softer endearments of a con-
> jugal life are only considered as a secondary object, there
> seems to be great propriety in such a choice ... those beau-
> ties are greatly heightened, or at least rendered more
> valuable, when the possessor is capable of dressing all
> kinds of skins, converting them into the different parts of
> their clothing, and able to carry eight or ten stone in sum-
> mer, or haul a much greater weight in winter (Hearne
> 1958:56-7).

Women were obtained as a "commodity" in ways other than by trading. It was not uncommon for Matonabee and other trade gangs to undertake raids on other Dene groups in search of women for transportation
work (Hearne 1958:80).

Alexander Mackenzie also made particular reference to Chipewyan
women being used for the purposes of trafficking, when he commented
that "[t]hey are frequently objects of traffic; and the father possesses the
right of disposing of his daughter." Mackenzie went on to comment on the
reason why the fathers were trading their daughters: "[t]hey do not, however, sell them as slaves, but as companions to those who are supposed to
live more comfortably than themselves" (Mackenzie 1970:151). This trade
took place with the leading Chipewyan traders, who would support numerous wives, as well as with the Europeans.

In the case of the Europeans, trafficking in women took place based
on the value of their labour and also on their sexuality. The trade in Indian
women as sexual objects was initiated solely by the Europeans because of
the absence of European women in Rupert's Land, together with the need
to retain the European labour force. The following description by Philip
Turnor, in 1792, is the clearest example of the intention to create a sexual
trade in Indian women:

> The Jepowyan [Chipewyan] Indians complain very much of
> the injustice done them by the Canadians in taking their
> women from them by force; some of the Canadians keep
> no less than 3 women and several 2 -- an instance hap-
> pened this day of the injustice of the Canadians in the traf-
> fic of the Fair Sex -- A Canadian that had 2 women before,
> went to their tents and took a young woman away by force,
> which was the only support of her aged parents. The old
> Indian her father, interfered, he was knocked down and
> dragged some distance by the hair of his head, altho so
> inform with age that he is obliged to walk with a stick to
> support himself ... all this is encouraged by their masters,
> who often stand as Pimps to procure women for their men,
> all to get the men's wages from them. -- The summer mas-
> ters role employ is in taking care of the men's women,
> which is, in my humble opinion, a very immodest employ,
> but be it as it will they make great profit, the Masters in
> the Traffic of the Females for the mens uses (Hearne and
> Turnor 1934:447).

There were no historical roots for the sexual exchange of Indian
women in communal society. It was completely a creation of the Europeans
(Hudson's Bay Company and North West Company). What we witness
with the above quote is the commodification of sexuality and labour power
in the person.   In situations like these, women themselves were not
exchanging their sexuality and labour power in return for material goods,
but were in fact taken possession of as sexual/labour slaves.   This form of
possession and trade was created by the officer class (entrepreneurs of sexuality) in order to keep their European male labour force resident in the
interior, to extract from their wages, and to lower the overhead costs of
labour with the creation of these domestic units.   The Chipewyan women
were either re-sold by the officers or the labourers themselves once they
moved on.   Such practice was part of the colonial subjugation of the Indian
and stood as an expression of the inferiorization and continued subjugation
of both Indian society and Indian women. The following observation of the
status of Chipewyan women by an officer of the North West Company
illustrates this bias:

> Those females are extremely prolific, notwithstanding the
> slavish life they lead with their haughty lads and masters
> who look upon them in no other light than as fit to be
> used as beasts of burden, to conduce to their sensual pleas-
> ures and to bring forth children... The women are obliged
> to do all the work at the tent, such as cutting wood for fire,
> poles to stretch the tent, clear away the mew, prepare the

victuals and when all this done his lordship sits down at his
care while the obedient wife takes off his shoes and puts on
dry comfortable ones for the night, brings him water to
drink and, in fact, does everything in her power to make
him easy; thus the life those poor wretches... (Masson Col-
lection:19-20).

There is no doubt that male domination of women occurred in Chipewyan
society, and possibly to a greater degree than in other Indian groups. Also,
there is no doubt domestic labour was physically demanding given the
struggle to survive in the natural environment. Nevertheless, these relationships were not exploitive and were not comparable to relationships Indian
women had with European men, which included their status as property.
Within Chipewyan society, women were responsible for and exercised
authority over domestic production as production for the greater society.
In this respect and in many other respects, Chipewyan women were autonomous. In relationships with European men, as in the above situation, the
domestic duties described were still an expression of women's control over
the household, but a household which was incorporated as a basic unit of
production into the nascent capitalist system. The extent that women
"waited" on Indian men is an open question subject to the bias of interpretation and the degree to which commodity production had already altered
social relations in favour of male authority.

The development of peripheral capitalist relations of production, in
the last twenty-five years of the eighteenth century, was concomitant with
the rise of the industrial revolution in Britain. Labour shortages there produced increases in the price of labour both within the Company's service
and in Britain (Glover 1948). The Company needed a source of labour that
was cheaper than constantly importing from Britain and, at the same time,
could be obtained without drawing upon the Indian population and thereby
breaking down the "pre-capitalist" (non-capitalist) relations of production
that were still required.

The source for this new labour was the product of intermarriages of
British men with Indian women. The basis for this intermarriage must be
seen within the dialectic around the division of labour: the unequal value
of Indian versus British labour power and the need to keep Indian labour
in primary production.

With forced colonialism and dependency, Indian women found themselves having to take advantage of the system in order to survive [36].
They gradually engaged in individual relationships with European men;
alternatively, the women were acquired through trade or capture [37]. In
either case, their labour within the mixed family units became a valuable
commodity to be exploited. Indian women's skills allowed them to do sup-

port work that could not be done by European women. The following describes Cumberland House in the 1790s:

> Left Cumberland House to proceed towards the Athapes-
> cow with two canoes and the following men, viz Mr. Mal-
> colm Ross... Mr. Ross had also his woman and 2 children
> with him. (An Indian woman at a House is particularly
> useful in making shoes, cutting line, netting snow shoes,
> cleaning and stretching Beaver skins, etc., that the Europe-
> ans are not acquainted with.) (Hearne and Turnor
> 1934:327).

Indeed, it is posited that Indian and Half-breed women placed in these colonial positions as "wives" must be seen in the context of the value of their labour power, i.e., the cost of reproduction of the labour force characteristic of fur trade society. Indian and Half-breed women provided cheap labour power in the reproduction of these mixed family units (European labour), to the support of the fur trade post, and in the procreation and reproduction of the internal wage labour force (Half-breed). In 1802 the Governor's council at York Factory clearly defined the value of Indian and Half-breed women to the fur trade post:

> We wish to remark that the women are deserving of some
> encouragement and indulgence from your Honors, they
> clean and put into a state of preservation all Beaver and
> Otter skins brought by the Indians undried and in bad con-
> dition. They prepare Line for snow shoes and knit them
> also without which your Honours servants could not give
> efficient opposition to the Canadian traders. They make
> leather shoes for the men who are obliged to travel about
> in search of Indians and furs and are useful in a variety of
> other instances, in short they are virtually your Honors
> Servants [38].

As peripheral capitalist relations took form, relationships between Indian women and European men marked the beginning of class formations among Indian women. As the first generations of Half-breed women came into being, the resident European officer class (particularly in the Hudson's Bay Company) found it more suitable to their class position to take a Half-breed woman as a companion rather than an Indian woman. This was more common around the "Bayside" where trade relations had been established for over one hundred years and Indian women were not necessary in maintaining trade relationships. The following communication, in 1783, signifies that Half-breed women were being taken as country wives and illustrates the circumstances in which these women were finding themselves:

> An infant that has the tenderest claims upon me, and looks
> up to me for protection and support, demands that I
> should not ... increase it by leaving him in this country, i.e.,
> helpless orphan, unprotected to the mercy of unfeeling
> Indians ... the request arises not from a sudden fit of affec-
> tion from the infant but from a long-wished-for desire;
> from a duty I owe him, as well as from the affection I bare
> him, and I the more strongly wish it as his Mother is the
> daughter of an Englishman and has few or no Indian
> friends to protect the child should any accident happen to
> me [39].

As peripheral capitalism began to unfold, a colonial elite of mixed-
blood women was created and reflected class and racial divisions among
Indian women as a whole. Mixed blood women were neither Indians nor
English. They were the creation of the English, half-castes or Half-breeds.
Indian women and Half-breed women born of the servant class were considered to be more suitable companions for the British working class, while
Half-breed women born of the officer class almost exclusively became the
country wives of officers. With the development of peripheral capitalism,
then, there emerged a further interwoven structure of race, class and gender.

Around some of the bigger "Bayside" posts, at the turn of the nineteenth century, this racist transformation was ideologically reinforced
through the education system and through Christianity. Education and
religion were directed at obliterating Indianness from young Half-breed
girls, since language and superstitions were seen as a reflection of the last
vestige of the evils of Indianness. The latter was seen as nature, an evil
propogated through women. The first generation of Half-breeds were
allowed to be raised as Christians but prevented from becoming British
Christians.

> Education and religion should be imparted without distinc-
> tion to the children of both Sexes and that the female
> youth in particular should experience that delicacy and
> attention to their person their peculiar situation requires.
> Native Women as attendant on these young persons seem
> improper their Society would keep alive the Indian lan-
> guage and with it its native superstitions which ought to be
> obliterated from the mind with all possible care. It is
> therefore, humbly suggested that a female from England of
> suitable ability and good moral character accompany the
> School master [40].

Fundamentally, the birth of the Half-breed arose from the colonial subjugation and exploitation of the Indian, and stood as a symbol of that subjugation. The emergence of the Half-breed was not just a question of fecundity, but the product of profound human disunion and inequality between Indian women and European men of two opposing classes. The fundamental condition of the intermarriage between European men with Indian women was the superiority of the European over the Indian arising from economic conquest and exploitation. As peripheral capitalism continued to take form, capitalist relations expanded upon the already existing classes and manipulated and took charge of this intermarriage. The process resulted in the further creation of classes and racial divisions.

Conclusion

In this article I have shown how, as capitalist relations of exploitation take form, race and gender divisions come to be inextricably bound with class divisions. The subjugation of Indian women has its antecedence in the development of capitalism with the fur trade. As commodity production of fur was created, Indian women themselves became valuable, first for developing trade relationships, and then for their labour power and sexuality. The role of Indian women in communal society was intricately bound with the relations of cooperation. To destroy the latter, the merchant capitalists had to simultaneously destroy the autonomous role of Indian women in society. Therefore, Indian women experienced forms of domination, subjugation and exploitation somewhat different than those experienced by Indian men.

The fundamental basis of the subjugation of Indian women's autonomy was the conquest of their labour power. In the process of conquest the gender division of labour was incorporated into capitalism. Pre-capitalist social relations of production (kinship) were transformed, incorporated and reproduced within the expanding capitalism of the fur trade. The continuation of natural subsistence by Indian labour provided inexpensive labour power. The dichotomization of the public/private sphere of production and the exploitation of the labour power of Indian women must be placed in this context. In the colonial transformation Indian women were subordinated to men -- first European and then, over a period of time, Indian. In the case of the latter, Indian men came to dominate Indian women -- but both were exploited.

In their dependent relations with European men, Indian women and later Half-breed women were exploited both as labour and as sexual commodities. Dependent relationships with European men led first to the creation of class differences between Indian women, and then to race differences with the emergence of Half-breed women. Thus, class and race divisions were imposed on Indian women through dependency relationships with European men and under the influence of colonial relations of domination.

In the last two decades there has been a plethora of scholarly works on Indian and Métis people in Canada. Roxanne Dunbar Ortiz has recently pointed out that, though revisionist works have advanced an understanding of Aboriginal peoples in the northern Americas, they are at the same time an expression of a larger neo-colonial movement by the ruling classes to redefine the subjugation of Aboriginal peoples [41]. Many of these scholarly works in Canada fit the neo-colonial model, in that they attempt to redefine historic relationships in a new light in order to retain the status quo [42].

The question at hand for socialist scholarship in general, and feminist (socialist, Marxist) in particular, is to advance a critical analysis of the historic and current interaction of class, race and gender in such a way as to offer an explanation of the forces underlying the oppression suffered by Aboriginal people in Canada. Since the focus is on Aboriginal women, to emphasize one form of oppression to the exclusion of the others essentially asks Aboriginal women to divide themselves as to their oppression. It is no small wonder that some sectarian factions of feminism are rebuked when they advance sisterhood only in the context of gender oppression and in their own image, to the exclusion of racial and class oppression.   The women's movement in Canada is predominately determined by white middle-class women in struggle for parity with white middle-class men. There has yet to emerge the leadership of working class women defining the agenda for women's liberation. Today it is becoming abundantly clear that human oppression is interconnected and embedded in our system of capitalism.   Although there are basic differences between the oppression of Aboriginal people in general and the oppression of women, there has yet to emerge a clear understanding of the parallels between the two and of how unity can be developed. One small step can be made if organizational ties are developed around specific issues which address in a concrete manner the social and economic basis of how class, race and gender are interrelated. It is reaching a time when we must go beyond the *Indian Act* and the illusion of rights defined under that *Act*. The *Indian Act* is, after all, race legislation developed to subjugate a free people.

Endnotes

*P.O. Box 33034, Regina SK. S4T 7X2.

1. Capitalistic relations of production take form when capital requires only the formal subordination of labour to itself. Capital takes labour power as it exists in pre-capitalist form and transforms it into the production of commodities for exchange and absolute surplus value. The means of production and means of subsistence are not entirely converted into capital. Instead, the exploited producers

still rely partly on natural subsistence and the manufacture of their own means of production. By the seventeenth century in Britain industrial capital predominated over merchants' capital and commerce in general. Pre-capitalist modes of production the world over were transformed to suit the needs of industrial capital and its world market. See Karl Marx 1976:975-1025; and 1977:332-34. We do not see class relations as forming immediately with the imposition of capitalistic relations of production. Instead they arise from the lengthy process involved in the breakdown of the communal mode of production and the kinship system. The transformation which takes place is a qualitative process that ultimately results in Indians comprising a social formation of labour exploited in the production of fur. In this capacity Indian women and men comprise a particular class position of fur producers. A flexible definition of class is offered by V.I. Lenin, which makes possible a comprehensive understanding of the class structure of a society at any given time. As Lenin says:

> Classes are large groups of people differing from each other by the place they occupy in a historically determined system of social production, by their relation ... to the means of production, by their role in the social organizaiton of labour, and consequently, by the dimensions of the share of social wealth of which they dispose and the mode of acquiring it (see V.I. Lenin 1974:421).

2. Peripheral capitalism can be defined as the formation of capitalist relations of production in the colonial areas coincident with the industrial revolution in Europe. Peripheral capitalism in the colonial areas is characterized by the accumulation of capital and the development of a free labour market. The accumulation of capital and the real subordination of labour to capital takes place as development -- but not at the same level as in Europe, particularly Britain. Hence capitalism in the colonial areas is peripheral to what takes place in Europe. See Amin 1976:199-203.

3. By Western feminism, it is taken to mean the varied expressions of Marxist, socialist and radical feminism which have emerged in the West. These expressions of feminism are largely a reaction to capitalism within the 'white' advanced capitalist societies. See Bandarage 1984:506.

It is beyond the scope of this article to analyze the different ideological currents of feminism. Such attention requires much more dedication than this article is able to afford. Our purpose using the methodology of historical materialism is to document how Indian women were incorporated into the initial stages of capitalism. In our discussion we reject any notion of a gender determined system operative within original human society and subsequently determining the development of social, economic and political systems. In fact, we reject any notion of a single cosmogony as a motor force of world history.

4. Leacock 1979 and 1981. Leacock points out that women's oppression is so pervasive in all societies that it is easy to assume and hence to argue that it has been universal to all societies at all times. She of course goes on to argue that this is not the case. Leacock also points out that race and sex oppression has been so interrelated with capitalist development that to deal with one at the exception of the other is to dichotomize those who suffer from that oppression. Oppression resulting from exploitation by class, race and sex is in itself pervasive in all capitalist societies. To theorize one to the exception of the other is destructive. Certain factions of feminism, namely radical feminism and even socialist feminism, are intolerant to dealing with racism. Race and class oppression are ideologically

defined as subordinate to gender oppression. See Murphy and Livingston 1985. A case in point is the 1988 Canadian Learned Societies meetings in which two sessions dealing with feminism and racism erupted into heated if not antagonistic debate. In the Socialist Studies session the discussion took two forms. At one level was the obvious threat that some socialist feminists feel when having to deal with racism, especially when confronted for propagating a Eurocentric middle-class feminism to the exclusion of women of colour and their racial oppression. At another level, and in response to the above, it was argued that exploitation and oppression are abstractions not based in material reality and as such divisive. As an alternative to material reality is offered a post-Marxism which, when explained, is a synthesis of vague socialist, and radical liberal and feminist positions. Such theorizing serves only to confuse and disguise objective conditions of exploitation and oppression experienced by many women in this country. It is no small wonder that politically conscious Aboriginal women at least raise objections to the feminism of the white middle class.

5. Caulfield 1977. These Marxist feminist anthropologists are critical of the dichotomization of women and men, including the notion of the universal oppression of women by men. They are interested in improving Marxist analysis of the role of women in pre-capitalist societies.

6. See *Critique of Anthropology* 3:9 and 10 (1977) and *Current Anthropology* 19:2 (1978). These editions contain a series of articles on communal (pre-state) egalitarian society and the status of women within them. Specific to the point raised by Eleanor Leacock that women in communal societies (hunting-gathering) exercised autonomy within the sexual division of labour and that this autonomy was materially based, the debate is almost evenly divided in agreement and disagreement. The complexity of the debate, however, requires attention beyond the spatial confines of this article. For those who are in disagreement there is an inconsistency in what is meant by domination and subordination. We contend that domination is historical, and also reciprocal between women and men, to communal societies. Universality of women's subordination is again posed in terms of the separation of domestic from public production and male control over biological and hence social reproduction. The communal family does not entail an absolute differentiation between public and private production. The biological reproduction of labour for its productive use-value in the survival of a collective is entirely different from its reproduction for exchange-value in the appropriation of surplus value by a class. It is important to understand that Leacock, in articulating the concept of egalitarian relations between women and men (differences without subordination), is addressing the anarchism and ill-defined radical liberalism which was emerging with the theorization of universal subordination. Leacock is also addressing the possibility of an egalitarian society for the future.

7. Mies 1986:13, 38, 66-71. It is our view that patriarchy does not exist in capitalism. Capitalism has developed its own form of male domination, based on the nuclearization of the family and separation of the public and private spheres arising from the development and predominance of the capitalist mode of production globally.

8. Hudson's Bay Company Archives (hereafter HBCA), London Correspondence Outwards - Official, A6/1, f.5.

9. Ibid., A6/1, f.77d, and A6/3, f.99.

10. Ibid., A6/2, f.72d.

11. The interpretation and emphasis on the Slave woman by the Officer in his journal suggests that she may have been exceptional. Her exceptionality was in fact an outgrowth of egalitarian society. The division of labour did not predetermine that women collectively or individually be subservient. Individualism and exceptionalism existed for women as it existed for men, but it was within the context of collectivism.

12. HBCA, Post Records - York Factory, B239/a/2, f.28d.

13. Ibid., B239/a/2, f.35d.

14. Ibid., B239/a/2, f.28-30.

15. HBCA, London Correspondence Outwards - Official, A6/3, f.133.

16. HBCA, Post Records - Albany, B3/a/1, f.25-9.

17. HBCA, Post Records - York Factory, B239/a/2, f.33d.

18. Ibid., B239/a/3, f.33.

19. Ibid., B239/a/3, f.23.

20. HBCA, Miscellaneous Records - Andrew Graham's Observations, E2/4, f.22d.

21. HBCA, Post Records - Moose Factory, B135/a/14, f.63-5.

22. HBCA, Post Records - York Factory, B239/a/1, f.27.

23. HBCA, Miscellaneous Records - Andrew Graham's Observations, E2/4,7, f.25, 2d.

24. HBCA, Post Records - York Factory, B239/a/50, f.3-7.

25. HBCA, London Correspondence Outwards - Official, A6/7, f.222.

26. HBCA, Miscellaneous Records - Andrew Graham's Observations, E2/7, f.5d.

27. Amin 1978:9, 11, 35; and 1974:134. Beginning with mercantilism when merchants capital is subordinate to industrial capital, the law of value as an economic law comes into effect, in which exchange is no longer seen as one of comparative advantage based on use-value, but on exchange value in which the value of a commodity is determined by the socially necessary labour that goes into its production, or its price of production.

28. See Muszynski 1986. Muszynski extends this argument to the capitalist mode of production as it develops with the west coast fisheries industry. The upshot of Muszynski's analysis is that during the colonial mercantile period relations of exploitation imposed on the resident Indian societies reproduced in distorted form many of their pre-capitalist relations of production including natural subsistence. The capitalistic relations of production which were created intersected with gender and ethnic divisions which defined Indian labour as cheap labour. Later these relations of production were further transformed and incorporated into the capitalist mode of production proper in which gender, race, and natural subsistence served to define Indian labour as cheap labour.

29. HBCA, London Correspondence Outwards - Official, A6/1, f.5.

30. Ibid., A6/1, f.16.

31. HBCA, Post Records - Prince of Wales, B42/a/5, f.7.

32. See HBCA, Post Records - Prince of Wales and Albany, B42/a/36, f.19-20 and B3/a/1, f.28. These and numerous other instances reveal the breakdown of the collective family, individual dependence on the fur trade posts and women's work as support labour for these posts.

33. See HBCA, Post Records - Prince of Wales, B42/a/56, f.44-7. In this case the death of a male left his family (woman and children) destitute and dependent on the post.

34. When the trade was first established via the Slave woman in the early 1700s (1714-1716) it was the men who were given and instructed in the use of the rifle and taught what quality of furs were needed.

35. Matonabee was born at Fort Prince of Wales of parents who had been retained by the Governor in the capacity of Homeguard Indians. Matonabee's father died while the son was young; the Governor of the Fort accordingly adopted him. The Governor shortly returned to England. Matonabee returned to the Chipewyan people and was raised by his father's relatives. On reaching adulthood, Matonabee was retained as a hunter in the service of the company. The point of the matter is that Matonabee acquired the knowledge and understanding of the mercantile system and was "employed" in such a capacity as a middleman. Furthermore, Matonabee operated outside the kinship system, although retaining many of its basic features in his life style. In short, Matonabee was mercantilized just as the different Indian societies were mercantilized with time.

36. Hearne and Turnor 191934:252-3. Philip Turnor's Journal of 1778-9 describes servants and officers of the North West Company acquiring women and supporting them at the expense of the Company. The same material support for women was practised by the Hudson's Bay Company.

37. Ibid., p. 449. Indian women were forcibly taken in payment full or in part of a husband's or father's debt. The women were in turn sold to the workers of the mercantile companies in order to retain their services.

38. HBCA, Post Records - York Factory, B239/6/79, f.39.

39. HBCA, London Inward Correspondence from Hudson's Bay Company posts, A11/4, f.208.

40. Ibid., A11/118, f.2.

41. Dunbar Ortiz 1984 and 1981. Ortiz is a Cheyenne, a Marxist and a feminist who does invaluable work on Aboriginal people throughout the Americas.

42. For two cases in point see Van Kirk 1980 and Brown 1980. Although providing valuable information on Indian and Métis women in the fur trade, their analysis is Euro-centric. They do not address Indian women in any context of their own society, nor do they acknowledge any relationships of domination and exploitation of Indians in general and Indian women in particular. Indian women are portrayed as providing a *functional* role to the fur trade. Furthermore, in various instances Indian women are portrayed as being liberated from the backwardness of Indian society through individual relationships with European men.

BIBLIOGRAPHY

Amin, Samir. 1980. *Class and Nation, Historically and in the Current Crisis*. New York: Monthly Review Press.

Amin, Samir. 1978. *The Law of Value and Historical Materialism*. New York: Monthly Review Press.

Amin, Samir. 1976. *Unequal Development*. New York: Monthly Review Press.

Amin, Samir. 1974. *Accumulation on a World Scale*. New York: Monthly Review Press.

Bailey, A.G. 1969. *The Conflict of European and Eastern Algonkian Cultures, 1504-1700*. Toronto: University of Toronto Press.

Bandarage, Asoka. 1984. "Women in Development: Liberalism, Marxism and Marxist-Feminism", *Development and Change* 15:14, pp. 495-515.

Bradby, Barbara. 1975. "The Destruction of Natural Economy", *Economy and Society* 4:2, pp. 127-161.

Brown, Jennifer S.H. 1980. *Strangers in Blood*. Vancouver: University of British Columbia.

Caulfield, Mina Davis. 1981. "Equality, Sex and Mode of Production". In *Social Inequality: Comparative and Development Approaches*, pp. 210-219. Gerald Berreman, ed. New York: Toronto Academic Press.

Caulfield, Mina Davis. 1977. "Universal Sex Oppression? A Critique from Marxist Anthropology", *Catalyst* 10-11, pp. 60-77.

Cox, Oliver C. 1964. *Capitalism as a System*. New York: Monthly Review Press.

Cox, Oliver C. 1959. *Caste, Class and Race*. New York: Monthly Review Press.

Driver, Harold E. 1969. *Indians of North America*. Chicago: The University of Chicago Press.

Dunbar Ortiz, Roxanne. 1984. *Indians of the Americas*. New York: Praeger.

Dunbar Ortiz, Roxanne. 1981. "The Context of Colonialism in Writing American Indian History". In *American Indian Issues*, Roxanne Dunbar Ortiz, ed. Los Angeles: UCLA American Indian Studies Research Center.

Engels, Frederick. 1975. *The Origin of the Family, Private Property and the State*. Introduction by Eleanor Leacock. New York: International.

Etienne, Mona and Eleanor Leacock, eds. 1980. *Women and Colonialization*. New York: Praeger.

Glover, Richard. 1948. "The Difficulties of the Hudson's Bay Company's Penetration of the West", *Canadian Historical Review* 29:3, pp. 240-254.

Graham, Andrew. 1969. *Andrew Graham's Observations on Hudson's Bay, 1767-91.* Glyndwr Williams, ed. London: The Hundson's Bay Record Society.

Great Britain, British Parliament. 1749. *Report from the Committee on the State of the Hudson's Bay Company.*

Hartmann, Heidi. 1976. "Capitalism, Patriarchy, and Job Segregation by Sex". In *Women and the Workplace*. R. Bloxall and B. Reagan, eds. Chicago: University of Chicago Press.

Hearne, Samuel. 1958. *A Journey from Prince of Wales Fort in Hudson's Bay to the Northern Ocean, 1769, 1770, 1771, 1772.* Richard Glover, ed. Toronto: MacMillan of Canada.

Hearne, Samuel and Philip Turnor. 1934. *Journals of Samuel Hearne and Philip Turnor.* J.B. Tyrell, ed. Toronto: The Champlain Society.

Hudson's Bay Company Archives (hereafter HBCA). London Correspondence Outwards - Official, A6/1, f. 5.

HBCA, London Inward Correspondence from Hudson's Bay Company Posts, A11/4, f. 208.

HBCA, Post Records - York Factory, B239/6/79, f. 39.

Leacock, Eleanor. 1981. *Introduction to Myths of Male Dominance.* New York: Monthly Review Press.

Leacock, Eleanor. 1979. "Women, Development and Anthropological Facts and Fictions". In *Women in Latin America: An Anthology from Latin American Perspectives*, pp. 7-16. Riverside: Latin American Perspectives.

Leacock, Eleanor. 1978. "Women's Status in Egalitarian Society: Implications for Social Evolution", *Current Anthropology* 19:2, pp. 247-275.

Leacock, E. 1975. "Introduction". In *The Origin of the Family, Private Property and the State*, by Frederick Engels. New York: International Publishers.

Leacock, Eleanor. 1974. "The Structure of Band Society", *Reviews in Anthropology* 1:2, pp. 212-222.

Leacock, Eleanor. 1954. "The Montagnais 'Hunting Territory' and the Fur Trade", *American Anthropological Association*, p. 7.

Lenin, V.I. 1974. *Collected Works, Vol. 29.* Moscow: Progress Publishers.

Mackay, Douglas. 1949. *The Honourable Company: A History of the Hudson's Bay Company.* Toronto: McClelland and Stewart.

Mackenzie, Alexander. 1970. *The Journals and Letters of Sir Alexander Mackenzie.* Kaye Lamb, ed. Toronto: MacMillan of Canada.

Marx, Karl. 1977. *Capital, Vol. II.* Moscow: Progress Publishers.

Marx, Karl. 1976. *Capital, Vol. I.* London: Penguin.

Masson Collection, Public Archives of Canada, MG16, C1, No. 3, pp. 19-20.

Meillassoux, Claude. 1972. "From Reproduction to Production", *Economy and Society* 1:4 (February), pp. 93-105.

Mies, Maria. 1986. *Patriarchy and Accumulation on a World Scale.* London: Zed Press.

Murphy, Lindsay and Jonathon Livingston. 1985. "Racism and the limits of radical feminism", *Race and Class* 26:4, pp. 61-70.

Muszynski, Alicja. 1986. "The Creation and Organization of Cheap Wage Labour in the British Columbia Fishing Industry", Unpublished Ph. D. dissertation, University of British Columbia.

Reiter, Rayna R., ed. 1975. *Toward an Anthropology of Women.* New York: Monthly Review Press.

Rey, Pierre-Philippe. 1982. "Class Alliances", *International Journal of Sociology* 12:2, pp. 1-120.

Rich, E.E. 1960. *Hudson's Bay Company, Vol. II.* Toronto: McClelland and Stewart.

Rich, E.E., ed. 1942. *Minutes of the Hudson's Bay Company, 1671-1674.* Toronto: The Champlain Society.

Rosaldo, Michele Z. and Lavine Lamphere, eds. 1974. *Women, Culture and Society.* Stanford: Stanford University Press.

Rubin, Gayle. 1975. "The Traffic in Women: Notes on the 'Political Economy' of Sex". In *Toward and Anthropology of Women*, pp. 157-210. Rayna R. Reiter, ed. New York: Monthly Review Press.

Sacks, Karen. 1979. *Sisters and Wives: The Past and Future of Sexual Equality.* Westport: Greenwood Press, Inc.

Siskind, Janet. 1978. "Kinship and Mode of Production", *American Anthropologist* 80:4, pp. 860-872.

Tyrrell, J.B., ed. 1931. *Documents Relating to the Early History of Hudson Bay.* Toronto: The Champlain Society.

Van Kirk, Sylvia. 1980. *Many Tender Ties.* Winnipeg: Watson and Dwyer.

7. Race, Class and Marginality in a Manitoba Interlake Settlement: 1850-1950

Nicole St-Onge*

It is the curious fate of people who have experienced the expansion of imperialism to be considered inherently incapable of so-called progress and development (Gupta 1983:23). The supposed backwardness of Canadian native people, for example, is often explained in terms of their inability to think beyond their group affiliations and to break through walls of "unprogressive" customs and traditions, due to some "racial" shortcoming (Giraud 1984, introductory comments). Researchers falling back on racial explanations for uneven socio-economic situations thus avoid any analysis of how society has developed and how it functions.

For many "Métis" in western Canada racism is a fact of life even though, as Lagassé points out, most Métis would escape identification if they were affluent and resided in predominantly white communities. Many European nationals have coarse black hair, high cheek bones, dark skin pigmentation, and deep brown eyes -- all traits used in describing the Métis (Lagassé 1959:5). In fact, instances of Manitoba's Métis "passing" for whites after socio-economic improvements are well documented. In a 1947 letter to the father provincial, the Oblate missionary for Abbeville, Manitoba, comments:

> Population catholique [est de] 164 personnes dont plusieurs ont l'humeur vagabonde. Dans 7 familles Métisses on parle encore sauteux. *Les 40 ou 50 Métis bien évolué devraient figure sous la rustique 'Canadien Francais'* ce qui ferait c.f. = 108, Métis peu évolué = 50, Ang.,ind., etc. = 6 (emphasis mine) [1].

When asked to define "Half-breeds", people evoke physical characteristics. The actual indicators are general lifestyle, living conditions, work performed, language spoken, and clothes worn. Dipankar Gupta's comment on the dominant society's perception of French Canadians holds true for the Métis: "Racism is the most comprehensive ideological weapon of domination and ... it does not always obey the protocol of color" (Gupta 1983:24).

This paper examines how, since the 1850s, capitalist development in Manitoba's Interlake area and the interpretation of this region's history have been heavily influenced by a western racist ideology. This ideology, coupled to the other political-social-economic dynamics of capitalism, led to the development and maintenance of racially distinct marginal communities. Racism alone, however, was used to explain the existence of these communities in terms of a perceived racial difference that affected the residents' culture, world view, and work habits. The specific community examined is a Métis settlement on the southern shores of Lake Manitoba.

The Mirage of Race: The Scientific Bases for a Theory of Human Races

What is meant by concepts such as "race" and "racism", and what should their position be in a materialist framework? Should these terms and the closely related and currently more popular, polite, and nebulous expression "ethnicity" be seen as *fundamental variables*, having a reality independent of our awareness of them? Or should they be seen as *objects of critical analysis*? Should ethnicity, race, and racism be analytical tools in studies of society, or should the key questions be how and why they have come to give an apparent (but erroneous) sense to the phenomenal world?

Robert Miles [2] points out that physical characteristics are still used to categorize people, without regard to other traits that set them apart. Certain phenotypical variations are interpreted using the word race, but the word is used in a diffuse way (Miles 1982:7) without regard to a formal or scientific definition. It is simply part of every day discourse, and is assumed (wrongly) to have a scientific basis referring to discrete categories of people separated by their physical characteristics. Social significance is attributed to these categories to justify or generate different patterns of behaviour (Miles 1982:10). Rebuttals of racial theories by geneticists and biologists have not trickled down from scientific discourse and, therefore, have not negated the belief in races nor the existence of a racist world-view within the western world's popular culture and ideology.

Miles' explanation for the persistence of these folk concepts is based on a fundamental distinction made by Marx between *phenomenal* form and *essential* relations (Miles 1982:14). The "phenomenal form" is the way in which the phenomena of the external, social world are perceived and represented in human experience while "essential relations" refers to the real conditions of existence of the phenomenal forms. For example, the differing experiences of the indigenous population to the advance and development of capital in what was called British North America have been ascribed to racial differences (Giraud 1984:introductory comments). But such analysis fails to examine the impact of imperialism, how it varies at the core and periphery, and what is experienced by populations differently situated within capitalist relations of production. As Miles points out:

> We must not unquestioningly incorporate in a scientific
> analysis the categories of description and analysis used in
> everyday discourse because, in so far as that discourse is
> uncritical and confines itself to the direct experience and
> appearance of the social world, then there is the possibility
> of creating a false and misleading explanation (Miles
> 1982:32).

Since race has no biological reality but is a social construct, authors basing
their analysis on the assumption of the existence of races confuse the phenomenal form in which economic and political conflicts appear, with the
underlying *structural* characteristics of these social formations [3].

Miles argues that race and racism cannot be traced directly to the
development of capitalism, since there is a great delay between the rise of
capitalism as a mode of production and the development of an ideology
seeing people of colour as inferior beings. It is also difficult to label it a
"child of imperialism" since such an explanatory framework would have
difficulty dealing with the development of racism within Europe, *vis-à-vis*
the Irish or the Jews for example (Miles 1982:146). Nevertheless, by the
second half of the 19th century, racism had become a central element in
the world view of large segments of the bourgeoisie and was influencing
the thinking of elements within the working class. Racism began to have
real material effects. It became what Marx termed a "material force", influencing and being influenced by the conditions of production.

In this context of capitalist expansion imbued with a racist ideology,
the Métis settlement of Saint-Laurent developed.

Saint-Laurent du Manitoba: General Background

In the Red River settlement (1821-1870) basic social divisions --
including the division of labour -- were understood to be the product of
racial or ethnic, not class, divisions. This racial perception and the resulting
fragmentation of labouring groups were caused by a deliberate policy of
Hudson's Bay Company (H.B.C.) officials, and not merely the product of
racist assumptions or the straightforward dictates of a mercantilist economy. As Ron Bourgeault notes in relation to the possibility of home guard
Indians being involved in wage labour around the fur trade post:

> Any change in productive relations such as allowing Indi-
> ans access to wage labour jobs around the posts, was for-
> bidden, since such change would contribute to the break-
> down of the peasantry. Together with an already highly
> developed ideology of racism among the colonizers, which

served to justify the nature of this exploitation, this division enhanced subjective racial ideas of differences among the European labourers around the posts. The difference was also maintained economially between the two divisions of labour, primarily through the tariff or the rate at which labour was exchanged or sold for goods. The tariff was much higher for the primary producer than for the wage worker (Bourgeault 1984:54).

Cultural differences were emphasized, defined as racial, and presented as having a direct bearing on the labouring potential of individuals. The English, the Orkneymen, the French-Canadians, French Roman-Catholic Métis, English Protestant Half-breeds, and finally the full-blooded Natives -- all were seen as occupying distinct socio-economic positions as a result of their "race". To what extent this was internalized by the actors involved is difficult to assess. Irene Spry has argued that class governed social interaction and blurred (some) of the racial distinctions in Red River to an extent greater than previously thought (Spry 1985:95-118). However, it is clear from existing archival material that the authorities' *perception* of the nature of the racial divisions affected the economic roles of individuals.

Between 1760 and 1821 a need emerged for a source of wage labour located within the territory. Indians or, more accurately, those engaged in the primary task of producing furs for exchange could not be recruited in large numbers since this would threaten the very existence of the fur trade. Thus fur trade officials turned to the mixed-blood children of European or Canadian workers and local women who had not been absorbed culturally and economically into the Indian class. Out of the curious combination of the demands of mercantilism for a local wage labour pool, and a pre-existing racist ideology, a new biological category imbued with specific social and economic characteristics crystallized:

> For reasons of class and race [they] were no longer to be considered as Indians and were not allowed to become English; they were, as their colonizers called them, "Half-breeds" (or the French equivalent, "Métis") (Bourgeault 1984:61).

With the merging of the H.B.C. and the North West Company in 1821 many in this evolving racial category could not be employed full-time in wage-labour occupations. The streamlining of the fur trade labour force, along with improved technology (the York boats), resulted in a rapid rise in the unemployed or underemployed Métis population of the Red River (Rothney 1975:62-113). This surplus population specialized in the production of commodities indirectly tied to the fur economy. A fluid Métis underclass of bison hunters, fishermen and salt makers emerged. They tried to diversify out of their precarious existence but met with only limited success. They were opposed by Company officials leary of any perceived threat to their reserves of labour and plain provision.

Only in the 1850s and 1860s did significant class differences occur *within* the population labelled Métis. An elite composed of small traders and farmers emerged, but their primary loyalties became (or remained?) class-oriented, not racial (St-Onge 1985:149-172): they remained largely passive during the 1869-70 events. The supporters of Riel framed their demands for socio-eonomic improvement and security in racial and nationalistic terms, but motivation came from their membership in an oppressed and increasingly marginalized class.

By the late 1820s, semi-permanent settlements were emerging in the Saint-Laurent, Duck Bay, and Oak Point areas where winter fishing could be carried out [4]. These areas also became rallying points in spring and autumn for Métis involved in the production of salt on the shores of Lake Manitoba. Settlers combined such activities with some buffalo hunting. These lake shore settlements were a direct result of market demands for certain staples; they *never* became self-sufficient.

Ten families (two from North Dakota) lived in Saint-Laurent by 1858. Their involvement in the hunt and the exploitation of the more northerly salt springs forced the Métis into a semi-nomadic existence, but they consistently came back to what was by then an Oblate mission area where good fishing grounds existed [5]. There is no archival documentation to suggest that much agricultural activity occured in Saint-Laurent prior to the early 1860s. Farming was barely a viable occupation (in terms of both output and market demands) in the heart of the colony let alone in the Interlake 'hinterland' (Sprenger 1972).

Race, Class and Missionaries' Perceptions:
Saint-Laurent, 1850-1900

Oblate missionaries imbued with a racist ideology perpetuated the process of racialization of Red River society, while emphasizing further distinctions along religious and linguistic lines. Missionary letters are filled with interpretations of existing economic situations using a racist worldview. These letters advocate specific actions that very much take the concept of race into account. For example, during the worst of the famine of 1867-1868 the local Saint-Laurent Oblate, Father Simonet, apparently unaware of the effects of starvation, attributed the Métis lack of interest in doing *corvee* work for the mission to their laziness and inherently indolent character [6]. The resident priest for the parish of Sainte-Claire, assessing the economic prospects for his parish, argued that even though the local Métis were reasonably well off:

> Quand aux métis qui composent en grande partie ma paroisse, à part de respectable exceptions, ils sont une bande de dégénérés, de jouisseurs ... la chose capitale pour l'avenir de Sainte-Claire est de *remplacer en grande partie les métis par des familles canadiennes-francaise, autrement nous aurons le même resultat qu'à Saint-Laurent* (emphasis mine) [7].

In other words: poverty, marginalization, and even simply cultural traditions were the result of the biologically inherited and unchangeable predisposition of the Métis, and were unrelated to the structural constraints of a peripheral staple producing economy. Solutions advanced were posited in terms of altering the "genetic" composition of the local population rather than in terms of addressing economic problems.

Whatever the merits of the ecclesiastial assessment of Métis character, these underclasses of labourers (H.B.C. hired hands) and staple producers experienced severe material hardship and social dislocation between 1865-1875 with the decline of the fur trade centered on the Red River, the decimation of the bison herds, and the transfer of power from the H.B.C. to the Canadian government. For Saint-Laurent, documented hardships began with the famine of 1867-8. The statistical summary produced by the Executive Relief Committee indicates that 17 households out of 36 were in need of immediate relief, even though most included able-bodied men [8]. Even among the non-indigent families only one or two reported possessing enough bushels of potatoes and heads of cattle to carry them through the winter. In the 1860s the vast majority of these people still counted on fishing and bison hunting to feed their families and produce an exchangeable commodity. Neither of these staples were in plentiful supply in the late 1860s.

It is therefore not surprising that the starving segment of the population took action:

> In March 1870, during the Riel Rebellion, the [Saint-Laurent and Oak Point] Half-breeds took possession of the H.B.C. post at Oak Point and killed 8 or 10 head of cattle, distributed the beef among themselves as well as some dry goods taken from the store [9].

They treated the clerk in charge kindly "furnishing him with fresh meat and staples". Seemingly as an afterthought, the chronicler (writing in 1895) comments that Father Camper was very much displeased with his charges.

This foray brought only fleeting relief for the desperate families. Commenting on the months following the March trading post take-over, Brother Mulvihill states:

> After March [came a] time of hunger. There was no flour to be found just dried jackfish. A métis, Francois Bonneau was suffering from extreme want and poverty. He once had been a buffalo hunter. [Bonneau tells chronicler] 'I have eaten nothing in the last 3 days save and except "des petites poires qui me donnent la chiche, mon corps est toujours lache et je suis bien faible'". Bonneau had been one of the bravest [hunters] on the plain [10].

Nevertheless the Métis stayed in Saint-Laurent, slowly giving up their bison hunting and salt making for lack of a product or market [11] while making the transition to *commercial* fishing, coupled with either dairy farming, trapping, wild produce harvesting, occasionally winter freighting on the lakes and, after World War I, farm labour [12]. Dairy farming became a viable alternative for some of the Saint-Laurent families because, unlike other areas of the province (St-Onge 1983), several of them were successful at securing letters patent for their land. Of 24 lots surveyed, 14 were at least partially patented in the name of the original claimants. But by no means did all of these 14 Métis patentees have sufficient capital, expertise, or market outlets to bring the land into production. Also, the number of families residing in Saint-Laurent had increased from 20 in 1866 to 130 in 1893, most presumably without title to the land they occupied.

After 1870 the writer of the Saint-Laurent *codex historicus*, in a curiously dichotomous manner of thinking, criticized the Métis for their lack of responsibility towards land ownership, while in the next text acknowledging their severe, crippling poverty which would impede any attempt at successfully bringing their land into production and would make the selling of scrip or sections of land for hard cash a frequent *necessity*. Commenting on the land speculators that were operating in the area, Brother Mulvihill states:

> Few if any of the Half-Breeds availed themselves of this good occasion to procure and secure additional property, no, but they sold their 'script' to speculators or land grabbers for whatever they could get for it. This script was sold for 35 cents on the dollars ... [also] The Half-Breeds of this parish as well as other parishes not only sold their script but also the 240 acre lot which each obtained ... not one of them owns a 240 acre lot just now in 1895 at least in this parish [13].

Yet in the same text the Brother expresses deep concern over the question of how the lakeshore inhabitants can make a living. In the spring of 1867 he anxiously notes that black flour is selling for $7.00 to $10.00 per 100 lbs sack [14]. In an entry made in 1875, Mulvihill comments that "the Fathers did not at all expect such crowds of people at the retreat, especially as the poor people *have to subsist from day to day* by the chase" [15] and therefore the participants were skirting famine by suspending such activities for several days (emphasis mine). Despite this pragmatic realization of the constraints under which the Métis inhabitants lived the overall tone is one of condemnation. In 1877 Father Lacombe o.m.i. writes to the Father Superior:

> La population de Saint-Laurent est composée presque exclusivement de métis qui habitent les bords du lac. Ils se sont bâti des maisons aux environs de la mission et cultivent chacun un petit morceau de terre. Anciens chasseurs de la forêt, ils gardent encore leurs vieilles habitudes et passent plusieurs semaines à poursuivre le gibier [16].

But even at this early date (1900) the Oblates' chronicles betray the existence of emerging class divisions in the settlement. While still making generalized deprecating racial remarks about the Métis, they noted that Saint-Laurent was fragmenting along occupational lines: "Il y en a cependant un certain nombre qui ne s'éloignent jamais de la mission et qui vivent du produit de leur jardin et de la pêche" [17]. Like the previously mentioned priest of Abbeville, the Oblates maintained a racist paradigm in the face of social change by whitening those of their charges who became economically successful and no longer fit the stereotype. When describing an exceptionally hard-working woman, Father Mulvihill makes the comment: "It may be added that Mrs. (Cecile Larivière) McLeod had been both tall and strong and good-looking and resembled a French-Canadian rather than a half-breed" [18]. By the 1900s the Oblates' lack of esteem for their Métis charges translated itself into an active campaign to recruit *farming* French-Canadian and Breton families for settlement in Saint-Laurent [19]. It was hoped that, by bringing in new blood, the parish would become a prosperous agrarian settlement.

These lay and clerical officials' (along with their French Canadian and Breton proteges') views of the Métis have been perpetuated and presented as truth in the literature published by ethnologists and historians. Giraud's lengthy, scathing condemnation of this class of people published in 1945 sums up 20th century attitudes towards this 'race':

> Il est logique que cette état de décomposition se traduise par l'isolement d'une grande partie de la société métisse

dans les provinces de l'Ouest. *On ne saurait attendre d'éléments reduits a ce degré de décheance qu'ils obtiennent, du moins en nombre appréciable, un droit d'accès à la société blanche.* Ou bien, lorsque les unions s'accomplissent, elles risquent fort de se faire entre éléments de même niveau, et de demeurer sans profit pour les métis. L'isolement se manifeste déjà dans les groupes que nous avons observés autour des lacs Winnipeg et Manitoba, dont la décadence est pourtant moins prononcée. *A Saint-Laurent, Francais et Canadien s'unissent dans un égal mépris du group de couleur. Leur hostilité s'y exprime en paroles malveillantes, presque haineuses, surtout de la part des familles francaises récemment introduites par les Pères Oblats:* la conduite de celle-ce, faite de travail et d'abnégation, ne saurait s'harmoniser avec les habitudes de vie des Métis. Les Canadiens n'adoptent pas une attitude plus conciliante, bien qu'ils n'atteignent pas au niveau de ces magnifiques familles du "vieux pays". Sans doute quelques unions sont inévitables ... Et il existe, nous l'avons vu, parmi les métis, des familles assez évoluées pour ne pas encourir sans injustice, l'hostilité systématique des Blancs. Mais les alliances qui s'opèrent entre les uns et les autres sont mal vues de ces derniers. Non seulement, elles ne dissipent point leurs préventions, mais elles paraissent les aggraver. C'est précisément des Canadiens dont les familles comptent une ou plusieurs unions de cette nature qu'émanent les critiques les plus sévères, comme *s'ils eprouvent une vive humiliation d'avoir à admettre parmi eux des réprésentants de ce groupe inférieur* (Giraud 1984:1271-72, emphasis mine).

Saint-Laurent du Manitoba, 1900-1945

If one rejects the biological explanation for the Saint-Laurent Métis second-class citizen status (or, more accurately, the labelling of the poorer section of the population as Métis) other avenues must be explored. What were the real underlying relations, coalescing between 1900-1945, that produced such antagonistic social groups whose very existence was justified and reinforced by racist ideology? Through written archival material and with the help of oral history, the impact of both a western concept of races and of capitalist expansion in the Interlake area, on the development of a "racially distinct marginal community" on the southern shore of Lake Manitoba can be assessed.

In 1900 Saint-Laurent was still experiencing the rapid capitalist penetration that had already resulted in socio-economic fragmentation during the closing years of the last century. The village's economy, essentially based on the production of staples, strongly resembled communities on the more northerly shores of the lake (Lagassé 1959: Vol. 3), with which it still had familial and business ties (as in the previous century with salt production) [20]. The village was linked to an international economy through its production of pelts and fish but, unlike the northern settlements, it was also tied to the provincial economy through the selling of dairy cream to Winnipeg [21]. This provincial connection was crucial in the rise of clear socio-economic differences in Saint-Laurent.

The Saint-Laurent farming segment was largely composed of recently arrived french immigrants but it also included a few families of Métis descent that had successfully passed into it during the interwar period. Unlike the families more fully tied to an international economy by a greater dependence on fishing and trapping for income, they were always reasonably assured of a fairly steady market for their products between 1870 and 1950. On the *average*, Manitoba farmers in 1936 had an overall net income of $303.12, a drop of 62% from their 1926 income, but still not nearly as great a downward trend as that experienced by other primary producers [22].

Between 1900 and 1945 most residents of Saint-Laurent fished commercially to some degree. The arrival of the railway in the early 1900s tied producers to international markets, especially Chicago (Zazlow 1971:92). This was a mixed blessing since, by pushing up demand and production, it threatened to further deplete fish stocks. As early as 1890 the Department of Indian Affairs had noted: "The lower portion of Lake Winnipeg and portions of Lake Manitoba have ceased to be good fishing grounds after having been operated upon by large fishing establishments for a comparatively short period of time" (Rothney 1975:153). This comment also reveals the direct competition that individual fishermen faced from large companies. Independent fishermen in Saint-Laurent had difficulty absorbing the loss of property and lives which occurred frequently through storms and treacherous ice conditions [23]. As one respondent noted, a person could live on independent fishing but he had never heard of one getting rich by it [24]!

The problems plaguing small family fishing outfits (between 1900 and 1945) were similar, in an exacerbated form, to those faced by farmers. Hundreds of competing petty commodity producers sold-out to a handful of companies that often cooperated with each other and exported most of the profits out of the region. As the Rothney-Watson report notes:

> Only 4 frozen fish companies [largely controlled by American capital] operated in Manitoba and by the 1930s they

were cooperating to reduce competition. The individual
producers were largely helpless in advocating for better
prices and efforts at organization largely failed [due to] difficulties of substaining collective mass solidarity within the
confines of a capitalist market ... [and] no permanent and
mutual group spirit emerges from an organization based on
motives of diversity, individualism and self-interest (Rothney and Watson 1975:41).

Intensified competition during favourable market periods and cyclical
slumps in prices due to an unstable international economy, meant a precarious existence for those of the Saint-Laurent fishermen who were heavily dependent on bought food staples. An example of fluctuating prices is
the 1914-1915 abrupt slump in demand. By early February prices were cut
50%; by the end of the month buyers had stopped buying (Rothney and
Watson 1975:57). This spelled disaster for fishermen who had gone in debt
to get onto the ice. But by 1920-21 the prices were the highest in living
memory [25] and most fishermen were able to make a profit -- making the
Métis villagers' continuing reluctance to pay church dues a mystery to the
religious authorities. This prosperity was not to last. By the 1930s prices
had once again plummeted:

Market conditions have changed considerably in the last
few years and what was once an extensive and favourable
market cannot now absorb present production at any price
and indeed can only take care of a fraction of the whole
production at any price which will net the fishermen even
a small profit (Rothney and Watson 1975:58).

Fishermen were faced with widespread seasonal debts (getting outfit-
ted, needing credit during a bad year, facing unexpectedly low prices) that
often left little room for capital accumulation (Rothney and Watson
1975:46). Though prices tended to rise, there is little evidence that fishermen's buying power increased at the same pace. Tables illustrating the
return to fishermen compared to market prices (1931-1956) indicate that
the prices received by the fish companies had risen *much* more rapidly.
Profits did not trickle down to primary producers (Lagassé 1959, Vol.
3:69-70). For some of the more common species of fish, such as whitefish,
prices based on sale to first buyer were to remain at a static low for decades (Leacy 1983: Section 'N').

Fishermen in Saint-Laurent never formed a distinct socio-economic
(or racial) grouping. Farmers, trappers, hunters and gatherers all participated in the winter fishing industry. What distinguished the participants
from each other was the *importance* of fishing in the family budget, the

scale on which it was undertaken, and the other staple producing activities linked to it. The so-called white familes -- those who had attained a certain degree of material well-being and social acceptability -- were combining fishing with dairy farming [26]. The revenues derived from these activities must have been considerable since the Church authorities in 1905 expected them to pay the greatest amount of tithes: $10.00 a year. Poor families were only expected to contribute $2.00 a year. Only 35 families out of a total of nearly 200 were considered well-to-do by the Oblates [27].

These farmer-fishermen sometimes put 200 nets under the ice and their outfits were comprised of at least one team of horses (later Bombardiers) and some hired hands. If the fishing season was good they were able to clear a substantial profit and reinvest it in other economic activities [28]. If the catch (or the market) was poor they could count on income from cream or hay sales to recoup their losses, honour their debts (at least partly), and pay their hired hands. Produce from their garden and cattle herd lessened their dependence on the merchants. Though differences existed in herd size, number of fish nets put out, extent of land and capital control and, last but not least, level of help (financial or other) received from religious authorities [29], all could weather several bad fishing seasons without being beggared.

At the other end of the socio-economic scale were the "Fort-Rouge" residents [30], most of whom also engaged in fishing. Fort Rouge was an impoverished fringe area of Saint-Laurent situated (literally) on the other side of the tracks from the main mission area and containing at its most populous perhaps 100 households. Several Métis villages had such small communities on their outskirts. These seem to have been given distinct names to emphasize their separateness (Lagassé 1959, Vol. 1:72). Respondents defined Fort Rouge as being somehow more traditional. The fishing-farming respondents considered them closer in appearance and custom to the Indians. Most spoke Cree or Saulteaux to each other and the older women still wore the black shawl and smoked corn pipes in the 1940s [31]. Though the origins of Fort Rouge are nebulous, indications are that it was populated at least partly by descendents of the families listed as indigent in the 1867-1868 famine, and also by families who had come to the settlement in the 1880s and 1890s when hunting and trapping no longer generated sufficient revenue. By this time, very little free land would have remained in the parish.

Well-to-do residents thought of Fort Rouge as a tough place, had few social contacts with its inhabitants and denied having any relatives [32]. In the clergy's eyes, these Métis had serious problems when it came to religious or moral obligations and duties [33]. Oblates would deplore their "savage mentality", their reluctance to obey directives given at the pulpit and their tight-fistedness when it came to paying church dues [34]. At the turn of the century the resident priest was already complaining:

> Il y en a toujours qui se plaignent. Ils [les métis] peuvent tout dépenser pour satisfaire leur vanité, leur orgueil, leur passions, leurs désirs déréglés, pour les plaisirs, pour la boisson, etc. ... et ils n'ont que des murmures et des plaintes à faire entendre quand on leur demande quelque chose pour le Bon Dieu [35]!

In defence, these impoverished people would point to the Oblates' prize winning dairy herd, large land holdings and stone buildings, and ask why they (the villagers) should have to pay tithes. Outside funds had established the church's presence in Saint-Laurent and, therefore, the Oblates should look elsewhere for money [36].

What really distinguished Fort Rouge people from other villagers was the chronic serious poverty, often resulting in hunger [37]. These Métis did not own land, did not have the money to build up a dairy farm, could not (because of their subsistence activities) plant large gardens and were, interestingly enough, even more sensitive to the vagaries of an international economy than their more established neighbours [38]. Interviews indicate that these people worked quite hard but that the very activities open to them, by and large, assured them a life of poverty [39]. In winter many ice-fished, but on a small scale. They did so with the help of dogs and sleighs on the edge of the lake, and rarely put out more than 20 or 25 nets. What was left, once the needs of the family (and the dogs) had been met, was sold to the fish companies. However, since prices were usually quite low, returns tended to depend on quantities harvested. Presumably in a good year some money could be made since these fishermen had little overhead cost [40]. But a series of bad years could be disastrous and, as Lagassé points out, alternative sources of income came into direct conflict with home gardening which would have lessened their dependence on often unscrupulous merchants for foodstuff (Lagassé 1959, Vol. 3:77-86).

Besides fishing, the Fort Rouge underclass engaged in trapping, berry picking, seneca root digging, and frog harvesting, coupled with some form of seasonal wage labour [41]. Other villagers also participated from time to time in such activities but viewed them as sources of *supplementary* income to be undertaken when time permitted [42]. For the Fort Rouge underclass, revenues generated by these occupations were crucial to their material well being. A decline in the supply of any one of them could easily spell material hardship for these people. The precariousness of their livelihood was exacerbated by the prices for these goods, which fluctuated wildly; moreover, the same events which adversely affected fishing often had an impact on the other products. For example, in 1914-1915 inspector Jackson wrote:

> The price of fur has been very low this season -- muskrats about 10 cents each, and to show what a drug (sic) in the market furs are one reliable indian informed me that he took some muskrat skins into the H.B.C.'s store and they refused to buy at any price (Rothney and Watson 1975:57).

Rothney and Watson also report a large slump in the demand for furs during the early years of the Great Depression (Rothney and Watson 1975:39). Both these periods (1914-1915 and 1929-1935) coincide with a downward trend in fish prices and the income generated by berry picking or seneca root harvesting could not be increased sufficiently to compensate for loss of revenues in other sectors (Lagassé 1959, Vol. 3:77-86). These were also periods when the fishermen-farmers with large outfits would be cutting back on their labour needs in an attempt to weather the "down" years. Marginal people (neither fully staple producers nor fully wage labourers) suffered the most when an economic slump, usually affecting both spheres, occurred.

Conclusion

From the data presented it can be concluded that, in the geographical area concerned, an impoverished underclass was created and reproduced between 1850 and 1945. One need not resort to race for the explanation. The lack of access to land, the lack of capital, and (in Saint-Laurent) the lack of clerical support marginalized many of these old settlers and led them into a cycle of debt-peonage to the merchant representatives of national and international economies. The producers of fish, fur and seneca root -- never seemingly able to generate enough revenue to reproduce themselves -- were dependent on traders for credit to see them through the year in food and equipment. In this manner, the very *means of production* were not owned by the Fort Rouge people even when they were not involved in a wage-labour relation [43]! A racist ideology hardened the attitudes of better-off settlers and authorities. Explanations for their decheance never went beyond perceived racial shortcomings. Consequently some options and opportunities which were opened to others were *a priori* out of reach for this group.

What is significant about the history of this underclass is that by the 1950s well over 80% of the descendants of 18th and 19th century Canadian-European workers and local native women did not perceive themselves, and were not perceived by others, as Half-breeds (Lagassé 1959, Vol. 1:77), having been fully integrated into so-called white society. Any obstacles encountered in their daily lives were not the products of a racist ideology (which they themselves often espoused). When Half-breeds and Métis were defined by society at large, some allusion to Indian ancestry was made and physical characteristics were noted but, in fact, these were given social significance *only* because of the life-style led by the individuals. A Half-breed/ Métis was poor, unschooled, lived in a shack, engaged in a variety of seasonal employments, was not very submissive to authority and formed very much a part of the reserve labour force of Manitoba (Lagassé 1959, Vol. 3:chapter 8). Once an individual was enmeshed in this cycle of poverty, a theory of racial determinism was invoked. Métis were poor because of inherited characteristics. If a (once defined as) Métis family became prosperous its white parentage would be emphasized until the day, at least in the Oblate parishes, when it would merge with the French-Canadian element.

The dynamic of capitalism produces an underclass. Many former colonies have a marginalized, staple-producing reserve labour force. Most individuals do not engage in staple production by choice. In Manitoba, when industrial jobs became obtainable there was a distinct tendency to abandon seasonal jobs in favour of employment which produced more predictable returns (Lagassé 1959, Vol. 3:52). In Saint-Laurent, as in most of the Interlake, this underclass became viewed as racially or ethnically distinct because of a series of specific socio-economic historical circumstances that affected relations of production and reinforced an emerging racist ideology. Slight phenotypical variations were negatively evaluated, and this evaluation (for the Métis in 20% of the cases) reinforced the very real impact of chronic material hardship. It became a part of society's common sense that "most poor people in the Interlake were Natives, and that most Natives were poor". To this day, the authorities, the public, and even the people affected think in terms of Indian and Métis problems or of injustices done to Natives, and posit solutions with ethnic boundaries in mind -- not realizing that they are buying into an ever-evolving racist paradigm. Such a paradigm moves critical analysis away from class-based issues and obscures the capitalist process of differentiating society between the haves and have-nots. This process occurs not merely in the sense of capital versus the working class but also of capital versus a marginalized, staple producing, reserve labour force: the *sub-class*.

Endnotes

*Départment d'histoire, Université d'Ottawa, Ottawa ON, K1N 6N5. A slightly different version of this article appeared in *The Political Economy of Manitoba*. Jim Silver and Jeremy Hull, eds. Regina: Canadian Plains Research Centre, University of Regina, 1990, pp. 73-87.

1. Oblats de Marie Immaculée (O.M.I.), Archives Deschatelets (A.D.). L641 M271 55 1947.

2. Robert Miles 1982:9. This section relies heavily on Miles' published works, the above quoted in particular.

3. Ward (1978) is an interesting example of a book based on the premise that 'racial' differentiation has an inherent impact on social behaviour.

4. H.B.C., P.A.M., B235 Nov-Dec 1828, Fort Garry Correspondence Book.

5. O.M.I., A.D., L381 M27C 1858-1895, Historical Notes; Parish of Saint-Laurent.

6. P.A.M., MG2B6 1868 Statistical Summary, Executive Relief Committee, District of Assiniboia (parish of Saint-Laurent).

7. O.M.I., A.D., L1074 M27L 4-17, Parish of San Clara.

8. P.A.M., MG2B6 1868 Statistical Summary, Executive Relief Committee, District of Assiniboia (parish of Saint-Laurent).

9. O.M.I., A.D., L381 M27C 1858-1895, Historical Notes; Parish of Saint-Laurent.

10. Ibid.

11. According to the tables compiled by D.N. Sprague and R.P. Frye in *The Genealogy of the First Métis Nation*, only 3 heads of family in Saint-Laurent had been H.B.C. employees.

12. P.A.M., Manitoba Oral History Project (M.O.H.P.) (1985) Interviews C385, C383.

13. O.M.I., A.D., L381 M27C 1858-1895, Historical Notes; Parish of Saint-Laurent, p. 66.

14. Ibid., p. 7.

15. Ibid., p. 28.

16. Missions de la Congrégation des Missionaires Oblats de Marie Immaculée (Rome: Maison Générale, 1878), pp. 171-175.

17. Ibid.

18. O.M.I., A.D., L381 M27C 1858-1895 Historical Notes; Parish of Saint-Laurent, p. 66.

19. O.M.I., A.D., L111 M27C3, Rapport du Vicaire des Missions de Saint-Boniface 1893, p. 9. Missions de la Congrégation des Missionaires Oblats de Marie Immaculée (Rome: Maison Générale, 1898), p. 281. Ibid., (1907), pp. 327-9.

20. P.A.M., M.O.H.P.(1984) interviews C341, C351-2, C349, C357.

21. P.A.M., M.O.H.P. (1984) Interview C 353.

22. Statistics are derived from F.H. Leacy 1983, section 'M'. Incomes from other staple producing activities will be discussed further in the text.

23. P.A.M., M.O.H.P. (1984-1985) Interviews C349, C382, C385.

24. P.A.M., M.O.H.P. (1984) Interview C349.

25. O.M.I., A.D., L381 M27R 9 (parish of Saint-Laurent), p. 58.

26. P.A.M., M.O.H.P. (1984) Interview C353.

27. A.D., O.M.I., L381 M27R 9, pp. 2-4. In this document the poor segment of the population is labelled Métis but the writer is quick to point out there are "good Métis" families who are fully capable of meeting these higher financial obligations.

28. Ibid.

29. P.A.M., M.O.H.P.(1984) Interviews C351-2, C356, C360. For a contrasting view on the clergy, listen to C342-344.

30. This area no longer exists. It would seem many of its families moved to Winnipeg in the 1950s and 1960s.

31. P.A.M., M.O.H.P. (1984) Interviews C342-3, C351-2, C357, C363, C364.

32. P.A.M., M.O.H.P.(1984) Interview C346 (even though Saint-Laurent inhabitants usually recognized quite distant kin ties).

33. Missions de la Congrégations des Missionaires Oblats de Marie Immaculée, (Rome: Maison Générale, 1920) p. 273.

34. O.M.I., A.D., L381 M27R9.

35. Ibid.

36. Ibid.

37. P.A.M., M.O.H.P. (1984) Interview C351-2, C364 (for an interesting, if biased, description of Fort Rouge type inhabitants, read: Missions de la Congrégation des Missionaires Oblats de Marie Immaculée, 1901, p. 85-98).

38. Walter Hlady comments in a draft version of Vol. 3 of the Lagassé report on Métis attitudes toward gardening: "For many the necessity to go out harvesting the seneca root, fishing, cutting pulpwood and taking casual employment, all of which usually meant leaving the home community for extented periods was a valid reason for not gardening."

39. For the larger picture read Lagassé 1959, Volumes 1-2-3.

40. For an interesting discussion on fish prices for the Lake Winnipeg fishermen see C383 interview.

41. P.A.M., M.O.H.P. (1984-85) Interviews C357, C363, C385.

42. Listen to C357 describing father's occupations.

43. Rothney and Watson 1975:66. For the description of a remarkably similar socio-economic situation involving non-natives staple producers, consult Faris 1967.

BIBLIOGRAPHY

Bourgeault, Ron. 1984. "The Indian, the Métis and the Fur Trade", *Studies in Political Economy* 12 (Fall).

Faris, Jim. 1967. *Cat Harbour: a Newfoundland Fishing Village*. St. John's: Institute for Social and Economic Research, Memorial University of Newfoundland.

Giraud, Marcel. 1984. *Le Métis Canadien*. Saint-Boniface.

Gupta, Kepankar. 1983. "Racism without Colour: the Catholic ethic and Ethnicity in Québec", *Race and Class* XXV:1.

Lagassé, Jean H. 1959 *The People of Indian Ancestry in Manitoba: a social and economic history*. Volumes 1, 2, 3. Winnipeg: Dept. of Agriculture and Immigration.

Leacy, F.H., ed. 1983. *Historical Statistics of Canada*. 2nd ed. Ottawa: Statistics Canada.

Miles, Robert. 1982. *Racism and Migrant Labour*. London: Routledge and Kegan Paul.

Rothney, Russell G. 1975. "Mercantile Capital and the Livelihood of Residents of the Hudson Bay Basin: a Marxist Interpretation". Unpublished M.A. thesis, University of Manitoba.

Rothney, Russ and Steve Watson. 1975. *A Brief Economic History of Northern Manitoba*. Northern Planning Exercise, July.

St-Onge, Nicole J.M. 1985. "Dissolution of a Métis Community", *Studies in Political Economy* 18 (Autumn), pp. 149-172.

St-Onge, Nicole. 1983. "Métis and Merchant Capital in Red River: the Decline of Pointe-à-Grouette, 1860-1885". Unpublished M.A. thesis, University of Manitoba.

Sprague, D.N. and R.P. Frye. 1983. *The Genealogy of the First Métis Nation*. Winnipeg: Pemmican Press.

Sprenger, Herman G. 1972. "An Analysis of Selected Aspects of Métis society, 1810-1870". Unpublished M.A. thesis, University of Manitoba.

Spry, Irene M. 1985. "The métis and mixed-bloods of Rupert's Land before 1870". In *The New Peoples*, pp. 95-118. Winnipeg: University of Manitoba Press.

Ward, Peter. 1978. *White Canada Forever*. Montréal: McGill-Queen's UP.

Zaslow, Morris. 1971. *The Opening of the Canadian North, 1870-1914*. Toronto: McClelland and Stewart.

8. Canada's Immigration Policy and Domestics from the Caribbean: The Second Domestic Scheme

Agnes Calliste*

Introduction

Employment in domestic service was one of the few ways by which black women from the Caribbean could immigrate to Canada before 1962. The role of domestic service in the immigration of Caribbean blacks has been historically significant. In the period 1922 to 1931, 74 percent of the 768 Caribbean blacks who immigrated to Canada came as domestics. Between 1955 and 1961 domestics comprised 44 percent of the 4,219 independent Caribbean immigrants; many of these immigrants also sponsored the entry of their family members to Canada [1]. The proportion of Caribbean domestics is even higher than these statistics indicate, since many of the sponsored wives of immigrants who are listed as "dependents" entered the labour market; they had to work because of economic necessity given their husbands' low wages (Arnopoulos 1979; Leah 1980). Despite the significance of domestic service for the immigration of Caribbean blacks, little has been written on Caribbean domestics in Canada [2].

This study examines the Caribbean Domestic Scheme in Canada from 1955 to 1967 and argues that the growing demand for cheap domestic labour in Canada was the crucial stimulus for the Scheme; at the same time, other economic and political factors played a role in the initiation and continuation of this immigration scheme. Caribbean people, both in Canada and in the Caribbean, had pressured the Canadian government to liberalize its discriminatory immigration policy and regulations against people from the area. The Department of Immigration agreed to the Domestic Scheme in order to maintain Canada's preferential trade and investment in the British Caribbean; this agreement also reflected imperial ties between Canada and the Caribbean [3].

The Domestic Scheme did not indicate liberalization of Canada's immigration policy; on the contrary, it showed the racial, patriarchal and class biases underlying Canadian policy. Prior to 1962 the entry of black immigrants had been severely restricted except when they were needed as a cheap pool of labour. They provided a reserve army of labour for predominantly unskilled work which white workers were not willing to do (these jobs included working in the coke ovens in the Sydney steel plant, and working as domestics) [4]. As the Superintendent of Immigration, W.D. Scott, stated to the Minister of Immigration:

Coloured labour is not generally speaking in demand in
Canada and it is not only regarded as the lowest grade, but
it is the last to be taken on and the first to be discharged in
most enterprises [5].

Scott's description of the 1918 situation was still relevant in 1955. Despite
the critical shortage of labour during the post-war industrial boom (Green
1976), Canada turned to the Caribbean as a dependable source of cheap
domestics only when it became evident that Europe could not satisfy the
urgent demand for domestics; adding to the problem, many Europeans who
emigrated as domestics left domestic work soon after their arrival in Canada [6].

Utilization of the Domestic Scheme reflected some of the strategies
adopted by Caribbean women (as well as other immigrant women) to enter
Canada in order to improve their economic and social position [7]. These
developments also provide some insights into race, class and gender relations in Canada. We will begin by outlining the conceptual framework for
this study of the Domestic Scheme. Then we will discuss Canada's immigration regulations and policy in relation to Caribbean blacks, focusing on
those factors which influenced the Domestic Scheme. Finally, we will
examine the operation of the Scheme and look at its impact on the lives of
Caribbean women.

Conceptual Framework

Canada's immigration policies have been shaped by the demand for
cheap labour, as well as racial, ethnic, gender and class biases which have
discriminated against women of colour, particularly black Caribbean
women. Recent studies (Burawoy 1976:1050-87; Castells 1975:33-66; Miles
1982; Portes 1978:1-48) suggest that international labour migration is a
result of uneven capitalist development: massive accumulation of capital
and concentration of productive resources in some countries and underdevelopment and dependence on those countries by others (i.e., the "centre-
periphery" relationship). This dependence is partly the product of direct
exploitation by the centre of the "periphery's" resources through colonialism and imperialism.

Sixteenth-century European settlers in the Caribbean first tried to
enslave indigenous people to cultivate tobacco. When this population
proved unsuited, the settlers brought over white indentured workers from
Europe. With the change of the primary crop from tobacco to sugar cane
in the mid-17th century, settlers began to import African slaves as a cheap,
abundant and easily controllable labour force to work on the sugar plantations. After emancipation and the end of an apprenticeship system in 1838,
indentured workers were imported predominantly from China and India

(Augier et al. 1960; Williams 1966). Colonialism and slavery moulded plantation societies in the Caribbean in the interest of the metropolitan countries. Their economic legacy in the Caribbean has been underdevelopment, with high levels of unemployment (over 25 percent in some countries [8]), limited opportunities, low wage levels and poverty for the majority of the population (Beckford 1972). Governments in the Caribbean encouraged emigration as a means of reducing overpopulation and unemployment, stimulating economic growth through remittances sent home by emigrants, as well as improving the economic condition of emigrants and their families [9]. Thus, Caribbean people have had a migratory tradition since the time of emancipation, as they responded to employment opportunities within the Caribbean (e.g. migration from the smaller Windward and Leeward islands to Trinidad, Guyana and Panama) and opportunities abroad to support themselves and their families (Beckford 1972; Lewis 1968).

The legacy of slavery produced a low status for blacks. While Africans were enslaved for economic reasons (Williams 1966), the ideology of racism -- that blacks were inferior -- was used to justify slavery. Colour was employed as an effective means of social control (Beckford 1972); the colour stratification in the Caribbean, which associated blackness with class disprivilege and powerlessness, was maintained after emancipation. In the Caribbean, as well as in Canada, blacks remain one of the most disadvantaged groups due to institutional racism and systemic discrimination. Colonialism and slavery have affected labour migration, race relations and gender relations. People from colonial and less developed societies, particularly blacks, were more vulnerable to exploitation; they were more likely to be perceived as inferior and therefore as undesirable immigrants. Thus, in their country of immigration blacks were more likely to be hindered by a position of subordination and to be subjected to economic, political and social control. Working class women of colour from colonial societies were the most vulnerable.

Despite Canada's demand for cheap labour, its immigration policies were selective in terms of race, ethnicity and gender -- according to the needs of the labour market. Race and gender ideologies were used to justify the domination, exclusion and restriction of blacks and other people of colour, particularly women. For example, prior to 1955, stereotypes about black women being promiscuous and single parents were used to restrict the immigration of Caribbean domestics [10]. The ideology of racism was constructed to justify slavery, colonialism and imperialism. As this ideology was reproduced, it perpetuated the belief that different racial and ethnic groups had inherent attributes which suited them to particular jobs (e.g. blacks as suited to service jobs and those which required heavy physical labour).

Racism interacted with sexism and class exploitation in the labour market. Racially contructed gender ideologies and images portrayed black women as "naturally" suited for jobs in the lowest stratum of a labour market segmented along gender lines. Thus, prior to the mid-1950s in Canada, black men were pictured mainly as porters and black women as domestics. The latter reflected the stereotype of the "black mammy" or the traditional Aunt Jemima (Davis 1983; Hooks 1981; *Winnipeg Tribune* Aug. 4, 1904, Aug. 20, 1905, and Jan. 30, 1906). In 1911, for example, some employers in Québec recommended the immigration of domestics from Guadeloupe, not only because they were cheap but also because they were "fond of children", "knew their place"; and they included the proviso that "they remain in the country as servants" [11]. The Québec mistresses' evaluation of their domestics also reflected class relations and the fragmentation of gender along class lines.

The ideologies of racism and sexism were so pervasive that even some British Caribbean people seemed to have shared the stereotypical conceptions about black women. For example, a Caribbean trade official in Canada criticized Canada's discriminatory immigration policy against British Caribbean people because of its refusal to admit domestics into "a field of employment" he believed to be "admirably suited to West Indians" (Bodsworth 1955). Similarly, another Caribbean minister made a proposal to the Department of Immigration to recruit Caribbean women as "children's nurses" because they were "temperamentally well suited" for these positions [12].

In advanced capitalist and patriarchal societies racism and sexism are used to maximize profits in several ways: through segregated labour markets where racial minorities and women, particularly women of colour and immigrant women, are concentrated in low status and low paying jobs; and through the split labour market where women of colour are paid less than white workers and men for doing the same work (Bonacich 1972:547-59 and 1975:601-628 and 1976:34-51; Phizacklea 1983). Specifically, Caribbean domestics have been paid less than their Canadian and European counterparts. In 1910-11, for example, Caribbean domestics received a monthly wage of $5.00, compared to $12.00-$15.00 paid to other domestics. Even when we add the $80.00 cost of transportation from Guadeloupe to Québec, Caribbean domestics were still cheaper to hire since they had two-year contracts [13].

The classic cycle of structural discrimination reproduces itself. Discrimination in employment affects the wider society; discrimination in the areas of education, housing and immigration serves to perpetuate inequality. Blacks were stigmatized as unassimilable and undesirable for permanent settling because of racist ideology. The Department of Immigration used the depressed conditions of blacks in Canada, particularly in Halifax, to justify its restrictive immigration policy against Caribbean people [14]. In reality, the low socio-economic position of blacks in Nova Scotia and more generally in Canada reflects a history of oppression: slavery, discrimination in employment and housing, as well as segregated schools. Black poverty, a result of structural conditions, was attributed by many whites to cultural and personal characteristics, such as laziness and inability of blacks to maintain themselves (*Black Worker* 1952; Clairmont and Magill 1970; Corbett 1957:36, 195; Tulloch 1975; Winks 1971).

Organized labour -- feeling threatened by a cheap labour pool of non-unionized workers that might depress wages [15] and because of racism -- has historically discriminated against blacks (including those from the Caribbean) and other people of colour by formally excluding them from unions or by relegating them to auxiliary and segregated locals (Calliste 1987:1-20 and 1988:36-52; Marshall 1965; Northrup 1944). Labour opposed liberal immigration policies. Thus, the working class was fragmented along racial lines.

Working-class immigrant women of colour face multiple oppression. Their immigrant status interacts with race, class and gender. Many immigrant women have been relegated to the worst jobs, such as domestic service (Leah 1980; Phizacklea 1983; Rothenberg 1988). With its low wages, social isolation and undesirable working conditions (Arnopoulos 1979; Leslie 1974:71-126), domestic service is increasingly being performed by women from the Third World (particularly the Philippines and the Caribbean) on work permits. Live-in domestics are super-exploited. As Arnopoulos points out,

> [they] usually earn less than half the minimum wage, work long hours with little time off, and are clearly the most disadvantaged group among immigrant women in the Canadian labour market (Arnopoulos 1979:23).

As in other aspects of the gender division of labour, the racial and class position and the immigrant status of women affect their reproductive role. Women provide "the future human and labour power and the citizens of the state" as well as the racial and ethnic collectivities (Anthias and Yuval-Davis 1983:62-75). The stereotype about working class Caribbean women as single parents has been used since 1911 to justify the restriction and exclusion -- even deportation -- of Caribbean domestics. In that year, for example, seven domestics from Guadeloupe were barred from entry because they were single parents. The immigration officer surmised that they were likely to become pregnant again and would probably become a public burden [16]. The stipulation that Caribbean domestics who came on the Scheme were to be young (ages 21 to 35), single and without children

[17] had economic advantages for both employers and the state. The women were likely to be strong and healthy. Without their families in Canada, they would be more dependent on employers. This also represented a substantial saving in social capital such as housing, schools, hospitals, transportation and other infrastructural facilities (Burawoy 1976; Miles 1982).

This policy reflected the double standard in society, as well as an ethnocentric and patriarchal bias in immigration policy. Leah and Morgan point out that male immigrants and migrants were not required to be single and without children (Leah and Morgan 1979:23-4). Immigration regulations and policy which prohibited the entry of Chinese women (except for the wives of those classes of Chinese that were exempt from the Act, i.e., members of the diplomatic corps, merchants and students; "An Act Respecting Chinese Immigration" 1923, Ch. 38:3-4) and the prohibited entry of American black migrant porters' wives and families prior to 1943 (Calliste 1987), suggest racial, class and patriarchal biases in immigration policy which have inhibited the reunification of families of people of colour. These biases in Canadian immigration policy have also shaped the migration of black women from the Caribbean as domestics.

Canadian Immigration Policy and the Domestic Scheme

Caribbean blacks began migrating to Canada in very small numbers at the turn of the century. In Nova Scotia they came to work predominantly in the Cape Breton steel mills and in the coal mines. The Caribbean women were in great demand as domestics: with industrialization and urbanization, Canadian women were leaving domestic service to work in the emerging manufacturing and service sectors (e.g. in factories and shops) which provided higher status and greater freedom because their work time was clearly established [18]. The first Caribbean Domestic Scheme consisted of the recruitment of approximately 100 women from Guadeloupe in 1910-11 to help fill the demand for cheap labour in Québec [19]. Despite favourable reports from employers, who recommended that the Scheme be continued as a solution to the chronic shortage of domestics, it was stopped ostensibly because of rumours that some of the women were single parents [20]. Another reason for discontinuing the Scheme was the view that domestic service was not vital to the economy.

In his recommendation to the Minister that the Scheme be discontinued, W.D. Scott (superintendent of immigration) also emphasized the need for the exclusion of black immigrants, especially from among the Americans going to Saskatchewan and Alberta as homesteaders [21]. An Order-in-Council, P.C. 1324 of 1911, was passed to prohibit black immigration for one year. However, the order was cancelled because "it was inadvertently passed in the absence of the Minister" [22]. Such an order would have raised undesirable diplomatic problems with both the United States and the Caribbean. It would have antagonized black voters in Ontario and Nova Scotia who had traditionally supported Liberal candidates. Moreover, the informal restrictions instituted by the Department were probably considered sufficient to exclude blacks (*Hansard* 1911, Vol. 1, col. 608; Brown and Cook 1974:62).

Some of the domestics from Guadeloupe and the British Caribbean were subsequently deported when it seemed likely they would become public charges. This occurred particularly during the recession in 1913-15 when it was reported that there were scores of unemployed Canadian women in the cities and towns who were willing to do domestic work. Moreover, immigration officers were instructed to exclude all Caribbean blacks (e.g. as likely to become a public charge) even when they complied with the Immigration Act [23]. The deportation of domestics, particularly from Guadeloupe, was used for decades to justify the restricted entry of Caribbean women [24].

Even when there was a demand for Caribbean domestics, for example during the wars, their immigration was strongly discouraged because they were not regarded as a "permanent asset" [25]. Blacks were stereotyped as lazy, backward, more criminally inclined and less productive than whites (Winks 1971:292-8). During economic slack, they were likely to be fired to make room for unemployed whites. As Scott argued during World War I, when there were many requests to nominate Caribbean domestics:

> .... It seems to me that Canada would be adopting a very short-sighted policy to encourage the immigration of coloured people of any class or occupation. At its best it would only be a policy of expediency and it is altogether unnecessary, in view of the present upheaval in Europe, which will unfortunately throw upon the labour market a large number of women of a most desirable class, who can be utilized for the permanent advantage of Canada ... there is no use booking these coloured domestics because they are bound to meet with difficulties [26].

One of the most effective regulations used to restrict the immigration of Caribbean blacks was Order-in-Council P.C. 1922-717 which prohibited the landing of immigrants except farmers, farm labourers and domestics, the wife and minor children of residents in Canada, and British subjects from white English-speaking countries (Britain, Newfoundland, New Zealand, Australia and South Africa) and American citizens [27]. This regulation practically excluded Caribbean blacks except dependents and domestics going to assured employment [28]. Thus, in the period before World War

II the entry of Caribbean blacks was small and sporadic. Altogether, between 1904 and 1931 only 2,363 were admitted -- largely as labourers and domestics [29]. Immigration almost ceased during the depression.

In the immediate post-war period, the immigration of Caribbean blacks was restricted to sponsorship by close relatives [30]. Section 61 of the 1952 Immigration Act gave the Governor-General-in-Council authority to exclude people on the basis of nationality, citizenship, ethnic origin, occupation, geographical area of origin and probable inability to become readily assimilated ("An Act Respecting Immigration" n.d.:262). This section of the act was rigidly and selectively applied to restrict black immigration. For example, Order-in-Council P.C. 1950-2856 defined British subjects eligible for admission as those born or naturalized in Britain, Australia, New Zealand and South Africa. British subjects from the Caribbean, and other non-white countries, could enter only under special arrangement or quota or if they satisfied the Minister that they were suitable immigrants (for example, that they could be integrated in the Canadian community within a reasonable time after their entry) [31]. The Order reduced immigration of Caribbean blacks from 105 in the fiscal year 1949-50 to 69 in 1950-51, although the number of applications had doubled. Ethnic origin, not geographical area, mattered. Therefore, whites from the Caribbean were admitted: in 1951-52, 414 whites compared to 65 blacks [32]. In addition to miscegenation (racially mixed marriage) being perceived as morally, socially and politically unacceptable in Canada, there was a fear of recessive genes. As a result, immigration policy required married white applicants to supply family photographs in order to avoid non-white wives and children coming through chain migration [33].

Pressures for Increasing Immigration from the Caribbean

The restriction of blacks and other people of colour from the British Caribbean antagonized Caribbean people, particularly after World War II. They put pressure on the Canadian trade commissioners in Jamaica and Trinidad, who were responsible for implementing immigration regulations and policy, to liberalize Canadian immigration regulations and policy. This intensified pressure resulted from the movement toward self-government, an increasing level of education and high unemployment [34], especially after the McCarran Walter Act of 1952 further restricted Caribbean immigration to the United States. The trade commissioners recommended to the Department of Immigration that it should develop a tolerant immigration policy which would permit the entry of a restricted number of people from the British Caribbean, irrespective of their ethnic origins; the commissioners also called for greater diplomacy in responding to applicants, particularly the influential professional and business people, in order to develop closer commercial relations. As the Canadian Trade Commissioner in Trinidad, T.G. Major, stated to the Acting Director of Immigration in 1950:

.... We must be very careful not to offend local susceptibilities .... It must always be kept in mind that the peoples of the British Caribbean when not hampered by exchange difficulties buy up to $40 per head per annum of Canadian goods, even now the figure is close to $25 per capita or about $43 million per annum. As the colonies are moving steadily in the direction of self government and federation Canadian public relations must be handled with care .... There have been occasions when I have not been too happy about the phraseology used in "refusal" letters sent directly from Ottawa and have had to sooth ruffled feelings .... Canada is looked upon as the "big brother" of the British Colonies in these parts ... the accumulated good will is such a valuable asset to Canada that it must be carefully tended. Sooner or later immigration from the British Caribbean will have to be dealt with in accordance with a yet to be determined policy rather than on an ad hoc basis [35].

In the period following World War II, Canada had, indeed, more trading and investment interests in the Caribbean than in any other Third World country. Over 1,500 Canadian firms and companies had commercial connections in the Caribbean with a volume of exports which, despite exchange difficulties during the war and immediate post-war period, ranged between $30 and $80 million [36]. Canada-Caribbean trade was very important to the Atlantic provinces. The Caribbean was the most important market for salt fish; Nova Scotia's exports in 1963 to the English-speaking Caribbean were valued at $14,246,000 or 10.8% of the province's total exports for that year. Moreover, Canada imported raw materials (e.g. petroleum, bauxite and sugar) from the Caribbean. But more important to the Canadian economy was Canadian investment, particularly in the field of banking and insurance. Canadian banks began to move into the British Caribbean by 1889 to serve the bilateral trade and spread quickly throughout the area. For many years, three Canadian banks (Royal Bank, Bank of Nova Scotia and Canadian Imperial Bank of Commerce), together with Barclays Bank of England, had a monopoly of the banking business of the Caribbean. While intended to serve the interests of Canadian traders, these Canadian banks soon became an indispensable internal banking service for the Caribbean -- only on the deposit side, since loans were generally restricted to traders (Fergusson 1966:32; Nash 1960:223-42). Consequently, "the West Indies suffered a net drain in funds that helped [to] perpetuate their underdevelopment" (Naylor quoted in Chodos 1977:110), at the same time that the Canadian economy was being developed. Moreover, the banks' entry into consumer loans in the 1950s and 1960s reinforced the region's heavy dependence on imports.

Canadian insurance companies began to move into the Caribbean in 1880, and controlled approximately 70 percent of the insurance business in the region by the 1950s. Since 1955 Canadian investment has also played an important role in mining and manufacturing, particularly the Aluminum Company of Canada (ALCAN). In its Jamaican operations alone, ALCAN has invested more than $130 million (Callender 1965; Chodos 1977; Fraser 1966:33-41).

Given Canada's economic interests in the Caribbean, it was important to appease Caribbean people, whether in the Caribbean or in Canada, who were very critical of Ottawa's discriminatory immigration policy. Thus in 1951 the Departmental Advisory Committee on Immigration recommended to the Minister that Canada establish an annual quota of 150 Caribbean blacks who were professionals, skilled workers or close relatives sponsored by residents and who would contribute to the economic and cultural development of this country. The committee expected such immigrants to become exceptional citizens and help making blacks more acceptable in Canada [37]. Although Cabinet did not agree to a formal quota, it decided to admit a small number of immigrants from the Caribbean "of exceptional merit" (i.e., professional and skilled immigrants) on humanitarian grounds and by executive direction [38]. Out of 122 applicants from the Caribbean admitted in 1952-53, for example, 56 were skilled and professional immigrants [39]. This class bias in immigration policy was designed to serve the needs of the Canadian economy.

Canada's refusal to agree to a Caribbean quota (similar to those for India, Pakistan and Ceylon [40]) reflected racism against blacks. It probably also reflected the Caribbean's colonial status which increased the probability that Caribbean people would be perceived as inferior (i.e., that they could not govern themselves). Moreover, as colonies they did not have representatives at the United Nations who could help to put international pressure on Canada. Besides admitting immigrants on "exceptional merit", the Department of Immigration decided to be more diplomatic and, if possible, more specific when explaining the rejection of Caribbean applicants on occupational grounds (i.e., where it appeared that applicants had no employment offer or that they did not have a skill which would make them readily employable in Canada [41]).

Given the insatiable demand for domestics, it became increasingly difficult to reject Caribbean domestics on occupational grounds. As labour force opportunities grew for women, they tended to leave domestic work because of undesirable working conditions, low wages and the low value placed upon domestic work (Arnopoulos 1979; Connelly 1976). The increased participation of women in the paid labour force (Connelly 1976), the affluence which accompanied the post-war industrial boom, and the baby boom also strengthened the demand for domestics. Canadians, particularly those who had visited the Caribbean, put pressure on the federal government for the admission of Caribbean domestics as a cheap and reliable labour supply [42]. The publicity given to the exclusion of Caribbean domestics (Bodsworth 1955; "Here's Ottawa's Side" 1952:12) probably also served to pressure the Canadian government to modify its immigration policy with respect to Caribbean domestics.

The pressure to change immigration regulations and policy came increasingly from within the Canadian black community. In the immediate post-war period this group had assisted Caribbean immigrants in trouble, particularly those threatened with deportation, and facilitated the immigration of relatives of residents in Canada. By 1954 the community had developed a program to challenge immigration policy. The Negro Citizenship Association coordinated the efforts of existing black organizations with the support of both mainstream and ethnic organizations, such as church groups, the Brotherhood of Sleeping Car Porters and the Ontario Labour Committee for Human Rights [43]. The association focused attention on immigration policy, arguing that it demonstrated second-class status and was a structural barrier to integration. The black community held public meetings and invited Caribbean politicians visiting Canada to give public lectures. They demonstrated and sent petitions to Ottawa. A delegation presented a brief to Prime Minister Louis St. Laurent in 1954 with explicit proposals for policy reform: equal treatment of applicants from the British Caribbean with other British subjects, definition of "exceptional merit", and the need for an immigration office in the Caribbean [44].

Racial provisions in the immigration regulations were challenged before the Supreme Court of Canada in 1955 when Narine-Singh's family was ordered deported to Trinidad because Caribbean people of South Asian origin could not be admitted to Canada unless they were sponsored by close relatives [45]. Although the appeal was dismissed with costs on the basis that the Immigration regulations which permitted exclusion or restricted entry because of ethnicity were legal, "the regulations were amended and 'Asian' was deleted." Thus, women of south-asian origin were eligible to apply to Canada on the Domestic Scheme. As the Director of Immigration informed the Labour Commissioner in Guyana, "there would be no objection to including a few" of them in the Domestic Scheme [46]. The discriminatory immigration policy against British Caribbean people was also periodically attacked by the official opposition (*Hansard* 1952, Vol. 3:2803-4; 1952-53, Vol. 4:4348-53; and 1957-58, Vol. 4:3382, 3670-71; Hawkins 1972). However, the Immigration Department did not liberalize the regulations and policy. It simply sought "to eliminate certain irritants" [47]. Thus, the Domestic Scheme was designed and shaped by economic, political and ideological interests. In addition to serving the needs of the

Canadian labour market, the Scheme was intended to further Canada's economic interests through trade and investments in the British Caribbean. It was also influenced by racism, sexism, local and international politics, and by the need to appease the official opposition and people from the British Caribbean, both in Canada and in the Caribbean.

The Second Caribbean Domestic Scheme

The second Caribbean Domestic Scheme was based on the Canadian government's racist and sexist assumptions about black Caribbean women. Against the background portraying black women as promiscuous or as single parents likely to become a public burden, the Domestic Scheme began as an experiment with black immigration acceptable only under certain conditions: a limited number of migrant workers would be allowed as a short-term solution to the chronic shortage of domestics. The Department of Immigration's original intent was to admit Caribbean domestics as migrant workers for one year, with a possible one year extension on the understanding that they would remain in domestic service. The ministers of Trade and Industry of Jamaica and Barbados, who negotiated the Domestic Scheme with the Department of Immigration through the Colonial Office, had guaranteed the return of the domestics at the end of their contract [48]. An economic advantage to such a rotating migrant system is that employers and the state would have the greatest possible degree of control over that labour power so that it could be utilized only for domestic service and no longer than justified by economic demand. The use of migrant domestics would thus ensure that Canada did not have to meet the cost of their original production (nurturing and educating them), nor the expense of maintaining them in times of recession (Burawoy 1976; Miles 1982). Furthermore, the Department of Immigration did not want the Domestic Scheme to open the door to Caribbean immigration. As late as January 1955, the Director of Immigration blatantly argued against an immigration agreement with the British Caribbean. In his words:

> .... It is from experience, generally speaking, that coloured people in the present state of the white man's thinking are not a tangible asset, and as a result are more or less ostracised. They do not assimilate readily and pretty much vegetate to a low standard of living ... many cannot adapt themselves to our climatic conditions. To enter into an agreement which would have the effect of increasing coloured immigration to this country would be an act of misguided generosity since it would not have the effect of bringing about a worthwhile solution to the problem of coloured people and would quite likely intensify our own social and economic problems [49].

However, the Immigration Department decided to admit Caribbean domestics as landed immigrants. This change was made for two reasons: first, in response to criticisms that admitting domestics as migrant labour was a discriminatory policy similar to indentured labour; and second, because officials thought that, unlike Europeans, Caribbean domestics were not likely to leave domestic service at the end of their one year contract. Moreover, the Department felt that administrative controls would provide sufficient sanctions to prevent abuse of the Scheme. For example, any domestic found "undesirable" (e.g. who might become pregnant during her first year) or who broke her contract was to be deported at the expense of the Caribbean government [50].

The perception of Caribbean women as career domestics was based on discrimination in the labour market and the stereotypical perception of black women as domestics. In 1963, for example, when the Ministry of Development, Trade, Industry and Labour in Barbados offered to recruit 300 nurses to supply the growing demand in Toronto, the Central District superintendent assumed that Barbados could not afford to send so many trained nurses. Based on a racist stereotype, the superintendent suspected that these women were either domestics or at best nurses' aides [51].

The emigration of skilled labour actually indicated the limited job opportunities available in Barbados; such emigration caused a brain drain from Barbados to Canada -- an economic loss incurred by Barbados from educating and training professional and skilled people who subsequently migrated without contributing directly to the country's economic activity. Canada, on the other hand, economized on the reproduction of high-cost labour by importing ready-made workers, since it is cheaper and quicker to import foreign nurses than to produce them domestically.

Caribbean governments facilitated the brain drain. They instituted a rigorous selection process to ensure that candidates for the Domestic Scheme would establish a good name for Caribbean people in Canada; in this way, the Domestic Scheme would continue. It was also felt that the selection process would reduce or eliminate the probability of Caribbean governments having to pay the return fare of any domestic who might be deported during the first year after her arrival in Canada [52]. Unlike preferred immigrants from northern and western Europe, Caribbean domestics were not eligible to apply for interest-free travel loans from the Canadian government under the Assisted Passage Loan Scheme [53] of 1950. Since the Domestic Scheme provided almost the only opportunity for many black women from the Caribbean to enter Canada, and given the lack of educational and employment opportunities in the Caribbean, some skilled and semi-skilled workers (e.g. civil servants, nurses and teachers) used the Scheme to immigrate to Canada in order to further their education and to seek other fields of employment [54]. Henry found in her study of 61 domestics in Montréal who came on the Scheme that only 12 percent of those previously employed had worked as domestics (Henry 1968). According to *The Trinidad Chronicle*, in the selection process Caribbean governments placed greater emphasis on the women's educational background and ambition than on their domestic skills (*Trinidad Chronicle* 1956). This policy of brain drain from the periphery to the centre to do unskilled work was depicted in a cartoon about Caribbean girls' aspirations: "I'll be a Civil Servant when I grow up and get a chance to go to Canada as a Domestic Servant!" (*Evening News* May 30, 1960).

In 1956 the Department of Labour described the Scheme as an excellent experiment that had provided the best group of domestics to enter Canada from any country since World War II. According to the government, all of the 100 women were still in domestic service and 84 percent were still in their first job approximately nine months after their arrival. Those who had transferred, did so for higher wages and better working conditions or to be located close to friends. Employers were enthusiastic about the Scheme. They found their employees to be more educated, "fond of children", obliging and less demanding than other domestics [55]. Thus, the Scheme was extended from 100 in 1955 to 200 in 1956 and to 280 by 1959 to include Guyana and the islands of the Caribbean Federation. Between 1955 and 1965, 2,690 domestics came to Canada on the Scheme. In 1966, the quota was increased to 500 [56].

Unlike their employers, many Caribbean domestics were very disappointed. They found the work harder, the working hours longer and the pay much less than they had expected. They were surprised that Canadians hired only one domestic -- a general domestic -- instead of several who would share the work load and perform specialized duties. The first group found it more difficult than subsequent groups to leave domestic work at the end of their contract. This might be attributed to several factors, including greater inequality in employment, the lack of recognition of education, skills and work experience from non-European countries, the stigma attached to people engaged in domestic work, and the lack of networks among Caribbean women. Thus, three years after their arrival, many of the women were still working as domestics -- they were trapped in dead-end jobs.

However, by the late 1950s different areas of employment were becoming accessible to blacks, due in part to post-war social changes and legislation. Some blacks were able to leave domestic service (*Prefix to Statutes* 1953:27-29; Potter 1949). Caribbean domestics developed their own networks in order to be supportive of one another and to prepare new arrivals for life in Canada. They met these women at the airport or train station, quickly exchanged addresses and telephone numbers and tutored them on working conditions and wages, in order to put them on their guard. One domestic told a new arrival:

> If you don't like your bosses, you are allowed to switch right away ... Thursday is the regular day off; they will try to change it when it's convenient for them, don't let them do it. For big jobs such as washing windows, walls and scrubbing floors, let them bring in a char.

Members of succeeding groups were more likely to assert their rights, to ask for higher wages, to transfer from one domestic job to another -- because of unsatisfactory working conditions or isolation in the suburbs or because it was too far to travel to night classes -- and to leave their position at the end of their contract [57].

Those who were skilled or semi-skilled in other occupations (approximately 25 percent) tended to leave domestic service at the end of one year, others did so at a slower rate -- as they upgraded their education through night classes or correspondence courses or tried to save money to sponsor some members of their family. Sixty percent of the 1958 group, for example, left domestic service in less than two years. Less than 25 percent of each group remained in domestic service after three years [58]. Caribbean women found employment in the following areas: the service sector; secretarial services; the textile industry; laundry; hairdressing and restaurants; as nurses and nurses aides in hospitals; and, to a lesser extent, in sales, accounting and teaching. In some cases the new job was more physically exhausting and the net pay was lower than in domestic service, but the women's work time was clearly established and they had greater freedom.

The educational qualification required of Caribbean domestics was changed from Grade 8 to some high school in 1961, to prevent the immigration of low-skilled people from the Caribbean through sponsorship and to facilitate the retraining of domestics, if necessary [59]. This change reflected the general educational upgrading of the labour force; it also recognized the likelihood that Caribbean women might leave domestic work.

Although Caribbean women remained in domestic service longer than Europeans who came on similar schemes, some officials of the Departments of Immigration and Labour were disappointed by the former group's high mobility rate out of domestic service, particularly during the downturn in the economy and the high unemployment rates in semi-skilled and unskilled jobs in 1958-59. Even more disturbing to the officials was the sponsoring by some women of their family members [60]. Although the number of Caribbean applications was negligible compared to the influx of unskilled immigrants from Southern Europe (Levitt and McIntyre

1967:90-101), immigration officials complained that Caribbean immigrants were swelling the semi-skilled and unskilled labour force through chain migration. In 1961 there were 107 applications from the 1959 and 1960 groups of Caribbean domestics to sponsor their fiances and close relatives, including five "illegitimate" and three "legitimate" children [61]. Since only single women without children were allowed on the Scheme, mothers with children, who had failed to list their children on their application forms, needed legal counsel if they wanted to sponsor them. The eventual case of the "Seven Jamaican Women" (who were ordered deported in 1977 when they applied to sponsor their children) occurred during a period of economic decline and after the establishment of a new policy of recruiting domestics on work permits. At this time, Caribbean women were considered to be expendable (Leah 1980).

Immigration officials' negative attitudes toward Caribbean women's sponsorship of their families reflected race, class and gender biases: the nuclear, patriarchal family was regarded as the norm in Canada and men were expected to be the main wage-earners. Order in Council, P.C. 1950-2856 provided for a resident to sponsor the entry of his fiancee "provided the prospective husband is able to support his intended wife" (*Hansard* 1950, Vol. 4:4450). This assumed that immigrant women were likely to be dependent. However, the evidence suggests that because of immigration policy regarding Caribbean blacks, namely a predominance of single women as domestics (and nurses), women were more likely to sponsor their prospective spouses and other relatives. Some of the Caribbean men who came to Canada, sponsored by women already immigrated on the Domestic Scheme, had difficulty finding work (Clarke 1967; Bled 1965). In these cases, the women were the main wage-earners. Black women have always worked (in paid occupations) proportionately more than white women. Similarly, black women have had responsibility for financially supporting their children and grandchildren more often than have their white counterparts (Brand 1984:26-43 and 1988; Davis 1983).

The need for professional and skilled immigrants, as well as racial selectivity in immigration policy, militated against the immigration of low-skilled Caribbean men. The Negro Citizenship Association made representations to the Department of Immigration to admit a comparable number of Caribbean males to balance the sexes. The Department responded that it would prefer to admit professional and skilled Caribbean men to better meet the needs of the labour market; given the class differences between the sexes, such immigration would not satisfy the women's needs for companionship and marriage [62].

There was, indeed, a gross disproportion of the sexes. The problem was even more acute since the young Caribbean men present in Canada were predominantly university students who wanted to keep their social distance, at least publicly, from domestics. Because of class bias some students did not welcome domestics at their parties and one student organization almost banned them from attending. Some members of another Caribbean student organization preferred to disband their choir because of inadequate numbers, rather than admit domestics to it. Some female students also kept their social distance from domestics because they did not want to be mistaken for having that profession, given the stereotype about Caribbean women as domestics [63]. Thus, race and gender were fragmented along class lines. This phenomenon was less common among students from the smaller islands where there was less anonymity and where they probably had met the women and/or their relatives before migrating to Canada. One woman recalled that a student, whom she had known in the Caribbean, allowed her and her friends to use his room on Thursdays until they rented their own room in the same building.

The loneliness and isolation of Caribbean domestics were partially counteracted by community and women's organizations such as the Coloured Women's club of Montréal, and by the women's own initiative. Some domestics in Toronto, Montréal and Ottawa organized their own clubs, which met at the Young Women's Christian Association (YWCA). Some domestics in Montréal started two netball teams. Another group, the Pioneer Club, met at the Negro Community Centre (NCC) where community workers organized activities such as sewing and craft classes, and arranged for visiting speakers. The Pioneer women organized some social functions at the NCC such as talent shows. The group which met at the YWCA in Ottawa occasionally attended the Pioneer Club's functions, thus widening the network [64]. The initial contact between the Centre and domestics was made by some employers in Québec living outside of Montréal (e.g. in Chateauguay) who were concerned about their employees' loneliness on Thursday afternoons. The Department of Labour's evaluation of the Domestic Scheme in 1956 indicates that some employers had expressed concern about the limited social contacts that domestics had outside of employment.

The immigration policy of recruiting single women, causing the black community to experience an imbalanced sex ratio in certain age categories, has implications for aging: in the next decade some of the women who came on the Domestic Scheme will have become senior citizens -- without having any immediate family in Canada. There is need for further research in this area.

Caribbean domestics traditionally preferred to work in Montréal and Toronto. These cities had higher wages, a greater demand for domestics, and better educational and employment opportunities; the women were also more likely to have friends and/or relatives in these cities. Between 1955 and 1961, 580 out of the 1600 women chose Montréal (Bled 1965). After 1958 deliberate efforts were made to place domestics across the country, albeit in small numbers. Based on a racist supposition, this was done to prevent racial concentration: domestics tended to "band together". Immigration officers sometimes spirited women away from their friends (meeting them at the airport in Montréal) who might have influenced them to remain in the city [65]. This manipulation of Caribbean domestics was probably intended to make them more controllable; it also served to fill requests for domestics in small towns and in western Canada. Historically, it was difficult to get domestics to work in small towns and rural areas. [66] Despite the wider placement, some domestics migrated to Montréal and Toronto. In the 1959 group, for example, 34 moved to Toronto during their first year [67].

Criticisms of the Domestic Scheme

By 1961 the Department of Immigration was becoming ambivalent about the benefits of continuing the Domestic Scheme. Some officials suggested that the Scheme should be discontinued because "the rapid movement" out of domestic service did not serve the long term economic need for domestics. Moreover, the Scheme, like other special group programs, was perceived to have become unnecessary because of the proposed changes to immigration regulations in 1962. The latter emphasized education, skills, the ability of immigrants to establish themselves successfully in Canada (e.g. with pre-arranged employment), and the elimination of explicit racial qualifications for admission [68]. This view was also supported by the Caribbean Association in Ottawa, which argued that "to enter into a formal agreement with a government of a predominantly white country in which non-whites enter this country in a socially inferior role" encourages racism. The association suggested that since there was no apparent need for the continuation of the Domestic Scheme, which labelled and condemned Caribbean women to second-class status in Canada, Caribbean governments should cancel it and domestics should be treated as a skilled group under Canada's preferred immigration policy [69]. A certain number of women from the Caribbean migrated as domestics under the new immigration regulations. In the Canadian government's assessment, though, eliminating or reducing the quota of Caribbean domestics would likely cause greater tension in Canada-Caribbean relations, since the new regulations had not led to a substantial increase in Caribbean immigration to Canada [70]. The deracialization in the regulations was more apparent than real. The evidence suggests that, apart from the Domestic Scheme, Canada did not actively recruit or officially encourage immigrants from the Caribbean until the introduction of the points system and the opening of immigration offices in Jamaica and Trinidad in 1967 [71].

The Scheme had other political benefits for Caribbean government officials who did the initial selection of domestics [72]. Although the Department of Labour wanted the Scheme to continue because of the need for domestics, some immigration officials thought that professional and skilled immigrants would be more beneficial to the Canadian economy [73]. The Canadian government's dilemma was well expressed by G.F. Davidson, Deputy Minister of Immigration:

> Our chief dilemma seems to be that we are ambivalent as to what it is we are trying to do. Are we trying to pick domestics whose attitude to household service is good and who will be content to remain in household service and be good domestics on a career basis? Or are we using the domestic movement as a means of selecting a higher class of girl who will not stay in domestic service any longer than necessary but will move out after a year into the occupation for which she is best suited, and be in the long run a greater credit to herself, her race, and to Canada [74]?

Support for the continuation of the Domestic Scheme as a means of maintaining Canada-Caribbean relations also came from Canadian government's representatives in the Caribbean. For example, the assistant Under-Secretary of State for External Affairs in British Guyana, Arnold Smith, was very patronizing in his support for the Scheme. In his words:

> ... nothing that Canada has ever done for B.G. is so well and favourably known, or has given Canada as much kudos as this Domestic Workers Plan, which has had the very modest achievement of sending for the past 10 years a total of 30 B.G. (per year) girls to work in Canadian homes as servants. I have noted Department of Immigration rumblings somewhere to the effect that they are considering discontinuing the plan. Notation is made here that if this becomes a real intention it must be combatted in the strongest possible fashion. Why should such a mild scheme -- which is working in doing something towards filling a labour shortage in Canadian homes, is doing much to prove no discrimination because of colour, and which is pleasing to the B.G. people -- be eliminated [75]?

Smith did not acknowledge the race, class and gender biases of the Domestic Scheme. However, these were clear to blacks, particularly during the Civil Rights Movement and the movement for political independence in the Caribbean.

The immigration issue was a constant source of embarrassment and friction in Canada-Caribbean relations, particularly on the politically independent islands. Eric Williams, Prime Minister of Trinidad and Tobago, criticized Canada and other predominantly white Commonwealth countries for discriminating against people of colour as if they were "poison or disease":

> Today the world has worked out the curious hybrid of juridical equality of states and racial inequality of peoples .... Canada eases its conscience by accepting a handful of domestic servants; in Britain the contemporary slogan is "keep Britain white," the very Britain which was built up by African and Asian labour in Africa, Asia and the West Indies. Whatever the Commonwealth may be in theory, it is in practice being increasingly tainted with a racial limitation (*Hansard* 1966 Vol. 3:2319, and Vol. 6:5963; *Globe and Mail* May 21, 1965).

Williams' criticisms prompted a Canadian Member of Parliament, David Orlikow, to propose the issuing of a white paper to amend the Immigration Act and regulations, eliminating racial discrimination and convincing people of colour that the Canadian government believed in racial equality (*Hansard* 1966, Vol. 3:2319).

Some blacks criticized the Scheme as a form of indentured labour in which Caribbean domestics were expected to work harder at much less pay than their Canadian and European counterparts. One critic estimated the wage difference at $150 per month (*New Nation* May 31, 1964). Blacks argued that the benefits of the Scheme were questionable for several reasons. First, the small number of women who emigrated under the Scheme could not significantly reduce unemployment and population pressure in the Caribbean. Second, the Scheme did not provide great opportunities for black women, since they often did not have the time to upgrade their education. The evidence suggests that after initial surprise at domestics' attending night classes, many employers agreed to give their employees time off for this purpose, even though they thought that the women's educational and occupational expectations were too high. Some employers, though, refused to do so; in a few cases the relationship became very strained once employers had found out that domestics were attending classes. Obviously, some employers held very negative stereotypes about Caribbean women which influenced their perceptions about what jobs were appropriate for them (Bled 1965). These negative stereotypes and employers' attempts to limit their employees' educational and occupational expectations reflected race, gender and class biases, as well as the desire for cheap and controllable labour. Such a mistress-servant relationship is a challenge to the women's movement (Arat-Koc 1989:33-58).

A third criticism of the Scheme was that Caribbean domestics were being treated as third-rate citizens in Canada who were not allowed to integrate. Caribbean governments were criticized for their sexism and for supporting the centre-periphery relationship by sending young women -- including skilled and semi-skilled workers -- to Canada as domestics. The editor of *The Barbados Advocate*, for example, argued that pay inequity in the Caribbean was pushing skilled and semi-skilled women to emigrate on the Domestic Scheme. He called for pay equity for women and an end to the brain drain (*Barbados Advocate* April 6, 1964; *New Nation* May 31, 1964). Thus, both Canadian and Caribbean governments were being asked to re-examine the effects of the Domestic Scheme.

Despite these criticisms the Domestic Scheme seemed to be popular in the Caribbean [76]; it gave some women the chance to emigrate to a legendary land of opportunity and it enabled them to send much needed remittances home [77]. Emigration was also perceived as a relief from unemployment and overpopulation.

In a remarkable development Guyana relinquished its annual quota of 30 domestics in 1965 as part of its repatriation program. The Guyanese government asked Ottawa to implement a program which would educate Guyanese women and men, and which would be mutually beneficial to the Canadian and Guyanese people (e.g. by training 25 women as stenographers and 25 men as agriculturalists to help meet the country's development needs) [78]. This request reflected a policy shift in Canadian-Caribbean relations -- from trade preference to an aid program [79]. The Caribbean Domestic Scheme was approved annually by Order-in-Council until 1967. In that year it was announced that the Scheme would be discontinued effective January 1968. Domestics would continue to enter the points system [80].

Since 1973 the Canadian Employment and Immigration Commission (CEIC) has been admitting domestics (and seasonal agricultural workers) predominantly on temporary work permits. This policy shift reflects two factors: the number of women leaving domestic work at the end of their contracts and the lack of industrial expansion. The goals of this new system are two-fold. First, it ensures that the women's labour power is utilized only for domestic work. Second, because domestics from the Third World are regarded as expendable, they can be sent back to their home countries when the demand for domestics falls. Thus, women on permits are even more marginalized than these women who came on the Scheme.

Caribbean women seem to be even more vulnerable than some other Third World women. Recruitment of domestics from the Philippines has increased significantly in recent years, while there has been a decrease from the Caribbean. For example, 30 percent of the 5,021 new entrants in 1985 were from the Philippines compared to 13 percent from Jamaica and Guyana, the two Caribbean countries included in the ten leading source countries. Filipinos comprised 42 percent of the 8,175 new entrants in 1987, with Jamaicans comprising only 2 percent. In 1986 and 1987 Jamaica was the only Caribbean territory in the ten principal countries of origin for domestics [81]. Plausible explanations for the employers' preference for Filipinos compared to Caribbean domestics are: the former tend to be younger, they are probably cheaper, and they are more likely to show, if not feel, deference to their employers. Research has shown that employers expect submissiveness from domestic workers (Martin and Segrave 1985; Rollins 1985).

Under the 1981 regulations live-in domestics who have been here for two years and who have achieved a potential for self-sufficiency are allowed to apply for landed immigrant status; however, older Caribbean women with children are less likely than others to be granted landed immigrant status (Ramirez 1983-84:17-19; Silvera 1983:29; *Winnipeg Free Press* Nov. 25, 1983). These disadvantages experienced by Caribbean women have several causes. Racism may be a factor, given that blacks are lower on the stratification ladder and have more negative stereotypes (e.g. they are likely to be single parents) than Asians. Moreover, CEIC officials may evaluate older Caribbean women with dependent children as less likely to become self-sufficient. Further research is needed on the current immigration policy, its implementation, employers' preference for domestics and the question of whether types of domestic service vary by ethnicity.

Conclusion and Evaluation

Although the Domestic Scheme provided opportunities for some Caribbean women and their families to emigrate to Canada, it reinforced the racial, class and gender stereotypes about black women being inherently suited to domestic work. This did not stop Caribbean women in their struggle for upward mobility. They upgraded their education and moved into jobs with higher status and pay. Currently, some of the women are in nursing, teaching, accounting, small business and secretarial services; at least one studied medicine after teaching for a number of years and two are educational administrators. Some of the women migrated to the United States.

On the whole, though, the Domestic Scheme reinforced the oppression of black working-class women. It also contributed to the Caribbean's dependency on Canada. While some Caribbean governments recognized that the Scheme was demeaning to black women, they regarded it as a partial solution to such domestic problems as unemployment and overpopulation. Despite some advantages of emigration, it could not significantly reduce unemployment or provide a solution to the Caribbean's under-development. Indeed, by sending some skilled and semi-skilled women on the Scheme, Caribbean governments were perpetuating their under-development and dependency through the brain drain. Caribbean women were thus being oppressed by colonialism and neo-colonialism in the Caribbean, and by racism, sexism and class bias in Canada.

Although we do not know the long-term psychological effects of the Domestic Scheme on the women and their families, the evidence suggests that some domestics found such work very demeaning, particularly those from a higher social class background in the Caribbean and those whose families had employed domestics themselves. Some Caribbean domestics described their jobs as being in a prison -- they felt as if they were trapped. Moreover, the stigma attached to doing domestic work, and the racism, sexism and class bias that the women had to endure, may well have contributed to psychological problems. Some women who have achieved upward mobility will not admit that they came on the Scheme; they would prefer to forget about it [82].

Keith Henry's study of black politics in Toronto indicated that the overwhelming majority of females -- particularly domestics -- were politically disadvantaged because of racism and sexism; women's participation occurred predominantly in the church and in social clubs (Henry 1981:35). While this may have been the case in the 1950s and early 1960s, since the late 1960s -- with the increased influx of people from the Caribbean to Canada and policies promoting multiculturalism -- some Caribbean domestics, whether current or former, have been very active on the boards and executives of community and women's organizations.   A few former domestics have even been elected national presidents of organizations, and some have served on provincial and federal advisory councils.

This paper on Canada's immigration policy and the second Caribbean Domestic Scheme is part of a larger study on the social history of Caribbean domestics in the period 1900 to the present. The paper also provides some of the historical background for understanding the experiences of some black Caribbean women in Canada. There is a need for further research on the social consequences of the Domestic Scheme for Caribbean women and their families, the effects of immigration policy on ethnic stratification, and the policy implications for the aging of Caribbean women. Given that domestic service was the job open to many black women before the late 1950s, it would be interesting and useful to conduct a comparative analysis of Caribbean domestics and indigenous black Canadian domestics. Such a study might focus on the experiences of black Nova Scotians who work in white communities adjacent to their black communities. Special attention should then be directed to the implications of domestic service for the family and the community.

Endnotes

*Department of Sociology/Anthropology, St. Francis Xavier University, Antigonish, NS, B2G 1C0. The author would like to thank the women and men whom she interviewed; members of the editorial collective and Esmeralda Thornhill for their useful comments. Unattributed material derives from confidential interviews from 1982 through 1988.

1.   Canada, Department of Immigration and Colonization, *Annual Report,* 1922-1931; Canada, Department of Citizenship and Immigration, *Annual Report,* 1955-1961; Public Archives of Canada (hereafter PAC), Immigration Branch Records, RG 76, Vol. 475, File 731832; Vols. 566-67, File 810666; Vol. 830, File 552-1-644; Vol. 838, File 553-36-563.

2.   For preliminary work or case studies on Caribbean domestics, see Bled 1965; Henry 1968:83-91; Silvera 1983; Turritin 1976:305-20.

3.   PAC, RG 76, Vol. 830, File 552-1-644; Vol. 838, File 553-36-556; File 553-36-644.

4.   Canada, Department of the Interior, *Annual Report,* 1906-1917; Department of Immigration and Colonization, *Annual Report,* 1918-1931; Department of Citizenship and Immigration, *Annual Report,* 1955-1961; PAC, RG 76, Vol. 566, File 810666, W.D. Scott to L.M. Fortier, August 10, 1916; Vol. 830, File 552-1-644; Vol. 838, File 553-36-556; File 553-36-644; RG 76, Acc. 83-84/349, Box 107, File 5750-5, Part 1, the Director of Immigration to Crerar, Minister of Immigration, April 17, 1942.

5.   PAC, RG 76, Vol. 566, File 810666, W.D. Scott to W.W. Cory, April 25, 1918.

6. PAC, RG 76, Vol. 838, File 553-36-644; Iacovetta 1986:14-18.

7. *Hansard,* 1948, Vol. 6, pp. 5811-12; Iacovetta 1986; PAC, RG 76, Vol. 838, File 553-36-644.

8. The official unemployment rate of 25 percent disguises seasonal patterns and underemployment.

9. PAC, RG 76, Vols. 566-67, File 810666; Bodsworth 1955:127.

10. PAC, RG 76, Vol. 475, File 731832; Vols. 566-67, File 810666; RG 76, Acc. 83-84/349, Box 107, File 5750-5, Pt. 1, the Director of Immigration to Crerar, April 17, 1942.

11. PAC, RG 76, Vol. 475, File 731832, G.A. Marsolais to W. D. Scott, May 20, 1911; E. Dufrersne to W.D. Scott, May 20, 1911; F.X. Dupius to W.D. Scott, May 22, 1911; R. Morin to W.D. Scott, May 22, 1911; A. Rivet to W.D. Scott, May 22, 1911; C. Laurendeau to W.D. Scott, May 23, 1911; G. Boudrias to W.D. Scott, May 23, 1911.

12. PAC, RG 76, Vol. 847, File 553-110, the Office of the Commissioner for Canada to the Under-Secretary of State for External Affairs, December 29, 1961.

13. *The Montreal Herald*, April 8, 1911. See also PAC, RG 76, Vol. 475, File 731832; Vol. 566, File 810666; Clarke 1967; *The New Nation*, May 31, 1964.

14. PAC, RG 76, Vol. 830, File 552-1-644, the Director of Immigration to the Minister, September 12, 1951.

15. PAC, RG 76, Vol. 830, File 552-1-644, the Director of Immigration to the Minister, September 12, 1951.

16. PAC, RG 76, Vol. 475, File 731832, W. Klein to W.D. Scott, July 21, 1911.

17. PAC, RG 76, Vol. 838, File 553-36-644, L. Fortier to the Permanent Secretary, Ministry of Labour, Jamaica, August 1955; C. Smith to R. Mapp, Minister of Trade, Industry and Labour, Barbados, July 25, 1956.

18. PAC, RG 76, Vol. 475, File 731832, M.D. to L.M. Fortier, c. May 22, 1911; Vol. 566, File 810666, F.B. Williams to W.D. Scott, June 29, 1909; J. Gilchrist to W.D. Scott, April 1, 1915; Barber 1980:148-72; Leslie 1974.

19. PAC, RG 76, Vol. 475, File 731832, E.B. Robertson to G.W. Elliott, August 15, 1910; G.W. Elliott to W.D. Scott, September 10, 1910; Regimbal to W.D. Scott, April 10, 1911; R. Morin to W.D. Scott, May 22, 1911; *La patrie* [Montréal], April 7, 1911; *The Montreal Herald*, April 7, 1911.

20. PAC, RG 76, Vol. 475, File 731832, W.D. Scott to F. Oliver, June 2, 1911.

21. Ibid.

22. PAC, RG 2/1, Vol. 769, P.C. 1324, "Prohibiting Negro Immigrants from landing in Canada", August 12, 1911; Vol. 772, P.C. 2378, October 5, 1911.

23. West Indians had the highest deportation rate, particularly in 1913-15 when 91 were deported. Between 1909 and 1916, one in every 30 West Indian was deported. PAC, RG 76, Vol. 566, File 810666, L. Fortier to W.D. Scott, June 30, July 27, 1914; W. Egan to J. Cormack, April 24, 1925; *The Canada Year Book 1915*, 1916:114.

24. PAC, RG 76, Vol. 566, File 810666, W.D. Scott to E. Mousir, secretary, the Canadian-West Indian League, September 8, 1914; Scott to W. Givens, November 11, 1914; Scott to Melville-Davis Steamship and Touring Company, September 24, 1915; Scott to F. Knight, April 25, 1916; Scott to J. Webster, May 16, 1916; Scott to F.B. Harrison, June 1, 1917; RG 76, Acc. 83-84/349, Box 107, File 5750-5, Pt. 1, the Director of Immigration to Crerar, April 17, 1942. 25. PAC, RG 76, Vol. 566, File 810666, W.D. Scott to Pickford and Black, June 17, 1915.

26. PAC, RG 76, Vol. 475, File 731832, W.D. Scott to Hone and Rivet, May 11, 1915.

27. P.C. 1922-717 was amended several times. e.g. P.C. 1923-183, P.C. 1931-695, P.C. 1950-2856. PAC, RG 76, Acc. 83-84/349, Box 107, File 5750-5, Pt. 1, April 17, 1942; Cameron 1943; *Hansard*, 1922, Vol. 3, pp. 2514-17; cited in *Hansard*, 1931, Vol. 4, pp. 3124-25.

28. Canada, Department of Immigration and Colonization, *Annual Report, 1922-31*; PAC, RG 76, Vol. 566, File 810666, F.C. Blair to the Royal Mail Steam Packet Company, September 20, 1922.

29. Canada, Department of Citizenship and Immigration, *Annual Report, 1954*. Department of the Interior, *Annual Report, 1906-17*. Department of Immigration and Colonization, *Annual Report, 1918-31*.

30. An average of 82 West Indian blacks were allowed in annually in the fiscal years 1945-52. Canada, Department of Mines and Resources, *Annual Report, 1945-49*; Department of Citizenship and Immigration, *Annual Report, 1950-52*; PAC, RG 76, Vol. 830, File 552-1-644.

31. *Hansard*, 1950, Vol. IV, pp. 4449-50; *Hansard*, 1922, Vol. 3, pp. 2514-7; *Hansard*, 1931, Vol. 4, pp. 3124-5; Cameron 1943; Moore 1985; PAC, RG 76, Acc. 83-84/349, Box 107, File 5750-5, the Director of Immigration to Crerar, April 17, 1942.

32. PAC, RG 76, Vol. 830, File 552-1-644, "Immigration from the British West Indies since World War 11 showing partial breakdown of ethnic origin", January 1, 1958.

33. PAC, RG 76, Vol. 567, File 810666, C. Smith to A. Joliffe, May 28, 1948.

34. PAC, RG 76, Vols. 567, File 810666, T. Major to H. Choney, January 26, 1948.

35. PAC, RG 76, Vol. 830, File 552-1-644, T. G. Major to the Acting Director of Immigration, May 17, 1950. See also, T.G. Major, "Immigration from the British Caribbean", August 31, 1951; E. M. Gosse to the Director of Immigration, October 9, 1951.

36. PAC, RG 76, Vol. 830, File 552-1-644, T.G. Major, "Immigration from the British Caribbean", August 31, 1951; E.M. Gosse to the Director of Immigration, October 9, 1951.

37. PAC, RG 76, Vol. 123, File 3-33-21, L. Fortier to Cabinet, October 13, 1951.

38. PAC, RG 26, Vol. 123, File 3-33-21, P. Baldwin to the Deputy Minister, December 22, 1951; C. Smith to the Deputy Minister, March 28, 1952; W. Harris, Memorandum to Cabinet, June 10, C. Smith to the Deputy Minister, May 26, 1954; 1952; D. Moore 1985.

39. Canada, Department of Citizenship and Immigration, *Annual Report*, 1953, pp. 34-35.

40. After India, Pakistan and Ceylon became independent, Canada agreed to accept 150, 100 and 50 immigrants from these countries, respectively. This decision was a result of international pressure. PAC, RG 26, Vol. 123, File 3-33-21, L. Fortier to Cabinet, October 13, 1951.

41. PAC, RG 76, Vol. 830, File 552-1-644, the Director of Immigration to the Minister, September 12, 1951.

42. PAC, RG 76, Vol. 567, File 810666; Vol. 838, File 553-36-644.

43. For information on the Ontario Labour Committee on Human Rights, see Bruner 1979:234-55; Calliste 1987.

44. PAC, RG 26, Vol. 123, File 3-33-21, the Director of Immigration to the Deputy Minister, May 26, 1954; Vol. 830, File 552-1-644 Brief presented to the Prime Minister by the Negro Citizenship Association, April 27, 1954; *The Black Worker* (March 1952); Moore 1985:87-120.

45. Harry Narine-Singh was a draughtsman who applied for landed immigrant status when he was on a visit to Canada. "Immigration and 'Race' " 1955:4.

46. PAC, RG 76, Vol. 830, File 552-1-644, the Director of Immigration to the Deputy Minister, September 12, 1958.

47. PAC, RG 76, Vol. 830, File 552-1-644, the Director of Immigration to the Deputy Minister, September 12, 1958.

48. PAC, RG 76, Vol. 830, File 552-1-644, W. Dawson to A. Brown, May 10, 1955.

49. PAC, RG 76, Vol. 830, File 552-1-644, the Director of Immigration to the Deputy Minister, January 14, 1955.

50. PAC, RG 76, Vol. 838, File 553-36-644, Department of Citizenship and Immigration to Cabinet May 1955.

51. PAC, RG 76, Vol. 847, File 553-110, Pt. 2, Central District Superintendent to the Acting Chief, Settlement Division, April 3, 1963; Note, April 17, 1963.

52. PAC, RG 76, Vol. 838, File 552-1-644, the Department of Citizenship and Immigration to Cabinet, May 1955.

53. The Assisted Passage Loan Scheme provided interest-free loans -- initially to single workers and heads of families migrating from Europe, and since 1955 also to their wives and dependent children -- to cover the cost of passage to their Canadian destination of those immigrants who qualified because they were in occupations which were considered to be in short supply in Canada.

54. PAC, RG 76, Vol. 838, File 553-36-644, Pt. 2, G. Haythorne to L. Fortier, March 13, 1956.

55. One woman who had changed jobs three times was making the highest salary in the group: $125.00 per month compared to the average wage of $75.00. PAC, RG 76, Vol. 838, File 553- 36-644, G. Haythorne to L. Fortier, March 13, 1956.

56. The increase in the quota of domestics from 250 to 500 was not really a concession. Rather, it allowed Canadian immigration officials greater control over the movement of immigrants from the Caribbean. The actual intake of Caribbean domestics increased by 100 or 25 percent since 150 domestics were admitted outside the quota. The increase was intended to include all domestics, including those who were selected under the 1962 immigration regulations. Further, Canadian immigration officials controlled the selection of 250 domestics. PAC, RG 76, Vol. 838, File 553-36-563; Acc. 83-84/349, Box. 75, File 5425-4-16, Memo. January 21, 1965; Box 135, File 5850-3-533, C.F. Rogers to the Director, Foreign Branch, December 21, 1966.

57. PAC, RG 76, Vol. 838, File 553-36-563, The West Indian Domestic Scheme, November 20, 1963; King 1958:178-83; Bled 1965.

58. PAC, RG 76, Vol. 838, File 553-36-556, W. Baskerville to R. Smith, January 5, 1960; File 553-36-560, C. Isbister to the Minister of Immigration, November 20, 1963; File 553-36-563, A. Ewen, "Household Service Workers from the West Indies and British Guiana", October 6, 1961.

59. PAC, RG 76, Vol. 838, File 553-36-560, W. Baskerville to R. Smith, December 12, 1961.

60. PAC, RG 76, Vol. 838, File 553-36-563, A. Ewen, "Household Service Workers from the West Indies and British Guiana", October 6, 1961.

61. Ibid.

62. PAC, RG 76, Vol. 838, File 553-36-563, The West Indian Domestic Scheme, November 20, 1963.

63. PAC, RG 76, Vol. 838, File 553-36-563, The West Indian Domestic Scheme, November 20, 1963; Bled 1965; Diebel 1973:38-39, 84, 86-88; Handelman 1964:40-45; Lamming 1961:27, 52, 54-56.

64. PAC, RG 76, Vol. 838, File 553-36-644, Pt. 2, G. Haythorne to L. Fortier, March 13, 1956; Bled 1965; Das Gupta 1986:57; King 1958.

65. PAC, RG 76, Vol. 838, File 553-36-563, Location of West Indian Domestics, 1961.

66. PAC, RG 76, Vol. 566, File 810666, J. Gilchrist to W.D. Scott, April 1, 1915; Barber 1980.

67. PAC, RG 76, Vol. 838, File 553-36-563, Location of West Indian Domestics, 1961.

68. Order-in-Council, P.C. 1962-86; *Hansard*, 1962, Vol. 1, pp. 9-12.

69. PAC, RG 76, Vol. 839, File 553-36-644, B. Myers to the Chief Minister, St. Lucia, December 2, 1964.

70. PAC, RG 76, Vol. 838, File 553-36-560, C. Isbister to the Minister of Immigration, November 20, 1963.

71. In 1961, 1,126 West Indians were admitted. In 1962, the number increased to only 1,480 and in 1963 to 2,227. In 1964 Canada permitted 112,606 immigrants to come to Canada. Of these only 1,493 were from the Caribbean. *Hansard*, 1966, Vol. 6, p. 5963; *The Globe and Mail*, November 5, 1963; Hawkins 1972:382; Levitt and McIntyre 1967:93; Satzewich 1989:77-97.

72. PAC, RG 76, Vol. 838, File 553-36-560, C. Isbister to the Minister of Immigration, November 20, 1963; File 553-36-563, the Deputy Minister of Immigration to W. R. Baskerville, June 16, 1961; W.R. Baskerville to the Deputy Minister, June 27, September 26, 1961.

73. PAC, RG 76, Vol. 838, File 553-36-563, W. Baskerville to the Deputy Minister, June 27, 1961; September 26, 1961.

74. PAC, RG 76, Vol. 838, File 553-36-563, G.F. Davidson to the Acting Director of Immigration, August 29, 1961.

75. PAC, RG 76, Vol. 838, File 553-36-560, A. Smith to C. Isbister, July 3, 1964.

76. PAC, RG 76, Vol. 838, File 553-36-560, S. Hubble to the Under-Secretary of State for External Affairs, May 7, 1965.

77. For a discussion of the importance of remittances to the Gross Domestic Product in the Caribbean, see Lewis 1968.

78. PAC, RG 76, Vol. 838, File 553-36-560, C. Merriman to M. Gregg, May 3, 1965; R. Curry to H. Moran, July 13, 1965; Note for file, July 13, 1965.

79. Canada's aid program in the British Caribbean began with the West Indian Federation in 1958 (Chodos 1977; Fraser 1966).

80. PAC, RG 76, Acc. 83-84/349, Box 135, File 5850-3-533, R.N. Adams to D. Henderson, April 5, 1972.

81. Canada, Employment and Immigration, "Foreign Domestic Movement: 1985 Statistics Highlights"; "Foreign Domestic Movement Statistical Review, 1986" (July 1987); "Foreign Domestic Movement Statistical Highlight Report, 1987 (December 1988).
In both years England and Germany ranked second and third respectively of the top leading source countries. In 1987 seven European countries and Australia accounted for 32 percent of the new entrants.

82. PAC, RG 76 Vol. 839, File 553-36-644, L. Fortier to A. Brown, June 8, 1960; Bled 1965.

BIBLIOGRAPHY

"An   Act Respecting Chinese Immigration". 1923. *Statutes of Canada*. Chapter 38. Ottawa.

"An   Act Respecting Immigration". n.d. *Prefix to Statutes, 1952*. Ottawa: Queen's Printer.

Anthias, F. and N. Yuval-Davis. 1983. "Contextualizing Feminism -- Gender, Ethnic and Class Divisions", *Feminist Review* 15, pp. 62-75.

Arat-Koc, S. 1989. "In the Privacy of our own Home: Foreign Domestic Workers as Solution to the Crisis in the Domestic Sphere in Canada", *Studies in Political Economy* 29 (Spring), pp. 33-58.

Arnopoulos, S. 1979. *Problems of Immigrant Women in the Canadian Labour Force*. Ottawa: Canadian Advisory Council on the Status of Women.

Augier, F., S. Gordon, D. Hall and M. Reckford. 1960. *The Making of the West Indies*. Trinidad: Longman.

Barber, M. 1980. "The Women Ontario Welcomed: Immigrant Domestics for Ontario Homes, 1870-1930", *Ontario History* 72 (September), pp. 148-72.

Beckford, G. 1972. *Persistent Poverty: Underdevelopment in Plantation Economies of the Third World*. New York: Oxford University Press.

Bled, Y. 1965. "La Condition des Domestiques Antillaises à Montréal". M.A. thesis, University of Montréal.

Bodsworth, F. 1955. "What's Behind the Immigration Wrangle?", *Maclean's Magazine* (May 14), p. 127.

Bonacich, E. 1976. "Advanced Capitalism and Black/White Relations in the United States: A Split Labor Market Interpretation", *American Sociological Review* 41, pp. 34-51.

Bonacich, E. 1975. "Abolition, the Extension of Slavery, and the Position of Free Blacks: A Study of Split Labor Markets in the United States, 1830-1863", *American Journal of Sociology* 81:3, pp. 601-628.

Bonacich, E. 1972. "A Theory of Ethnic Antagonism: The Split Labor Market", *American Sociological Review* 37, pp. 547-59.

Brand, D. 1988. "A Conceptual Analysis of how Gender Roles are Racially Constructed: Black Women". M.A. thesis, O.I.S.E.

Brand, D. 1984. "A Working Paper on Black Women in Toronto: Gender, Race and Class", *Fireweed* 19 (Summer/Fall), pp. 26-43.

Brown, R. and R. Cook. 1974. *Canada 1896-1921*. Toronto: McClelland and Stewart.

Bruner, A. 1979. "The Genesis of Ontario's Human Rights Legislation: A Study in Law Reform", *University of Toronto Faculty of Law Review* 37:2, pp. 234-55.

Burawoy, M. 1976. "The Functions and the Reproduction of Migrant Labor: Comparative Material from Southern Africa and the United States", *American Journal of Sociology* 81:5, 1050-87.

Callender, C. 1965. "The Development of Capital Market Institutions in Jamaica", *Social and Economic Studies* 14:3 Supplement.

Calliste, A. 1988. "Blacks on Canadian Railways", *Canadian Ethnic Studies* 20:2, pp. 36-52.

Calliste, A. 1987. "Sleeping Car Porters in Canada: An Ethnically Submerged Split Labour Market", *Canadian Ethnic Studies* 19:1, pp. 1-20.

Cameron, J. 1943. "The Law Relating to Immigration". L.L.M. thesis, University of Toronto.

Canada. 1953. *Prefix to Statutes 1952-1953*. Ottawa: Queen's Printer.

The Canada Year Book 1915. 1916. Ottawa.

Castells, M. 1975. "Immigrant Workers and Class Struggles in Advanced Capitalism: The Western European Experience", *Politics and Society* 5:1, pp. 33-66.

Chodos, R. 1977. *The Caribbean Connection*. Toronto: James Lorimer.

Clairmont, D. and D. Magill. 1970. *Nova Scotian Blacks: An Historical and Structural Overview*. Halifax: Institute of Public Affairs, Dalhousie University.

Clarke, A. 1967. *The Meeting Point*. Toronto: Macmillan.

Connelly, M.P. 1976. "Canadian Women as a Reserve Army of Labour". Ph.D. dissertation, University of Toronto.

Corbett, D. C. 1957. *Canada Immigration Policy: A Critique*. Toronto: University of Toronto Press.

Das   Gupta, T. 1986. *Learning From Our History*. Toronto: Cross-Cultural Communication Centre.

Davis, A. 1983. *Woman, Race and Class*. New York: Vintage Books.

Diebel, L. 1973. "Black Women in White Canada: The Lonely Life", *Chatelaine* (March), pp. 38-39, 84, 86-88.

Fergusson, C.B. 1966. "The West Indies and the Atlantic Provinces: Background of the Present Relationship". In *The West Indies and the Atlantic Provinces of Canada*. Halifax: Institute of Public Affairs, Dalhousie University.

Fraser, D. 1966. "The West Indies and Canada: The Present Relationship". In *The West Indies and the Atlantic Provinces of Canada*. Halifax: Institute of Public Affairs, Dalhousie University.

Green, A. 1976. *Immigration and the Postwar Canadian Economy*. Toronto: Macmillan.

Handelman, D. 1964. "West Indian Association in Montréal". M.A. thesis, McGill University.

Hansard -- Debates of the House of Commons, various volumes.

Hawkins, F. 1972. *Canada and Immigration: Public Policy and Public Concern*. Montréal: McGill-Queen's University Press.

Henry, F. 1968. "The West Indian Domestic Scheme in Canada", *Social and Eonomic Studies* 17:1, pp. 83-91.

Henry, K. 1981. *Black Politics in Toronto since World War I*. Toronto: The Multicultural History Society of Ontario.

"Here's Ottawa's Side of Negro Ban Story". 1952. *The Financial Post*. July 12, p. 12.

Hooks, B. 1981. *Ain't I a Woman*. Boston: South End Press.

Iacovetta, F. 1986. "'Primitive Villagers and Uneducated Girls': Canada Recruits Domestics from Italy, 1951-52", *Canadian Women Studies* 7:4, pp. 14-18.

"Immigration and 'Race'". 1955. *Canadian Labour Reports*. (July-Aug.), p. 4.

King, V. 1958. "Calypso in Canada", *Canadian Welfare*. (Nov.), pp. 178-83.

Lamming, G. 1961. "The West Indians: Our Lonliest Immigrants", *Maclean's Magazine* (November 4), pp. 27, 52, 54-56.

Leah, R. 1980. "Immigrant Women: Double Victims -- A Study of Working Class Immigrant Women in the Canadian Labour Force". A paper presented at the Annual Meeting of the Canadian Sociology and Anthropology Association, Montreal.

Leah, R. and G. Morgan. 1979. "Immigrant Women Fight Back: The Case of the Seven Jamaican Women", *Resources for Feminist Research* 8:3, Pt. 2 (November), pp. 23-4.

Leslie, G. 1974. "Domestic Service in Canada, 1880-1920". In *Women at Work: Ontario 1850-1930*. J. Acton, P. Goldsmith and B. Shepard, eds. Toronto: Canadian Women's Educational Press.

Levitt, K. and A. MacIntyre. 1967. *Canada-West Indies Economic Relationship*. Montréal: Centre for Developing-Area Studies, McGill.

Lewis, G. 1968. *The Growth of the Modern West Indies*. New York: Modern Reader Paperbacks.

Marshall, R. 1965. *The Negro and Organized Labor*. New York: John Wiley.

Martin, L. and K. Segrave. 1985. *The Servant Problem: Domestic Workers in North America*. Jefferson, N.C.: McFarland Publishers.

Miles, R. 1982. *Racism and Migrant Labour*. London: Routledge & Kegan Paul.

Moore, D. 1985. *Don Moore: An Autobiography*. Toronto: Williams-Wallace.

Nash, E. 1960. "Trading Problems of the British West Indies". In *The Economy of the West Indies*. G. Cumper, ed. Kingston: United Printers.

Northrup, H. 1944. *Organized Labor and the Negro*. New York: Harper.

Phizacklea, A., ed. 1983. *One Way Ticket: Migration and Female Labour*. London: Routledge and Kegan Paul.

Portes, A. 1978. "Migration and Underdevelopment", *Politics and Society* 8:1, pp. 1-48.

Potter, H. 1949. "The Occupational Adjustment of Montréal Negroes 1941-48". M.A. thesis, McGill University.

P.A.C. (Public Archives of Canada). Various volumes.

Ramirez, J. 1983-84. "Good Enough to Stay", *Currents* 1, pp. 17-19.

Rollins, J. 1985. *Between Women: Domestics and Their Employers*. Philadelphia: Temple University Press.

Rothenberg, P., ed. 1988. *Racism and Sexism: An Integrated Study*. New York: St. Martin's Press.

Satzewich, V. 1989. "Racism and Canadian Immigration Policy: The Government's View of Caribbean Migration, 1962-1966", *Canadian Ethnic Studies* 21:1, pp. 77-97.

Silvera, M. 1983. *Silenced*. Toronto: Williams-Wallace.

Tulloch, H. 1975. *Black Canadians: A Long Line of Fighters*. Toronto: N.C. Press.

Turritin, J. 1976. "Networks and Mobility: The Case of West Indian Domestics from Montserrat", *Canadian Review of Sociology and Anthropology* 13:3, pp. 305-20.

Williams, E. 1966. *Capitalism and Slavery*. New York: Capricorn Books.

Winks, R. 1971. *The Blacks in Canada: A History*. Montréal: McGill-Queen's University Press.

9. Linking the Struggles: Racism, Sexism and the Union Movement [1].

Ronnie Leah*

Introduction

This article analyzes how women of colour in the Ontario labour movement are organizing against racism and sexism. Based on the experiences and concerns of women of colour, I have focussed on the process of building an anti-racist women's movement within the Ontario labour movement, one in which struggles against racism are integrated with struggles against women's oppression and workers' exploitation. Based on interviews with trade union activists, this research reviews recent labour struggles against racism and sexism, the role being played by women of colour in unions and the obstacles to their full participation in the labour movement. A case study of CUPE Local 79 provides evidence of how unions are addressing issues of discrimination and defending the rights of all workers.

Generally, union struggles against racism and sexism have proceeded in separate spheres: women's committees have organized against sexism, focussing on women's rights; race relations or human rights committees have organized against racism, focussing on minority workers' rights. This division has been especially harmful to women of colour: their particular concerns may not be taken up by either group. Women of colour and immigrant women experience racism and sexism in their daily lives, and both forms of oppression need to be challenged simultaneously by the labour movement.

Both women and minority workers have made significant gains in the Ontario labour movement in the last decade. By the early 1980s, women were consolidating their positions in the labour movement: they had established an organizational base in the Ontario Federation of Labour with the formation of the OFL Women's Committee; they had won labour support for a number of key women's demands such as daycare, equal pay and affirmative action; women's committees had been established in many affiliated unions; and women had gained valuable experience in learning how to organize as trade unionists.

In the 1980s, issues of racism and discrimination received growing attention from the labour movement. As non-white and immigrant workers came together in formations such as the Ontario Coalition of Black

Trade Unionists (OCBTU), as well as in union race relations and human rights committees, they challenged workplace racism and discriminatory policies, lobbied for stronger human rights legislation, and demanded equal rights within the labour movement itself.

Within this climate of growing labour opposition to racism and sexism, women of colour have come forward. They have challenged the women's movement, the anti-racist movement and the labour movement as a whole to address their specific concerns about the combined effects of racism and sexism. They have argued that issues of discrimination against women and minorities need to be placed on labour's agenda and treated as high priority issues for the union movement.

This paper reflects my experiences and concerns as someone who has been actively involved with the women's movement, the trade union movement and the struggle against racism. I have undertaken this research from the vantage point of working class women of colour, in order to document their experiences in the trade union movement. As a white woman who is seriously committed to building an anti-racist feminist movement, I feel it is important to ensure that our research and practice reflects the experiences and concerns raised by women of colour. In feminist analysis and practice, there has been a tendency to universalize women's oppression, failing to account for how racism and discrimination combine with gender and class-based oppression. In reviewing my earlier research on women and unions which essentially traces white women's organizing in the Ontario labour movement (Leah 1986), I've concluded that the picture isn't complete without taking the question of racism into account. This current research on women of colour in the unions reflects my efforts to develop a more fully integrated analysis of gender, race and class in the Ontario labour movement. While I cannot claim to speak for black women, Asian women, Native women and other women of colour, I have approached this work from their standpoint. My goal is to contribute to the growth of an anti-racist women's movement in the unions; this will be an essential part of building a strong labour movement that defends the interests of all workers.

I have generally used the term "women of colour" to refer to black, Native, Asian and other non-white women. This is the expression many women of colour currently use to describe themselves. Some of them may also be recent immigrants to Canada, although not all immigrant women are women of colour. Non-English-speaking immigrant women in English Canada (French in Québec) face additional problems because of language difficulties. While the term "visible minority" is the official designation currently used in goverment documents -- and also in many trade union documents -- it is generally not the term preferred by non-white women.

We need to keep in mind that these terms are socially constructed and may reflect relations of power and domination in Canadian society. Moreover, caution is needed when using inclusive terms to refer to women from many different communities, with their unique histories of racism and struggle. In general, this article refers to women who are non-white, non-European and/or non-English speaking, encompassing women who experience relations of gender, class, race and ethnicity in a variety of ways [2].

In becoming more active as feminists and trade unionists, black women and other women of colour have raised serious questions about feminist practice. They have challenged the universalistic assumptions of the mainstream women's movement: that addressing women's issues in general will take account of the concerns of all women. While substantial gains have been made by union women in recent years, women of colour assert that these gains have, on the whole, been limited to white women: the trade union women's movement has failed to adequately address their specific concerns about racism and sexism [3].

This critique of feminist practice has also been directed against feminist analysis using a "one-dimensional theory of gender and patriarchy" that ignores the multiplicity and diversity of women's oppression and silences "other" women whose experiences in Canadian society have been shaped by relations of race, ethnicity and class (Bannerji 1987:11). In addition to an oppression that is class determined, working class women of colour also experience oppression based on race and ethnicity. Bannerji points out how "organization by race (or racism) is a fundamental way of forming class in Canada"; she notes that this formation of class is also "fully gendered". Brand similarly identifies the "racially-gendered hierarchies" that perpetuate the exploitation of black women's labour, explaining how "Black women experience their race, class and sex consciously and simultaneously" (Bannerji 1987:12; Brand 1987:29). While some recent efforts have been made to incorporate an understanding of race relations into the analysis of gender and class relations, much work remains to be done [4].

This article reports on the efforts being made by trade unionists to link together the issues of racism and sexism. In particular, I have examined the trade union women's movement, questioning whether the substantial gains made by women in the labour movement have also benefitted women of colour. The research is based on interviews with several trade union activists, including June Veecock, present Director of Human Rights/ Race Relations for the Ontario Federation of Labour (OFL), and members of the Ontario Coalition of Black Trade Unionists (OCBTU). A number of union documents are reviewed as well [5].

I have highlighted a recent struggle by Local 79 of the Canadian Union of Public Employees (CUPE), in which the union effectively challenged the systemic discrimination faced by women of colour. Local 79 organized a campaign in defense of nursing attendants (the majority of whom are black and Asian women) when Metro Toronto took steps to replace full-time vacant positions with part-time casual hours. CUPE Local 79, with 8,000 members the largest municipal local in Canada, was the first union to organize a bargaining unit composed entirely of casual part-time workers; the majority of these 1,500 workers are women, half of them women of colour. This case study points the way to effective labour strategies for representing and defending women of colour. It demonstrates that unions can and will fight on behalf of all their members [6].

In the next section of this paper, I will review the material conditions of racism, sexism and exploitation faced by women of colour in the Canadian labour force. Then I will turn to an analysis of recent union organizing efforts against racism and sexism. I will focus on the demands being raised by women of colour within the labour movement, the efforts being made to build an anti-racist women's movement, and the development of labour strategies that challenge racism and sexism.

Material Conditions of Racism, Sexism and Exploitation

Experiences of racism and sexism have shaped the lives of women of colour: in their communities, in their workplaces and within the union movement itself. Their exploitation as workers has been shaped by Canadian capitalists' demands for cheap labour, combined with racist and sexist immigration policies and state practices. Immigrant women -- especially non-white and non-English speaking women -- are concentrated into the lowest paid, most insecure and least organized sectors of traditional female occupations. Black women (both Canadian born and immigrant) are segregated into the lowest status service jobs, while Native women are largely excluded from the paid labour force. Discriminatory government policies and workplace practices serve to maintain this extreme form of exploitation. Women of colour face many obstacles to unionization, and within the union movement itself they face continuing discrimination. It is these lived experiences of racism, sexism and exploitation that have shaped the demands being raised by black women, Asian women, Native women and immigrant women -- as they organize and demand that the labour movement take up their concerns.

Historical patterns of systemic discrimination have led to the development of a labour force that is segregated by gender, race and ethnicity. Women of colour suffer from the inequality faced by all working women: low wages, part-time employment, little job security, occupational and industrial segregation in women's job ghettos, sexist discrimination on the job and high unemployment rates [7]. Women of colour also face inequality based on the history of racism and discrimination against Native peoples, immigrants and Canadians of colour.

The arrival in the last two decades of large numbers of working class women from southern Europe and the Third World (non-English-speaking and non-white) has been encouraged by labour market demands for unskilled workers; immigration policy was directed towards these same ends. For example, non-English speaking women have entered Canada as "dependents" of male labourers from southern Europe; black women from the Caribbean emigrated to Canada under the Jamaica-Canada domestic agreement (this plan was later replaced by recruitment of domestic workers on temporary visas); more recently, Filipina women have been recruited for minimum wage jobs in the Canadian garment industry. Most immigrant women and women of colour are employed in the labour-intensive low-wage sectors, utilized as a reserve labour force, subject to intense exploitation, and often denied the most basic labour rights [8].

Non-English-speaking and non-white immigrant women, constituting a segregated, fragmented and marginalized labour force, are employed mainly in three areas of work: private domestic service, service industries and light manufacturing. About half the workers in the garment and textile industries are immigrant women. Wages are low, there are few fringe benefits, and job security hardly exists. Domestic workers and farmworkers face even worse conditions; they are excluded from many of the labour standards other workers take for granted [9].

Many immigrant women in the public sector are employed as cleaners, cafeteria workers, nurses' aides and lower level clerical workers. Most black women work at low-status jobs in homes and institutions, doing "black women's work":

> cleaning white people's houses, bathrooms and hotel rooms; serving white people breakfast, lunch and dinner in private homes, in office cafeterias, hospitals; lifting, feeding, minding, washing white people's children and older white people; sweeping, boxing, scouring, washing, cooking (Brand 1987:35).

CUPE Local 79 has noted the high concentration of black and Asian women in Metro Toronto Homes for the Aged, with a third of Metro's non-white workers being employed as Nursing Attendants (an entry-level, low-wage position). The union points out that more than half the nursing attendants are black or Asian and 93% of them are women [10].

This segregated labour force results in low pay, few benefits and little job security. While women workers generally earn only 50 to 60% of men's wages, women of colour are concentrated into the lowest paying jobs [11]. Women employed in private domestic service -- many of them recent immigrants or visa workers from Jamaica and the Phillipines -- generally earn below the minimum wage. Average hourly earnings of workers in the textile and garment industries ranged from $5.31 to $6.44 in 1980, compared with an average hourly manufacturing wage of $8.19. Native women have the lowest overall income of any group in Canada [12].

Related to their marginal labour status and low earnings, a high proportion of immigrant and non-white women are employed in part-time or casual jobs. The growing trend of women's part-time work has been well documented; Ontario statistics indicate that, in 1983, 26% of working women had part-time jobs and 71% of all part-time workers were women (*Ontario Statistics 1984*, Table 5.25). For women of colour the problem is even more acute. The "First Equal Employment Opportunity Report", issued by Metro Toronto in June 1985, pointed to a 492% growth in temporary and part-time employment between 1977 and 1985; 79% of these part-time workers are women and/or members of visible minority groups. Out of 1500 workers in Local 79's part-time bargaining unit, 90% are women and over half the workers are black, Asian or Native people [13]. A survey of its part-time members undertaken by Local 79 indicated that "75% are working part-time not by choice, but because there are not enough full-time jobs" [14].

The segregation of women of colour into such low paid, low status and insecure jobs reflects historic patterns of racism and sexism. CUPE has argued that the "historical and continuing concentration" of black and Asian women hired as casual workers in Metro Toronto Homes for the Aged reflects this pattern of discrimination:

> The concentration of Black and Asian women in this and
> related service occupations itself stems from long-standing,
> deeply-rooted and continuing systemic discrimination
> which has meant that relatively few occupations have been
> open to Black and Asian women in significant numbers
> [15].

CUPE's campaign to prevent Metro Toronto from converting full-time jobs, as they fell vacant, into part-time hours was based on the discriminatory effect this policy would have on women of colour. A detailed account of this campaign is given later in this paper.

Working class immigrant women are concentrated in dead-end jobs, with few opportunities for further training or advancement. Discriminatory government policies and practices maintain immigrant women's powerlessness, by denying access to language training, employment programs, or support services that would enable them to qualify for better paying, more secure, unionized jobs. Despite the fact that most immigrant women will enter the paid labour force, the majority of immigrant women enter Canada as dependents ("family class"); they are thus ineligible for English or French language training (and they may also be denied many social benefits such as social assistance, subsidized housing or subsidized daycare). Working women rarely have access to language training unless it is provided in the workplace, since family responsibilities generally prevent them from attending language classes after work. Language has been identified as a key issue for immigrant women, who remain isolated in job ghettos, separated from other workers and unable to fully participate in union activities [16].

The double burden of women's work places immigrant women and women of colour in a vulnerable position. Women may be forced to work at jobs with flexible hours, or to accept shift work or night work, in order to juggle paid work with domestic labour and childcare responsibilities. Beyond the problems faced by all working women in combining family responsibilities with paid labour force participation, the options for working class immigrant women are even more limited -- given their oppressive conditions of work, low wages and discriminatory government policy. This double burden of work leaves many women of colour with little time or energy to upgrade their employment or language skills, or to become involved in union activities.

Immigrant and visible minority women have looked to the union movement as an important means of improving their conditions of work, although the union movement has been slow in responding to their particular concerns -- as workers, as women and as minorities. At the same time, the material conditions of work experienced by women of colour have contributed to their difficulties in unionizing and becoming active in the labour movement.

Immigrant women and women of colour are concentrated in occupations which have traditionally been unorganized; except in the garment and textile industries, few are unionized. Many of the factors that obstruct unionization of working women are magnified for women of colour who face additional problems of racism and discrimination [17]. Structural barriers to unionization of immigrant and minority women workers coincide with the characteristics of the job market to which they have been relegated: fragmentation of the labour force; segregation into sex-typed, unskilled job ghettos; concentration in part-time and temporary jobs; and lack of access to language training.

Employer resistance to unionization of minority and immigrant workers is a major factor.   In addition to the strategies employed against women's unionization in general, immigrant workers are especially vulnerable to employer intimidation and harassment (Brand and Bhaggiyadatta 1986, Section 3). Inability to communicate and lack of knowlege about workers' rights add to immigrant women's vulnerability. Language differences and ethnic differences are often taken advantage of by employers as a means of dividing the workforce; employers exploit these divisions by deliberately hiring immigrant workers who can't speak English. Specific strategies have been proposed for organizing immigrant workers, such as the development of a Garment Workers' Action Centre for immigrant women in the garment industry that would serve as "a stepping stone to organize the unorganized" (Winnie Ng 1987:302).

The problems of organizing are magnified when it comes to unionizing part-time and casual workers, many of who are non-white and/or immigrant women.   Part-time workers are preferred by employers, not only because they are cheaper to hire (due to low pay and lack of benefits), but also because management has greater control over the workforce. Labour laws in Canada operate to the disadvantage of workers (especially part-timers) trying to organize.   According to the Ontario Labour Relations Act, union activity is prohibited during working hours; essential information may be witheld from unions, including the number of eligible workers in the bargaining unit and the names of workers to be signed up.   Moreover, the employer is able to flood the potential bargaining unit with new workers; casual workers are called up at the whim of management, they may work intermittently, and they are subject to intimidation for union activity.   Firings during union drives are common, but it's very difficult to prove to the Labour Relations Board that workers (especially casual part-timers) have been let go for signing a union card [18].

In the face of these obstacles, CUPE Local 79 conducted a successful organizing drive of part-time casual workers in Metro Homes for the Aged in March 1983.   Their campaign was "quick and quiet" and took Metro by surprise: after two months spent painstakingly collecting the names of the casual workers, 55 specially trained CUPE members personally approached the workers; within 25 days they had signed up 70% of the eligible casual employees and the union had applied for certification (Spink 1985:15). Local 79 thus became the first union in Canada to represent part-time casual workers. Subsequent collective agreements negotiated by CUPE for the bargaining unit set a standard in terms of winning benefits and seniority for part-time and casual workers [19].   These gains were a major step forward for women, minority workers and especially women of colour -- concentrated in such jobs -- who have faced great difficulties in unionizing and negotiating job security, better pay and decent working conditions.

In addition to the structural obstacles to unionization, women of colour have criticized the labour movement for its lack of effort in organizing the unorganized. They have also challenged unions for their lack of attention to the special concerns and needs of immigrant women, and their discriminatory attitudes towards women of colour. They charge that "the organized labour movement has always seen the concerns of visible minority and immigrant women as secondary, compared to those of male, white workers" (Das Gupta 1987:13). The next section of this paper will address some of these issues.

Despite many obstacles, immigrant women have become active in their local unions, playing an important role in union struggles for better pay, improved working conditions and an end to discrimination. These demands have emerged from the material conditions of racism, sexism and exploitation faced by women of colour and immigrant women in the workplace. Women of colour have looked to internal union action against racism and sexism and for union support in their struggles against discrimination in the workplace. They have argued for a stronger effort to organize the unorganized, for English language training in the workplace, for universal daycare, and for effective affirmative action policies [20].

Union Organizing Against Discrimination

Within the unions, immigrant women and women of colour have begun to organize and express their demands, making the unions aware of "how we haven't really sufficiently addressed racism" (Gallagher 1987:353). Women of colour have also become politicized through their involvement in community organizing. Their activity has gained momentum from recent events within the labour movement -- with the development of a trade union women's movement in the 1970s and growing anti-racist organizing in the 1980s.

Women of colour and immigrant women have played an active role in the labour movement, taking part in strikes and other workplace struggles, such as strikes at Puretex Knitting Mills, Bell Canada, Irwin Toys, and Ontario hospitals. The hard-won fight to retain union rights for cleaners at First Canadian Place in Toronto demonstrated the determination of the workers -- most of them Portuguese immigrant women [21]. A 1985 strike of Punjabi factory workers organized by the Communications and Electrical Workers union demonstrated the militance of South Asian women: "Contrary to prevalent ideology, women from the Indian Subcontinent are

not timid and they fight for their rights as workers and as women" (Aggarwal 1987:43).

Union support for workplace struggles has been negligible at times,
leaving women of colour to look elsewhere for help. Das Gupta notes that
"we have been successful in achieving our rights as workers largely by support from our own communities" (Das Gupta 1987:14). Women of colour
have been engaged in a variety of struggles in their communities, arising
out of their diverse experiences of race, ethnicity, gender and class. In
recent years, community groups and grassroots organizations have become
more conscious about their rights, speaking out and fighting discrimination.
Through organizing around a broad range of issues in the community,
women of colour have become politicized around their specific needs and
concerns. Such activities have empowered women in their struggles against
the structures of sexism, racism and class oppression, while developing
their leadership skills, political experience and self-confidence. Government initiatives in the 1980s to organize conferences and formations of
immigrant women and visible minority women also contributed to growing
labour awareness about issues of racism and sexism, at a time when Native,
black, South East Asian and South Asian women were becoming "a constituency to be recognized". These activities have contributed to the activism
of women of colour in the labour movement [22].

Other factors contributing to the growing politicization and organization of women of colour in Canada include the "rapidly increasing immigration in the 1970s, the revolutionary movements sweeping the international scene, and the popularity given women's issues by the women's
movement" (Carty and Brand 1988:40). In many of their organizing
efforts, women of colour do not exclusively focus on "women's issues";
rather, they often address broader social and political issues that affect
their daily lives. For example, the anti-apartheid struggle has profoundly
affected black women in Canada, and Native women have been active in
their peoples' fight for self-determination. Through such experiences,
women of colour bring a different perspective to the labour movement,
joining together issues of women's equality, racial equality and social justice.

Union activity by women of colour reflects their particular concerns as
workers facing the combined effects of racist and sexist discrimination.
Veecock explains: "we are talking about our experiences -- what we live as
women of colour" [23]. In addition to sexism, black women have experienced racism in their daily lives. Veecock notes that "racism is going on all
the time." She explains how the ongoing racial harassment and racial slurs
have victimized people and rendered them powerless -- until they organize
to speak out against racism and discrimination.

Working women have recently made significant gains in the labour movement as they became an organized force and succeeded in having their particular concerns taken up as trade union issues. By 1975 union women in Ontario began to organize collectively in order to effectively challenge male domination of the labour movement and to establish a base for organizing around concerns of importance to women. With the establishment of the Ontario Federation of Labour Women's Committee in 1978, women gained a collective base within the structure of labour. Activist union women were then able to put pressure on the labour leadership to take action on women's issues (e.g., day care, affirmative action) while at the same time mobilizing women in the affiliated unions around these demands [24]. They now had access to financial resources, staff support, communication networks, and the membership of affiliated unions.

Daycare was the first major women's issue to gain the support of labour. The adoption, at the 1980 Annual Convention, of the OFL *Statement on Daycare* (for free, universal, publicly-funded, quality childcare) indicated a significant development in the growth of labour support for women's concerns, as well as a new commitment by the traditionally male dominated labour movement to women's equality. The OFL Women's Committee subsequently gained official endorsement of a major policy paper on *Women and Affirmative Action* at the 1982 convention, which called for mandatory affirmative action at work and equal representation of women in the unions [25].

The OFL's support for daycare, affirmative action and other issues such as pay equity, parental leave and reproductive rights reflected the growing strength of women in a labour movement which was becoming more responsive to their demands [26]. While women still remain underrepresented in unions, they are becoming more aware of their power and demanding recogition as trade unionists on an equal footing with men. Women have learned effective tactics, how to plan strategically, and how to build a movement; they have learned "how to organize, how to fight" (Gallagher 1987:352).

Women's growing involvement in unions has had a positive impact on the labour movement, injecting a new vitality and democracy and serving as a force for progressive change in the unions (see Briskin 1983; Edelson 1987). While trade unionists have observed that women and minorities should be natural allies in their efforts to democratize the unions and make them more representative of groups traditionally excluded from power, much work remains to be done in terms of opening up the labour movement to immigrant and minority workers [27].

Black women and other women of colour have been critical of the mainly white women's movement for its failure to understand and support their struggles. Although there is some progress, Veecock notes the long way to go in bridging the gap:

> The women's movement is by and large very far removed from immigrant women and visible minority women: the women in the plant who speak very little English; the women in the garment industry; the women on the line in the factory -- the women who are most oppressed [28].

In both the community and the labour movement, racism has been seen by the women's movement as an issue that diverts attention away from traditional women's issues. There has been a tendency by women activists to say: "first we make these gains for women, then we'll deal with racism -- your turn will come." But, Veecock notes, "it isn't first one group and then the others -- we move together."

One of the better known advances of the past few years has been during International Women's Day (IWD), an event which includes the active participation of many trade union women. In 1986 IWD had a central focus on racism: "Women Say No! to Racism, from Toronto to South Africa". This event marked a "turning point" for the women's movement when "a major form of oppression faced by immigrant, visible minority and Third World women was ... recognized by all women" and "the link between racism and sexism was clearly defined" by women of colour and supported by progressive white women (Das Gupta 1986:44).

International Women's Day 1987 focussed on building a multiracial women's movement that would integrate the struggles against racism and sexism. There was a focus on issues "which affect the lives of women of colour, Black women and Native women"; about one third of the activists in the 1987 coalition were women of colour who took the initiative for building a stronger anti-racist consciousness in the women's movement" (Egan et al. 1988:44).

However, there were continuing concerns about how to address the issue of racism, and differences arose between black feminists and the IWD coalition. Veecock recalled some of these:

> Black feminists had difficulty working with mainstream feminists around IWD. The problem is, there is not a real sharing by the women's movement, they don't really listen to what black women say. The women's movement couldn't connect, they didn't really understand racism.

Black trade unionists have also raised concerns that anti-racism in the women's movement is still a "special event movement", where the issue of racism is raised only once a year on International Women's Day. Veecock notes that the danger of "tokenism" also arises if events which include black women as speakers do not really address the concerns of black women.

Some of these concerns have been taken up by groups of minority workers in the unions. However, women of colour report that they have been marginalized to some extent in these formations of minority workers, as well as in the trade union women's movement.

In the 1980s, issues of racism and discrimination began to receive growing attention from the labour movement. Black workers and other non-white workers organized within the OFL, eventually joining together in formations such as the Ontario Coalition of Black Trade Unionists (OCBTU) and union human rights committees; they challenged workplace racism and discriminatory policies, lobbied for stronger human rights legislation, and demanded equal rights within the labour movement. An OCBTU member explains that, as a result of these activities, trade unions have accepted the fact that racism exists: racism is now on the union agenda.

At the same time that minority trade unionists have challenged racist practices in the workplace, they have also challenged racism in the labour movement itself. The OFL, as a result of such pressures, has taken some steps to combat racism through the appointment of staff, the development of policies and action programs, and the allocation of resources. Still, workers of colour remain dissatisfied with the slow pace of change in the labour movement.

When resolutions on racism were brought forward at the 1981 OFL Convention, the labour federation committed itself to a campaign against racism by endorsing the *Statement on "Racism Hurts Everyone"*. The resolution focussed on both public education and internal union education; it called for regional forums on racism, stronger human-rights legislation, and workplace affirmative action programs. The OFL's "Racism Hurts Everyone" campaign saw the commitment of labour resources and staff, and racism was highlighted as a priority issue for labour (see OFL Information 1984). Mutale Chanda was hired on contract by the OFL to coordinate the campaign against racism, working with the Human Rights Director. However, when Chanda's contract was not renewed, the campaign against racism suffered a setback, according to some trade unionists.

There was growing pressure for the OFL to appoint a second Human Rights Director so that there would be a separate Director for Race Relations in addition to the Director of Women's issues. Veecock recalls that the OFL Women's Committee worked really hard on this; they lobbied for the separation of the two areas of work, so that racism would receive equal attention with women's issue. In addition, minority workers argued that it was important to have a person of colour coordinating the race relations work. Subsequently the OFL appointed June Veecock, herself a black woman, to this position.

The OFL's anti-racism campaign focussed on internal union education as a means of combatting racism in the workplace. Educational materials were produced, including fact sheets on racism and a handbook for shop stewards [29]. The Federation also initiated union courses on combatting racism, with local union activists from OFL affiliates trained as instructors. Union conferences were organized, including an Ontario-wide meeting on racism. The OFL's April 1986 conference "Building the Participation of Workers of Colour in our Unions" served as a catalyst for anti-racist work in the Ontario labour movement.

At about the same time, Black workers and other non-white workers founded the Ontario Coalition of Black Trade Unionists in order to focus on racism in the workplace; they wanted to "share the resources and coordinate the particular struggles waged by Black, Chinese and south Asian trade unionists". With membership in the OCBTU open to "all workers who are not white", the coalition's objectives were to "educate and raise the profile of Black workers in Ontario" (*OCBTU Newsletter* 1987-8).

The OCBTU developed out of the growing militancy of non-white trade unionists. Veecock recalls that the OFL's 1986 conference of workers of colour provided the impetus for the formation of the OCBTU. During the conference, there was discussion about a coalition of black trade unionists in the States, a list was sent around for people interested in such a structure, and this provided a direct impetus to organize in Ontario. OCBTU members note that dissatisfaction with the slow pace of change in the Ontario labour movement played a role in the formation of the Coalition. Among other issues, they point to the OFL's non-renewal of Mutale Chanda's contract as an issue which contributed to minority workers dissatisfaction. Since its formation in 1986 the OCBTU has challenged racism and discrimination in the workplace, and it has provided non-white workers with a base for further anti-racist organizing in the labour movement; the coalition also encourages black workers to become more involved in their unions.

Within the OFL, a second resolution on Racism and Discrimination was adopted at the 1986 OFL Convention. This resolution specifically addressed the problems faced by women of colour, Native women and immigrant women. Union locals were urged to eliminate barriers to the full union participation of "women, minorities and the differently abled".

The 1986 OFL policy paper addressed a number of areas with implications for women of colour. In addition to issues raised earlier (e.g., human rights committees, union education), emphasis was put on challenging racist and discriminatory practices (e.g., racist jokes, racial harassment). Unions with large numbers of immigrant workers were urged to translate collective agreements and to provide classes for English in the workplace.

Endorsement of formal policies was only one part of mobilizing workers against racism. Further work needed to be done at the rank and file level. For example, Veecock recalled that a weekend school on racism had to be cancelled because of poor registration. In other actions, the Federation organized a series of forums across the province in order to move the whole question of racism higher on labour's agenda. They targetted heads of unions and the district labour councils to participate and speak at the forums, indicating that "the labour movement is taking this issue seriously" (Veecock).

The recent development of Women's Committees and Human Rights Committees in the OFL has helped to ensured that the concerns of both women and minorities will be raised in the labour movement. However, it is not always clear which constituency has responsibility for addressing the concerns raised by women of colour. Most women's committees in unions do not include visible minority women, and the committees don't really address issues of racism. While visible minority women tend to be represented on human rights committees, these committees do not often address women's issues. In Veecock's opinion, the work should not be narrowly defined: "Discrimination knows no boundaries -- it's a question of exploitation of all the workers."

A key question relates to the location of women of colour: are they seen as part of the women's movement, or as part of "that group of visible minorities" outside the women's movement. Veecock argues that if women of colour have not shared in the recent gains made by women in the labour movement, then they shouldn't be claimed by the women's movement: "Don't count me in the statistics if I'm not going to share in the benefits."

Immigrant and minority workers continue to be under-represented in the union movement and their need for a more effective representation and protection within and by the labour movement has been identified by working class women of colour as a pressing issue. The 1986 OFL resolution on *Racism and Discrimination* provided impetus for internal change in the labour movement, to ensure that "visible minorities can become involved at all levels of the union movement." This emphasis was continued in the 1987 policy paper *A Statement on Equal Action in Employment.* As an employer, the labour movement was urged to examine its "own system of hiring" and to "encourage and facilitate membership participation in all levels of union office in order to remove any internal barriers."

Some resistance exists to the growing participation of minority workers in the labour movement; according to OCBTU members, their Coalition has been seen by some OFL leaders as a threat rather than as a positive opportunity for getting more black unionists involved. In the last few years black workers and other non-white and immigrant workers have become involved at various levels of the labour movement; however, the numbers are still extremely low. There is evidence that in recent years more women have been appointed to staff positions and elected to union positions within the Ontario labour movement. Similar progress is not yet occurring for women of colour. Veecock notes that there are very few women of colour in prominent labour positions; the hiring and promotion of minority women "has only just started" [30].

Union activists in the OCBTU have pointed to the problem of competition between women and minority workers. They note that in some cases women have felt that their positions and power are being threatened by minority workers who are demanding their own representation. Black women have identified the problem of racism in the women's movement: that instead of trying to see differences among women as an enhancement to women's struggle, (white) women see differences in a negative way. Thus, it has been a struggle to get progressive women to recognize that racism is a women's issue. An OCBTU member points out that, instead of seeing black women as a threat, "women should welcome us to the struggle." She notes that if women isolate other minorities, it will create a struggle within a struggle.

Members of the OCBTU have also noted problems of careerism: some workers have become co-opted into positions of power and then lose touch with their roots with the rank and file membership -- the people to whom they should be accountable.

Minority workers in the OCBTU have criticized the racist attitudes implied in telling women of colour that they "don't have the skills" and that they "are not ready" to take leadership in the labour movement. Similar arguments have been used against women when they were first organizing in the unions. In contrast, the experience women have had in fighting discrimination should serve to heighten their awareness about the need to struggle against racism.

Despite these continuing problems a number of positive developments have occurred in union struggles against racism. More unions have developed human rights programs, trained instructors, set up human rights and race relations committees, and provided race relations workshops. However, union activity on racism is still not commonplace [31].

The growing number of race relations and human rights committees established in local unions have further encouraged the union activity of minority workers. A black trade unionist has noted the importance of support for these committees at the shop floor level, particularly when issues of racism are being taken up with the employers; care must be taken that the committees do not become isolated.

Veecock relates how a union workshop on race relations was particularly effective as a means of involving immigrant workers and their families:

> The union members were invited to bring their relatives . . . And it was held on Saturday (a family day for immigrant workers). Immigrant workers walked in with their interpreters. It was very moving . . . to see families together, grandmothers and children, children translating for their parents. It was very successful, over 3 dozen people attended. They combined a social and learning experience. Foods from the different countries were prepared and served by the workers and their families.

This workshop effectively broke down the language barriers; it also helped to build links between union work and family life -- especially important for immigrant women who combine paid work with family responsibilities. Such strategies help to involve immigrant women and women of colour in union activity.

However, there is still a long way to go in the struggle against racism. In the opinion of black trade unionists, the fight against racism has only just started. Veecock notes that there are some unions that still don't see racism as a problem. In unions that have established policies on racism, these policies sometimes exist only at the leadership level without filtering down to the local membership. The fight has to be waged at the top and at the bottom -- at the leadership level and on the shop floor.

Black trade unionists feel that the involvement and leadership of black and minority workers will lead to "a different agenda for labour". Workers of colour in the OCBTU want to "break through the barriers" in order to provide leadership to the whole labour movement on more than just human rights issues. Minority workers need to be more active in the unions. Veecock notes: "We need to have people there with a real sense of what our struggles are." Black workers have noted that racism exists within the union movement just as it exists in the larger society. For example, OCBTU members report of being told they need "Canadian union experience" in order to get involved in the labour movement -- in the same way that immigrant workers are told they need "Canadian experience" in the workplace. Black workers conclude that the labour movement has not been particularly effective in fighting racism and has been especially weak in supporting women of colour.

Within the labour movement, women of colour challenge trade union women to incorporate an anti-racist perspective into the struggle for women's equality. Recent developments in the OFL indicate that the Women's Committee and the Human Rights Committee have begun cooperating in a number of areas, raising issues of discrimination as they apply to both women and minorities. The Women's Committee organized a one-day "think tank", facilitated by Dionne Brand, in order to bring together the Women's Committee and visible minority women in unions to address the issues of racism and sexism: "We identified what some of the issues were; women of colour and the Women's Committee came together."

The Human Rights Committee and the Women's Committee jointly developed the OFL's 1987 *Statement on Equal Action in Employment*. The Statement, endorsed as formal OFL policy, proposed affirmative action for four target groups: the Disabled, Native People, Visible Minorities and Women. The document demonstrated the connections between racism and sexism, noting that for visible minority, immigrant and native women, the barriers to women's equality are compounded by racism. The program of action incorporated demands that have come forward from both the race relations and women's committees [32].

The focus of the 1987 OFL policy paper was on mandatory affirmative action programs for all target groups in order to achieve a "truly representative workplace in Ontario". In addition to a strong focus on racism and systemic discrimination against visible minorities -- issues raised by the OFL Human Rights Committee -- the policy document emphasized a number of issues previously raised by the OFL Women's Committee. The program of action called for continuing efforts toward mandatory affirmative action (see the 1982 OFL *Statement on Women and Affirmative Action*) and urged unions to work for childcare subsidies and workplace childcare (see the 1980 OFL *Statement on Day Care*). Union locals were urged to work with women's and human rights committees, and to establish such committees where none exist. As a follow-up to this policy paper, the Women's Committee and the Human Rights Committee have organized forums together, focussing on equal rights in employment.

Within the Ontario Coalition of Black Trade Unionists (OCBTU), women have pushed for an affirmative action policy. Executive positions have been shared equally by women and men [33]. Yvonne Bobb, a black woman active in OPSEU, was recently elected president. And women like Madhu Das Gupta, a founding member of the Coalition, have been active for many years. Efforts have been made to focus on women's issues; for example, the 1987-8 *OCBTU Newsletter* had a special section on "Women and Work", emphasizing women's double discrimination and their struggle for equality. Bobb reports that men in the OCBTU have generally been supportive of women -- they "understand the struggle". However, she notes that women have generally not played a very visible role within the coalition. Bobb hopes to politicize black women, so that they develop leadership skills and take more leadership roles within the Coalition and within their unions.

Many important questions still need to be addressed. We need to look at the reasons why women of colour have not shared fully in the gains made by union women and why the women's movement has not more effectively addressed the specific concerns raised by women of colour. Both of these problems can be traced to racism within the labour movement and within the women's movement -- racism which reflects and reproduces racism in Canadian society.

Linking the Struggles: CUPE Local 79

Black trade unionists have identified the many dimensions of racism that persist in the labour movement, especially for women of colour who face both racism and sexism. A lot of work remains to be done in the unions and many trade unionists are dissatisfied with the slow pace of change. There are, however, some positive examples of unions that are challenging racism and sexism. A number of trade unionists have pointed to CUPE Local 79 as exemplary in this regard. Through its campaign to defend the jobs of black and Asian women employed as nursing attendants in Metro Toronto Homes for the Aged, Local 79 has -- in very practical terms -- challenged both racism and sexism in the workplace. This case study highlights some of these efforts and suggests how a stronger labour movement might be built that cuts across divisions of race and gender.

Local 79 took a major step forward in defending the interests of women of colour when it organized the casual part-time workers in Metro Homes; 90% of them are women, mostly from the black, Asian and Aboriginal peoples communities.   Unable to win an acceptable first contract through negotiations, the union was forced to go to arbitration to seek benefits parallelling those for full-time workers in the Homes.   Local 79 was successful and the contract set a precedent for part-time health care workers; further gains were made in the 1987-88 collective agreement, similar to those won by members of the full-time unit.   Part-timers in Local 79 became eligible for pro-rated health benefits, sick pay, maternity leave, holiday pay, increments and overtime pay.   The 1987-88 contract showed more improvements such as guaranteed shifts for part-timers with seniority, OHIP, and employer-paid maternity leave top-up [34].

These benefits were significant gains for casual part-time healthcare workers.   June Small, coordinator of the organizing drive at Greenacres Home, commented: "We're jubilant. The part-timers were getting fed up with being treated as second class citizens. At last they'll be getting benefits. We've waited two very long years for this" (CUPE Local 79 Press Release, Feb. 22, 1985).

In response to the union's argument that part-time employees with seniority should automatically move into full-time positions as they became vacant, the arbitrator had ruled that Metro was to consider seniority when filling full-time positions.   This was also an important advance for the workers (and would prove to be signficant in the union's subsequent campaign for jobs).   The coordinator of the organizing drive at Kipling Acres, Muriel Collins, stated: "We're very happy. Some of our part-timers have been waiting for years for a full-time job here. This signals the end of Metro's bringing in people from outside. Now they'll have to give the part-timers a chance at those precious full-time positions" (CUPE Local 79 Press Release, Feb. 22, 1985).

However, within a short time Local 79 became involved in a major campaign to prevent Metro's conversion of full-time nursing attendant jobs into part-time hours upon these positions becoming vacant.   Part-time workers in Local 79 filed grievances because their access to full-time jobs -- guaranteed through seniority provisions in the collective agreement -- was being circumvented through these cutbacks; the union also filed a policy grievance.   The proposed job cuts were confirmed by Metro's budget projections for the Homes [35].   A 1985 report had documented Metro's increasing use of part-time employment and the high concentration (79%) of women and/or visible minority workers in part-time positions (CUPE Local 79 Fact Sheet, 1986).

The union campaign against Metro's efforts was based on the "adverse and disproportionate" effect this would have on the black and Asian women who predominate in these entry level jobs -- and who work part-time only because there are not enough full-time jobs. While Metro Toronto was publicly committed to employment equity, the reduction in full-time jobs would constitute "a set-back for employment equity" for women, members of visible minority groups, and especially for women of colour [36].

The union argued that the reduction in full-time jobs would reinforce longstanding systemic discrimination:

> The issue for Local 79 and for the Black and Asian com-munities is that any reduction in the growing number of full-time jobs in an occupation where there is an historical and continuing concentration of Black and Asian women would automatically reduce the job prospects for these women, many of whom are sole-wage earners. The con-centration of Black and Asian women in this and related service occupations itself stems from long-standing, deeply-rooted and continuing systemic discrimination which has meant that relatively few occupations have been open to Black and Asian women in significant numbers. And given that other areas of work are not opening up appreciably, the conversion of full-time jobs into part-time hours is bound to increase poverty and hardship in these communi-ties [37].

In its public campaign against the cutbacks, Local 79 pointed to the contradiction between Metro's stated policy on employment equity and its actual staffing practices. The union noted that Metro's Equal Employment Opportunity Office had not even been informed about the staff cut-backs, although its role was to evaluate proposed changes in staffing policies that might affect equal employment.

The union also contrasted Metro's treatment of black and Asian healthcare workers with that of women in management. While Metro had approved an equal-pay adjustment for 315 women in the latter group (rais-ing salaries by as much as 33%), the reduction in the number of full-time positions for nursing attendants was a "move backwards" for employment equity. The union declared that "the real test of Metro's commitment to employment equity is how it treats employees at the bottom of the wage scale, most of whom are women and members of visible minority groups" (CUPE Local 79 Fact Sheet, 1986).

In building support for this struggle, Local 79 enlisted the aid of immigrant, women, community and seniors' groups, as well as support from other labour bodies. This fight against systemic discrimination attracted widespread support from groups representing women of colour [38]. Metro backed down on the conversion attempts and the union regained the majority of lost nursing attendant positions [39].

There were a number of factors that contributed to Local 79's successful campaign against systemic discrmination. By examining some of these factors we may identify effective labour strategies that link together struggles against racism and sexism.

There is evidence of a high level of political awareness on the part of the union leadership, the staff and the membership. Local 79 developed a clear analysis of systemic discrimination and then based its struggle on this analysis. According to Dionne Brand, Local 79 set a precedent for labour through its analysis of "the sexual division of labour as racially structured in institutionalized domestic work" (Brand 1987:36). Local President Steven David (himself an immigrant) consistently addressed the issues of racism and sexism, as illustrated by his response to Metro's 1987 report on Equal Employment Opportunity:

> We think that "socialization, education and social factors" like "factors which might exist in the workplace" are themselves both the result of and the means of perpetuating institutionalized racism and sexism and that these, too, must be addressed... [40].

Local 79's commitment to employment equity is consistent with CUPE's official policy of fighting discrimination against women and minorities and attacking the "systemic discrmination embedded in the policies and practices of our workplaces and other institutions in society", as stated in the union's affirmative action manual [41].

The Local had only recently organized the casual part-time workers in the Homes -- the organizing drive itself illustrated the union's commitment to the most disadvantaged workers in the healthcare system. Therefore, the union leadership and staff knew the membership well and they were quite aware of the racism and sexism faced by the black and Asian women employed as nursing attendants.

Even more important, the struggle against Metro's systemic discrimination would not have been successful without an active union membership. If workers had not grieved, the union would not have known about the job cuts in time to take effective action. It would have been more difficult to challenge the cuts in full-time jobs if the union had waited until Metro's budget had been passed.

Another indication of the union's commitment to fighting racism and sexism can be seen in the composition of the union leadership and staff. As the largest municipal local union in Canada, Local 79 includes six bargaining units, with an overall membership that is two-thirds women. Women hold close to half the leadership positions and all the staff positions, an unusual record among labour organizations:

> Women make up 42% of our Executive Committee and Executive Board, 53% of our Stewards' Body, 50% of our Bargaining Committees, 45% of our Chairpersons and Deputy Chairpersons of Committees, 49% of our Committees, 100% of our Support Staff and 100% of our Consultants [42].

While the union doesn't keep records by race, there are indications that minority workers are active at the leadership level. The Metro full-time unit officer is a black woman born in South America, and the Metro part-time unit officer is a francophone woman; both are nursing attendants in Metro Homes. Of the fourteen Executive Board members, three are black or Asian; one of the three Auditors/Trustees is black [43].

A commitment to fighting discrimination in the workplace often goes hand in hand with a commitment to equality within the union structures. Local 79's record indicates that it has a solid commitment to fighting racism and sexism in both spheres. According to union consultant Pat Murphy, "this struggle wasn't in support of minority workers -- this was *our* struggle."

Local 79 developed a strategy that demonstrated the benefit of employment equity and fair employment practices to all workers -- not just the black and Asian employees directly affected by Metro's actions. The union had explained to full-time workers how they would also gain by winning benefit provisions for part-time workers; this would then reduce Metro's financial incentives to replace full-time jobs with part-time jobs [44]. Had Metro been able to get away with reducing full-time jobs for nursing attendants, other groups of workers would also have been at risk.

Through its actions, Local 79 has demonstrated solid labour support for working women, linking together the issues of racism and sexism. The union successfully addressed the particular concerns of women of colour, fighting for union protection, for benefits and for full-time jobs [45].

Conclusion

This paper has examined the material conditions of racism, sexism and exploitation faced by working class women of colour. I have reviewed the union organizing efforts undertaken by women and minority workers, focussing on the concerns raised by women of colour. Furthermore I looked at problems of racism that exist within the women's movement and considered strategies for building an anti-racist women's movement in the unions. Finally, some tentative conclusions were drawn about effective strategies for fighting discrimination, based on our case study of CUPE Local 79.

This is only preliminary research; clearly more substantive work needs to be undertaken in this area, particularly by women of colour. I hope that the conclusions drawn from this research will stimulate debate on the issues, provide an impetus for further research and, most importantly, contribute to the growth of an anti-racist women's movement.

Unless feminist analysis seriously addresses issues of economic and racial oppression, it will not be relevant to women of colour (see Thornhill 1982). And until women's organizing activities in unions include women of colour and address both racism and sexism, such efforts will not reach their full potential. As June Veecock has stated: "We will be a powerful force if all women come together ... so very powerful."

Endnotes

*Department of Sociology, University of Lethbridge, Lethbridge AB, T1K 3M4. Acknowledgments: I would like to thank the trade unionists who shared their experiences with me, and provided me with information and documentation. I hope that this paper accurately reflects their concerns and their struggles against racism and sexism. Special thanks go to Yvonne Bobb, Madhu Das Gupta, Pat Murphy, and June Veecock. The analysis in this paper developed out of numerous discussions with trade unionists, community activists, academic colleagues and students. Many people have contributed to my understanding of the issues, particularly the black women, Native women and other women of colour who have spoken out against racism. I would also like to thank the trade unionists and the editors of *Socialist Studies* who provided me with feedback on earlier drafts of this paper; their suggestions were most valuable in making revisions. Any errors which remain in this paper are my sole responsibility.

Finally, I would like to acknowledge the support of the Advisory Research Committee of Queen's University at Kingston, which provided funding for this research, conducted while I was a member of their Department of Sociology.

1. This article was originally published as "Linking the Struggles: Racism, Feminism and the Union Movement". However, the current title more accurately reflects the focus of this article on racism and sexism.

2. Roxana Ng and Alma Estable note that the "common sense usage" of immigrant women refers to "women of colour, women from Third World countries, women who do not speak English well, and women who occupy lower positions in the occupational hierarchy" (1987:29). Linda Carty and Dionne Brand point out that "visible minority" is a designation that has been constructed by the State. They argue that debates at recent government organized conferences -- about the question of who constitutes a visible minority -- have served to divide women from different communities (1988:39-42).

3. Gains being made by union women have been well documented by a number of academics and trade unionists. See, for example, studies and reports by: Acheson 1980; Briskin 1983; Crombie 1986:22-25; Gallagher 1987; Leah 1987; Swarbrick 1988; White 1980. Concerns about the limitations of these gains have been articulated in a number of articles on immigrant women. See, for example: *RFR*, special issue on "Immigrant Women", 1987; Cumsille et al. 1983. Similar concerns about racism have been raised by some trade unionists, e.g. Gallagher 1987.

4. See, for example, *RFR* 1987; Gannagé 1986; Brand 1987. This *Annual* has been undertaken to address these very concerns.

5. June Veecock was interviewed on October 3, 1988. Veecock, a black woman, is one of the few women of colour with a staff position in the Ontario labour movement; she is the leading staff person responsible for work on race relations in the OFL. Discussions were held with members of the Ontario Coalition of Black Trade Unionists (OCBTU) on several occasions. Yvonne Bobb was interviewed on May 27, 1989. Bobb, a black woman active in OPSEU (Ontario Public Service Employees Union), recently became President of the OCBTU. Informal discussions were also held with members of CUPE (Canadian Union of Public Employees) and OPSEU. Statements by trade unionists are indicated in the text; they are identified by name (e.g., Veecock) or by position (e.g., OCBTU member).

6. Information and documentation about CUPE Local 79 has been provided by Pat Murphy, a consultant with the union. I have reviewed union documents including correspondence, fact sheets, press releases and reports.

7. For discussion of women's inequality at work, see Pat and Hugh Armstrong 1984: Chapter 2. See also Leah 1986: Chapter 4.

8. For further discussion of immigration policies, see Arnopolous 1979; Ng and Estable 1987. For information about domestic workers, see Calliste in this volume; Leah and Morgan 1979. For information about Filipino garment workers, see York 1989.

9. For discussion of the garment industry, see Arnopolous 1979; Ng and Estable 1987. On farmworkers, see Stultz 1987. On domestic workers, see Hernandez 1987; Cohen 1987:36-38.

10. See Metro Toronto, "First Equal Employment Opportunity Report", June 1985, cited in CUPE Local 79 Fact Sheet, Dec. 1986. See also letter from Local 79 President S. David to Ontario Women's Directorate, Sept. 16, 1988.

11. According to Statistics Canada, women working full-year in 1984-85 earned 60.9% of men's earnings. See Labour Canada 1987:47. The precise figures vary, depending on whether one compares full-time, full year workers, or all workers -- including part-time and temporary workers. A high proportion of the latter category are women of colour, who have comparatively lower earnings.

12. Average hourly earnings are reported in Armstrong and Armstrong 1984:30. According to unpublished data from the 1981 census, Native women have the lowest employment income of any ethnic group: Native women earned an average of $6,375 in 1981, compared with $8,863 for the female labour force. Study by J. Podoluk, cited in Stasiulus 1987:5-9 (p. 8, Table 1). This figure underestimates poverty among Native women, however, since a high proportion of them are not part of the paid labour force.

13. See letter from Times Change Women's Employment Service to Ontario Women's Directorate, Aug. 8, 1988, regarding CUPE Local 79.

14. Canadian data for 1980 indicates that 58% of women part-time workers wanted full-time work. See Armstrong and Armstrong 1983:265, Table 19. Local 79 survey is reported in CUPE Fact Sheet, December 1986.

15. Letter from Local 79 President S. David to Metro Chairman Dennis Flynn, Dec. 7, 1987.

16. For discussion of these issues, see Cumsille 1983; Ng and Estable 1987; Paredes 1987:23-27; Rodriguez 1981:34-35.

17. For discussion of the obstacles to women's unionization, see Armstrong and Armstrong 1984; Gallagher 1982; Ritchie 1983; White 1980.

18. Problems of organizing part-time workers were discussed by Pat Murphy (in correspondence) and Spink 1985.

19. See letter from Times Change to Ontario Women's Directorate, Aug. 8, 1988.

20. Legislative and policy changes recommended by immigrant and non-white women include: improvements to employment standards, health and safety, immigration laws, job training and language training, and mandatory employment equity. See section on "Women and Work", compiled by Dionne Brand, in the *OCBTU Newsletter* (published by Ontario Coalition of Black Trade Unionists, Toronto, 1987-8).

21. This 1986 fight was won because of strong union and community support, media attention and direct intervention by the provincial government. See Neal and Neale 1987:39-41.

22. Carty and Brand 1988:41; they point out how state initiatives may have served to direct and contain women's struggles at a time when women in many communities were becoming organized. For discussion of immigrant women's organizing, see also Das Gupta 1986.

23. Statement by June Veecock, OFL Human Rights Director. See Note #5, above.

24. For more detailed discussion of women's organizing in the OFL, see Leah 1987.

25. A subsequent OFL Convention approved expansion of the Federation Executive to include additional seats reserved for women.

26. Acheson 1982:5. Acheson was OFL Human Rights Director at that time.

27. See, for example, comments of trade unionist quoted by Leah 1986:424.

28. See also comments by Brand 1987; Das Gupta 1986; Egan et al. 1988:20-47; Stasiulus 1987.

29. Eight Fact Sheets on Racism were produced by the OFL Human Rights Committee, in seven languages. The fact sheets covered such topics as the climate of racism, racial harassment, minority workers, the collective agreement, establishing Race Relations-Human Rights Committees, and educational resources for unions. The OFL also produced *Steps to Resolving Racial Conflict at the Workplace*, a handbook for shop stewards.

30. See Moore 1987, reported in the *OCBTU Newsletter* (1987-8). According to Moore, in June 1987 there were three other non-white women on staff with the OFL in addition to Veecock (two secretaries and one executive assistant).

31. For example, Moore reports that according to a Labour Council survey of Hamilton unions, 92% of unions did not have human rights committees, 75.6% did not have non-discrimination clauses in the collective agreement, and 65.5% of locals did not have minorities on their executive. At the same time, 65.2% of these Hamilton locals were workers from minority groups (*OCBTU Newsletter* 1987-8).

32. This information was provided by June Veecock.

33. See listing of 1987-8 executive in the *OCBTU Newsletter*.

34. See letter from Times Change to Ontario Women's Directorate, Aug. 8, 1988; Local 79 Press Release, Feb. 22, 1985.

35. Information from Pat Murphy.

36. Letter from Local 79 President Stephen David to Ontario Women's Directorate, Sept. 16, 1988.

37. Letter from S. David to Metro Chairman Dennis Flynn, Dec. 7, 1987.

38. Groups supporting the campaign included: Immigrant Women's Job Placement Centre, Black Women's Collective, Black Secretariat, Kababayan Community Centre, Ontario Coalition of Visible Minority Women, Congress of Black Women, Cross-Cultural Communications Centre, Centro Para Gente de Habla Hispana, Latin American Community Centre, Times Change Women's Employment Service, Immigrant Women's Centre, Jamaican-Canadian Association, Council of Jamaicans in Ontario, Women Working with Immigrant Women, Ontario Coalition of Black Trade Unionists, and Organized Working Women. Two newspapers, *Chinese Daily News* and *Share*, contained articles opposing the cutbacks. See Local 79 Fact Sheet, "Groups opposing cut-backs" (n.d.).

39. There was also continuing union pressure on Metro to develop an employment equity policy to be used in assessing the impact of changes in employment practices. While this had been recommended by Metro's "First Equal Employment Opportunity Report" in June 1985, such a policy had not yet been developed. See Letter from Times Change to Ontario Women's Directorate, Aug. 8, 1988. See also Local 79's response to a Report by the Director of Equal Opportunity ("Reduction in the Number of Full-Time Nursing Attendant Positions - Homes for the Aged", Nov. 26, 1987), letter from S. David to Metro Chairman Dennis Flynn, Dec. 7, 1987.

40. Letter from S. David to Metro Chairman, Dec.7, 1987.

41. CUPE, *Equality in the Workplace: An Affirmative Action Manual*, (Ottawa, CUPE National Office, n.d.).

42. Letter from S. David to Ontario Women's Directorate, Sept. 16, 1988.

43. Information from Pat Murphy. See also letter from S. David to Ontario Women's Directorate, Sept. 16, 1988.

44. Remarks by S. David, Local 79 Press Release, Feb. 22, 1985.

45. Most recently, Local 79 has mounted a campaign against Metro's internal human rights complaints procedure. Arguing that workers have a right to work-places free from all forms of harassment and discrimination, the union has charged that the internal complaints procedures are designed to undermine hard-won rights under the collective agreement and the Ontario Human Rights Code. Information provided by Pat Murphy; see also Local 79 correspondence.

BIBLIOGRAPHY

Acheson, Shelley. 1982. "Daycare in the 80's: the Experience of the OFL". Remarks to the Equality Forum, CLC Convention. Toronto: OFL Women's Committee, May.

Acheson, Shelley. 1980. Report. *Women's Rights Bulletin*. Toronto: OFL, November.

Aggarwal, Pramila. 1987. "Business as Usual in the Factory", *RFR* 16:1 (March), pp. 42-43.

Argue, R., C. Gannagé and D.W. Livingstone, eds. 1987. *Working People and Hard Times*. Toronto: Garamond Press.

Armstrong, Pat and Hugh. 1984. *The Double Ghetto*. Toronto: McClelland and Stewart.

Armstrong, Pat and Hugh. 1983. *A Working Majority: What Women Must Do for Pay*. Ottawa: CACSW.

Arnopoulos, Sheila. 1979. *The Problems of Immigrant Women in the Labour Force*. Ottawa: CACSW.

Bannerji, Himani. 1987. "Introducing Racism: Notes Toward an Anti-Racist Feminism", *RFR* 16:1 (March), pp. 10-12.

Bourne, Jenny. 1984. *Towards an Anti-Racist Feminism*. Race and Class pamphlet No.9. London: Institute of Race Relations.

Brand, Dionne. 1987. "Black Women and Work", *Fireweed* 25 (Fall), pp. 28-37.

Brand, Dionne and Krisantha Sri Bhaggiyadatta. 1986. *Rivers Have Sources, Trees Have Roots: Speaking of Racism.* Toronto: Cross Cultural Communications Centre.

Briskin, Linda. 1983. "Women and Unions in Canada: A Statistical Overview". In *Union Sisters.* Linda Briskin and L. Yanz, eds. Toronto: Women's Press.

Briskin, Linda and L. Yanz, eds. 1983. *Union Sisters.* Toronto: Women's Press.

Calliste, Agnes. 1989. "Canada's Immigration Policy and Domestics from the Caribbean: the Second Domestic Scheme", *Race, Class, Gender: Bonds and Barriers, Socialist Studies* No. 5 (this volume).

Canadian Labour Congress (CLC). 1983. *Human Rights and Trade Unions.* Ottawa: CLC, Labour Education and Studies Centre, April.

Canadian Union of Public Employees (see CUPE).

Carby, Hazel. 1982. "White Women Listen!". Centre for Contemporary Cultural Studies. *The Empire Strikes Back: Race and Racism in 70's Britain.* U. of Birmingham: Centre for Contemporary Cultural Studies.

Carty, Linda and Dionne Brand. 1988. "'Visible Minority' Women -- a Creation of the Canadian State", *RFR* 17:3 (September), pp. 39-42.

Cohen, Rina. 1987. "The Work Conditions of Immigrant Women Live-In Domestics: Racism, Sexual Abuse and Invisibility", *RFR* 16:1, pp. 36-38.

Crombie, Stuart. 1986. "What Have Women Done" (Looking back on 10 years work with the OFL Women's Committee), *Our Times* 5:2 (March), pp. 22-25.

Cumsille, Alejandra, et al. 1983. "Triple Oppression: Immigrant Women in the Labour Force". In *Union Sisters.* Linda Briskin and L. Yanz, eds. Toronto: Women's Press.

CUPE (Canadian Union of Public Employees). 1988. Letter from Times Change Women's Employment Service to Ontario Women's Directorate (Re: Nomination of Local 79 for 1988 Achievement in Employment Equity Award), August 8.

CUPE. 1988. Letter from Local 79 President Stephen David to Ontario Women's Directorate, September 16.

CUPE. 1987. Local 79. Correspondence: Letter from Local 79 President S. David to Metro Chairman Dennis Flynn (Re: Director of Equal Employment Opportunity's Report, "Reduction in the Number of Full-Time Nursing Attendant Positions -- Homes for the Aged", November 26, 1987), December 7.

CUPE. 1986. Local 79 Fact Sheet. "Some Facts About Metro and Employment Equity". December.

CUPE. 1985. Local 79 Fact Sheet. Metro Toronto. "First Equal Employment Opportunity Report". June.

CUPE. 1985. Local 79. Documents: Press Release (Re: Arbitration award for Local 79, first collective agreement for part-time workers), February 22.

CUPE. n.d. Local 79 Fact Sheet. "Groups opposing cut-backs".

CUPE. n.d. *Equality in the Workplace: An Affirmative Action Manual*. Ottawa: CUPE National Office.

Das Gupta, Tania. 1987. "Unravelling the Web of History", *RFR* 16:1 (March), pp. 13-14.

Das Gupta, Tania. 1986. *Learning From Our History: Community Development with Immigrant Women, 1958-86*. Toronto: Cross Cultural Communications Centre.

Edelson, Miriam. 1987. *Challenging Unions: Feminist Process and Democracy in the Labour Movement*. Feminist Perspectives No. 8. Ottawa: CRIAW, February.

Egan, Carolyn and L. Yanz. 1983. "Building Links: Labour and the Women's Movement". In *Union Sisters*. Linda Briskin and L. Yanz, eds. Toronto: Women's Press.

Egan, C., L.L. Gardner and J.V. Persad. 1988. "The Politics of Transformation: Struggles with Race, Class and Sexuality in the March 8th Coalition", *Socialist Studies* 4, pp. 20-47.

Estable, Alma. 1986. *Immigrant Women in Canada: Current Issues*. Ottawa: Canadian Advisory Council on the Status of Women.

Fireweed: A Feminist Quarterly. 1987. "The Issue is Class", Issue 25 (Fall).

Fireweed: A Feminist Quarterly. 1983. "Women of Colour", Issue 16 (Spring).

Gallagher, Deirdre. 1987. "On Affirmative Action". In *Working People and Hard Times*. R. Argue, et al., eds. Toronto: Garamond Press.

Gallagher, Deirdre. 1982. "Getting Organized...in the CLC". In *Still Ain't Satisfied: Canadian Feminism Today*. M. Fitzgerald, et al., eds. Toronto: Women's Press.

Gannagé, Charlene. 1986. *Double Day, Double Bind: Women Garment Workers*. Toronto: Women's Press.

Hernandez, Carmencita. 1988. "The Coalition of Visible Minority Women", *Socialist Studies* 4, pp. 157-168.

Hernandez, Carmencita. 1987. "Organizing Domestic Workers". In *Working People and Hard Times*. R. Argue, et al., eds. Toronto: Garamond Press.

Khosla, Prabha. 1983. "Profiles of Working Class East Indian Women", *Fireweed* 16 (Spring), pp. 43-48.

Labour Canada. 1987. *Women in the Labour Force*, 1986-87 Edition. Ottawa: Ministry of Supply and Services, Canada.

Labour Council of Metro Toronto (LCMT), Women's Committee and Human Rights Committee. n.d. *The Equality Project for Union Women.* Pamphlet. Toronto: LCMT.

Leah, Ronnie. 1990. "Daycare, Trade Unions, and the Women's Movement: Trade Union Women Organize for Change". In *Making Knowledge Count.* Peter Harries-Jones, ed. Montréal: McGill-Queen's University Press.

Leah, Ronnie. 1987. "Organizing for Daycare". In *Working People and Hard Times.* R. Argue, et al., eds. Toronto: Garamond Press.

Leah, Ronnie. 1986. "The Day Care Issue and the Development of a Trade Union Women's Movement". Unpublished Ph.D. thesis, University of Toronto.

Leah, Ronnie and Gwen Morgan. 1979. "Immigrant Women Fight Back: the Case of the Seven Jamaican Women", *RFR* VIII:3 Part 2 (November).

Moore, Cleve. 1987-8. "Partial Statistics on Employment Inequity in Unions", *OCBTU Newsletter.*

Neal, Rusty and V. Neale. 1987. "As Long As You Know How to Do Housework: Portuguese-Canadian Women and the Office Cleaning Industry in Toronto", *RFR* 16:1 (March), pp. 39-41.

Ng,   Roxana and Alma Estable. 1987. "Immigrant Women in the Labour Force: An Overview of Present Knowledge and Research Gaps", *RFR* 16:1 (March), pp. 29-33.

Ng,   Roxana and Tania Das Gupta. 1981. "Nation Builders? The Captive Labour Force of Non-English Speaking Immigrant Women", *Canadian Woman Studies* 3:1, pp. 83-89.

Ng,   Winnie. 1987. "Garment Workers Action Centre". In *Working People and Hard Times.* R. Argue, et al., eds. Toronto: Garamond Press.

OCBTU Newsletter. Published by Ontario Coalition of Black Trade Unionists, Toronto, Ontario.

One   Sky Report. 1984. "The Triple Oppression of Immigrant Working Women", Special Issue, December.

OFL   (Ontario Federation of Labour). 1987. *A Statement on Equal Action in Employment.* November.

OFL. 1986. *Racism and Discrimination.* November.

OFL. 1984. Information, "OFL Press Conference -- Anti-Racism", January 23.

OFL. 1982. *Statement on Women and Affirmative Action.* November.

OFL. 1981. *Statement on "Racism Hurts Everyone".* November.

OFL. 1980. *Statement on Day Care.* November.

OFL. 1978. *A Woman's Place is in her Union.* November.

OFL. 1975. Resolutions of Annual Conventions. *Statement on Women.* November.

OFL. n.d. Human Rights Committee, publications: Fact Sheets on Racism, Nos. 1-8.

OFL. n.d *Steps to Resolving Racial Conflict at the Workplace*. Handbook.

Ontario Statistics 1984. 1984. Toronto: Ontario Ministry of Treasury and Economics.

Paredes, Milagros. 1987. "Immigrant Women and Second Language Education". *RFR* 16:1 (March), pp. 23-27.

Resources for Feminist Research (RFR). 1988. "Feminist Perspectives on the Canadian State", 17:3 (September).

RFR. 1987. "Immigrant Women", 16:1 (March).

RFR. 1981. "Women and Trade Unions", X:2, Part 2 (July).

Ritchie, Laurell. 1983. "Why Are So Many Women Unorganized?". In *Union Sisters*. Linda Briskin and L. Yanz, eds. Toronto: Women's Press.

Rodriguez, Maria Luisa. 1981. "An Immigrant Woman Speaks", *RFR* X:2, pp. 34-5.

Silvera, Makeda. 1983. *Silenced*. Toronto: Williams-Wallace.

Spink, Marilyn. 1985. "Bring in the Part-Timers". *Metro Toronto Labour*.

Stasiulus, Daiva. 1987. "Rainbow Feminism: Perspectives on Minority Women in Canada", *RFR* 16:1 (March), pp. 5-9.

Stultz, Erma. 1987. "Organizing the Unorganized Farmworkers in Ontario". In *Working People and Hard Times*. R. Argue et al., eds. Toronto: Garamond Press.

Swarbrick, Ann. 1988. "Recent Developments for Union Women". Presentation for Workshop on Union Women Organizing for Change, Society for Socialist Studies, Windsor, June.

Thomas, Barb and C. Novogrodsky. 1983. *Combatting Racism in the Workplace: A Course for Workers*. Toronto: Cross Cultural Communications Centre.

Thornhill, Esmeralda. 1982. "Black Women's Studies in Teaching Related to Women: Help or Hindrance to Sisterhood?", *Fireweed* Issue 16.

White, Julie. 1980. *Women and Unions*. Ottawa: Ministry of Supply Services Canada.

York, Geoffrey. 1989. "Winnipeg seamstress, others snarled in deportation dilemma", *Globe and Mail* [Toronto], January 9.

10. Métis Women and the Economy of Northern Saskatchewan

Irene A. Poelzer*

Introduction

Métis women in northern Saskatchewan are related to the economy in three distinct ways. A few Métis women, fortunate enough to be in paid employment, are directly related to the capitalist wage economy. However, most Métis women find themselves related indirectly to the capitalist economy through volunteer work, transfer payments (welfare), or both.

Like wage labour, volunteer labour is intricately related to capitalist development. In non-capitalist and/or pre-capitalist societies, although people often have a tradition of sharing and helping, this cannot be termed volunteer work because essentially volunteer work means work that could be waged work but is non-paid work. Since in non-capitalist or pre-capitalist societies there is no waged work, volunteer work as non-paid work is conceivable only in a society in which there is waged work.

Similarly, social welfare understood in terms of transfer payments cannot be conceived in a non-capitalist society. This phenomenon is possible only in a society where some people do not earn a wage and, hence, are in need of transfer payments in order to live in such a society. A significant number of Métis women are related to the wage economy through the volunteer work they do or through the transfer payments they receive.

On the surface, Métis women's connection to the economy is not unlike that of other women across Canada: some are employed in the work force, some do volunteer work, and some need social assistance. The difference between the Métis women studied here and other Canadian women, however, lies in the fact that Métis women of northern Saskatchewan are locked into an economically depressed region in which waged employment opportunities are virtually non-existent; in which race and class considerations operate invisibly in the decisions of governments and multinationals to deny the development of a viable economy in northern Saskatchewan; and in which gender determines the kinds of jobs and low wages open to Métis women. Unlike the general Canadian female population, Métis women very seldom, if ever, have the opportunity of choice in job selection. They also lack the means and power to demand higher wages for the few jobs available: for every Métis woman who might conceivably refuse a job for reasons of low pay, there are countless others waiting in the shadows to accept the job at low pay simply out of necessity. They lack

security and mobility and must be content to accept any available employment at hand. Finally, Métis women have neither the facilities nor the
opportunities to equip themselves for any but the lowest paid jobs, mostly
in the service sector.

Gender, race, and class are often studied to show the broad social and
economic tensions, along with the injustices that exist in society, particularly those arising from economic development schemes. The disadvantaged
situation of women should, then, not be thought of as natural, inevitable,
or even inescapable. Furthermore, it is not enough for Métis women, for
example, to know just the geography of the situation of their lives, that is,
to be conscious of their condition. It is of utmost importance that the genesis of their situation, as well as its possible alternatives, be understood.
Only then is it possible to have a critical grasp of Métis women's situation
in its entirety: what it is, how it comes about, what it ought to be, and how
it can be changed. The feminist sociologist Dorothy Smith suggests that,
by perceiving the everyday world as problematic, it is possible to make an
objective investigation of how the social relations of the everyday world of
women are joined to the social relations of the larger social organization
which shape and determine that everyday world. Smith further suggests
that such an investigation begins from the standpoint of women and with
their own articulation of their everyday world (Smith 1981).

In this paper the articulations of Métis women concerning their everyday life situations in seven different communities are utilized for the purpose of disclosing the taken-for-granted social relations of the capitalist
economy that are the major determinants of their lives. These social relations are prior to the level at which the Métis women speak. By making the
connections between the social relations of the capitalist economy and the
social relations of the everyday world of Métis women, it is possible to gain
a deeper and more complete picture of the effects of such factors as gender, race and class on these women's lives, and also to point to possible
ways of changing their situation. Essentially, this paper presents a methodology for understanding the impact of the capitalist economy on the everyday lives of Métis women.

To provide a backdrop for the examination of the lives of Métis
women in northern Saskatchewan and the economic relationships in which
they find themselves, a brief history follows of the impact of uranium mining and of government intervention in the introduction of a wage economy
in northern Saskatchewan.

In northern Saskatchewan, during the first half of the twentieth century, there was no widespread nor established waged economy. People were
isolated and lived off the land. A few white-dominated tourist resorts and

one or two mining ventures constituted what little waged economy there was in the region. Beginning in the 1960s, vast amounts of uranium were found in the area; both government and multinational corporations became involved in capital intensive resource extraction. Massive state participation in uranium mining was justified as a scheme for diversifying and stabilizing the provincial economy -- hitherto solely dependent on agriculture. With the establishment of the Saskatchewan Mining Development Corporation, the provincial government was brought into "alliance with multi-national corporations intent on little more than the exploitation of energy resources" (Gunn 1982:4). What followed was the rapid introduction in northern Saskatchewan of capitalist social organization based on a wage economy.

The imposition of a wage economy on northern communities and the accompanying establishment of necessary bureaucratic, organizational and social structures did not, however, transform the northern region into a population of waged labourers, as might have been expected. While government and multinationals were intent on discovering and extracting uranium, neither was committed to community building. Few native people were hired in the initial construction stage of the various mines, and very few in the later operational stage. Highly trained outside experts held the lucrative positions available at the mine sites. Generally, big capital had little interest in developing a viable economic base for the communities of the north, or in being supportive participants in the social development of these communities. With the exception of Uranium City, which would still end up as a ghost town, major uranium corporations carefully avoided any substantial long-range commitment to northern communities. Instead, a free air commuter system (facilitating rotation work schedules) was established to bring in workers who lived outside the North. Although these labour practices were expensive, corporations maintained that, in the long run, they were more efficient. Investing money to develop a viable economic base for native communities was an expense and risk that mining corporates were unwilling to take.

Since the multinationals provided relatively few full-time jobs for native people, and had little interest in the social and economic conditions of northern communities, any social and economic changes that did transpire within communities were largely due to government intervention, particularly during the decade of the seventies. The government provided state capital for infrastructures and social services needed by both the mining corporations and northern communities. Facilities in the areas of transportation, roads and airstrips, communication, energy, and mine site housing for workers were necessary for the efficient function of mining enterprises. Other projects, such as general housing, sewer and water facilities, recreational units, schools, a few restaurants and motels were central to northern community infrastructure. Government buildings and offices were also needed for the staff who implemented policy and monitored activities. The public infrastructure connected to health, education, and social welfare was also established during this decade. The service sector jobs associated with these government activities provide the major source of employment for native people. However, the number of positions available is far below that necessary to sustain a healthy economy in northern communities. The employment situation in the town of La Loche illustrates this point very well. According to a survey conducted in 1984, this town of approximately 2000 people had 82 people employed full time and 54 part time (Collins et al. 1985). This depressing situation is found in most northern communities.

The Experience of Métis Women in Northern Saskatchewan

Let us now examine women's actual experience as *waged labourers*, as *volunteers* and as *welfare recipients* [1]. What is it they speak about? What are some of the things they do? How are their lives shaped? We will attempt to discern how their experiences are shaped by the mega-capitalistic system through the infrastructure at the community level. Three different sets of excerpts will be examined. The first set is taken from conversations with women who were employed in waged labour. The second set comes from interviews in which the women indicated that they did volunteer work on a regular or occasional basis, that is, they were employed in non-waged labour. The third set is taken from conversations with women who were unemployed. This group received transfer payments in some form or another, i.e., unemployment insurance, welfare cheques, or various types of pensions.

Métis women employed in waged labour

In a waged economy, participation in the labour force is an expected activity, if not a fundamental right. Only in relatively recent history has the participation of women in the labour force been encouraged on a wide scale. A significant number of Canadian women in the labour force are there out of necessity; others are there by choice. In contrast, *every* northern Saskatchewan native woman who is fortunate enough to have a waged job, works because of necessity. Welfare is the only other choice for the vast majority of native women.

How do these employed native women perceive and experience their situation? Here are a few excerpts from their articulations.

> I work at whatever I can get. I used to do a cook job ... I did nurses' aide for awhile ... I'd like to do some kind of secretarial job, but I don't know about typing anymore...

[When you have a job] it's pretty hard to find a babysitter to really look after the kids. It takes a lot out of my pay cheque to pay for a regular babysitter... Besides, you can't always trust a babysitter... Even with the babysitter, when I come home from the job,I have lots to do with the kids and the house.

When asked why she didn't stay home to care for the children:

You have to work now. Money means everything. You can't live without it. Women didn't work before. But now lots of the women try for jobs because you have to pay for the light bills, the power and everything. Expenses are high, like $75-$100 for electricity every month. And the oil bill in the winter. It takes money. Now we have water and telephone. Everything is just paying bills, buying clothes, buying food.

For a woman with kids, working is hard because it means to take on so much. I'm held up eight to ten hours working at the restaurant cooking, and serving people, and I can't find time for other things -- like what's going on in the community. It's hard 'cause I get tired. You know, to get home and do everything there. The men don't understand they need to help in the home, too. The woman always has the supper to do and things like that in the house. My husband has a trap line. Some winters he might make $500. He doesn't want to lose his trapping rights, so he's away a lot in the winter. But when he is here he will babysit the kids so I don't have to pay someone then.

About the wage she received:

I get minimum wage, like most of the women who work around here. My friend started this place. She got a money loan or grant from the government to get started. She had to wait a long time. Lots of times people don't like to wait that long and do all the red tape stuff. But she stuck it out. I work long for her everyday, but I'm glad for the money I get. Not everybody gets jobs. There is really nothing for women in the north. Cooking, working in a store, secretary at the LCA [Local Community Authority office] or at the government places, I even saw a woman working at the garbage collecting. But, in the winter I think it will be too cold for a job like that for a woman. So I'm glad I have my job.

Another women stressed the scarcity of jobs for women, the high cost of living, and the effects of poverty on children:

> Jobs in the North are very scarce. What we have is more under social services. We call it social service jobs. Minimum wage only. Part of my job here is interviewing and counselling those who want to get in on these jobs. Lots of them are part-time jobs, or maybe full-time but only for a couple of months. Most are men jobs. Not very much for women around here. I used to work as an aide at the school. Then I worked at the hospital from 1:30 to 8:00. Now I work here at the social services office. I am not young anymore, but I have to work because the money is always short. Short for groceries. Short for vehicles. Short to make ends meet. Even when I work, I save the food and clothes for the children and won't buy clothes for myself ... just do on less, for the kids' sake. I think very much that the mothers keep families together. I do most of the sewing for the family. I have an old sewing machine, a pedal one; and I do knitting. My children wear outgrown clothes. It's handed down from the older ones. The mother of a poor family has sorrow if children are hurt in school, too: "How come you're wearing used jacket? How come you're wearing patched jeans? How come you are wearing old pair of shoes?" The child comes home and the mother takes on the hurt. It hurts very bad. Really hurts when children at school do that to other children. There's nothing I can do.

When asked if she couldn't do something when she was an aide at the school:

> It doesn't make any difference. Women don't have a say, like the principal. It's like working at the hospital. You work but you have no say. So you can't do much but talk to your kids and tell them not to pay attention when the others tease. Just walk away or something.

Do women work at the mine? Does that pay well?

> I heard of one women who did baking up there, but she didn't stay long. She said the work was too long, you had

to get so much done, like so much baking, before you finished your day. I also know of a young woman who is a heavy duty equipment worker. She has her training and all that just like the men, but she can't get a job up there. I don't know why. I think the women can do the heavy equipment jobs and the driving of those big trucks, too. They're just as good as the whites, and maybe better. They need training.

Are you satisfied with the work you are doing now?

I like to work but it is also hard because you are away from the family. I worry about people drinking with my husband; about the children drinking too. Lots of people drink now, even women. It's not good. But once you start drinking it's hard to sober up. I was there myself, but I've been sober now for over three years. I went to the rehab centre in ... . Drinking is no good. People fight and get hurt. The woman gets beat up and the kids aren't cared for when the parents are drinking. There's lots of tragedy when people drink: fights, car accidents and people getting hurt. Drinking is no good. It wasn't always like that. Before the road, the booze was more bootlegging stuff. Only the men drank, and then on special occasions when there should be a celebration. Not like now. If the man drinks it's really hard on the mother and kids. If both the man and woman drink the kids get hurt. That's why I'm afraid about the kids when I am at work. Maybe my husband will be drinking and the kids aren't taken care of. I am afraid that the kids don't eat proper foods ... all this potato chip stuff. I get scared that the house might be getting on fire. I don't like the shows for the children to see on the T.V. I don't like the children watching that because they learn, get messages. I would rather they see native shows but you don't get that on T.V. It affects me as mother. I don't have enough time to talk to them because you have to work when you get home. The kids say, "Mother, you're old fashioned". Where do they get that?

Another woman talks of how the community laundromat has changed her routine. She also speaks of the expensive shopping trips made to southern towns where things are cheaper.

When I first had a job I used to do washing clothes almost every night, and stay up late sometimes to bake, and keep

the house good. Now I wash on Saturdays at the laundromat. With seven kids it takes sometimes three to four
hours. You have to get there early and you have to stay
there until all your clothes are done. It's nice to talk to the
other mothers there. Sometimes I listen to the radio when I
am there. I don't bake so much any more neither. I buy
bread and sometimes the sweet rolls for a change. When
my pay cheque comes in I go more to ... to shop. Things
are cheaper there in the south. There are no sales here.
Before the school starts I always go down south for the
sales to buy school clothes and the stuff they need at
school. Sometimes I go with others in a taxi. It costs about
fifty dollars, but you aren't paying it all by yourself. Other
times we go together in a truck or car. Maybe, when some-
body is going there anyway you can catch a ride. It's quite
a long trip, but you leave early in the morning, and sometimes you stay overnight.

It is not surprising that the majority of the waged women workers speak of
low-paying employment such as "interviewing", "counselling", "helping the
nurses", "cooking", "serving people" and "typing". At first glance, these
activities reflect the immediate social relations of their work day, and how
they relate to and/or serve people in their jobs. However, the activities also
indicate another set of social relations: that of employer and employee.
This is an unequal relationship in position and power. Referring to these
positions the women state that "women don't have much say" and "you
work, but you have no say". This employer-employee relationship is an
essential part of the work organization in a waged economy. These
employed women stand at the point of intersection between two sets of
social relations: that which is more personal and immediate emanating
from their family organization, and that which is structured by the wider
capitalist economy in which they sell their labour to an employer for wages.

Women seem to work by default, since it is believed that there is
"really nothing for women in the North"; "most are men (sic) jobs". Even
a woman trained in "heavy duty equipment" operation was not able to find
work. Nevertheless, if they had the job training, these women felt they
could be "just as good as whites".

Outside of the workplace, the waged-work relationships in which
labour is bought and sold as a commodity, penetrates and organizes the
everyday lives of Métis women. When these women speak of "wages"
earned by their labour, it is generally in terms of "minimum wage". This
is not unexpected because jobs in the service, sales and clerical sectors are
characterized by low wages. Métis women recognize and talk about the

importance of money, stating that "money means everything" and "you can't live without it". In the same breath, women speak of *having* to work, even for minimum wages, because they need money. For them, "money is always short ... short for groceries ... short for vehicles ... short to make ends meet". Some attempt to achieve this through "sewing for the family", "knitting", and recycling clothes in the tradition of hand-me-downs from the older children to the younger children. Obviously their minimum wage is simply not enough for their needs. So they are forced to compensate by taking on various other extra activities, or to "make-do" or "do-without".

Their waged work also cuts into time for community involvement. They "can't find time for other things -- like what's going on in the community."

More importantly, involvement in waged labour alters attitudes and schedules with respect to work in the home. First, the women begin more and more to accept and internalize the capitalist definition of work as paid employment and now note that "women didn't work before". They have internalized the modern notion that what women do in the home does not constitute real work.

Second, involvement in the labour force creates a double day for employed Métis women. These women feel the effects of market relations in the dual work they now shoulder: "When I come home from the job I have lots to do with the kids and the house." They note that "men don't understand [they] need to help in the house too." Household and family remain essentially female responsibilities.

Working also produces stress for the women when they are "away from family". Some are "afraid about the kids" when they are at work. They worry about their children not eating "proper foods" and needing to have their TV-watching monitored, about the house "getting on fire" and about the husband drinking.

Working at low wages may also necessitate an overnight trip to another centre to get the best prices for clothing, groceries and household effects. Because of their job activity, the women also participate in the transformation of particular social relations that were previously grounded in tradition or culture. For example, those who work for wages now need "a babysitter to really look after the kids". They pay for these services and, thus, create a market relation out of a traditional relationship within the extended family where child care is often performed by grandparents or other relatives. Similarly, the activity of washing clothes becomes a market relationship at the laundromat. Although these employed women may have washing machines at home, using the laundromat on Saturday gives

them the opportunity of "doing two or three loads of clothes" simultaneously. Thus, it saves them time but, coincidentally, their everyday social
relations become determined by the laundromat schedule.

Since home and child care are still the major responsibility of women
(whether or not they are working in the labour force) this role of home-
maker becomes more burdensome for those with low-paying jobs. It also
creates a barrier to employment, especially for single or divorced mothers.

Women who need to engage in waged work are caught by the nature
of their jobs. Their positions in the labour force are those typically characterized by low wages, high turnover rates, few educational requirements,
few opportunities for promotion and considerably fewer for long-term
advancement. None of the jobs are managerial. Women are locked into
these jobs, located at the lowest levels of the infrastructure. Their labour is
bought and sold as part of the process of accumulation of state/corporate
capitalism.

Ideally, capitalism ought to provide a whole range of job opportunities
for all employable adults in a society, both men and women. However, this
has never been the case. In northern Saskatchewan, since the structure
and operation of government and corporate enterprises has not built a stable economic base from which widespread permanent employment could
arise, job opportunities are at a premium. Thus, Métis women (and men)
do not even constitute an army of reserve workers as do certain groups in
other parts of Canada. They have been made into a surplus population
struggling to co-exist with the giant of government-corporate joint ventures.

Métis women engaged in volunteer work
(non-waged employment)

The following excerpts are taken from interviews in which the women
spoke of performing essentially volunteer work. While there may not be
any volunteer agencies as such operating in the north, volunteer work is
being done. In the southern portion of the province we are familiar with
people who provide their services, at no charge, to agencies (such as the
Saskatoon food bank) set up for specific purposes. Volunteers do jobs similar to paid workers, or assist paid workers, without being paid themselves.
In northern Saskatchewan, although there are no institutions or agencies
listed as dependent on volunteer work for meeting their objectives, community structures and programs exist that would not fare well, and perhaps
even fold, if it were not for volunteer work. The following excerpts pinpoint some of those areas that depend, to some extent at least, on volunteer
labour, and describe how women supply that labour.

Today I did many of the usual things ... what a woman does everyday, like get the kids up and off to school, make the meals and lunches, clean up the house, have coffee with my friend at her house. After the kids came from school I did bottle collection for a few hours. I drive the kids around in the truck so that they can collect bottles for their bottle drive. It might take a couple of evenings to finish the collecting. Then we sort the bottles and maybe clean up a few and then they are cashed in. The money made goes for hockey equipment for the little boys' team.

With your family, how do you find time for this?

You make time. I get stuff for supper around early before I drive the kids in the truck. That's for those that are home. Sometimes it's late when we get back. The dishes are waiting and all that. So maybe I'll do them after the kids are in bed. When you do something like bottle collection you just work around it. It has to be done when the kids can come along. It's their bottle drive.

Another woman provides insight into the incredible amount of time required of Métis women involved in volunteer projects.

I often help with the rummage sales to make money for the recreation programs. This summer we are sending 23 boys to the hockey school in Alberta. A rummage sale is not just selling clothes. It means taking a day off maybe at home and first sorting out the family's clothes to find which ones you are going to give to the sale. Then you take that in, and go around and help collect clothes from other families. After that, all those clothes have to be sorted and marked for price. It all takes time. Only then are you ready to have the sale. A lot of times people think that rummage sales are easy to put on, but it is more work than it seems.

When asked why rummage sales were necessary, and why the Recreation Board did not send the kids to hockey school:

Well, the recreation director doesn't get as much money as before for programs. We used to get $300,000, but now it is down to $50,000 or $30,000 they say. Before we were getting the rink built and all that, so it cost more. But now we have it, and the programs are the big thing. But there isn't enough money to cover everything so groups get together and work on funding. The women do things like bake sales, rummage sales, and bottle drives. Sometimes they get permission for a bingo, but it's not a big bingo. Big bingos are those that are held on the night of the day that the welfare cheques come in. There's money then and people will spend it at the bingo. Some people win big prizes. The men put on the big bingos. They also put on the smokers. That is dances where there is a bar, and liquor is sold. It usually has a good crowd.

Volunteer work is not all geared towards fund-raising, as the following woman makes clear. Taking care of the elderly who are now in homes for senior citizens requires a different schedule for women than in former years when elderly people lived with the family.

Some of us go and visit the old folks and make sure that they have what they need, and take them shopping and things like that. We have a worker at the senior citizens' home but it is not enough, so the families or friends keep an eye on their needs. In some other communities they have separate homes for each old couple, but it still means that someone has to look in on them every day or so.

Before our grandparents often lived with the family at home. In some ways it was easier then. They helped out with the kids and with the work around the place. In some ways it was harder, especially if they were sick and you had to take care of them, or if they didn't see the way you were bringing up the kids. If the kids didn't like something, they would go to grandfather and get out of what you wanted them to do. It's better to have your kids brought up by yourself. There's only one boss. Grandparents are good to have around, but sometimes it made things harder.

When asked if it didn't cut into the day's routine by now having to check in on them regularly:

It takes time, especially if they have to be taken to the clinic, or maybe go for extra shopping. Sometimes you do the shopping for them. But you have to see that everything is all right at their place. Maybe you will clean up or something like that. And you always talk and visit. After that you come home and do your work.

Recreation needs are not the only focus of volunteer fundraising. Church and school also expect unpaid work from women.

> In our community we do fund raising for the school. There is always this or that needed. Maybe they want to go on a trip with the kids. All kinds of things. The women also put on sales for church funding. Mostly bake sales. You make the cakes and things at home and bring them to the sale. The men don't put on sales like this. They have the bingos mostly.

Some Métis women become involved in volunteer work in certain fields because it is seen as an avenue for getting a paid job at a later date.

> I had a teaching job at a different community for one year, but it didn't work out so I came back here. I didn't have my own house, but rented and all that, so it was expensive. And then some things at the school didn't suit me so I left after a year. I hope to get a job here. After my two girls come home for lunch at noon each day, I go to the school for volunteer work from 1:00 to 3:00 each afternoon. I work on a one to one basis with the children. Now I am thinking of volunteering with the noon supervision. By doing that volunteer work, I keep in touch with my teaching methods, and I also have a better chance of getting a job if there is ever an opening here. Doing that work makes my mornings more busy since I try to fit in the things I would otherwise do in the afternoon. But it is not much different from teaching full time. There you have to come back and do all your housework besides spending the whole day at school. I have two girls. I'm separated from my husband. So in some ways it is harder than if the separation hadn't been. But no matter, you still have to do the home making and all that. That's the woman's job.

Again, the things and activities these women decribe are connected to the infrastructure and, ultimately, with the corporate and state ventures in mineral extraction in northern Saskatchewan. Some of the activities they mention are: rummage sales, money for recreations programs, bingos, "smokers", bottle drives, bake sales, visits to old folks, housework, volunteer tutor, and church fundraising. The work connected with these activities entails: sorting clothes, selling clothes, marking prices, making money, visiting the old folks and keeping "an eye on their needs", extra shopping, cleaning up, doing housework, and making "the cakes and things".

All of these jobs require change in their daily schedules. For example, rummage sales mean "taking a day off maybe, at home, and first sorting out the family's clothes to find which ones you are going to give to the sale." It means taking time to go "around and help collect clothes" and, after that, the collected clothes need "to be sorted and marked for price". As the women suggest, this all takes time and work. Only a few specify how their home schedule has been set aside and adjusted in order to do this volunteer work. "You make time. I get stuff for supper around early before." When you return from collecting clothes "the dishes are wait-ing". They are done "after the kids are in bed". Volunteer work means that daily house chores are done in the evening, or that meals are pre-pre-pared for the time that mothers are away, or that the women get up earlier than usual in order to do their regular work. All this may mean family upset, and/or strained family relations for a period of time. It also means fatigue for the women.

But how are these rummage sales connected with the infrastructure? The purpose of these sales is usually connected with the recreation pro-gram: "sending the boys to hockey school" or buying uniforms or equip-ment, and so forth. If more employment were available in the north, parents could have adequate funds for their children's recreational needs and would not have to be involved in raising money for these purposes. But jobs are hard to come by in the north, and whatever jobs there are, they generally pay poorly. Thus parents are forced to find other means of equipping their youngsters or for sending them to hockey school.

During the past decade organized recreation has become more and more prominent in northern Saskatchewan communities. This phenom-enon is connected with the changeover to a wage economy. It is a predic-table outcome of the way capitalist society is run, where most activities are organized around the notions of work time and non-work time. It is *because* work time is regulated to eight hours each day or forty hours each week that non-work time appears. This is true not only for the market place but also for other types of activity. For example, schools and other educational institutions are the "workplace" of youth and students. The "work hours" in these places roughly correspond to that of the wage-labour arena, with the same creation of non-work time. Participants in both the waged-work world and the youth-student world thus have "time on their hands" after their work day, or work week, is completed. It becomes nec-essary therefore to fill this non-work time with "meaningful activity".

Before the waged economy was brought to northern Saskatchewan, there was no time-defined organization of work and recreation. These often overlapped, or transpired as the need and opportunity arose. Recrea-tion was more dependent on the creative imagination and capacities of the participants. But in a society based on a waged economy, work and non-work time are clearly delineated. Furthermore, since capitalist society has provided families with electric lighting, oil or gas heating, and plumbing services, many of the "chores" of earlier times have been eliminated, thus leaving an extra gap in the day after work hours, work days or work weekends. In capitalism, "time is valuable". One does not and should not "waste time". Organized recreation thus fills non-work time. Organized recreation is, more often than not, commercialized recreation. It not only occupies people, it also generates profit. People no longer rely on their creative imaginations and capacities for recreation but depend on outside agencies to organize and make it available.

Organized recreation is part of the infrastructure at the community level of northern Saskatchewan, funded by government. The imposition of this waged economy coincided with, and was the outcome of, corporate capital ventures in the region. Volunteer work for recreational funding purposes thus intersects with market relations within recreational programs. As one woman stated, previously they received much larger grants for recreation purposes. Beginning in the sixties and early seventies, the government provided funding for community halls, rinks, and town offices. Part of this is in keeping with the government's role of legitimation in the capital accumulation process of joint venturism in the uranium industry.

Volunteerism is often incorporated into the programs and social service institutions that are products of the legitimation process. It is generally perceived by the public to be purely philanthropic or charitable group endeavours for the social good. It is seldom perceived as a way in which the state saves money in its amelioration and legitimation roles in advanced capitalism. For example, in 1983 the value of volunteer work in Canada was estimated at $2.0 billion, or 1.3% of all wages and salaries (Ross 1983). Nor is volunteerism generally seen to be a method whereby state and capital draw attention away from an elementary fact: that capitalism does not support all the population through waged labour, but that it stands in need of free labour to alleviate certain situations consequent on capitalism and to maintain certain aspects of the system such as social services. Volunteer labour is similar in some ways to domestic labour in that it is done for free, and in that it plays a significant role in the reproduction of workers, as well as a role in commodity consumption and, therefore, in the reproduction of capital -- be it on ever so small a scale. Volunteerism in respect to child care and recreational programs is significant in the reproduction of future workers, as well as the maintenance of market relations and commodity consumption.

For example, let us examine the role of volunteerism with respect to organized hockey programs. The government has also been very supportive of hockey leagues and other such recreational activities in the north.

This support has been taken as evidence of the government's interest in health and exercise. Hockey to most people is perceived as an exciting game, not as part of big business. "Hockey" is a fun game that is good exercise and that keeps youngsters occupied in an approved way. From the perspective of parents and community it is part of the everyday social relations of families. People enjoy hockey games whether as spectators or participants.

On the other hand, "hockey" is part of a million dollar business. Here it is viewed in its market relations. In the first place, the facilities that are needed (rink, ice, seating accommodations, dressing rooms, and so forth) cost money. Waged labour is employed in the construction of these facilities. Commodities such as lumber, glass and other supplies are bought and sold. All this is part of the capitalist market system, and it generates profit. Furthermore, the equipment (skates, helmets, sweaters, knee pads, puck, and hockey sticks) is all capitalist-produced, costing money and providing profit. Finally, when hockey games are played people pay money to become spectators. In that way the game itself becomes a commodity.

So, when we see Métis women volunteering their work to raise funds for hockey purposes, their labour is directly linked to the market relations of the hockey business. Their work is also directly linked to the fact that the recreational infrastructure at the local level, at first so well funded by government grants, is now underfunded. Their work fills the gap which was created by the withdrawal of funds. In a very real way, the government is relieved of its initial responsibility for maintaining good recreational facilities by providing sufficient job creation so that communities can adequately handle their own recreational programs and needs without being subsidized by volunteer work.

The irony of the situation is that in former years the native people used to meet regularly at Ile à la Crosse for a summer camp at which the game of lacrosse was the main attraction and activity. The Indian foremothers of present day Métis women probably helped pitch camp at the site and joined in the fun. The difference between them and today's Métis women who do volunteer work at fund raising for hockey -- a game closely resembling lacrosse -- is that the Indian forebears were in charge of the whole gathering, and the work they did in preparation of the games was done for purposes and objectives that they had determined. Today, Métis women work to provide money that is spent not by them and not for purposes determined by them. Rather, the recreation directors and, indirectly, the market relations of the hockey business determine that.

For a portion of the population, volunteer work offers an opportunity for co-operative community work in response to social needs, as an outlet for boredom and as an antidote to a sense of meaninglessness on the part of individuals. The operations in which volunteer work is utilized are generally supported and/or partially funded by the state. Volunteer work keeps people occupied. Often it gives them a sense of personal or collective accomplishment. Because of this feeling of doing something worthwhile, people seldom question the reason for volunteer work in a capitalist society in the first place. Volunteers generally are not aware of the fact that persons for whose welfare such work is done are, in a subtle manner, made dependent on legitimation programs initiated and sponsored by the government for capitalist reasons.

Métis women who are unemployed and on welfare

For the portion of the population that is unemployed and thus unable to subsist without help, social assistance programs -- often in the form of transfer payments -- are instituted. Before capitalist expansion into specific regions, it can be argued, the people who now find themselves in the welfare recipient group were just as able to maintain their livelihood as were those who now have permanent employment. The class divisions of waged, non-waged and welfare recipients within the actual and potential labour force are part of the larger process of capitalism. One effect is that persons finding themselves in the welfare assistance group constitute surplus population or surplus labour. As well as being outside the workforce, they are totally dependent on public agencies for cash needed for such government-supplied amenities as light, water, housing, gas and telephone, and to pay for necessities such as clothing and food. They are caught in a cycle of poverty. On the one hand, they are not able to sell their labour in the capitalist system, and, on the other hand, they cannot opt out of the social system developed by capitalist enterprise. They are forced to live their lives without any real options, or any real control over the shape of their lives.

A surplus population is a powerless population dependent on the "good graces" of government and/or capital for "handouts" and "occasional jobs". When a large portion of a population becomes a surplus population, as is the case in northern Saskatchewan, it becomes necessary for the government to alleviate this social "dis-ease", at least to some extent. If this is not done, whole groups of people would revolt or die in utter poverty.

From the point of view of capitalism, a surplus population (which in itself results from the profit-making process) is seldom considered redeemable. Rather than "waste profits" on developing a stable economic base for this population, it is easier to provide "handouts". This latter process effectively manipulates large groups of people and maintains their powerlessness. The "handouts" in northern Saskatchewan are generally provided by the government partner in the corporate resource extraction industry.

Since governments stand to make large profits from joint venturism, they will not generally make things difficult for the corporate partner. Hence, they will not compel corporate capitalism to establish a viable economic base, especially in the extraction industries, for this surplus population so that it can become self-sufficient. This would not be profitable for the corporations. Crisis management becomes the function of the state particularly in advanced capitalism. Given the situation in northern Saskatchewan, therefore, the institution of transfer payments for large sectors of the population is the expected role of the government. It is a way of placating people. It holds them in hopeless hopefulness, while at the same time distracting them from knowing and understanding the real reasons for their plight.

How do Métis women who are on welfare perceive and experience their situation? Here are a few excerpts from interviews with them.

> I used to have a job   but not any more, so I have to depend on welfare for awhile ... I hope it is only for awhile. I worked in an office before. So I still do some things that I learned there. I will list the things that I have to get done each day and then priorize the work, what you will do in the morning and what you do in the afternoon. Otherwise you forget so many things and you don't get many things done, and the day is gone. It depends. I just sort of work it like ... if I have washing to do, I do that that day. I wash clothes usually twice a week. It used to be a big job when the kids were small, but not so much any more. It used to be about ten or fifteen dollars a week, but now it's different. Maybe two or three dollars. I go to the laundromat. I have a Hoover machine but it broke down. The spinner is not working. But it's hard to get it fixed up. There's only one appliance place that fixes things as far as I know. And it is all the way across town. So the washer just sits there more often than getting fixed up. Now I have to pack my clothes and take it to the laundromat. It takes about an hour or an hour and a half. If it is busy it takes more time. When I'm there I usually read or I knit. Going to the laundromat is really inconvenient. Before when I was working for awhile and my machine was still working I could do the washing right at home and, while that was going on, I could do a thousand things in the house while you're washing, you know. The laundromat has certain hours. You have to go there at those times.

Since I have been out of work I have learned how to knit. My friend said come over and I will teach you. Now I knit scarves, headbands and all that. It helps to take up the time after I have the cleaning-up done in the house. Some of the women I know visit and play cards. Some drink, too. Others watch T.V.. I don't have T.V. since it is too expensive, and also I don't like the children to watch so much that is on T.V. I let them go to the neighbours to see a T.V. show sometimes.

I take my children along when I grocery shop. They kind of enjoy it. I grocery shop in different places. La Ronge has a few more stores than in other communities. Usually I watch the flyers and the sales. Economical pressures ... (laughs). So I go to different stores to get the best prices. The IGA often has sales. I buy milk, sugar, flour in bulk. I bake a lot of my bread. It takes a good part of my day sometimes. That saves on the grocery bill, because bread is a dollar or more a loaf now. Except when the price war was on, then we were getting it half price. I bought the white loaves then, because that was usually on sale. I buy unbleached flour. The other is hard to come by, you know, whole wheat. I like this other flour sometimes. It's not altogether whole wheat, but a mixture -- 50% or something. I realize the food value so I try to get that kind for the kids.

My kids don't get much junk food, although they want it. It's a constant battle because other kids have it. But we have to live on less. I try to give them an allowance but it's not much. It's a battle. Maybe it's because, I wonder, because the kids around them have so much, eh. They always want it.

I have an old sewing machine. I sew some clothes for the children. Now I am teaching my girls. They can operate it. It's quite simple and basic.

When asked how she got around in the town in respect to transportation:

Around here you almost have to have a good car like a new car, because of the cost of repairs. The second hand car of mine everything seems to go wrong. And you go in there and you come out with a bill of over a hundred dollars. It's real expensive to do a little bit of work, eh. Some-

times it will sit there, like one time it sat there for two
weeks. All it needed was a battery, and they couldn't figure
out what was wrong, so they kept it for two weeks. We
have about three services stations now for car repair. But I
found that I could not afford having a car after awhile,
especially if it was a car that didn't really work that good.
You were always paying these extra bills every month. So I
had to walk or when the kids were small, use a taxi, but
that's expensive too.

Though welfare may seem to bring ease in one sense, generally it is very
hard on families. As another woman stated:

In some ways welfare makes things easy for us. It wasn't
like that with our parents. We can sit back and enjoy our
assistance. They didn't have it. They had to earn their
money the hard way. They had to do it by themselves,
even to get groceries.

In some ways it is hard to be on welfare. You always
have to pay cash when you shop -- no credit. And prices
are very high. Clothing prices are high even for seven-
and eight-year olds. Three pairs of jeans means $100
almost. Sometimes I get second-hand clothes to wear. Power bills go high. My last electric bill was way over $30.
Lots of times it's $70 to $100. The water and sewer costs,
too, and the oil in the winter because we don't have the
wood stoves anymore. We have to pay every month on the
DNS house. I think it is like twenty years that we pay.

I would like to have a job, but there aren't many jobs
around for women, even for men. And you have to have
money now to pay for what you buy. If my husband or me
don't have a job then we have to go on welfare. We need
the cash. Everything costs money, you know.

When the Métis women speak about their everyday situation as welfare
recipients, they usually preface their remarks by talking of "*having* to
depend on welfare" or that they "*have had* to go on welfare". These statements imply that being on welfare is not what they personally choose, but
it is something of a "last ditch" situation they can't avoid.

Some of the things Métis women talk about are "the Hoover machine"
that "broke down", "the spinner" that "is not working", the "grocery bills",
"having to live on less", the "old sewing machine", "the old car", the high

"clothing prices", and "water and sewer costs". The "economic pressures" and the "lack of credit" constitute their greatest concerns. Some of the activities of which they speak are "using the laundromat", "knitting", "cleaning the house", and shopping for "the best prices" for food. Although one woman suggests that "welfare makes things easy" relative to what their parents experienced in times of non-welfare, being on welfare takes its toll -- not just in work but also in worry. Their life is filled with work and frustrations, because they must daily try to make ends meet with old appliances. They become weary from the work of shopping for the best prices, from the work of managing a household on less, from the work of walking to wherever they need to go, and from the work of cleaning the house and taking care of the children. Their work is different from that associated with paid employment in that it is not a nine-to-five schedule; it is unpredictable (for example, appliances break down and work schedules change abruptly); it does not, in the end, provide a paycheck, nor does it provide a sense of independence and achievement. Although women on welfare have much the same family responsibilities and domestic work as women who are in paid employment, they cannot afford a babysitter to bring them occasional relief. These welfare women are caught in a vicious circle of work, worry and frustration.

When one examines the things and activities these women talk about, it is possible to discern the connections between their situation and the mega-structures of a waged economy. Take, for example, the necessity of going "to the laundromat" because the washing machine "broke down". When one considers this activity on the level of personal relations and convenience, the laundromat may be seen as a place where women can meet and chat while waiting for the clothes, or a place where one may "read or knit" or gain a little rest during the waiting time. In this sense, the laundromat takes on the characteristic of a social or personal haven. But the very term "laundromat" implies a set of market relations that is prior to the speaking and on which the very essence of the laundromat as a commodified service is grounded. The laundromat is the locus of the exchange of commodities. The laundromat sells a commodified service to women. The women, whether waged or non-waged workers or welfare recipients, are in reality consumers who pay for this commodity. At the laundromat they become tied into the infrastructure as consumers while pursuing an activity necessary for clean clothes in the family. Behind the laundromat are different sets of market relations. For example, we find the whole production process of Maytag, Westinghouse, or other washing machine manufacturers. There are also the market relations of the capitalist enterprise of producing and selling detergents, bleaches, and softeners. In addition, there are the market relations connected with the maintenance and operation of the laundromat itself.

Laundromats have been established in some northern communities because a market for such services can be built up, first, among people who don't have washing machines (often those on welfare) and, second, in those communities where houses are not wired adequately for the installation of home washers and dryers. (Again, the occupants of these dwellings are often on welfare.) Both these situations are related to government and corporate activities or, in other words, to the mega-structure of society. Welfare populations, on the one hand, are a product of the inability of capitalism to employ the whole of the labour force. On the other hand, welfare is a government institution that arises from the amelioration role of government in joint venturism. The fact that the majority of able-bodied native persons in the North are unemployed is a function of the inability of capitalism to generate universal employment. These people do not even constitute a reserve army of workers. They are simply a surplus population. Within this population, Métis women become a doubly disadvantaged segment of the surplus population in comparison to men. There are at least two reason for this. First, many northern women's relations to the larger economy is not mediated by a husband's waged employment. Second, many women are husbandless by choice of circumstance. This is a recent phenomenon in the north. These women still have to maintain themselves and their children. They are alone, unemployed, unpaid; or they are alone, employed in the service sector and underpaid. In either case, they are doubly disadvantaged.

The fact of laundromat services in a northern community often shapes and changes Métis women's everyday lives. Some find that "going to the laundromat is really inconvenient"; others point out that "the laundromat has certain hours" and "you have to go there at those times". In addition, it is costly, "$10 to $15 a week" for one respondent. Although some Métis women (and in this case those on welfare) must utilize the community laundromat they may not realize how it (and the market relations behind it) shape their lives. They may believe that it is the necessity to have clean clothes that is shaping their lives. That it is a more personal and existential reason grounded in domestic social relations. It is, however, the more powerful mega-structure making its connections to the micro-world through the community infrastructure, that is the dominant shaper of Métis women's everyday lives.

Although native people comprise a surplus population, they are still caught in dependency on consumer goods that are peddled into the North. Bakeries, food chains, furniture business, laundromat companies, and service industries -- all have expanded their markets into the North. Purchasing these products eats up a large share of the transfer payments made to the local population. Many of the goods are unnecessary, manufactured to become obsolete in a short time and of inferior quality. Consumer goods and services have all too profound effects on the everyday life of native families.

On Power (and the Lack of It)

The everyday lives of Métis women who live in northern Saskatchewan communities are greatly affected by the recent rapid northern economic development, a corporate capitalist enterprise supported by the joint venturism role of the state. All too frequently, however, what transpires in the everyday lives of Métis women is thought to have its source in personal, family and/or community relations. Thus, when Métis women take on extra activities to "make ends meet", or when the children need clothes, or the recreation committee needs help to send little boys to hockey school, or the church groups need funding, or the school needs new athletic equipment, or the family needs food, or the house needs repair, these activities are all generally regarded as practical answers to needs which find their source in the immediate situation.

Much of the real source of these everyday experiences for employed women is found in the taken-for-granted reality of receiving only a minimum wage which is insufficient for them to provide adequately for their families. This source often remains invisible. Likewise, for unemployed women subsistence welfare cheques cannot cover all family needs. For the unpaid volunteers the underlying invisible reality of working for free is one of the main factors that shapes their everyday lives. This invisibility of the concrete impact of state and corporate enterprises on the everyday social relations arises because people's everyday lives are often viewed as being isolated or separated from the dominant economic structure of the world of business and development.

It is assumed that the reality of everyday lives generates its own set of independent social relations. Any troubles are "private" (rather than "public") issues. These assumptions are erroneously based on a belief in a real separation between the home as private sphere and the workplace as public sphere. This, though, is a conceptual and not a real separation. The two are very much connected and interrelated. The public sphere, or in the case of northern Saskatchewan the mega-structure of state and corporate capitalism, indeed dominates and determines the so-called private sphere of Métis women's everyday lives in innumerable ways. What transpires in many aspects of the private sphere is, thus, frequently a public issue.

People generally don't know how the activities of corporate capitalism affect their personal, family and community lives: they don't know what corporate capitalism is doing in their region. They are not involved as labourers in corporate activities and corporations don't share information.

A reason for not having native people involved is grounded in the fact that corporate capitalism feels no responsibility toward them. It does this under the guise of neutrality of interest with respect to the engagement of labour, the establishment of industry sites, and the specific corporate activity pursued. Hence, corporate capitalism doesn't have to support native communities that grow up around the industry, nor necessarily provide jobs for native people. While its actions and activities are legitimized on the basis of technological imperative and efficiency, the purported neutrality creates invisibility.

This neutrality is misleading. It simultaneously exonerates corporate and government development schemes from considering Métis women (and men) as full participants in the development of the North. In addition, it provides corporate and government enterprises with a neutral but false rationale for their activities. Furthermore, since responsibility for the overall activity of a corporate industry is not invested in individuals but in a Board of Directors, any critical analysis or social objection to the corporation's operation and purpose is effectively diffused.

The powerlessness of Métis women (and men) also flows from their structural economic position. For example, Métis women fortunate enough to be engaged in waged labour find themselves structurally powerless. They are kept in certain employment sectors and in low-status positions within these sectors. Métis women are hired in predominantly low-wage positions. These low-paying jobs force them to concentrate on sustenance activities with little energy or opportunity for activities that are related to important decision-making in their communities or in the wider northern community. Métis women are thus effectively removed from the locus of orchestration of power (which deals with infrequent but important decisions) and, at best, exercise implementation power (consisting of frequent but unimportant decision-making).

Métis women engaging in volunteer (non-waged) work are also structurally powerless. Through the governmental function of legitimation they are subtly caught in the process of life-compartmentalizing programs often initiated by government. For example, the recreational program in the North functions to give legitimation in its own way to the capitalistic venture. Northern recreational programs have seldom grown out of the needs and/or visions of the native people. Instead they are initiated from the South and patterned on programs in the South. By doing volunteer work in such a program, Métis women are continuing and maintaining a program based on a different set of social values: those of money making and control. Their position is, in effect, one in which they become the very means of maintaining and continuing a process which keeps them structurally powerless. The position in which they find themselves requires their labour to "make money" for the program, but it gives them no control over the utilization of that money. Such volunteers, in effect, simply raise money and hand it over to someone else who makes the important decisions about the product of their labours.

Volunteer work has no personal economic rewards in our current system. It is questionable how someone in our waged economy can build publicly recognized self-worth from giving to people, without receiving the monetary recognition upon which our normative reward system is based. Volunteer work is essentially exploitative labour where one has little power or status in the decision making process connected with the creation, operation, and purpose of "the job". A volunteer worker can never accumulate seniority or other benefits allowing one to move or change advantageously within the labour force. A volunteer remains virtually powerless.

Métis women on welfare are in a similar position. Caught in a dependency syndrome, they are utterly powerless to change their oppressed condition. This oppression is both financial and psychological. They are always in debt or "beholden" in the sense that they stand in need of money handouts or other assistance. Furthermore, they are completely at the mercy of government bureaucrats who may delay or even cancel their transfer cheques. When they initially receive welfare, they are hooked into all the rules, regulations and "red tape" linked with the government role of amelioration. For example, a single or divorced woman on welfare loses that benefit if a man is living with her since the male is assumed to be the head of the family; in such an arrangement she is thus judged as being supported. In addition, welfare recipients cannot better themselves with job training because they lack money and opportunity. Neither sufficient nor adequate job training programs exist in the North. Finally, if women on welfare are to survive they cannot criticize the welfare system because, again, they may lose the needed assistance. They have to "put up" and "shut up".

Their position is psychologically oppressive for many reasons. Métis women on welfare are "kept down" by oppressive societal definitions and self-definitions of "what welfare folk are like". The process of legitimizing capitalistic values includes the norm that "one earns one's own way" because "jobs are open to anybody and everybody". If people are not working, it is for not "wanting a job" and/or for being personally too shiftless, irresponsible, and so forth, to "hold down a job". Such a perspective also regards being jobless as a "personal or private trouble" rather than a "public issue". Consequently Métis women on welfare take on the guilt for their situation. Once they have internalized the perspective that the individual "could do something about it but doesn't", they are unable to throw off this oppressive psychological burden.

Concluding Remarks

The powerlessness of Métis women, whether due to lack of knowledge or to their structural positions, is part of the problematic situation of people in northern Saskatchewan. If women want to take back the position of being subjects in their lives, they need to recognize, identify and articulate their powerlessness. They need encouragement to develop alternatives to (and within) this system that dramatically shapes and determines their everyday lives but excludes them from positions of power.

As they become more conscious of the fact that their situation is not natural, inevitable, and inescapable; as they move beyond being merely aware of insult and inferiority to becoming conscious of the contradictions in the social order; and as they begin to perceive the injustices they experience as no longer tolerable, Métis women are finding the solution to their situation within the situation itself: and they take power to themselves.

Endnotes

*College of Education, University of Saskatchewan, Saskatoon, SK, S7N 0W0.

1. The author spent many months in northern Saskatchewan over a span of five years, during which time she had intensive interviews with over 100 Metis women in the communities of Stony Rapids, La Loche, Turnor Lake, La Ronge, Cumberland House, Sandy Bay, and Ile-à-la-crosse.

BIBLIOGRAPHY

Collins, M., A., Kowalczyk and R. Regnier. 1985. *Assessment of an Adult Basic Education Program*, Job Orientation Training (J.O.T), La Loche, Saskatchewan.

Gunn, J. 1982. *The Political and Theoretical Conflict over Saskatchewan Uranium Development* (M. A. Thesis, University of Regina, October).

Ross, D. 1983. "Some Financial and Economic Dimensions of Registered Charities and Volunteer Activity in Canada". Ottawa: Secretary of State (unpublished, mimeo).

Smith, Dorothy E. 1981. *The Experienced World as Problematic: A Feminist Method* (University of Saskatchewan Sorokin Lectures, No. 12).

11. Living The Gospel Through Service To The Poor: The Convergence of Political and Religious Motivations in Organizing Maquiladora Workers in Juarez, Mexico

Kathryn Kopinak*

Introduction

This paper focusses on the organization of women workers in one community in the Special Enterprise Zone in Mexico, just south of the Mexican-U.S. border. The possibility of a Canadian government instituting Special Enterprise Zones (also known as Free Trade Zones, Export Processing Zones and Free Enterprise Zones) first arose in British Columbia in 1983. On the advice of the Fraser Institute, the Social Credit provincial government introduced a neoconservative budget and legislative package in reaction to the changes occurring in the world economy. Special Enterprise Zones were promoted as part of this program to attract investment to the province. The proposal was immediately condemned by the B.C. Federation of Labour as a method of eroding wages and working conditions, lowering them to levels found in less developed parts of the world. Economists from different ends of the ideological spectrum debated the issue from their respective think tanks. Herbert Grubel, of Simon Fraser University and a member of the Fraser Institute's editorial board, was the main spokesperson promoting the zones, while David Donaldson and Jacqueline Maund, at the University of British Columbia, countered his arguments from the B.C. Economic Policy Institute (Grubel 1983; Donaldson and Maund 1984; Donaldson 1985). Even though the provincial government had strong allies within the Conservative cabinet in Ottawa to help lobby for these proposals, the zones never became a reality because of fear over the political damage which might have resulted from a national debate on the issue. Also, the federal government was more committed to its plans to negotiate a bilateral Free Trade Agreement with the United States, rather than allowing each region to make its own arrangements.

A few years later, Canadians in southwestern Ontario had mostly forgotten these debates, and responded with anxious awareness when they witnessed industry fleeing from their region to Free Trade Zones on the Mexican-U.S. border and in the Sunbelt. International Business Consultants of Canada, a firm which advises companies on how to make such a move, is based in Leamington. In 1988, my casual reading of newspapers revealed that Bendix Heavy Vehicle Systems moved one-half of its jobs away from London, Fleck Manufacturing closed in Centralia, and D.G. Trim Products left Petrolia. A systematic survey would undoubtedly turn up many more. These moves make it clear that Special Enterprise Zones did not have to be introduced in Canada in order for capital to discipline labour, but that a similar effect could be accomplished by putting Canadian workers in direct competition with those from Mexico and the southern U.S. In the following quotation, Dillon attributes the Conservative government's advocacy of free trade to pressure from Canada's most powerful corporate lobby, the Business Council on National Issues, which is made up of the chief executive officers of the 150 largest corporations operating in Canada:

> When BCNI members look south they like what they see. They envy the business climate in the United States where only 17% of the workforce is unionized compared to 39% in Canada. They reason that competition from the 'right-to-work' states of the U.S. sunbelt would be more effective in weakening Canadian labor laws than their own lobbying efforts (Dillon 1988:7).

A longstanding bias of modernization theories that is sometimes shared with the cross-cultural study of movements for social change is the idea that societies which are 'behind' will follow the established patterns of resistance and struggle in the democratizing process. We should not assume that strategies for defending workers' rights that have been successful in Canada should or can be exported through some form of international trade unionism. Rather, we need to examine state and union structures in other parts of the world before we generalize from our experience.

This paper attempts to take the specificity of the situation in one community on the Mexican-U.S. border into account and to describe the bases of resistance to exploitation that have developed there. First, a brief history of the formation of the Export Processing Zone is set in economic and political context. Next, the potential of unions to protect workers' rights is evaluated, followed by a review of the existing literature on the formation of a women's centre. Finally, the author's findings about the religious dynamics of working women's organization are integrated to round out the story. The site of this research is Juarez, Chihuahua, located midway between the Pacific and the Gulf of Mexico. Along with its twin city on the U.S. side of the border, El Paso, it is an urban complex of over 2 million people. It is also the only border city in Mexico to have a centre for working women.

The Origin and Context of the
Mexican Border Industrialization Program

The strip of land 20 miles wide and 2,000 miles long which encapsulates the border between Mexico and the U.S. has a unique regional identity, predating the international division and surviving into the present (Miller 1981). Its contemporary character has been shaped by economic and political developments emerging since World War II, creating a new set of infrastructures within which the inhabitants live and work. On the U.S. side there has been an increase in investment, population, and urbanization with the growth of the Sunbelt economy which, Davis notes, favours this area because of the existence of a pool of cheap, unorganized labour (Davis 1984:12-13).

While the U.S. borderlands constitute the poorest area in the U.S., they have always attracted Mexican migrants who find greater opportunities there than in their homeland. Circular migration of rural Mexican males has been so essential to the agricultural economy of the American southwest, that its annual return was safeguarded in law by the Bracero Program originating in the 1940s. When the U.S. government unilaterally decided in 1964 to abruptly stop farm labour's migration northward, the Mexican government instituted the Border Industrialization Program (BIP) in order to alleviate high unemployment rates among Mexican men in the North. This program allows foreign companies to import the materials for production, assemble them using Mexican labour, and then export them -- paying taxes only on the value added, i.e., the cost of labour. Industrial parks, providing buildings, water, energy sources, etc., have been established on both sides of the border to enhance the 'business environment'.

While the BIP was instituted by the Mexican government in immediate response to the end of the Bracero Program, it is consistent with long-standing state policies which attempt to bring capital to the north. As early as the 1930s the federal government established Free Trade Zones along the border with the U.S. in order to encourage industrialization (Fernandez-Kelly 1983a:25). As the following quotation indicates, the purported reasons for successive regimes' support for the program have changed over time:

> The in-bond industry is one of the few positive aspects to Mexico's troubled economy. Although the creation of employment was its initial intention, generation of foreign exchange has become increasingly important as the program has matured. In his August, 1983 presidential decree, President de la Madrid also acknowledged the industry's contribution in providing training for workers

and   supplementing   the   internal   Mexican   market
(U.S.-L.D.C. 1984:82).

Thus a system of twin plants has been set up from Matamoros/
Brownsville to Tijuana/San Diego, with goods warehoused on the U.S. side
of the border and assembled on the Mexican side. The first *maquiladoras*,
as these factories are called in Mexico, opened in Juarez in 1966. That city
remains one of the sites of greatest *maquiladora* concentration. While the
program was broadened legally in 1972 when the Mexican government
extended it to the entire country, most of its impact continues to be felt at
the border since it is convenient for companies and their U.S. personnel to
keep one foot in the U.S. The increasingly rapid devaluation of the peso
since 1982 has acted as a further attraction to capital in search of cheap
wages. Baker reported that the total number of *maquiladoras* in Juarez
alone would reach 250 in 1988, bringing the number of employees in that
city to 110,000 (Baker 1988:49). This represents approximately one-third
of the total *maquiladora* work force in Mexico.

Male rural migrant workers, for whom the program was purportedly
designed, are still highly unemployed since the companies moving to Mexico under these new regulations have chosen to hire young women, a group
not strongly represented among waged workers previously. While 63 per
cent of all Mexican waged workers are female, it has been estimated that
from 75 per cent to 90 per cent of BIP workers are women (Seligson and
Williams 1981:25-27). Their ages range narrowly between 16 and 25. Fernandez-Kelly argues that a new segment of the labour force has been created, activating "daughters and wives whose principal activities took place in
the school or in the home prior to the existence of the in-bond plant program" (Fernandez-Kelly 1983a:45). When the needs of capital have con-
flicted with those of *maquiladora* workers, the state has generally ruled in
the interests of the former. For example, after the worldwide recession
from 1974 to 1975, when many *maquiladoras* closed or laid off workers,
the Mexican government exempted them from legislation protecting workers (Tiano 1987:22). However, more consideration may be given to workers since the ruling party came close to losing the 1988 election.

While there are several different kinds of products assembled in
maquiladoras -- electronic components (60 per cent), electrical goods and
automotive parts (15 per cent each), textiles, toys, and medical goods (10
per cent) -- the one factor which is a common drawing card is cheap
labour. It has been estimated that the average annual savings of a company's move to Mexico was $20,000 (U.S.) per employee in 1985
(U.S.-L.D.C. 1984:87). Workers must be paid at least the minimum wage
set by the Mexican government. The question of which capitalists (Mexican
or foreign) are responsible for keeping Mexican wages low is a hotly debat-

ed one. Baker, Vogel and Bard present data from the U.S. Labor Department to show that "U.S. employers pay Mexican workers about half of what Mexican companies pay them" (Baker et al. 1988:102, 106). One of the results is a high turnover in the work force, with workers going to whichever plant offers the best benefits. They also argue:

> But exploitative wages aside, *maquiladoras* still make poor models for Mexican development. Much of the income they bring to Mexico comes from building and selling the plant shells, not running them. A mere 2% of the components come from Mexican suppliers. And the work itself is low skilled, so workers receive little training. 'The *maquiladora* does not transfer technology,' Salinas told BUSINESS WEEK during the presidential campaign last summer [1988] (Baker et al. 1988:102).

Juarez's current mayor, Jaime Bermudez, was a pioneer in the BIP, building the first Mexican industrial park in Juarez. His company now operates five other industrial parks in more southerly locations in Chihuahua. The advantages that the program has brought to Juarez include jobs, tax revenue, and international prestige, but it has also put an unbearable strain on the city's infrastructure. Basic public services take second place to industries' needs for drainage, energy, and particularly drinking water, causing resentment among *Juarenses*. Even though observers estimated that the city's capacity for *maquiladoras* was saturated four years ago, their numbers keep increasing. So great was the Mexican government's need to legitimize itself that it announced plans for a special tax on *maquiladoras* one week before the election in 1988, only to postpone the implementation of the tax shortly after.

Election times suggest the possibility of change and often reveal internal dynamics of a society which are not ordinarily visible. The hierarchy of the Roman Catholic Church was moved to publicly criticize the lot of workers under the BIP when socialist candidates for the Presidency began to make headway in the base communities and organizations of young Christian workers. In June of 1988 a press release from the Archbishop's office recognized that the Roman Catholic Church had been absent from labour struggles and committed that institution to finding some way of encarnating the gospel's message in the workers' world. It also condemned the injustices suffered by *maquiladora* workers, naming these as unfair wage scales, inhuman hours, obligatory double shifts, excessive pressure on workers to meet unreasonably high standards of production, and repression of workers independently organized ("Preocupa a la Iglesia" 1988). The bishop of Juarez urged foreign management in the *maquiladoras* to pay workers a living wage, saying that "natural law imposes greater demands than merely human laws" (Thompson 1988). In the face of such moral authority, even those on the side of *maquiladora* management admitted how difficult the situation was becoming for Juarez workers:

> Don Nibbe, editor of Twin Plant News magazine in El Paso, agreed with the bishop that inflation in Juarez is not on the wane despite government claims to have brought it under control. In Juarez, Nibbe said, 'It's getting harder and harder to put food on the table.' Nibbe, whose monthly magazine is aimed at twin plant managers, said that when benefits and wages are totaled, most *maquiladoras* now are paying 70 percent more than Mexico's minimum wage of just under $4 a day (Thompson 1988).

This position of the Roman Catholic Church of advocating on behalf of *maquiladora* workers is a new one and, while it deserves the attention of observers in the contemporary situation, it was not previously a political force. The absence of the Church from public life is a legacy of the Mexican Revolution of 1910-17 which was inspired, in no small part, by liberal revulsion against the previously privileged position of the Church. Since that time the Church has legally been denied any institutional role in national affairs, being forbidden to own property and having its clergy disenfranchised. This has begun to change as the mandate of the Vatican Council (1962-65) to engage in action in areas of moral importance is finally acted upon in Mexico. While a new course for the participation of the Catholic Church in civil society has definitely been set, this has not occurred without severe criticism from other sectors which fear that it will re-establish its pre-revolutionary position (Goulet 1988).

Neither has the Mexican labour movement been effective in protecting *maquiladora* workers' rights in the past, with only ten per cent of them belonging to unions. This extremely low rate can be understood in the more general context of the Mexican polity. The *Partido Revolucionario Institucional* (PRI) has been in power ever since its founding in 1929. During the Cardenas administration (1934-40, a period of economic growth) a great deal of popular support for the state existed and most of the country's mass organizations were incorporated into the official party. This included support from the working classes and incorporation of the unions. Subsequent capitalist development in Mexico depended on corporatism through which labour could be controlled. The most frequent tools for keeping independent labour organizations in check were the replacement of militant leaders with those subservient to the state (known as *charrazos*), the distribution of benefits to state organizations only and, failing all else, the destruction of independent organizations with military force (Olsen 1987:5-32).

A good example of the suppression of independent unions can be seen in the strike at Appliances and Components in June of 1988. Workers joined an independently organized union, denying affiliation with any political party, and went on strike because this company only paid the minimum wage ($25 U.S./week) and had poorer benefits than other *maquiladoras*. When 1,200 of the 1,400 workers started to walk out of the plant, security guards tried to stop them by firing tear gas at them. The next day these workers blocked one of the international bridges between El Paso and Juarez for one hour in protest; when they withdrew they were beaten by city police. The Juarez Office of Reconciliation and Arbitration declared the strike illegal and authorized the company to fire, without compensation, 300 workers who had been involved in illegal activities.

The largest labour federation in Mexico is the *Confederacion de Trabajadores Mexicanos* (CTM), led by 89-year-old Fidel Velazquez. Claiming 5 million members, it has been one of the three main sectors of the PRI for 43 years. Pena (1983) and Van Waas (1981) provide good analyses of how unions affiliated with the CTM do more to discipline *maquiladora* workers than to protect their rights, often using sexual harassment to control female workers. From its position inside the state the union movement was convinced in the early years of the BIP to limit its organizing of *maquiladora* workers; in return the regime agreed to declare any independent unions illegal. The *Comite de Defensa Popular* (CDP) is the largest left-wing organization in Juarez and a growing political force especially among the poor in the *colonias*, particularly the new city districts with makeshift homes (and without basic services) that have sprung up on the outskirts of Juarez. It has not, however, attracted *maquiladora* workers.

While the union movement and the Church cannot be considered very important in the past organization of *maquiladora* workers, the near loss of the PRI in the 1988 election has clearly changed this. Union identified candidates were especially unsuccessful and it has been predicted that the labour movement will undergo a restructuring with more *maquiladora* workers being unionized as part of this plan. Along with the Church, the unions will constitute a more active civil society outside of the state structure. Because of this turning point, the present time is an especially good one in which to bracket past experience for analysis.

Even this very brief review of the Mexican political and economic context of the Export Processing Zone makes clear some important distinctions between the societies which border the U.S. on the north and the south. As noted above, there are strong proponents of Export Processing Zones in Canada. They have been unsuccessful -- even in British Columbia where the political structure has been most supportive of such ideas. While Mexico may have some very good labour legislation on the books, comparable laws in Canada are implemented to a much greater degree. Unions and political parties function much more as open, participatory, mass organizations in this country than they do in Mexico, although this may not be as true for Canadians from minority backgrounds as it is for those from the dominant Anglo groups. As Clement and others have pointed out, Canada differs from several Latin American countries because of our distinction between public and private power, and our liberal democratic traditions (Clement 1977:300). Canadians have not been able to block continental economic integration through their use of these liberal democratic institutions, however. The place of Canada in the world economy is extensively debated by dependency theorists and neo-Marxists. For more on this issue, see Williams (1988:107-140).

The Organization of Maquiladora Workers
On the Basis of Gender

The group that is best known for organizing *maquiladora* workers in Juarez is the *Centro de Orientacion de la Mujer Obrera* or COMO. Its founding and success is usually attributed to Guillermina Valdez de Villalva who herself comes from a privileged class background in Juarez. She was educated in U.S. schools, doing postgraduate work at the University of Michigan. Her doctoral research led her to adopt many ideas from Fromm and Freire whose theories she has applied in the contemporary Mexican situation (Pena 1983:443). She is influential within the PRI and is a charismatic Catholic.

Many of the socially concerned U.S.-based researchers who have published on the subject of *maquiladora* workers gained access to their research subjects through COMO. For them the organization has also become an object of study, and their orientation to it ranges from very positive (Pena 1983; Fernandez-Kelly 1983b:41-45) to mildly critical (Staudt 1987; Yudelman 1987; Young 1987). Stoddart has contracted to do most of his research for *maquiladora* owners, and does not focus on COMO except to call it a "working women's indoctrination center" (Stoddard 1987:57). Firmly established at the University of Texas at El Paso for many years, he has apparently forgotten the adage about people who live in glass houses and throw stones.

A review of this literature, with the inclusion of information from my own informants, will allow us to consider the actual empowerment and organizing processes of women *maquiladora* workers in Juarez. In a 1981-82 self-evaluation, COMO staff categorized the history of their organization into four stages which are also utilized by some of the above authors. The multiple class interests which gave rise to the organization were evident in its founding period between 1968 and 1974. This cross-class collaboration is described by Pena as resulting from the joint efforts of Villalva who, for her part, wanted to "develop a new pedagogical approach for Mexican education which would be responsive to the psycho-social reality of contemporary Mexico", and Maria Villegas, a nurse who had worked at RCA for three years (Pena 1983:443-5). As a result of her working experience, the latter felt that women workers needed an organizational form which would allow their self-orientation, and had to develop from a cultural core that was their own. While women working in the *maquiladoras* did influence the organization, its predominant ethos in this early period seemed to be that of *asistencialismo* and *beneficiencia* which imply a mutual helping characteristic of conservative conceptualizations of social work.

COMO's projects included publication of a journal for working-class women -- containing articles on assertiveness, consciousness raising, and social problems -- and the organization of a youth centre offering a variety of seminars and room and board to 70 *obreras*. In this first stage, COMO also worked closely with *maquiladora* management, teaching courses inside the plants on the social imagery of working women and on problems of drug abuse, alcoholism, marital conflict and health care. Five different factories contracted with COMO to teach a total of 13 courses called "What it is to be a Woman". These were consciousness raising sessions in which women talked about the changing role of women, family relations, marriage, and the world of work. Their success as politicizing vehicles is evidenced by the fact that, after 1975, the plants refused to hire COMO to teach the courses again because they perceived COMO staff as militant for criticizing health and safety conditions. They also believed the courses to be "a source of potential labor organizers" (Yudelman 1987:21). When President Luis Echeverria visited Juarez in 1972, COMO proposed a number of government actions which would begin to meet some of the social costs of the BIP. One result of this lobbying was that the government remodelled an existing government building and gave the legal title to COMO for its use. Thus, after having been rebuffed by capital, COMO received institutional support from the state.

Pena studied COMO in detail because he viewed it as the embodiment of the circulation of struggle from the factory to the community (Pena 1983:441). He looks first, then, at the work place where the occupational hierarchy is rigidly stratified by gender and ethnicity. Those positions with the least power, operatives and sometimes group chiefs, he found filled by Mexican women, whereas all jobs above this level were performed by Anglo men. *Maquiladora* management hires young, friendly, attractive and well educated men as direct supervisors of women workers. Practices of sexual harassment are common on the shop floor and outside of work. Supervisors invite workers out socially after working hours (sometimes at company expense) and often succeed in forging friendship networks through which they control workers and encourage them to produce even more. These social relations are reflected in the fact that production line workers are reported to commonly call the men who supervise them *mi ingeniero o mi ingenierito* (my engineer or my dear engineer; COMO 1984:37).

Patriarchal relations of domination are resisted by operatives through the creation of friendship networks among workers, and it is these networks which COMO's educational programs reinforce and extend. Pena argues that because Anglos have a more universalistic value orientation, they are less likely to be drawn into shop floor networks which are based on more particularistic personal alliances common to Mexican culture. Group chiefs, who are also often Mexican women, do become part of workers' networks of resistance because of cultural affinity and because they are recipients of the same forms of sexual harassment as operatives. Pena finds that these networks were used to resist management's control of the labour process, to sabotage production, and to restrict output. He also found that workers most likely to be engaged in such forms of resistance have more militant attitudes, favouring strikes and independent unions.

As a woman's organization whose programs focussed on the gender of workers, COMO was able to build on the gender solidarity originating in the work place. Mexican unions, which reproduce the same patriarchal practices as are present in management, could not defend women workers' rights because of their own mysogyny. This will continue to be an important dynamic of the organizing process of *maquiladora* workers until Mexican unions change and/or more men are hired as operatives. Because high unemployment among men is such an explosive political issue, claims have been made that more men are being hired. Researchers have not been able to substantiate these claims, however (Yudelman 1987:17-18).

This form of gender solidarity is not uniquely Mexican and was familiar to me as a Canadian researcher. Feminist ideology has been redefining normative expectations for gender roles in Canada ever since women began entering the labour force in large numbers after the Second World War. As Herrera-Sobek notes, this has not been the case in Mexico. Although working-class women have been a source of cheap labour since the rise of Mexican capitalism at the turn of the century, their integration into the work force has not been accompanied by a redefinition of sex role expectations that would culturally support them in this activity (Herrera-Sobek 1979:59-60). Thus, women who work in factories are assumed to be sexually compromised and less than decent.

It is because of the greater strength of the women's movement in Canada that unions here have become relatively more open to women's participation and to the inclusion of sexual harassment and other gender-specific clauses into contracts (Attenborough 1983; Field 1983). As Navarro has explained, women's movements emerged later in Latin America than in North America for a number of reasons, including the presence of authoritarian political regimes which stifle all forms of political participation, anti-feminist propaganda identifying the North American women's movement with oppressive colonial regimes, the hegemony of *la dependencia* as a theory which does not focus on gender, etc. (Navarro 1979:111-120). The growth of an indigenous Mexican feminism can no longer be denied, though, and will increasingly inform political life. *Nueva Cultura Feminista* (FEM), the main organ of grass-roots feminism in Mexico, began publication in 1976 and is still in print, with past issues containing articles on Mexican and Chicana feminism (Acevedo et al. 1980:7-26; Morales 1985:41-44). The building of international solidarity among women workers must consider how North American and Latin American feminism can be linked.

Back in the first stage of COMO's development, from 1968 to 1974, little conscious concern existed about the need for an indigenously Mexican feminism among *maquiladora* workers. When the economic recession at the end of this period caused plant closures and increased unemployment among women, they began to realize that their employment in the *maquiladoras* was very likely to be temporary. COMO's strategy was to teach *maquiladora* workers to improve their lives by helping each other and by assisting other sectors of the community, rather than becoming dependent on foreign capital to provide them with jobs. This was a way of implementing the founder's Freirian philosophy of education (Fernandez-Kelly 1983b:43) and was extended to scavengers at the Juarez dump who for some years had lived off what they could get for selling scraps. Entrepreneurs had been given concessions at the dump by the government and when the material handlers sold their pickings to them, they received very little in return. In comparison to material handlers at the dump, *maquiladora* workers are relatively well educated and have experienced a higher standard of living. Their assistance in the material handlers' efforts to build a worker-owned cooperative was a strong statement about their own belief in the necessity of Mexican self-sufficiency.

The second stage of COMO's development from 1975 to 1977 is identified by Pena as a time of consolidation and formalization with workers taking over the administration of the organization (Pena 1983:447). Yudelman indicates that, in terms of the organizing process, "[t]he numbers of students grew to 300, some of whom stayed to volunteer their time" (Yudelman 1987:21). This was in an economic context of recession, when *maquiladoras* were not able to provide stable employment, and a political context of increased feminist influence after Villalva attended the first International Women's Year conference. It is important to acknowledge this ideological influence of feminism: COMO did not operate in a political vacuum, but was in fact being harassed by the official union movement which felt threatened by the possibility of COMO becoming a woman's union. The unions had been petitioning the government to take away the building it had given to COMO, until Villalva happened to meet Velazquez by chance and convince him that COMO was not a threat to his organization.

The tasks completed during this period are impressive. The course curriculum was expanded vocationally to try to retrain workers expelled from the *maquiladoras*. It was also during this period that COMO's assistance to displaced workers began to crystallize in the form of worker-owned cooperatives. *Sociedad Coperativa de Selecionadores de Materiales* (SOCOSEMA) is a cooperative owned and operated by garbage dump workers and their families, and GUILLE is a garment cooperative made up of unemployed seamstresses. COMO's ability to create these organizations reflects its shift in orientation from philanthropy to community organization and development.

In its third period from 1978 to 1981 "COMO underwent major transformations in its scope of activities, organizational structure, and funding bases" (Pena 1983:449). COMO workers saw the results of these years as

> systematization and restructuration of the educational program, acceptance of workers trained by COMO in new labor markets, and acceptance of COMO by UCECA, CONAFE, and a variety of other public agencies. But the underlying accomplishment was clearly the process of self-management and linkage-building with the working-class community (Pena 1983:446).

The first part of this quotation refers to the development of *promotores externas*, workers acting as community organizers and social activists. These external promoters made COMO's presence felt in the working-class community by helping to organize cooperatives, developing outreach intensive education centers known as CEBIs (*Centros de Educacion Basica Intensiva*). Yudelman notes: "The CEBI program had been started by a nongovernmental organization in the city of Chihuahua and expansion was also put in the hands of nongovernmental organizations" (Yudelman 1987:24). These centers allowed COMO, under contract from the *Comision Nacional de Fomento Educativo* (CONAFE), to establish schools in some of the most impoverished areas of Juarez. They also continued to support, advise, and counsel industrial workers.

In order to develop new programs to teach these organizational and research skills to *maquiladora* workers, COMO incorporated itself formally in 1978 and received registered recognition from the federal state agency *Unidad Coordinadora para el Empleo, Capacitacion y Adiestramiento* (UCECA), which allowed them to provide on-the-job training to industrial workers. This registration, along with their work in the CEBIs, "solidified COMO as a viable organization and increased its legitimacy" according to Pena (Pena 1983:449). He also uses the events of these years to extend his analysis of the organization as "a dimension of political recomposition which emerges from the worker's self-activity in the factories" (Pena 1983:445).

Indeed, *maquiladora* workers' involvement at two factories (Converters and Acapulco Fashions) increased COMO's involvement in industrial conflicts. In the latter case COMO assisted the independent workers' union with logistical support, advice on tactics, promotion of support networks, fundraising, and public relations. By the end of this period over 14,000 workers had been associated with COMO. They often continued their activities after completing COMO programs, forming informal groups which undertook their own independent courses of action.

COMO was assisted in the achievements of this period by two grants of less than $200,000 (U.S.) each from the Inter-American Foundation. These grants were essential in leadership development because they allowed many of the *maquiladora* workers who had worked at COMO as volunteers to leave their factory jobs and become paid staff members. Yudelman provides interesting details of how this worked:

> COMO began to transform itself from an ad-hoc operation of forty-two volunteers and nine paid staff members into a more formal organization. By 1978 COMO had an eight-member board of directors and departments of administration, promotion, special training courses, technical assistance to cooperatives, social work and community services. COMO also established a fifteen-member workers council made up of three board members, staff responsible for each of the programs, and a worker-student elected by participants in each of the program tracks (Yudelman 1987:23).

In the fourth period outlined by Pena, which begins in 1981 and reaches to just before the publication date of his work in 1983, COMO made advances in conducting its own research on a broader scale on topics which would allow workers to transfer skills learned in the factories to worker-controlled cooperatives. He sums up succinctly:

The organization has succeeded in synthesizing self-management principles with a blend of change agent, community organizing, and Freirian pedagogical tactics. COMO is
not a trade union, yet it promotes labor organizing through
support and linkage of independent worker coalitions and
informal networks. COMO is not a political party, yet it
promotes political involvement and articulates political
demands, sometimes much more effectively than leftist
parties. In many ways, COMO bears striking similarities to
the Polish workers' Solidarity movement (Pena 1983:461).

Yudelman, who has been with the Inter-American Foundation for two
decades, provides the most recently published account of COMO's history.
She labels the next stage "crisis, diaspora, and new beginnings"; I will number it the fifth stage. She diagnoses the cause of the crisis as overextension
and attributes it to the emphasis on participation and self-management
which left administrative structures underdeveloped and Villalva too central as Director. Two evaluations of COMO identified such problems, and
the Foundation decided to provide only a limited amount of 'bridge' funding until COMO could restructure itself and find some other source of support. The ministry of education and the PRI offered to take COMO under
their wings, but both offers were rejected out of fear for "loss of control,
bureaucratization, politicization, and loss of credibility among its constituency" (Yudelman 1987:106). The director and staff decided in 1984 to
"liquidate personnel according to law with remaining funds and allow those
who wished to continue to do so as volunteers, supporting themselves with
other employment" (Yudelman 1987:27). The cooperatives continued to
have offices in *Edificio COMO* their rent paid for building maintenance
and a secretary's salary. Those who had been employed in COMO programs found other jobs with government and local agencies in the private
sector.

The sixth stage of development, which I have derived from Yudelman's account, is described as co-optation by the PRI.

In mid-1985, Dr. Valdez was asked by the federal government to organize a program for women in Juarez. The
implementing organization was to be COMO. Subsequently, $50,000 was made available for six months, and former
staff members working for government or state agencies
were seconded to COMO for the duration of the project
(Yudelman 1987:28).

By the next year there were the equivalent of twelve staff members who
taught leadership and organizational training as well as courses in sewing,

public speaking, etc. According to Yudelman, the government expected COMO to deliver the women's vote to them. An ex-*obrera* became the Director for this stage. Guillermina Valdez de Villalva headed a government sponsored research agency (CEFNOMEX).

The Organization of Maquiladora Workers On the Basis of Religion

My curiosity about possible religious bases of resistance to gender exploitation was first aroused when a charismatic Catholic colleague brought Laurentin's *Miracles in El Paso?* to my attention [1]. The title refers to a group of charismatic Catholics who celebrated Christmas in 1972 by bringing dinner to the material handlers at the Juarez dump. The alleged miracle involved the inexplicable multiplication of food supplies. While Laurentin gives Guillermina Valdez de Villalva a leading role in his account of the religious events, he does not mention COMO and strongly denies that there is any political dimension.

In response to this new piece of information, I read through the literature cited above once again and found hints that there was another side to this story, which had not yet been told. For example, in the quotation by Pena above, we are told that "COMO bears striking similarities to the Polish workers' Solidarity movement." He then goes on to demonstrate that there are parallel strategies and tactics, but says nothing about comparable religious motivations. In her study of empowerment, Staudt does not count religious participation which predated the student's entry into the program or group membership centred around proselytizing (Staudt 1987:167). Even so, two of the four examples of women she describes at length as examples of the "more fully empowered" are members of evangelical church groups. She raises absolutely no questions as to why this might be so, failing to take cognizance of these data.

In order to better understand the relationship of the political and religious in women's organizing, the author interviewed two people who had been involved: Guillermina Villalva and Jean Soto [2]. They have known each other since girlhood, and Jean Soto was a member for eight years of an American prayer group which visited the garbage workers. Both were highly critical of Laurentin's account, saying that it incorrectly gives the leading roles in the unfolding of events to Americans and that it gives a negative impression of Juarez. Having visited Juarez on several occasions before reading his book, I agreed with the latter criticism. Laurentin's book was never translated into Spanish or published in Mexico, and Mexican protests to the French clergy with whom Laurentin worked prompted them to sponsor the making in 1983 of a videotape called "Pepenadores -- Down, But Not Out", to set the record straight. It has been shown throughout the world (in Egypt, most notably) as a model of how cooperatives can be formed by garbage- and other workers.

The picture that emerges from these new sources of data highlights the political and economic change that was taking place in northern Mexico from the late sixties onward, and the lack of internal differentiation in civil society which would give people a sense of belonging and rootedness. As noted above, the bargain that had been struck between foreign capital, the ruling party and the labour movements for the sake of social harmony meant that limited numbers of *maquiladora* workers were unionized. Because of the unions' participation within government, they could not serve very effectively as interest groups to lobby government on behalf of workers. The Catholic Church had not been an important public institution since the revolution and, in the 1960s, was suffering from a decline of clergy as priests became dissatisfied with their role within the institution and left.

Rick Thomas was ordained to the priesthood as a Jesuit in the early 1960s. While his vocation had always inclined to the poor, he did not become a believer in the charismatic renewal movement until a decade later. Laurentin says that although his ministry had been efficient and well organized up until this time, it remained barren (Laurentin 1982:54-55). The Catholic hierarchy in both El Paso and Juarez was opposed to meetings where people prayed in tongues. While the Bishop of El Paso left Thomas's group free to call meetings in that city, "glossalalia" proved more offensive to religious sensibilities prevalent in Mexico, and the Bishop there ordered that Thomas discontinue the prayer meetings he had been holding in Juarez.

Villalva was an intellectual who had had a lifelong commitment to social justice; while she herself was an atheist, she had been intellectually interested in how U.S. Blacks and Chicanos had used religion in their respective civil rights' movements. She was socially involved in her community giving lectures from a Marxist perspective in the technical schools and colleges on issues such as Mexican migrant labourers to the U.S., commuting workers, etc. Her work with priests who were also committed to reducing the sense of anomie in Juarez led to discussions about whether the holy spirit could be seen as the new person who needed to emerge in order to deal with societal changes. Retreating into a period of reflection during an illness in the early 1970s, she began to seriously study the Scriptures and for the first time entered into dialogue with people in the Catholic charismatic movement.

These were members of the American prayer group, led by Father Rick Thomas. Jean Soto, a U.S. friend with whom she had attended an exclusive Catholic girls' high school in El Paso, belonged to this group, as did many poor Chicanos. Villalva says she learned a great deal from interacting with the latter about the simplicity of a life of faith. She saw their economic well-being, in comparison to the situation of the poor in Mexico, as giving them a comparative freedom that the Mexican poor did not have. Their emotional depth provided a balance for her more intellectual approach, and eventually she herself converted. Her husband and mother had done so before her. She said of this time: "I was born with a hunger and thirst for justice, but had to learn love" [3]. With the bishop's authorization she resumed prayer meetings in the basement of her husband's Juarez office; they were still not allowed in a church. The bishop appointed her the leader of Catholic charismatics in Juarez.

Because of her lifelong commitment to social justice Villalva had been working for some time with the *basureros*, the material handlers at the Juarez dump. After her conversion, she led the American prayer group to the people she knew at the dump. These visits were still continued by some members of the U.S. group in 1988. They include joint bible study and the sharing of American food and clothing -- with the study, fellowship, and sharing being equally valued. While it was Guillermina who was responsible for the prayer group's visits to the dump, they were strongly supported by the U.S. leader, Father Thomas.

The prayer group held their meetings in a room that overlooked Juarez. Such views are quite common in El Paso, if one chooses to look. During my field work in July 1988, I stayed in a student residence at the University of Texas at El Paso. To the north of the building I could see the Sunbowl football stadium and a very beautiful campus designed in Tibetan fashion [4]. Beyond this is the 'West' side of El Paso, where the middle class lives and does business. From the other side of the building is a panoramic view of Juarez -- a vast city spreading out over the valley, where the buildings are much smaller, fewer streets paved, and less green in evidence because of less irrigation. All that separates UTEP from Juarez are the freeway and the Rio Grande in whose toxic waters Mexican children play to cool off. The profound contradiction involved in standing on the roof of the student residence and simply turning my head was quite overwhelming. But many Americans do not look south, and when they do it is too often through ethnocentric glasses which cloud their perception. Jean Soto said that it was the genius of Father Rick Thomas to recognize the obvious -- the interfacing between the "developed" and the "underdeveloped", the "affluent" and the "poor". The U.S. prayer group considered that sharing their lives with the poor would be a way of concretely embodying their love of God. Their attitude was one of openness to the Lord, to receptivity to how God was calling their community to act. Holding their meetings in a room overlooking Juarez, they knew God to be calling them there. This was the motivation for their visit in Christmas of 1972.

In the videotape describing this involvement with the material handlers, Guillermina Villalva says:

> The first time I came to the dump, I was a Marxist. I couldn't stand such a situation. The second time, I came with my bible in hand and I didn't see injustice, I saw beyond the injustice. I saw, felt, the presence of the Lord, and then I understood that it was a sign for me (Barry 1983).

This new religious orientation reinvigorated Villalva's approach to social problems in the community. There were other religious women in Juarez who were similarly predisposed, since church life in Mexico had been largely left to women. Not only were men absent from Church affairs, but this institution was the only one where it was socially approved for women to be active outside the family.

Since Villalva was already deeply involved in building COMO when she underwent her conversion, she began to link the religious and the political in her work there, developing a systematic leadership training process which incorporated both. This was a female leadership because women were more likely to be *maquiladora* workers and to be religious. When I interviewed her in 1988, she said that she did not agree with Mother Teresa that one should follow people to the grave without political help and support. Villalva considered it naive to think that religious ideas do not have political ramifications. The process by which this leadership developed can be illustrated with the *Team Manual for Life in the Spirit Seminars*, which Jean Soto said was

> the most widely used method of introducing people to the Catholic Charismatic renewal. It was translated into several languages and used all over the U.S. and the world. We did not use it ... but it was an important reference book for us ... . We thought that the manual lacked sufficient emphasis on social justice issues [5].

Given these caveats, it is still possible to get a sense of how people could be empowered in reference to this source. "To accept Jesus Christ into your life means to allow him to take the center . . . . To those who accept him in this way, Jesus gives the gift of the Spirit and a new life" (Clark 1971:43) The gifts of the spirit include speaking in tongues, prophecy, teaching, administrative abilities, healing, words of wisdom, and more. A fully developed community or prayer group will have a person with each of the gifts of the spirit, or will be on the lookout for someone gifted by the spirit in a way that would complete their community. Being baptized in the Spirit is a great leveller because it puts those who are socially unequal because of class, gender etc., on an equal footing in the eyes of the Lord. Priests, husbands, and other men withheld objections to women's leadership when it was seen in this way. Because the gifts of the spirit are from God, a community or prayer group feels a duty to receive them and receive them well. This created openings for the development of new women's leadership. It was, in Jean Soto's analysis, similar to the female leadership of some Baptist sects in the pre-revolutionary southern colonies, which "had great faith in the immediate teaching of the spirit and permitted women to speak at their public meetings" (Spruill 1972:247). On the individual level the person was encouraged by many steps in the process. For example, the following is from the *Team Manual*'s "Expanded Outline for Seminar #4: Receiving God's Gift":

> Turning to him: faith (belief) A.2) when we see the fact that God promised something, we can expect it to happen to us
> - we need more than just doctrinal belief; we need to claim the promises of God
> B. We can expect God to baptize us in the Spirit
> - because he told us he wants it for us (Lk 11:9-13),
> because he loves us and wants us to be united with him
> - we can have it because of what Jesus did for us, not because we can earn it or deserve it (Clark 1971:76)

The *Manual* also gives detailed instructions on how members of the team can encourage, assist and support new people at every step of the way.

Villalva has tailored a process for developing female leadership in five steps which move the focus from the individual person's situation to general social conditions, and stress empowerment by being in partnership with God. When individuals come to the group with a personal problem, it is not interpreted in terms of an individual's sin and her need for salvation but in terms of public issues. When the guilt attached to the explanation of personal sin is removed, a person is more likely to reorient herself in a constructive social manner. Villalva has shared this religious politicizing process internationally with people of faith.

When the bishop of Juarez commissioned Guillermina Villalva in the early 1970s as official leader of charismatics in Juarez, it marked the beginning of a ten-year period of tremendous support in the diocese for women's activism. While tension existed between female leaders and some male priests who were not accustomed to working with women with greater authority, the support for the growth of a female leadership continued because it filled a vacuum in the larger society. Villalva's religious convictions were purposely kept hidden from the public's view of COMO because of the historic separation of church and state in Mexican society. It would have been frowned upon to have religious people educating workers, and COMO was afraid of losing its registration with UCECA which allowed it to provide workers with education. She also feared that if people were aware of her religious beliefs, COMO would be stereotyped as headed by a middle-class "do gooder". This would not have helped to fulfill COMO's goal of being self-managed.

The specific structure formed by the group of religious people gathered around Guillermina Villalva and her husband was a base community called the St. John the Baptist Community. A great deal of overlap existed between membership in this base community and in COMO, and the video narrator says that it was the Church which asked Guillermina Villalva to found COMO for working women. The real cohesion between these people came from their religious ties, while COMO and SOCOSEMA were lay institutions where they could practise their religion. Members of the St. John the Baptist Community understand themselves as living the gospel through service to the poor.

The videotape which was made to correct Laurentin's account of Guillermina's activities is the clearest publicly available document showing how these organizations interlocked. In this program Guillermina's husband Antonio summarizes the work of COMO in two points by saying that its first goal is to evangelize and that, secondly, it aims to reduce the chasm between the rich and the poor. The construction of many cooperative organizations is attributed to the charismatic Catholic leaders within COMO, including SOCOSEMA, the seamstress's cooperative GUILLE, *Valle Nuevo* (an agricultural cooperative), as well as the CEBI classes set up by COMO under the government CONAFE umbrella. All of these cooperatives are portrayed as owned and managed by their members, with COMO helping primarily in the beginning -- and later when requested. People working as nurses, social workers, teachers, and community organizers attest to having come to work at COMO because of their commitment to the Christian faith.

Religion has been useful in this situation as a space for the empowerment of working women because in these particular historical circumstances men were absent. Guillermina Villalva estimates that in the 1986 elections in Juarez, for example, 86 per cent of the people from the base communities were involved in political campaigns of all three major political groupings [6]. She sees this as an evolution in women's political participation. I do not believe it to be a direct route to women's liberation, since no women from the base communities were elected. Many, however, were more politically active than ever before.

Events in the last few years in Juarez also indicate that an inevitable increase in the political involvement of women from the base communities cannot be assumed. Beginning in 1983, there was a movement in the Mexican Church away from women's leadership. Conservative groups within the Church expressed doubts about the prominent roles women filled. As a result, much of the lay inspired female leadership was displaced by men (especially from middle-class backgrounds) and priests. This meant that St. John the Baptist Community women left COMO and got jobs in other lay or secular organizations. For example, four people from the St. John the Baptist Community now work with Guillermina Villalva in her present position as Director of the *Colegio de la Frontera Norte*. About 45 of them still meet formally as a prayer group although they earn their livelihood in different places. She did not oppose this change because she sees the more appropriate site of women's struggle as being in the larger society. When women have equal rights in the larger Mexican society, she argues, the Church will have to respond. Women who began their public activism in base communities have moved into leadership positions in community organizations, government, and local agencies in the private sector (Yudelman 1987:28).

Villalva says that now there are two COMOs. Men are the visible leaders of the government funded COMO, and it serves young men who work in the informal sector as well as women and men *maquiladora* workers. Guillermina Villalva, while no longer involved in the daily management of COMO, played a role in planning the goals of COMO for the years before the nearest election. In fact, her official political work is now much more internal to the Mexican government than in the early days of building COMO, as she takes a leading role in planning policy for the social development of the border region for the next six years.

I believe that the second COMO of which she spoke is the one described in the videotape, the one which the Church asked Guillermina to form and with which she developed her own religious politicizing process. The second COMO is the St. John the Baptist Community which is still a prayer group but whose members are no longer employed by the government-funded COMO. Villalva says that it was the economic crisis and the political stress it has caused in Mexico since 1986 that has created the separation and distance between the two COMOs. The PRI does not understand the St. John the Baptist Community, according to her, and distrusts it because it contains supporters of other political parties. She has been asked by government officials to write papers on religious phenomena such as "resting in the spirit". They have not been convinced by explanations that rely on faith rather than science. The St. John the Baptist Community has continued, however, as an independent religious movement on its own.

It is difficult to predict whether the state's cooptation of COMO and its most prominent activist marks the permanent loss of independence for the women workers' movement described in this paper. The only author in the literature available who addresses this issue is Yudelman, who is highly critical of PRI's control over the COMO program. She argues that the commitment of the women workers at the core of COMO is too strong to disappear, and that the social energies which fuelled their movement will emerge again in another, perhaps different, movement (Yudelman 1987:28-29). Within the Mexican Left, two currents (both of which broader than any particular organization) take opposing positions on whether the government can be an arena for social struggle. Those who see the state as satisfying the needs of national development as well as representing the interests of capital believe they should compete for positions within the government, rather than waste their energy attacking it. On the other hand, those who see the Mexican state as authoritarian and bourgeois argue that it is only capable of repression through its labour bureaucracy (Semo 1986:20). I have found observers on both sides of the Mexican-U.S. border thoroughly convinced of either position in regard to COMO, and would have to observe the situation further to evaluate their analyses.

Conclusion

The very unique events in Juarez described in this paper demonstrate the possibility of combining goals from several very different sets of beliefs usually observed to be distinct: feminism, theology of liberation, and the charismatic renewal. As a case study, it can sensitize us to broadening our expectations of how resistance to exploitation emerges among women in non-Anglo cultures. It may make an interesting comparison to other situations throughout Latin America, where people have formed base communities as part of a general process of activism. While they do so for genuinely religious reasons, there are political consequences which very naturally follow. This has special import for women who often constitute the majority of base community members, because in Latin America their power is restricted in other areas of society like the home and the public realm.

The example presented by this paper may also point to the need for Canadian scholars to take a more serious look at similar processes emerging here. When I presented an earlier version of this paper at the 1988 conference of the Canadian Research Institute for the Advancement of Women, Madeline Parent was in the audience and informed me after the session that similar dynamics had been at work in Québec, i.e. in the Catholic Women Teachers' Union which preceded the contemporary union of teachers. My work in Mexico brings me back to Canada asking for more from quotations like the following:

Despite their conservative and sometimes confessional origins, public sector unions, particularly those in the Québec Common Front, have proved to be both militant and relatively open to women's demands (Maroney 1987:88).

Did their openness to women's demands develop in spite of confessional origins, or because of them? Among which other Canadian women might we expect such dynamics to have been, or still be, at work? Immigrant women from Catholic countries might be a good place to begin, especially because many of them are employed in Canadian jobs most similar to *maquiladora* employment.

This look at working women's organizing efforts elsewhere on the North-American continent stimulates further comparison because of its ability to throw new light on the work of Canadian scholars and political activists. When free trade emerged as the central issue in the 1988 election campaign, the destinations of fleeing industry were first mentioned by critical commentators. This provided an opportunity for Canadian attention to be focussed on the question of where industries are going when they leave this country and why they are going there. As the two examples below show, however, this opportunity was largely missed.

One of the earliest activists on this issue is John Ralston Saul. In an article entitled "Canada today, Mexico tomorrow..." in *If You Love This Country*, he explains why Mexican labour represents impossible competition for Canadians without once noting that the majority of the Mexican workers he is talking about are women. This blindness to the importance of gender as a factor making superexploitation possible is inexcusable in view of the literature which has emerged in the last fifteen years on capitalism and patriarchy.

Only as an afterthought, in his response to a negative review of his portion of the book, does Saul recognize gender. Buried as it is in his letter to the editor of *Saturday Night*, it by no means gives this factor the attention it deserves, but it does reveal some biases that are all too familiar:

> That admission revealed a profound misunderstanding of how competition must be and is carefully defined when trading zones are created. The purpose of such definitions is to avoid *rawer*, more *backward* forms of competition in one country being used to undermine more *advanced* forms of competition in another. In concrete terms, this means avoiding the problem of young *girls*, who are exploited at less than a dollar an hour in Mexico and at less than seven dollars an hour in the southern states without

> any attached social costs, being used to undercut reasonable
> wage levels and social programmes in Canada (Saul
> 1988:5-6, emphasis added).

By identifying "girls" with "rawer, more backward forms of competition"
in Mexico and the southern U.S. and "more advanced forms of competition" with Canada, he introduces a racist subtext identified in feminist literature by authors like Carby, and Amos and Parmar (Carby 1982; Amos
and Parmar 1984:3-20). They argue that we are all too ready to assume
that black and Third-World women are passive and politically immature,
and that they lack a history of struggle, when in fact they have been (and
continue to be) among the first and strongest resistors of imperialism.

"Common Frontiers", published by the Latin American Working
Group in the middle of the election campaign, says in the very first sen-
tence that workers in the Mexican Export Processing Zone are "mostly
women". They say very little about gender subsequently, though, and what
they do say is questionable in light of findings of more in-depth research
conducted by border scholars. In the third paragraph, they state:

> As most families are headed by single mothers, children as
> young as 13 or 14 are forced to drop out of school and fal-
> sify birth certificates to obtain employment. Since the
> companies are short of workers they only ask for photoco-
> pies of birth records, making it easy to change the dates
> (Latin American Working Group 1988:1).

I am not quarrelling with the fact that this happens, but when it is the only
thing said about how workers' gender is relevant, it may inadvertently reinforce the stereotype that relationships between Latin American men and
women are not sanctioned by law often enough, or that the Latin American
family is weak. COMO found that by steadily raising the educational
requirements necessary for their largely female work force between 1966
and 1983, the *maquiladoras* had reversed the Mexican family's traditional
preference for educating boys rather than girls (COMO 1984). Ten years
after the Export Processing Zone was instituted young working-class
women were found to have an average of nine years of education, while
their male counterparts remained at the national average of three and one-
half years. This did have an effect on marital status because it upset traditional courtship patterns, with young working-class men feeling very
resentful at the rejection they received from women with more education
and better jobs.

The family is a much more important unit of social organization in
Latin America than it is in Anglo America, and while nuclear households

are more common than they used to be, people still survive largely through the support of family networks. Single mothers on the Mexican-U.S. border are more likely to be part of extended households than those in Canada. Also, Pena found that the household structure was often reorganized to suit the kind of work women were doing outside the home, with the appearance of households with multiple female heads (Pena 1983).

To the extent that writing of this kind ignores or misrepresents issues of gender, sexuality, and family structure, it fails to empower Canadian workers in forging relationships of solidarity with their Mexican counterparts. In his review of how research on Mexican *maquiladoras* contributes to the rethinking of international solidarity from a feminist perspective, Mitchell points out that solidarity has been "conceived of both as a unity of condition and as a form of social action (Mitchell 1989)." The work of Saul and LAWG does not allow a full consideration of the unity of condition between Mexican and Canadian workers because it is narrowly aimed at the state, the electoral process, political parties, and trade unions. The present work provides further support for Mitchell's challenge of the traditional literature on international solidarity for its emphasis on male workers, trade unions, and conventional macroeconomic criteria. Because past understanding of international solidarity is grounded in a materialist conception of class politics, it tends to view religion as an inevitably conservative justification of exploitative conditions. Recent literature has begun to educate the secular Left on the importance of the religious Left, but this needs to be further developed among those who view solidarity both as unity of condition and a form of social action [7].

Endnotes

*Department of Sociology, King's College, The University of Western Ontario, 266 Epworth Avenue, London, ON, N6A 2M3.
This is a revised version of a paper prepared for the 12th Annual Conference of the Canadian Research Institute for the Advancement of Women on "Women and Development", November 11-13, 1988 in Québec City, Québec, Canada.

Acknowledgements: The research on which this paper is based began in 1984 when I was a visiting scholar at El Paso Community College. I am indebted to EPCC for their support and to King's College for research grants awarded annually since that time to continue the work. Interviews with Guillermina Valdez de Villalva and Jean Soto were invaluable in reaching the analysis contained in this paper. Jean Soto also provided important feedback on previous versions of this work. Judy Soles, at the El Paso Times was very generous in granting me access to their library and permission to quote the newspaper. Juan Sandoval was very helpful in finding sources at the library at the University of Texas at El Paso. Ronnie Leah and Ed Silva were helpful in my revision of the paper for this volume. Eric Mitchell also read and commented on previous drafts. Last but not least, I would like to thank Cathy Mendler for typing and partially editing this manuscript. Any errors contained herein are the sole responsibility of the author.

1. I would like to thank Arnold McKee, Department of Economics, King's College for raising the issue.

2. Guillermina Valdez de Villalva was interviewed in August and again in October of 1988, when the author heard her presentation on "Women in the Latin American Catholic Church" at the meeting of the Society for the Scientific Study of Religion in Chicago. Jean Soto was interviewed in July of 1988, and I have corresponded with her since.

3. This was communicated to the author by Guillermina Villalva in our interview in August of 1988.

4. The story of how UTEP was designed in Tibetan style is that, on the day the University of Texas' first president was leaving home for the meeting which would make architectural decisions for the future campus, he consulted his wife. She happened to be reading an article on Tibet in National Geographic and thought that, since the El Paso landscape looked like the pictures she saw of Tibet, their building design would also be suitable.

5. Letter to the author from Jean Soto, January 8, 1989.

6. This information comes from the presentation by Guillermina Villalva entitled "Women in the Latin American Catholic Church" at the meeting of the Society For The Scientific Study of Religion in Chicago in October of 1988.

7. See the special double edition on religion and the Left, *Monthly Review* 36:3 (1984).

BIBLIOGRAPHY

Acevedo, Marta, Marta Lamas and Luisa Liguori. 1980. "Mexico: Una Bolsita De Cal Por Las Que Van De Arena", *FEM* 4:13 (March/April), pp. 7-26.

Amos, Valerie and Pratibha Parmar. 1984. "Challenging Imperial Feminism", *Feminist Review* 17:3, pp. 3-20.

Attenborough, Susan. 1983. "Sexual Harassment: An Issue for Unions". In *Union Sisters*, pp. 136-143. Linda Briskin and Lynda Yanz, eds. Toronto: Women's Press.

Baker, Stephen. 1988. "The Magnet Of Growth In Mexico's North", *Business Week*, June 6, pp. 48-50.

Baker, Stephen, Tod Vogel and Adrienne Bard. 1988. "Will The New *Maquiladoras* Build A Better *Manana*", *Business Week*, November 14, pp. 102, 106.

Carby, Hazel V. 1982. "White woman listen! Black feminism and the boundaries of sisterhood". In *The Empire Strikes Back*, Centre for Contemporary Cultural Studies, pp. 212-235. London: Hutchinson.

Clark, Stephen. 1971. *Team Manual for the Life in the Spirit Seminars*. Notre Dame: Charismatic Renewal Services.

Clement, Wallace. 1977. *Continental Corporate Power: Economic Elite Linkages between Canada and the United States*. Toronto: McClelland and Stewart.

Centro de Orientacion de la Mujer Obrera, A.C. (COMO) 1984. *Primer Taller de Analisis sobre Aprendizaje en la produccion y transferencia de Tecnologia en la Industria de Maquila de Exportacion*. Cd. Juarez, Chih.: Centro De Estudios Fronterizos Del Norte De Mexico.

Davis, Mike. 1984. "The Political Economy of Late-Imperial America", *New Left Review* 143, pp. 6-38.

Dillon, John. 1988. "U.S.-Canada Free Trade. Latin America is Next", *NACLA* 22:4, pp. 7-9.

Donaldson, David. 1985. "Does B.C. Need Special Enterprise Zones?", B.C. Economic Policy Institute Paper No. P-85-01. January.

Donaldson, David and Jacqueline K. Maund. 1984. "British Columbia's high technology policy", B.C. Economic Policy Institute Paper No. P-84-12. September.

Fernandez-Kelly, Maria Patricia. 1983a. *For We Are Sold: I And My People. Women and Industry in Mexico's Frontier*. Albany: State University of New York Press.

Fernandez-Kelly, Maria Patricia. 1983b. "Alternative Education for 'Maquiladora' Workers", *Grassroots Development. Journal of the Inter-American Foundation* 6:2 and 7:1, pp. 41-5.

Field, Debbie. 1983. "A New Look at Co-worker Harassment". In *Union Sisters*, pp. 144-160. Linda Briskin and Lynda Yanz, eds. Toronto: Women's Press.

Goulet, Denis. 1988. "The Mexican Church: Into The Public Arena". Paper read at the annual meeting of the Society for the Scientific Study of Religion, October 28-30, in Chicago. Mimeographed.

Grubel, Herbert. 1983. *Free Market Zones: Deregulating Canadian Enterprise.* Vancouver: The Fraser Institute.

Herrera-Sobek, Maria. 1979. "Mothers, Lovers, And Soldiers: Images of Woman In the Mexican Corrido", *Keystone Folklore Journal* 23, pp. 53-77.

Laurentin, Rene. 1982. *Miracles In El Paso?* Ann Arbor: Servant Books.

Latin American Working Group. 1988. "Common Frontiers", *LAWG LETTER* 10:2 (November).

Maroney, Heather Jon. 1987. "Feminism at Work". In *Feminism And Political Economy*, pp. 85-108. Heather Jon Maroney and Meg Luxton, eds. Toronto: Methuen.

Miller, Tom. 1981. *On The Border.* New York: Harper and Row.

Mitchell, Eric. 1989. "Rethinking International Solidarity From A Feminist Perspective: Contributions From Research On Mexican *Maquiladoras*". M.A. Research Review, York University.

Morales, Patricia. 1985. "Feminismo Chicano", *FEM* 39, pp. 41-44.

Navarro, Marysa. 1979. "Research on Latin American Women", *Signs* 5:1, pp. 111-120.

Olson, Wayne. 1987. "Crisis Politics in Mexico, 1968-85", *The Insurgent Sociologist* 14:1, pp. 5-32.

Pena, Devon Gerard. 1983. "The Class Politics Of Abstract Labor: Organizational Forms And Industrial Relations In The Mexican *Maquiladoras*". Ph.D. dissertation, University of Texas at Austin.

"Preocupa a la Iglesia la Injusticia en que Viven 1988 los Obreros". 1988. *El Fronterizo* June 14, p. 1.

Saul, John Ralston. 1988. Letter to the Editor. *Saturday Night*, July, pp. 5-6.

Saul, John Ralston. 1987. "'Canada today, Mexico tomorrow...'". In *If You Love This Country: Facts and Feelings on Free Trade*, pp. 188-192. Laurier LaPierre, ed. Toronto: McClelland and Stewart.

Seligson, Mitchell A. and Edward J. Williams. 1981. *'Maquiladoras' and Migration. Workers in the Mexico-United States Border Industrialization Program.* Austin, Texas: Mexico-United States Border Research Program.

Semo, Enrique. 1986. "The Mexican Left And The Economic Crisis". In *The Mexican Left, the Popular Movements, and the Politics Of Austerity*, pp. 19-32. Barry Carr and Ricardo Anzaldua Montoya, eds. San Diego: Center For U.S.-Mexican Studies.

Spruill, Julia Cherry. 1972. *Women's Life and Work in the Southern Colonies*. New York: Norton.

Staudt, Kathleen. 1987. "Programming Women's Empowerment: A Case from Northern Mexico". In *Women on the U.S.-Mexico Border. Responses to Change*, pp. 155-176. Vicki L. Ruiz and Susan Tiano, eds. Boston: Allen and Unwin.

Stoddard, Ellwyn R. 1987. *Maquila*. El Paso: Western Press.

Thompson, Chandler. 1988. "Twin plant pay upsets bishop", *El Paso Times* June 23.

Tiano, Susan. 1987. "Women's Work and Unemployment in Northern Mexico". In *Women On The U.S.-Mexico Border. Responses To Change*, pp. 17-40. Vicki L. Ruiz and Susan Tiano, eds. Boston: Allen and Unwin.

U.S.-L.D.C. Trade Link Policy Research Project. 1984. *U.S. Finance and Trade Links With Less-Developed Countries*. Austin: University of Texas.

Van Waas, Michael. 1981. "The Multinationals' Strategy For Labour: Foreign Assembly Plants in Mexico's Border Industrialization Program". Ph.D. dissertation, Stanford University.

Williams, Glen. 1988. "On Determining Canada's Location Within the International Political Economy", *Studies in Political Economy* 25:2 (Spring), pp. 107-140.

Young, Gay. 1987. "Gender Identification and Working-Class Solidarity among Maquila Workers in Ciudad Juarez: Stereotypes". In *Women On The U.S.-Mexico Border. Responses To Change*, pp. 105-28. Vicki L. Ruiz and Susan Tiano, eds. Boston: Allen and Unwin.

Yudelman, Sally W. 1987. *Hopeful Openings. A Study of Five Women's Development Organizations in Latin America and the Caribbean*. West Hartford, Connecticut: Kumarian.

Videotape

Barry, G. H., Editor and Director. 1983. *Pepenadores -- Down, But Not Out*. International Foundation for Economic, Social, and Spiritual Development.

Abstracts

Roxana Ng -- Sexism, Racism and Canadian Nationalism

This paper addresses the problem of treating gender, race and class in social science research as abstract categories, which informs political praxis in the Left and in the women's movement. It makes use of a method of thinking derived from Marx and feminist interpretations of Marx, which insists on reconceptualizing gender, race and class as social relations arising out of people's struggles over the means of production and reproduction. Through historical examples, the paper shows that sexism and racism are constituent features of nation-building, as men from the British Iles colonized Canada and as they attempted to assert hegemony through the consolidation of state power. With this understanding of the interpenetration of gender, race and class relations in the Canadian state formation, the paper ends by exploring how the Left could develop a praxis for eradicating sexism and racism.

Esmeralda Thornhill -- Focus on Black Women!

Women have many common concerns, but their experiences and their histories are often vastly different. Esmeralda Thornhill challenges White Womanhood to examine the special situation in which Black Womanhood finds itself, always keeping in mind the ultimate goal of Women's solidarity. She states that as long as White Women do not recognize their own racism, their own advantages and the way in which they oppress other Women, Black Women will remain on the sidelines of the Women's movement. She further states that, when it comes to actual planning and strategy, Women cannot allow the more privileged White Women to speak for all Women, for fear that affirmative action programs and other government initiatives will be tailored toward White Women who make themselves heard and with whom bureaucrats have become familiar.

Esmeralda Thornhill credits the history of Blacks with the unique experience that Black Women bring to the overall collection of Women's experiences -- slavery and oppression have made Black Women strong; Black Women generally do not know the problem of being financially dependent on men; Black Women have been systematically exploited by all those with authority over them, including White Women. She calls for a new dialogue between all Women, one that will focus on differences as well as similarities, because such a dialogue can help to clarify the mechanics of oppression.

Marlee Kline -- Women's Oppression and Racism:
A Critique of the "Feminist Standpoint"

This article provides a critique of the "standpoint" approach to feminist theory from a perspective attentive to concerns of race and racism. It demonstates how this approach -- with its emphasis on women's commonalities rather than their differences -- serves to focus attention on the concerns and priorities of white middle-class women, and obscure the forms of oppression experienced by women of colour. The white privileged status of most contemporary feminist theorists is considered, and it is concluded that those engaged in feminist theorizing and practice need to confront, rather than fear or ignore, the complexity of women's oppression and the consequent differences in women's priorities and interests, and thus maintain a historically-based and contextual approach to analyzing, strategizing and actively working for women's liberation.

Alicja Muszynski -- What is Patriarchy?

It is generally acknowledged that the relations of exploitation and oppression connected with race, class and gender are complex. Orthodox Marxists insist that class analysis can be used to explain racism and sexism in capitalist societies, while many radical feminists have argued that patriarchal oppression is prior to and underlies class exploitation; they have rejected class analysis. The argument in this paper urges the necessity of treating race, class and gender as related phenomena that nevertheless carry their own dynamic. By re-examining the concept of labour contained in Marx's labour theory of value, the need is demonstrated to broaden the concept of labour more widely. Specifically, the way in which women's labour was separated from that of men and rendered "animal-like" (tied to necessity) at the dawn of Western civilization must be given equal treatment with the manner in which labour power is commodified in the capitalist mode of production. Patriarchal oppression and class exploitation are interrelated, but they carry their own set of dynamic processes which act upon each other. In turn, they also help to define racism within capitalism.

Ron Bourgeault -- Race, class and gender: colonial domination of Indian Women

The object of this paper is to explain the manner in which Indian and Métis women were incorporated into capitalism under colonial relations of domination. It is argued that the oppression and subordination of women to men is not a universal phenomenon. In the case of non-white women in particular, and colonial women in general, it is the direct result of colonially imposed capitalist relations of production and exploitation, which also include race oppression and racism as an ideology that explicitly expounds racial superiority.

Consistent with other pre-capitalist societies in the seventeenth and eighteenth centuries, the various hunting-gathering social formations of the sub-arctic region were transformed in the interests of commodity production. Indian labour was formally subordinated to capital and subjected to capitalistic relations of exploitation. It is argued that formal subordination of Indian labour to capital could not take place at the level of the economic. Instead, extra-economic (violent) coercion took place directed at the egalitarian communal societies, which included also coercion against the autonomy of Indian women within their societies. As commodity production took root the gender division of labour within the social formations was transformed and incorporated into capitalistic relations of exploitation. Indian women were slowly subordinated in relationships with European men, and then to Indian men. The imposition of capitalist relations of production in the form of peripheral capitalism at the turn of the nineteenth century resulted in the creation of the Euro-Indian, the Métis, as a "new race". Under peripheral capitalism miscengenation between Indian women in dependent economic relationships with European men resulted in class and race differentiation among Indian women.

Nicole St-Onge -- *Race, Class and Marginality in a Manitoba Interlake Settlement: 1850-1950*

This paper examines how, since the 1850s, capitalist development in Manitoba's Interlake area and the interpretation of this region's history have been heavily influenced by a western racist ideology. This ideology, coupled with the other political-social-economic dynamics of capitalism, led to the development and maintenance of racially distinct marginal communities. Racism alone, however, was used to explain the existence of these communities in terms of a perceived racial difference that affected the residents' culture, world view, and work habits. The specific community examined is a Métis settlement on the southern shores of Lake Manitoba.

Agnes Calliste -- *Canada's Immigration Policy and Domestics from the Caribbean: The Second Domestic Scheme*

This paper examines the Caribbean Domestic Scheme in Canada from 1955 to 1966 and argues that, although the urgent demand for cheap domestic labour in Canada was the crucial stimulus for the Domestic Scheme, other economic and political factors also played a role in the initiation and continuation of the Scheme. Caribbean people, in both Canada and the Caribbean, had pressured the Canadian government to liberalize its discriminatory immigration policy and regulations against people from the British Caribbean. The Department of Immigration agreed to the Domestic Scheme partly to maintain Canada's preferential trade and investment in the British Caribbean; this agreement also reflected imperial ties between Canada and the Caribbean. The Domestic Scheme reflects, as well, how immigration policy has historically been shaped by racial, class and gender biases.

Stereotypes of working class Caribbean women as career domestics and single parents had been used to justify the restriction and exclusion of Caribbean domestics since 1911. Since the Domestic Scheme provided almost the only opportunity for many black women to enter Canada, and given the lack of educational and employment opportunities in the Caribbean, some skilled and semi-skilled workers used the Domestic Scheme to emigrate to Canada in order to further their education, to seek other fields of employment at the end of their contract and to sponsor the entry of their family members. Although Caribbean women tended to remain in domestic service longer than their European counterparts, Canadian government officials who had expected Caribbean women to be career domestics -- a legacy of slavery -- questioned the long-term economic benefits of the Scheme for Canada, given the women's high mobility rate out of domestic service and the sponsorship of some of their family members. Some blacks, however, criticized the racial, class and gender biases of the Domestic Scheme and questioned its benefits for Caribbean women who were paid less than their Canadian and European counterparts, and who were treated as second-class immigrants. They also questioned the benefits of the Scheme for the Caribbean, particularly because of the brain drain.

Ronnie Leah -- *Linking the Struggles: Racism, Sexism and the Union Movement*

Women of colour have challenged the dominant assumptions in feminist practice: they have called for an approach that links together struggles against racism and sexism, and addresses the specific experiences and concerns of working class black women, Native women, South Asian women, and other women of colour. The mainly white feminist movement has tended to marginalize women of colour and the general gains made by women in the union movement have often not extended to women of colour -- who face both racist and sexist discrimination.

This paper discusses some of the issues currently being raised by black women and other women of colour in the Ontario labour movement. The gains made by union women, combined with growing labour opposition to racism and discrimination, have contributed to increasing participation and militancy by women of colour in the unions. At the same time, women of colour have identified a number of obstacles that continue to impede their progress in the labour movement -- as women, as minority workers and as trade unionists.

The author examines strategies that might help build an anti-racist feminist movement among working people -- a movement that links together the issues of racism and sexism and fully incorporates the concerns of women of colour. The recent fight waged by CUPE Local 79 to maintain full-time jobs in Metro Toronto Homes for the Aged -- for a workforce mainly composed of black and Asian women -- exemplifies how unions defend the interests of all workers by taking up struggles against racism and sexism.

Irene Poelzer -- Métis Women and the Economy of Northern Saskatchewan

In this article the author presents a method for examining the effects of the wage economy on the lives of Métis women in northern Saskatchewan. By interviewing Métis women in seven northern communities, the author was able to gather information about the life situations of Métis women who are in waged employment, of those who do volunteer work, and of those who are unemployed and on welfare.

Utilizing an approach from the work of the feminist sociologist Dorothy Smith, the author examines the articulations of the Métis women in order to uncover the connections between the mega structure and what happens in everyday lives of these Métis women. For those in waged employment, the author pinpoints direct relationships betwen the powerlessness of Métis women and their position in the labour market. By their labour participation Métis women also share in the transformation of particular social relations that used to be grounded in tradition or culture; for example, the care of children within the home is now transformed into the labour relations of babysitting. Furthermore, the volunteer work of Métis women is shown to be directly connected to capitalist structures; for example, organized recreation becomes commercialized recreation in the non-work time within the capitalist system. Often the volunteer work of Métis women is directly connected to the market relations of corporate enterprises in the recreational field. Finally, Métis women on welfare become part of a powerless surplus population (an effect of the profit-making process of capitalism), a population which is dependent on the "good graces" of government and/or capital for "handouts" or "occasional jobs". The author argues that the powerlessness of Métis women is a function not only of lack of knowledge about the effects and purported neutrality of corporate capitalism, but also a function of the structural position held by Métis women with respect to the economy. The author concludes by saying that the very situation of powerlessness in which Métis women find themselves is also the locus of activity that can be transformed from being demeaning to being empowering.

260

Kathryn Kopinak -- Living the Gospel through Service to the Poor:
The Convergence of Political and Religious Motivations in Organizing
Maquiladora Workers in Juarez, Mexico.

Canadian, American, European, and Japanese manufacturers of textiles, garments, and electronic components have increasingly been drawn to the Mexican-U.S. border for over two decades, where the Export Processing Zone has created a corridor of twin plants. Unassembled components are warehoused on the U.S. side and assembly itself takes place on the Mexican side in factories called *maquiladoras.* El Paso/Juarez is the largest urban population complex on the border, and Juarez has always been one of the sites of greatest *maquiladora* concentration. Multinational capital has been attracted by the 'favourable business climate' surrounding the twin plants, which includes the availability of services in industrial parks and cheap female labour. Only a small proportion of working women have been organized into unions, and many have found the unions' abilities to defend their rights weakened by state control and the easy availability of cheap labour. In Mexico, the ruling PRI maintains tight control of the CTM and suppresses more militant independent unions. While this damages the position of workers in general, women workers are made even more vulnerable by the fact that unions often utilize the same patriarchal organizational forms as capital.

This paper examines how a women's centre emerged as a response to this situation. *Centro de Orientacion de la Mujer Obrera* (COMO), in Juarez, has been the focus of previous research, but no one has yet brought to light the central role of religion in that organization's development. This paper extends and corrects accounts of COMO's development available in already published works. New data indicate that the most active members of the Juarez working women's centre combined ideas from the theology of liberation and the Catholic charismatic renewal movement. While base communities have helped people throughout Latin America to read and act on the political events in their societies, none has formed people's consciousness of gender-related issues in exactly this way.

Abrégés

Roxana Ng -- **Sexisme, racisme et nationalisme canadien**

Cette communication traite la manière dont les chercheurs en sciences sociales étudient le sexe, la race et la classe comme des catégories abstraites, qui animent les pratiques politiques de la gauche et des mouvements féministes. Elle s'inspire d'une méthodologie qui découle de Marx et des interprétations féministes de Marx, et qui insiste sur la reconceptualisation du sexe, de la race et de la classe comme des rapports sociaux résultant des luttes pour décider des moyens de production et de reproduction. S'appuyant sur des exemples historiques, la communication démontre que le sexisme et le racisme ont présidé à la création de la nation que les colons britanniques ont fondée au Canada où ils ont esayé d'affirmer l'hégémonie par la consolidation du pouvoir de l'état. Après avoir étudié l'interpénétration des rapports de sexe, de race et de classe dans la formation de l'état canadien, la communication s'achève par des considérations sur la manière dont la gauche pourrait mettre sur pied une pratique qui supprimerait le sexisme et le racisme.

Esmeralda Thornhill -- **Mise au point: La femme noire!**

Les femmes ont beaucoup de préoccupations communes, mais leurs expériences et leurs antécédents sont souvent très différents. Esmeralda Thornhill défie les Blanches d'examiner la situation particulières des Noires en vue de renforcer l'idéal de la solidarité des femmes. Elle déclare qu'aussi longtemps que les Blanches ne verront pas leur propre racisme, leurs privilèges et la facon dont elles oppriment les autres femmes, les Noires demeureront en marge du mouvement des femmes. Elle signale également que, sur le plan des stratégies pratiques, les femmes ne peuvent pas permettre aux Blanches privilégiées de parler au nom de toutes les femmes, de peur que les programmes d'action positive et les autres initiatives des gouvernements ne soient concus uniquement à l'intention des Blanches qui se font entendre et que les bureaucrates connaissent bien.

Esmeralda Thornhill se fonde sur l'historie des Noirs pour décrire l'expérience unique que les Noires apportent au collage de l'expérience générale des femmes -- l'esclavage et l'oppression ont rendu les Noires fortes; les Noires ne connaissent pas en général le problème d'être à la charge financière des hommes; les Noires ont été systématiquement exploitées par tous ceux qui ont eu autorité sur elles, y compris les Blanches. Elle revendique un nouveau dialogue entre toutes les femmes qui devra porter sur leurs différences autant que sur les traits communs, puisqu'un tel dialogue aidera à éclairer les mécanismes de l'oppression.

Marlee Kline -- **L'oppression des femmes et le racisme: une critique de l'approche "standpoint"**

Cet article offre une critique de l'approche "standpoint" en abordant la théorie féministe et le fait d'une perspective qui est attentive aux problèmes de race et de racisme. L'article montre comment, en mettant l'accent sur les intérêts que les femmes ont en commun plutôt que sur leurs différences, cette approche sert à fixer l'attention sur les problèmes et les priorités des Blanches de la classe moyenne et à masquer les formes d'oppression subies par les femmes de couleur. Le statut privilégié de la plupart des théoriciennes féministes contemporaines de race blanche est pris en considération et on a déduit que plutôt que de craindre ou d'ignorer la complexité de l'oppression des femmes et les différences entre les priorités et les intérêts des femmes qui en résultent, celles qui sont engagées dans l'élaboration de la théorie et la pratique féministes doivent y faire face et, ce faisant, élaborer une approche basée sur l'histoire et le contexte qui inspirera leurs analyses, l'élaboration de leur stratégie et leur engagement dans la lutte pour la libération des femmes.

Alicja Muszynski -- Qu'est-ce que le patriarcat?

En général, on reconnaît que les rapports entre l'exploitation et l'oppression qui on trait à la race, à la classe et au sexe sont complexes. Les marxistes orthodoxes soutiennent que l'analyse de classe peut être employée pour expliquer le racisme et le sexisme dans les sociétés capitalistes, alors que bien des féministes radicales affirment que l'oppression patriarcale y est antérieure, même que c'est elle qui est à la base de l'exploitation de classe et elles ont rejeté l'analyse de classe. La prise de position de l'auteur de cette communication est de faire valoir la nécessité de traiter la race, la classe et le sexe comme des phénomènes connexes qui, malgré leur connexité, ont chacun leur propre dynamique. En réexaminant le concept du travail tel qu'avancé par Marx dans sa théorie qui préconise la valeur du travail, on voit la nécessité d'élargir considérablement le concept du travail. En particulier, il faut traiter sur un pied d'égalité la façon dont, dès l'aube de la civilisation occidentale, le travail des femmes était séparé de celui des hommes et puis doté d'une "animalité" (c'est à dire: lié au besoin) et la façon dont ce pouvoir du travail est réifié dans le mode de la production capitaliste.

L'oppression patriarcale et l'exploitation de classe sont étroitement liées l'une à l'autre, mais chacune possède sa propre série d'opérations dynamiques qui agissent les unes sur les autres. A leur tour, elles aident également à définir le racisme à l'intérieur du capitalisme.

Ron Bourgeault -- Race, classe et sexe: la domination coloniale des femmes indiennes.

Le but de cette communication est d'expliquer la façon dont les Indiennes et les Métisses ont été incorporées au capitalisme sous les rapports coloniaux de domination. Nous soutenons que l'oppression de la femme par l'homme et sa subordination à celui-ci n'est pas un phénomène universel. Dans le cas des femmes de couleur en particulier, et des femmes coloniales en général, elles sont le résultat direct de rapports capitalistes de la production et de l'exploitation imposés par le colonialisme; elles comprennent également l'oppression de la race et le racisme en tant qu'une idéologie qui expose explicitement la supériorité raciale.

Comme d'autres sociétés précapitalistes des dix-septième et dix-huitième siècles, les diverses organisations sociales de la région subarctique, qui pratiquaient la chasse et la cueillette, ont été tranformées pour assurer la production des marchandises. La main d'oeuvre indienne a été officiellement subordonnée au capital et soumise aux rapports d'exploitation capitalistes. Nous soutenons que la subordination officielle de la main d'oeuvre indienne au capital n'aurait pas pu se réaliser au niveau de l'économie. Au lieu, on a pratiqué une contrainte extra-économique (violente) à l'égard des sociétés collectives égalitaires, et qui comprenait également une contrainte mise en action contre l'autonomie des femmes indiennes au sein de leurs sociétés. Au fur et à mesure que la production des marchandises prenait racine, la notion de la division du travail selon le sexe du travailleur qui s'implantait au sein des organisations sociales, a été transformée et intégrée aux rapports d'exploitation capitalistes. Les Indiennes ont été peu à peu subordonnées aux

Européens dans leurs relations avec ceux-ci et ensuite aux hommes indiens. L'imposition des rapports de production capitalistes sous forme de capitalisme périphérique à la fin du dix-neuvième siècle a abouti à la création d'une "nouvelle race" euro-indienne ou métisse. Sous le capitalisme périphérique le croisement d'Indiennes ayant des rapports économiques dépendants avec des Européens avaient comme résultat l'établissement de différences de classe et de race entre les Indiennes.

Nicole St-Onge -- *Race, classe et marginalité dans un peuplement de la région Entre-lacs au Manitoba: 1850-1950*

Cet article examine comment, depuis le milieu du dix-neuvième siècle, de développement capitaliste de la région Entre-lacs au Manitoba, aussi bien que l'interprétation de l'histoire de cette région ont été influencés largement par une idéologie raciste occidentale. Cette idéologie, jointe aux autres dynamiques politiques-sociaux-économiques du capitalisme, a mené au développement et à la continuation de communautés de faible rendement qui sont distinctement racistes. Une interprétation raciste, néanmoins, a servi à expliquer l'existence même de ces groupements en function de différences perçues au plan racial, différences qui affectaient la culture, la perception du monde et les habitudes de travail des residents. Le regroupement dont il est question ici est une peuplade métisse de la rive Sud du Lac Manitoba.

Agnes Calliste -- *Le Deuxième Plan les concernant la politique canadienne d'immigration et les employées de maison en provenance des Antilles*

Cette étude analyse le Plan concernant les Employées de Maison en provenance des Antilles en vigueur au Canada entre 1955 et 1966 et soutient que, bien que la demande pressante au Canada d'employées de maison à bon marché fût le ressort principal de l'inauguration du Plan Employées de Maison, d'autres facteurs économiques et politiques ont également joué un rôle dans la mise sur pied du Plan dans sa longévité. Les Antillais tant au Canada qu'aux Antilles avaient fait pression sur le gouvernement canadien et demandé qu'il libéralise sa politique et ses règlements discriminatoires en concernant l'immigration des originaires des Antilles britanniques. Le département de l'immigration a consenti au Plan concernant les Employées de Maison en partie pour assurer le commerce préférentiel et les investissements du Canada aux Antilles britanniques; cet accord reflétait également les liens impériaux entre le Canada et les Antilles. Le Plan concernant les Employées de Maison montre également la facon dont, au cours des années, la politique d'immigration reflète les préjugés, de race, de classe et de sexe.

Le stéréotype de l'Antillaise de la classe ouvrière comme domestique de carrière ou mère de famille célibataire a été évoqué pour justifier la restriction et l'exclusion des domestiques antillaises depuis 1911. Puisque le Plan concernant les Employées de Maison offrait à beaucoup de Noires presque leur seule possibilité de venir au Canada, et étant donné le manque de perspectives d'avenir faute d'études et de débouchés sur le marché du travail aux Antilles, certaines ouvrières spécialistes et expérimentées se sont servies du Plan concernant les Employées de Maison pour immigrer au Canada dans le but d'entreprendre des études avancées de chercher du travail dans d'autres domaines à l'échéance de leur contrat et de parrainer l'entrée des membres de leur famille. Bien que les Antillaises aient eu tendance à rester employées de maison plus longtemps que leur contre-parties européennes, les fonctionnaires canadiens qui s'étaient attendus à ce que les Antillaises soient des domestiques de carrière -- un héritage de l'esclavage -- ont mis en question les avantages économiques durables du Plan, étant donné la rapidité avec

264

laquelle ces femmes qui ont abandonné le service domestique tout en parrainant quelques membres de leur famille. Cependant, Noir(e)s certain(e)s ont critiqué les préjugés de race, de classe et de sexe du Plan concernant les Employées de Maison et ont mis en doute les avantages que pourraient en tirer des Antillaises qui étaient moins bien rémunérées que les domestiques d'origine canadienne et européenne, tout en étant traitées comme des immigrées de deuxième classe. Ils ont aussi mis en question les avantages que les Antilles pourraient tirer du Plan, vu que c'était surtout les plus intelligentes qui partaient.

Ronnie Leah -- *Le lien entre les luttes:*
racisme, sexisme et le mouvement syndical

Les femmes de couleur ont protesté contre les suppositions dominantes de la pratique féministe: elles ont reclamé une approche qui rattache la lutte contre le racisme et la lutte contre le sexisme et qui traite les expériences et les problèmes particuliers aux ouvrières noires, amérindiennes, asiatiques, et les autres ouvrières de couleur. Le mouvement féministe, à majorité blanche, a eu tendance à marginaliser les femmes de couleur et les progrès réalisés par les femmes dans le mouvement syndical ont rarement été assurés aux femmes de couleur qui font face à la double discrimination raciste et sexiste.

Cette communication discute quelques-uns des problèmes soulevés à l'heure actuelle au sein du mouvement ouvrier en Ontario par les Noires et d'autres femmes de couleur. Les progrès réalisés par les femmes syndiquées et l'opposition toujours plus forte des travailleurs au racisme et à la discrimination ont encouragé de plus en plus des femmes de couleur à participer au mouvement syndical et à y jouer un rôle toujours plus important. En même temps, les femmes de couleur ont identifié un certain nombre d'obstacles qui continuent d'entraver leurs progrès dans le mouvement syndical -- en tant que femmes, en tant que travailleuses minoritaires et en tant que syndicalistes. L'auteur va donc examiner des stratégies qui pourraient aider à créer un mouvement féministe anti-raciste parmi les travailleurs -- un mouvement qui relie la question du racisme et la question du sexisme et qui tienne compte des problèmes des femmes de couleur. La récente dispute menée par la section 79 du SCFP en vue d'assurer des emplois à temps plein dans les Hospices de Vieillards de Toronto métropolitain où les effectifs sont en grand partie des femmes noires et des asiatiques -- montre comment, en soutenant la lutte contre le racisme et le sexisme, les syndicats défendent la cause de tous les travailleurs.

Irene Poelzer -- *Les Métisses et l'économie du nord du Saskatchewan*

Dans cet article l'auteur propose une méthode d'examiner les conséquences de l'économie salariale dans la vie des Métisses du nord du Saskatchewan. Dans des entrevues avec des Métisses dans sept communautés du Nord, l'auteur a pu recueillir des renseignements sur la situation des Métisses qui ont un emploi rémunéré, de celles qui travaillent comme bénévoles et de celles qui sont en chômage et qui touchent des prestations sociales.

Utilisant une approche inspirée des travaux de la sociologue féministe Dorothy Smith l'auteur examine "l'articulation" des Métisses dans le but de mettre à découvert les liens entre la mégastructure et ce qui arrive dans la vie quotidienne de ces femmes. Pour celles qui ont un emploi rémunéré, l'auteur met le doigt sur les rapports directs entre l'impuissance des Métisses et leur situation dans le marché du travail. A cause de leur participation au travail les Métisses ont également leur part dans la transformation de certains rapports sociaux qui, auparavant, étaient ancrés dans la tradition ou la culture. Par exemple, la garde des enfants à la maison est maintenant transformée en babysitting par des relations de travail. De plus, on trouve que le travail bénévole des Métisses est le résultat direct des structures capitalistes. Par exemple, à l'intérieur du système capitaliste la détente organisée devient une détente commercialisée en dehors des heures de travail. Souvent le travail bénévole des Métisses est directement lié aux rapports de marché des entreprises des grandes sociétés dans le domaine de la détente. En dernier lieu, les Métisses qui touchent des prestations sociales font partie d'une population impuissante et superflue (ce qui est une conséquence de la manière dont on réalise des bénéfices dans le système capitaliste). Cette population dépend des "bonnes grâces" du gouvernement et/ou du capital pour "l'aumône" ou des "emplois intermittents". L'auteur soutient que l'impuissance des Métisses n'est pas seulement en fonction du manque de connaissances qui concernent les conséquences et la neutralité prétendue du capitalisme des grandes sociétés, mais également en fonction de la place des Métisses dans la structure de cette économie. L'auteur termine en déclarant que c'est cette même situation d'impuissance dans laquelle se trouvent les Métisses, qui est le foyer d'une activité avilissante qui, cependant, pourrait faciliter leur accès aux pleins pouvoirs.

Kathryn Kopinak -- Vivre selon l'évangile en venant en aide aux pauvres: La convergence des mobiles politiques et religieux dans l'organisation des ouvriers et ouvrières des Maquiladoras à Juarez, au Mexique.

Depuis plus de deux décennies, les fabricants canadiens, américains, européens et japonais de textiles, de vêtements et de pièces constituantes électroniques sont de plus en plus attirés par la frontière mexicaine-américaine où la zone de transformation des exportations a créé un couloir d'installations jumelles. Les pièces détachées sont emmagasinées du côté américain de la frontière et l'assemblage lui-même se fait du côté mexicain dans des fabriques appelées *maquiladoras*. El Paso/Juarez est le plus important complexe urbain situé de part et d'autre de la frontière et Juarez a toujours été l'un des emplacements où l'on trouve la plus grande concentration de *maquiladoras*. Le capital des sociétés multinationales a été attiré par le "climat favorable aux affaires" des installations jumelles, à savoir l'accès aux services dans les zones industrielles et à la main-d'oeuvre féminine à bon marché. Il n'y a qu'un petit pourcentage des ouvrières qui soient syndiquées, et beaucoup d'entres elles ont constaté que les syndicats peuvent à peine défendre leurs droits face au contrôle de l'état et vu la grande disponibilité de main-d'oeuvre à bon marché. Au Mexique le PRI, qui est au pouvoir, a assujetti le CTM à un contrôle sévère et réprime les syndicats indépendants plus militants. Alors que ceci nuit à la situation des ouvriers en général, les ouvrières deviennent encore plus vulnérables parce que les syndicats ont souvent les mêmes régimes d'organisation patriarcaux que le capitalisme.

Cette communication analyse la manière dont on a créé un centre pour les femmes pour faire face à cette situation. Les chercheurs ont déjà étudié le *Centro de Orientacion de la Mujer Obrera* (COMO) à Juarez mais jusqu'ici personne n'a mis à jour le rôle central de la religion dans l'évaluation de cette organisation. Cette communication amplifie et corrige les comptes-rendus du développement du COMO dans des travaux déjà publiés. De nouvelles données montrent que ceux et celles qui militaient en faveur du centre des ouvrières à Juarez se sont inspirés à la fois de la théologie de la libération et du mouvement pour le renouvellement charismatique du catholicisme. Tandis que des communautés de base ont aidé les habitants de l'Amerique latine à comprendre les événements politiques dans leurs sociétés et à agir en conséquence, aucune d'entre elles n'a réussi à éveiller les gens et à leur faire prendre conscience des problèmes liés au sexe de cette façon précise.

About the Authors

Ron Bourgeault is a Ph.D. student in sociology at Carleton University. He holds degrees in mathematics and sociology, and taught from 1985 to 1987 in the Department of Native Studies at the University of Saskatchewan. Ron's research interests pertain to early capitalism and current imperialism in relation to the indigenous people of Canada, and the common roots of racial segregation in Canada and South Africa. His publications are: "The Struggle of Class and Nation: The Canadian Fur Trade, 1670s to 1870", *Alternate Routes* Vol. 8, 1988; "Race and Class Under Mercantilism: Indigenous People in Nineteenth-Century Canada" in *Racial Oppression in Canada*, 2nd ed., B. Singh Bolaria and Peter S. Li, eds., Toronto: Garamond Press, 1988; "The Development of Capitalism and the Subjugation of Native Women in Northern Canada", *Alternate Routes* Vol. 6, 1983; "The Indian, the Métis and the Fur Trade: Class, Sexism and Racism in the Transition from 'Communism' to Capitalism", *Studies in Political Economy* No. 12, Fall 1983. Address: Ron Bourgeault, P.O. Box 33034, Regina SK, S4T 7X2.

Agnes Calliste is a professor of sociology at St. Francis Xavier University. She holds a doctorate (sociology in education) from the University of Toronto, in addition to several degrees from universities in Canada and the West Indies. Before coming to Antigonish, Agnes taught at York University, in the Black Cultural Heritage Program (Toronto Board of Education), and at the University of Manitoba. Agnes published "Sleeping Car Porters in Canada: An Ethnically Submerged Split Labour Market", *Canadian Ethnic Studies* 19:1 (1987), pp. 1-20, and "Blacks on Canadian Railways", *Canadian Ethnic Studies* 20:2 (1988), pp. 36-52, and she is also working on such topics as three generations of black women in domestic service in Canada, ethnic organizations and integration, and black communities in the Americas. Among her social and scholarly functions and affiliations are Liaison Officer for Black and Native Students, St. Francis Xavier University; President, Society for the Study of Ethnicity in Nova Scotia (1985-6); Prairie Representative, National Black Coalition of Canada, and President of the Winnipeg chapter (1982-4); Member, Manitoba Advisory Council on the Status of Women (1983-4). Address: Agnes Calliste, Department of Sociology and Anthropology, St. Francis Xavier University, Antigonish, Nova Scotia, B2G 1C0.

Tania Das Gupta teaches in the Department of Sociology at Atkinson College, York University. She previously taught in the Department of Community Work of George Brown College in Toronto and served as community coordinator with the Cross Cultural Communication Centre between 1984 and 1987. Tania holds a doctorate from the University of Toronto in Sociology in Education (1986) and is interested in comparative perspectives of women and politics, specifically India and Canada, South-Asian women in Canada and multicultural cross-cultural approaches. Among her publications are: *Learning from Our History: Community Development by Immigrant Women in Ontario, 1958-86, a tool for action*, Toronto: Cross Cultural Communication Centre, 1986; "Nation Builders? The Captive Labour Force of Non-English Speaking Immigrant Women", *Canadian Women's Studies*, 3:1 (1981), co-authored with Roxana Ng. Tania's community involvement includes the South Asian Women's Group (which she helped found in 1982). She also worked with the Coalition of Visible Minority Women (1983-7) and is a past-chairperson of Women Working with Immigrant Workers. Address: Tania Das Gupta, Department of Sociology, Atkinson College, York University, 4700 Keele Street, North York ON, M3J 2R7.

Marlee Kline teaches feminist legal theory and property in the Faculty of Law at the University of British Columbia. She holds a Master's of Law degree from Osgoode Hall Law School. Her thesis, entitled "Child Welfare Law, Ideology, and the First Nations", investigates structures of racism in Canadian law. Marlee has published "Race, Racism and Feminist Legal Theory", *Harvard Women's Law Journal* 12 (1989), pp. 115-150, and "Challenging Privilege: Women, Knowledge, and Feminst Struggles", *Human Justice* 2 (1991), pp. 1-36 with Dawn Currie. She is a member of the Law Union of B.C., the West Coast Law and Society Association and the National Association of Women and the Law. From 1988 to 1989 Marlee was involved with the Socialist Feminist Collective of the Law Union of Ontario. Address: Marlee Kline, Faculty of Law, University of British Columbia, 1822 East Mall, Vancouver, B.C., V6T 1Z1.

Kathryn Kopinak has been a professor of sociology at King's College (University of Western Ontario) since 1976. She holds a Ph.D. in sociology from York University where she specialized in women's studies, communication, social movements, gender, and political sociology. Among her publications are: "Gender Differences in Political Ideology in Canada", *Canadian Review of Sociology and Anthropology*, 24:1 (February 1987), pp. 23-38; "Women in Canadian Municipal Politics: Two Steps Forward, One Step Back", *Canadian Review of Sociology and Anthropology*, 22:3 (August 1985), pp. 394-410; "A Business Unlike Others: A Review of the Royal Commission on Newspapers", *Studies in Political Economy*, 12 (Fall 1983), pp. 143-152. Kathryn is currently investigating the effects on women of continental integration. She is involved with several scholarly organizations (particularly those connected with Latin America and the Caribbean), served on the Board of the Cross Cultural Learners Centre in London (1987-89) and just finished a term as president of the U.W.O. Caucus on Women's Issues. Address: Kathryn Kopinak, Department of Sociology, King's College, 266 Epworth Ave., London, Ontario, N6A 2M3.

Ronnie Leah is a professor of sociology at the University of Lethbridge where she teaches courses in women's studies. Prior to her appointment in 1990, Ronnie taught at Queen's University and various other universities. Ronnie studied at SUNY (Buffalo campus) and Toronto, and received her doctorate from the Ontario Institute for the Study of Education (sociology in education) in 1986. Very concerned with building an anti-racist women's movement and a strong labour movement, she has written extensively about immigrant women, women's trade union organizing, and coalition building: "Saskatchewan Women Respond to Cutbacks: The Founding of a Provincial Women's Coalition", with C. Ruecker, in *Women and Social Change: Feminist Activism in Canada*, J. Wine and J. Ristock, eds. Toronto: James Lorimer, 1991; "Daycare, Trade Unions and the Women's Movement: Trade Union Women Organizing for Change", in *Making Knowledge Count: Advocacy and Social Science*, P. Harries-Jones, ed. Montréal-Queen's, 1991; "Organizing for Daycare", in *Working People and Hard Times: Canadian Perspectives*, R. Argue, C. Gannage and D.W. Livingstone, eds. Toronto: Garamond, 1987; "Women's Labour Force Participation and Daycare Cutbacks in Ontario", *Atlantis* 7:1 (Fall 1981); "Immigrant Women Fight Back: The Case of the Seven Jamaican Women", *Resources for Feminist Research* VIII:3, Part 2 (November 1979). Ronnie continues her research in a number of areas such as: racism, sexism and the union movement; women's organizing --- analysis of gender, race and class; women's work --- interconnection of family, labour force and daycare; coalition building --- organizing the popular sectors. She coordinates sessions at the Learned Societies Conferences of the Society for Socialist Studies and other scholarly organizations, while working with and lecturing to academic, labour, women's and activists' groups in those areas. Address: Ronnie Leah, Department of Sociology, University of Lethbridge, 4401 University Drive, Lethbridge, Alberta, T1K 3M4.

Alicja Muszynski's research in the sociology of labour led in 1987 to a doctorate from the University of British Columbia. She has been teaching at the University of Regina since 1984, is interested in the political economy of the provincial agri-

268

cultural sector, and participates in an international research project on family farms in Canada, France, Poland, Tunisia and Brazil. Alicja's publications include: "The Organization of Women and Ethnic Minorities in a Resource Industry", *Journal of Canadian Studies* 19:1 (Spring 1984), pp. 89-107; "Class Formation and Class Consciousness: The Making of Shoreworkers in the B.C. Fishing Industry", *Studies in Political Economy* 20 (Summer 1986), pp. 85-116; "Race and Gender: Structural determinants in the formation of British Columbia's salmon cannery labour force", *The Canadian Journal of Sociology* 13:1/2 (Winter-Spring 1988), pp. 103-120. Since 1987 she has been on the Programme Committee of the Society for Socialist Studies (which plans the annual Learned Societies conference of this organization) while she is currently the Saskatchewan representative on the executive of the Canadian Research Institute for the Advancement of Women (CRIAW). Address: Alicja Muszynski, Department of Sociology, University of Waterloo, Waterloo ON, N2L 3G1.

Roxana Ng received her Ph.D. from the University of Toronto in 1984, specializing in the area of immigrant women and the state. Following teaching stints at various universities (Saskatchewan, Queen's, New Brunswick) she is now a professor at the Ontario Institute for the Studies in Education. Roxana's research interests lie with the history of immigrant women's organizing in Canada, along with race relations and multiculturalism. Principal publications are: *Immigrant Housewives in Canada*, with Judith Ramirez. Toronto: Immigrant Women's Centre, 1981; *The Politics of Community Services. Immigrant Women, Class and State*, Toronto: Garamond Press, 1988; *Community Organization and the Canadian State*, Roxana Ng, Gillian Walker and Jacob Muller, eds., Toronto: Garamond Press, 1989. Roxana has been active in the immigrant women's movement since 1976. She is currently working, with practitioners in the field, on the development of anti-racist and anti-sexist teaching methods. Address: Roxana Ng, Sociology of Education, OISE, 252 Bloor St. West, Toronto, Ontario, M5S 1V6.

Irene A. Poelzer has been involved in research relative to Métis women in Northern Saskatchewan for the past nine years. She is the co-author of the book *In Our Own Words (Northern Saskatchewan Métis Women Speak Out)*. She has been involved in post-secondary education in Saskatoon for over twenty years. During part of that time Irene was an instructor at La Ronge in the Northern Teachers Training Programme. This is where she first became interested in the situation of Métis women in Northern Saskatchewan. The paper printed in this *Annual* forms the basis for a chapter in her forthcoming book, *The Dynamics of Economic Development on Métis Women's Lives*. In addition, Irene is a potter, dabbles in poetry. and is a feminist. Address: Irene Poelzer, College of Education, University of Saskatchewan, Saskatoon, Saskatchewan, S7N 0W0.

Nicole St-Onge teaches history at the Collège Universitaire de St-Boniface. She is a graduate of Trent University and the University of Manitoba, where she received her M.A. in anthropology in 1985. She is currently completing her doctoral dissertation in history at the University of Manitoba, from which the article in this volume has been extracted. Address: Nicole St-Onge, Département d'histoire, Collège universitaire de St-Boniface, 200 avenue de la Cathédrale, St-Boniface, MB, R2H 0H7.

Esmeralda Thornhill is an agente d'éducation with the Direction de l'éducation of the Commission des droits de la personne du Québec. Address: 360, rue Saint-Jacques, Montréal, Québec, H2Y 1P5.

7: THE CRISIS IN SOCIALIST THEORY, STRATEGY AND PRACTICE ($19.95)
(forthcoming)

Paul Browne: *Reification and the Crisis of Socialism*

Max Nemni: *Marx and Engels and the Exhaustion of "Scientific Socialism"*

Herb Gamberg: *What is Socialism?*

Frank Cunningham: *Democracy and Marxist Political Culture*

Gerry van Houten: *Socialism Today: Renewal or Retreat*

Axel Dorscht: *Politics of Transformation and the Process of Social Change*

Margaret Luxton: *The Crisis of Socialism and Feminism*

Lois Corbett: *Environmental Crisis and the Socialist Response*

Cy Gonick: *Socialism: Past and Future*

Jos. Roberts: *Conclusion*

**To order, send cheque or money order for $19.95 to
Society for Socialist Studies, University College
University of Manitoba, Winnipeg R3T 2M8, Canada.**

6: REGULATING LABOUR: THE STATE, NEO-CONSERVATISM AND INDUSTRIAL RELATIONS ($19.95)

Larry Haiven, Stephen McBride, John Shields

Larry Haiven, Stephen McBride, John Shields: *The State, Neo-Conservatism and Industrial Relations*

Bob Russell: *Assault Without Defeat: Contemporary Industrial Relations & the Canadian Labour Movement*

John Shields: *Building a New Hegemony in British Columbia*

Larry Haiven: *Hegemony and the Workplace: The Role of Arbitration*

Stephen McBride: *Authoritarianism Without Hegemony? The Politics of Industrial Relations in Britain*

Banu Helvacioglu: *The State in the Reagan Era: Capital, Labour and More?*

Gregg M. Olsen: *Swedish Social Democracy and Beyond: Internal Obstacles to Economic Democracy*

Jerry White: *The State and Industrial Relations in a Neo-Conservative Era: A Thematic Commentary*

To order, send cheque or money order for $19.95 to
Society for Socialist Studies, University College
University of Manitoba, Winnipeg R3T 2M8, Canada.

4: SOCIAL MOVEMENTS/SOCIAL CHANGE ($15.95)

Frank Cunningham -- Sue Findlay -- Marlene Kadar -- Alan Lennon -- Ed Silva

Carolyn Egan, Linda Gardner, Judy Vashti Persad: *Race, Class and Sexuality in the March 8th Coalition*

Laurie E. Adkin & Catherine Alpaugh: *Labour, Ecology, and the Politics of Convergence*

Monique Simard: *Coalition Politics: The Québec Labour Movement*

Sharon D. Stone & Joanne Doucette: *Organizing the Marginalized: The DisAbled Women's Network*

Susan Prentice: *"Kids are Not for Profit": The Politics of Childcare*

Patricia Antonyshyn, B. Lee, & Alex Merill: *The Campaign for Free-Standing Abortion Clinics in Ontario*

Carmencita R. Hernandez: *The Coalition of Visible Minority Women*

Tim McCaskell: *The Bath Raids and Gay Politics*

David Langille: *Building an Effective Peace Movement: One Perspective*

Kari Delhi, John Restakis & Errol Sharpe: *The Rise and Demise of the Parent Movement in Toronto*

Alexandra Devon & Ron Hayley: *Kick It Over: The Evolution of a Journal*

Dieter Hoehne: *Self-Help and Social Change*

To order, send cheque or money order for $15.95 to
Society for Socialist Studies, University College
University of Manitoba, Winnipeg R3T 2M8, Canada.

3: WORK AND NEW TECHNOLOGIES: OTHER PERSPECTIVES
($11.95)

Chris DeBresson -- Margaret Lowe Benston -- Jesse Vorst

C. DeBresson & M. Lowe Benston: *Introduction: Work & New Technologies --
Other Perspectives*

PART 1: PERSPECTIVES ON LABOUR RESEARCH ON NEW TECHNOLOGIES
D'Arcy Martin: *Canaries and Cargo Cults -- Worker-Oriented Research in the
Silicon Age*
Ken Hansen: *Focus of Union Research on Technological Change*
M. Lowe Benston, M. White & M. Cohen: *Community Based Research Around
Technological Change*
Jim Peterson: *The Shop Floor -- Design and Control for Self-Management*
Elaine Bernard: *New Initiatives, New Technology, New Labour*
Summary of a Conference Discussion

PART 2: THREE EXPERIENCES
C. Micklewright: *Video Display Terminals, Health Hazards, Electronic
Surveillance*
Omer Chouinard: *Resistance of the Coastal Fisherman to Structural
Transformations in Northern and Eastern New Brunswick, 1965-1986 (in
French)*
Paul-André Lapointe: *Crisis in the Employment Relationship at Alcan's
Jonquière Plant (in French)*

*PART 3: CONCEPTUAL PROBLEMS OF RESEARCH ON TECHNOLOGICAL
CHANGE*
Pierre Doray: *Skills & Workers' Contributions - A Critique of Braverman's
Deskilling Thesis (in French)*
Alfred Dubuc: *Technical Choices, Social Choices - Numerically Controlled
Machine Tools*
M. Lowe Benston: *Marxism, Science, and Workers' Control*
C. DeBresson: *The Ambivalence of Marx's Legacy on Technological Change*

DISCUSSION SECTION: Max Nemni: Nationalism, Socialism and Democracy (in
French)

**To order, send cheque or money order for $11.95 to
Society for Socialist Studies, University College
University of Manitoba, Winnipeg R3T 2M8, Canada.**

2: CRITICAL PERSPECTIVES ON THE CONSTITUTION ($10.95)

Guest Editor: Robert Martin

G. Starr: *Popular Rights In (and Out Of) The Constitution*

S. Rush: *Collective Rights and Collective Process -- Missing Ingredients in the Canadian Constitution*

Ch. Campbell: *The Canadian Left and the Charter of Rights*

L. McDonald: *The Supreme Court of Canada and the Equality Guarantee in the Charter*

R. Martin: *The Judges and the Charter*

H. Glasbeek, M. Mandel: *The Legalisation of Politics in Advanced Capitalism*

G. Raphanel: *Justice and Sexual Politics -- Legal Rights in the Charter of Rights and Freedoms*

Chr. Boyle: *Home Rule for Women -- A Contribution to the Feminist Analysis of Representation*

J. Tait: *Section 15 -- Time to Prepare*

N. Zlotkin: *Aboriginal Peoples and a Constitutional Reform*

L. Mandell: *The Union of British Colombia Indian Chiefs Fights Patriation*

V. di Norcia: *Social Reproduction and a Federal Community*

S. Ryerson: *A New Pattern for Canada? Hardly*

Y. Bélanger, P. Beaulne: *La Constitution -- Enjeux Economiques*

N. Penner: *The New Federalism; Or How the Liberal Concept of National Unity was Transformed*

H. Milner: *The Constitution and the Reform of Québec Education Structures*

R. Whitaker: *Democracy, Federalism, and the National Political Communities in Canada*

G. Stevenson: *Constitutional Amendment -- A Democratic Perspective*

DISCUSSION SECTION: J. Sher: The NEP Debate Revisited

**To order, send cheque or money order for $10.95 to
Society for Socialist Studies, University College
University of Manitoba, Winnipeg R3T 2M8, Canada.**

1: MARXISM, FEMINISM, THE STATE ($9.95)

Frank Cunningham: *C. B. Macpherson and Stanley Ryerson on Marxism and the Eighties*

Varda Burstyn: *Economy, Sexuality, Politics -- Engels and the Sexual Division of Labour*

Barbara Cameron: *The Sexual Division of Labour and Class Struggle*

Geraldine Finn: *Feminism and Fiction -- In Praise of Praxis, Beyond Bodily Harm*

Bert Young: *Witness to Reality*

L. Blais: *Socialist Organizing in the '80s - The Experience of Building the Comité des Cent/Mouvement socialiste*

Paul Stevenson: *The State in English Canada -- The Political Economy of Production and Reproduction*

Jean-Guy Vaillancourt: *The Political Economy of Québec -- A Selective Annotated Bibliography*

Julian Sher: *The NEP -- Patriotism of Profits*

M. Watkins: *The NEP and the Left -- A Commentary on Sher and Others*

**To order, send cheque or money order for $9.95 to
Society for Socialist Studies, University College
University of Manitoba, Winnipeg R3T 2M8, Canada.**